D. J. B. Trim

A Passion for Mission

A Passion for Mission

Newbold Academic Press

Author: David John Ballard Trim

Cover design: Any Kobel, Switzerland

Layout: Manfred Lemke

Printing: Lightning Source

© November 2019

The opinions expressed in our published works are those of the author(s) and do not necessarily reflect the opinions of Newbold Academic Press or its Publishing Panel.

Except as otherwise permitted under the Copyright, Designs and Patents Act 1988 this publication may only be reproduced, stored or transmitted in any form or by any means, with the prior permission of the publisher, or in the case of reprographic reproduction, in accordance with the terms of a licence issued by The Copyright Licensing Agency. Enquiries concerning reproduction outside those terms should be sent to Newbold Academic Press, Bracknell, Berkshire, RG42 4AN, UK.

ISBN 978-1-9162888-0-5, Softcover

Table of Contents

Table of Contents	I
Acknowledgments	III
Abbreviations	V
List of Illustrations	IX
Figures	IX
Maps	X
Photographs	XI
List of Tables	XVII

Introduction:
   Chapter 1   1

PART ONE: Origins
   Chapter 2: Foundations   33
   Chapter 3: Beginnings   55

PART TWO: The First Forty Years
   Chapter 4: 'A Solemn Responsibility':
   Depression and World War, 1929–1946   69
   Chapter 5: 'A Passion to Win Men and Women to God':
   The Refoundation, 1946–1950   109
   Chapter 6: 'Evangelism in Every Community':
   Years of Stability, 1951–1970   133

PART THREE: The Last Half Century
    Chapter 7: 'Saying Goodbye with Heavy Hearts':
        Separating from Sub-Saharan Africa, 1969–1980   167
    Chapter 8: 'A Caring Community':
        Unity and Diversity, 1976–1991   189
    Chapter 9: Organising for Mission, 1991–2015   217

PART FOUR: Analysis
    Chapter 10: Institutions   257
    Chapter 11: Engaging with Society   285
    Chapter 12: Adaptation and Innovation   315

Conclusion:
    Chapter 13   355

Appendix I: Countries and Ecclesiastical Organisational Units   421

Appendix II: Division Administration 1929–2019   427

Appendix III: Division Headquarters Locations   421

Bibliography, Part I:
Select Bibliography on Adventist History in the TED   433

Bibliography, Part II:
Additional Primary and Secondary Sources Cited   443

Acknowledgements

I am grateful to the three executive officers of the Trans-European Division for commissioning me to write the division's ninetieth-anniversary history: President Raafat Kamal, Secretary Audrey Andersson, and Treasurer Nenad Jepuranović. In particular, I am greatly beholden to Audrey Andersson, whose concept this history was, who has overseen it since 2014, and without whom this literary vessel would not have been brought safely into harbour.

I gratefully acknowledge Manfred Lemke of Newbold Academic Press, who oversaw the actual production of the volume. I am obliged to the Press's peer reviewers for their comments, corrections, and suggestions. I also thank Taylor & Foote, which carried out the copy editing.

All historical research projects are collaborative to a greater or lesser extent. At the General Conference Archives, I am grateful to Benjamin Baker, Ashlee Chism, Daniel Fults, Kenrie Hylton, Chelsy Tyler, and Michael Younker, for assistance with finding or verifying documents, photographs, maps, and statistics. At Newbold College, I am indebted to Per Lisle and Lynda Baildam for facilitating research in the Roy Graham Library's archival and manuscript collections, and for numerous stimulating conversations about Adventist history in the last two decades or so. My thanks go to Merlin Burt and Judymae Richards at the Center for Adventist Research, for supplying scanned copies of files in the Center's collections; and to Rainer Refsbäck, Audrey Anderssson, and Dean Papaioannou, for providing references to and/or copies of documents at the headquarters of the Swedish Union of Churches and in the archive of the Trans-European Division. Finally, I am much obliged to the staff of the Barker Research Library (Durham University Library), where I consulted a number of books and documents, and where the first drafts of several chapters were written.

History-writing, too, is by its nature collaborative. Not for the first time, I make thankful homage to Harry Leonard, who read the whole book in draft (and helped me to become an historian). The book in manuscript was also read by, and improved by the comments of, Reinder Bruinsma and Patrick Boyle, both of whom I appreciatively acknowledge. A heavily condensed version of the book, with its main arguments, was given as the TED Ninetieth-Anniversary Lecture at Newbold College on 18 May 2019; I am grateful to Raafat Kamal, who arranged the lecture, to all in the audience, and especially to those who shared thoughts and questions afterwards. I am grateful to Kevin Burton for his comments on a draft of Chapter 5. Finally, I am, as ever, deeply indebted to Wendy Trim, for literally invaluable assistance in completing this project and for much else besides.

Abbreviations

ADCOM	Administrative Committee
ARH	Adventist Review & Sabbath Herald [also published variously over the period as Review & Herald and Adventist Review]
ASR	Annual Statistical Report
ASTR	GC Office of Archives and Statistics (to 2011)/Office of Archives, Statistics, and Research
ASWA	Adventist Seminary of West Africa
AVS	Adventist Volunteer Services
BAM	British Advent Missions Ltd
BMB	BAM Minute Book
BUC	British Union Conference
CAR	Center for Adventist Research, Andrews University, Berrien Springs, Mich., USA
CED	Central European Division
DUL	Durham University Library, Archives and Special Collections, Durham, UK
EAD	Euro-Africa Division
EAUM	East African Union Mission
ENUC	East Nordic Union Conference
fld.	Folder
GC	General Conference of Seventh-day Adventists

GC Ar. Archives of the General Conference of Seventh-day Adventists, Silver Spring, MD, USA

GCB General Conference Bulletin

GCC General Conference Committee/Executive Committee

-Proc. GCC 'Proceedings' [i.e. minutes: this title was given to minutes, which were in bound volumes up to 977]: GC Ar., RG 1

GCOM GC Officers' Minutes: GC Ar., RG 2

HRSDAE Heirs of the Reformation: The Story of Seventh-day Adventists in Europe, ed. Hugh Dunton, Daniel Heinz, Dennis Porter, and Ronald Strasdowsky (Grantham, UK: Stanborough Press, 1997)

HUC Hungarian Union Conference

mins. Minutes

MEUM Middle East Union Mission

NAUK The National Archives, Kew, UK

NUC Netherlands Union Conference/Union of Churches

NED Northern European Division

NEDCOM NED Committee (including Minority Committee)/Executive Committee: GC Ar., RG NE 1, boxes 6630-39

-WCM NEDCOM Winter Council minutes [up to the early 1950s, a separately paginated series from main minutes, but filed with them]

NEWAD Northern Europe–West Africa Division

NEWAEC NEWAD Executive Committee

NNESC	NEWAD Northern Europe Section Committee
NWASC	NEWAD West Africa Section Committee
NWDM	NEWAD Committees (NEWAEC, NNESC, NWASC) Minutes Collection: GC AR., RG NW 1, boxes 6639-42
-ECM	NEWAEC Minutes
-ESC	NNESC Minutes
-WSC	NWASC Minutes
PDC	GC Provisional Division Committee for Detached Missions
PUC	Polish Union Conference
RG	Record Group
RHPA	Washington, D.C.: Review and Herald Publishing Association
RGL	Roy Graham Library, Special Collections, Newbold College, Bracknell, UK
SDAE	Seventh-day Adventist Encyclopedia, 2nd revd edn (Hagerstown, Md.: RHPA, 1996)
SED	Southern European Division
SEEUC	South-East European Union Conference
SUC	Swedish Union Conference/Union of Churches
ScUC	Scandinavian Union Conference
TED	Trans-European Division
TEDArc.	TED Archives
TEDEC	TED Executive Committee
TEDMC	TED Committees Minutes Collection: GC Ar.,

		RG TE 1, boxes D12.46, MIN370-371, R1982
	-AC	TED ADCOM Minutes
	-EC	TEDEC Minutes
WAUM		West African Union Mission
WNUC		West Nordic Union Conference
WWAM		World Wide Advent Missions Ltd
YB		Seventh-day Adventist Yearbook [published since 1929; exact titles differ]
YPMV		Young People's Missionary Volunteer Department [later Youth Ministries]

List of Illustrations

Figures, Maps, Photographs

Figures

1	Division Nomenclature, 1929–2019	7
2	NED Membership, 1951–1969	155
3	NED Membership in Africa and Europe Contrasted, 1951 and 1970	156
4	Membership in Africa and Europe, NED, 1951–1970	157
5	Distribution of Membership and Share of Accessions, Northern Europe and West Africa Sections, 1970–1980	180
6	NED Membership, 1981–1985	192
7	Growth Rate, NED/TED, 1982–1991	207
8	Pakistan Union Section Membership, 1986–2010	232
9	MEUM Membership under the TED (two-year moving averages)	234
10	Sudanese Membership in Relation to Membership Across the Middle East	234
11	MEUM Membership (less Sudan) under the TED	235
12	Membership in TED, 1991–2011, Excluding Pakistan and the Middle East	241
13	Growth Rate Trend in the TED, 1929–2018	342
14	Membership Trajectories in the TED's Core Countries since 1929	365
15	TED, Current Territory, Membership on New Year's Day, 1929–2019	372

Maps

Map 1.1 The Southern European Division in 1929	3
Map 1.2 The Northern European Division's African Mission Fields in 1929	4
Map 1.3 The Euro-Africa Division in 2001	5
Map 2.1 The Northern European Division in 1929	46
Map 2.2 The NED's European Territory in 1929	47
Map 4.1 The NED's African Mission Fields in 1935	77
Map 5.1 The NED after the 1946 GC Session	117
Map 6.1 The NED's African Mission Fields in 1954	136
Map 8.1: The End of NEWAD: The NED after the 1980 GC Session	190
Map 8.2: The Trans-European Division in 1986	196
Map 9.1: The TED in 1993	220
Map 9.2. The Creation of Two Unions in Former Yugoslavia, 1998	227
Map 9.3. The TED in 1996	229

Photographs

Note: An online archive of TED Ninetieth Anniversary photographs is available at URL TBC

Photographs are all found between pp. 379–414.

1.1 General Conference President W. A. Spicer at Malamulo Mission Station
1.2 Baptism in Victoria Nyanza

2.1 Delegates to the European Division Council, Darmstadt, 1928
2.2 Oliver Montgomery, GC vice-president
2.3 Lewis H. Christian, first NED president
2.4 William A. Spicer, GC president, 1929
2.5 Christian Pedersen, first NED treasurer
2.6 Walter E. Read, first NED secretary
2.7 'British Missionaries 1907–1927'

3.1. The new NED office building, 1929
3.2. Another view of the new NED headquarters
3.3. Christian and Read with British church leaders outside Number 10 Downing Street

4.1 Ernest D. Dick, NED secretary (1932–1936)
4.2 James I. Robison, NED secretary (1936–1941)
4.3 Ellis R. Colson, NED treasurer (1935–1941)
4.4 A. S. ('Uncle Arthur') Maxwell, Editor of Present Truth
4.5 Paul M. Knudsen, NED secretary-treasurer, 1941
4.6 William T. Bartlett, NED field secretary, 1942
4.7 William H. Branson, GC president (1950–1954)

4.8 William McClements, missionary to West Africa (1943–1951)
4.9 and 4.10 Ruben and Hanna Bergstrom, pioneer missionaries to Cameroon
5.1 Gustav A. Lindsay, NED president (1946–1950) and treasurer (1950–1958)
5.2 Alf M. Karlman, NED treasurer (1946) and secretary-treasurer (1947–1950)
5.3 Edwin B. Rudge, NED secretary (1950–1958)
5.4 A. Floyd Tarr, NED president (1950–1962), in 1962

6.1 George D. King, NED secretary (1956–1962)
6.2 Tarr on an itinerary somewhere in Africa, 1946
6.3 Tarr in the early 1950s
6.4 Tarr in Ethiopia, 1961
6.5 Erwin E. Roenfelt as a young man
6.6 Roenfelt, when NED president (1962–1966)
6.7 W. E. Read, in later life, while GC field secretary
6.8 Roy A. Anderson, evangelist and administrator
6.9 Harry W. Lowe, GC field secretary (1962–1966)
6.10 William G. C. Murdoch, educator and theologian
6.11 E. E. (Eddie) White, educator and administrator
6.12 Edward Heppenstall, influential theologian
6.13 George D. Keough, missionary and theologian
6.14 Keough with Newbold students, early 1960s
6.15 Emanuel W. Pedersen, NED secretary (1962–1966)
6.16 Stanisław Dabrowski, Polish church leader
6.17 W. Duncan Eva, NED president (1966–1973)

7.1 Robert H. Pierson, GC president (1966–1978)
7.2 Walter R. Beach, GC secretary (1954–1970)
7.3 Magdalon E. Lind, Afro-Mideast Division president (1970–1975)

7.4 Charles D. Watson, Afro-Mideast Division president (1975–1980)
7.5 John Muderspach, NED/TED treasurer (1980–1990)
7.6 Reinder Bruinsma, TED Secretary (1995–2001)
7.7 Bert B. Beach with map of NEWAD's Northern Europe Section

8.1 Jan Paulsen, NED/TED president (1983–1995), in 1985
8.2 GC President Pierson in 1977
8.3 Orville Woolford, TED departmental director (1985–2005)
8.4 Cecil R. Perry, British church leader

10.1 Newbold College of Higher Education
10.2 Skodsborg Badesanatorium
10.3 Nigerian Training College, 1954
10.4 Kwahu Hospital School of Nursing and Midwifery, c.1960s
10.5 Newbold Missionary College, c.1950
10.6 Adventistički Seminar Dvorac Maruševec (Yugoslavian Adventist Seminary), c.1986
10.7 Netherlands Missionary School, Huize 'Zandbergen', 1950
10.8 Hlíðardalsskóli (Iceland secondary school), 1962
10.9 Toivonlinnan Kristillinen Opisto (Finland Mission School), 1960
10.10 Vejlefjord Højskole (Danish Mission School), 1954
10.11 Ekbyholmsskolan (Swedish Junior College and Seminary), 1962
10.12 Tyrifjord Høyere Skole (Norwegian Junior College), 1962

10.13 Adventistički Teološki Fakultet (Adriatic Union College), Maruševec, Croatia, 2018
10.14 Ile-Ife Hospital, c.1960s
10.15 The Hydes, missionary family, at Jengre, 1933
10.16 Jengre Seventh-day Adventist Hospital, c.1960s
10.17 Nurses at Kwahu Hospital, c.1970
10.18 Hultafors Sanitarium, 1946
10.19 NED Secretary Bert Beach, 1979
10.20 Beach pictured in 1970, when NED Education departmental secretary
10.21 Northern European Division Teachers Convention, 1965

11.1 William E. Nelson, GC treasurer (1936–1950)
11.2 John-Jacob Strahle, Director of European Relief (1946–1950)
11.3 Food Depot in Vienna, 1946
11.4 Trucks Carrying Food Parcels from Copenhagen to Vienna, 1946

12.1 C. Dunbar Henri, missionary to Africa and GC general vice-president
12.2 Henry L. Rudy, GC vice-president (1950–1958)
12.3 Alf Lohne, NED secretary and president, GC vice-president
12.4 Walter R. L. Scragg, NEWAD/NED president (1975–1983)
12.5 Jan Paulsen, 1991
12.6 Bertil Wiklander, TED president (1995–2014)
12.7 John F. Coltheart, evangelist and administrator
12.8 Bert Beach, 1999
12.9 Mark A. Finley, evangelist and administrator
12.10 Raafat Kamal, TED president since 2014

12.11 Bernard Seton, NED secretary (1966–1967)
12.12 Victor Cooper, GC Communication associate director (1973–1988)
12.13 Ray Dabrowski, GC Communication Department director (1994–2010)
12.14 Harald Wollan, TED secretary (2001–2010)
12.15 Bryan Ball, church historian and South Pacific Division president
12.16 Jan Knopper, missionary and publishing leader
12.17 V. Norskov Olsen, church historian and institutional leader
12.18 Gottfried Oosterwal, influential missiologist
12.19 Estonian Conference officials, including laypeople, c.1926
12.20 Margaret Wharrie, union treasurer in African mission fields (1929–1935)
12.21 Amanda Nuka, church leader in Eastern Europe and Africa (1929–1959)
12.22 Else Luukkanen and Aino Lehtoluoto, Finnish evangelists, 1964
12.23 Anna-Liisa Halonen, TED treasurer (1990–1992)

List of Tables

2.1 Distribution of European Division Components in Three New Divisions — 44
2.2 Major Ecclesiastical Organisational Units in the Northern European Division, 1929 — 48
4.1 Major Ecclesiastical Organisational Units in the Northern European Division, 1933 — 76
4.2 Membership in European Division(s), 1928–1938 — 99
4.3 Membership in Europe and Attached Mission Fields, 1928–1938 — 101
13.1 Ninety-Year Trend: January 1929 to 1 January 2019 — 364

A.1 Nations, Dependencies, and Autonomous Polities in the Northern European Division, 1929 — 421
A.2 Unions and Polities in Northern European Division, 1933 — 423
A.3 Major Ecclesiastical Organizational Units in the Reorganised Northern European Division, 1951 — 423
A.4 Nations, Dependencies, and Autonomous Polities in the Northern Europe–West Africa Division, 1971–1980 — 423
A.5 Major Ecclesiastical Organizational Units in the Northern Europe–West Africa Division, 1971–1980 — 423
A.6 Major Ecclesiastical Organizational Units in the Northern European Division, 1981 — 424
A.7 Ecclesiastical Organizational Units in the Northern European Division, 1991 — 424
A.8 Major Ecclesiastical Organizational Units in the Northern European Division, Early 1995 — 425
A.9 Major Ecclesiastical Organizational Units in the Northern European Division, 1999 — 425
A.10 Nations, Dependencies, and Autonomous Polities in the Trans-European Division, 2019 — 426
A.11 Major Ecclesiastical Organizational Units in the Trans-European Division, 2019 — 426

Chapter 1
Introduction

> *The unwarned millions make their pathetic appeal and in view of the nearness of the coming of Jesus we must certainly lay plans for a larger work.* – Adventist Church leaders in Northern Europe, November 1928

The final day of 1928 was also the last day of the European Division of the General Conference of Seventh-day Adventists. On New Year's Day, 1929, four new divisions came into existence: the Soviet Russian, Central European, Southern European, and Northern European Divisions. In 2019, the last of these is the only survivor from 1929 and celebrates its ninetieth anniversary. While its name and territory have changed, the Trans-European Division (TED) as it is now called, is the only division of the four that has enjoyed a continuous existence ever since. The TED is an enduring feature of the ecclesiastical-organisational landscape of the Seventh-day Adventist Church, its influence felt far beyond Europe's shores.

The continuity embodied in the TED is noteworthy not least because the nine decades since it was created have been ones of enormous change, both in the Adventist Church and in the wider world. When the Northern European Division (NED) was created, the European Division had existed for nearly twenty years, one of the first 'divisions' created by the Seventh-day Adventist Church. Conceived of as sub-divisions of the General Conference (GC), the overarching organisation of the Adventist world church, three divisions were created in 1909: North American, European, and Asiatic. In 1928, the European Division was one of eight world divisions of the Adventist denomination. Nine decades later, the TED is one of thirteen world divisions. At the time the European Division was divided, Adventists in Europe totalled 32 per cent of the global membership and were equivalent to 80 per cent of the membership in the North American

1

Division (NAD). With just over 24,400 members, the newly created NED was the third-largest world division in terms of membership but, excluding its African mission fields, the division's membership in Europe, the territories of which are still with TED today, was just over 21,000; with members in Hungary and the Balkans, the 1929 membership in the TED's territory today was just over 24,300: this constituted 8 per cent of the global membership, equivalent to 19 per cent of the North American membership. Today, the number of church members in the TED has increased by 260 per cent; but ninety years on, its nearly 90,000 members are 0.4 per cent of world reported membership, equivalent to 7 per cent of the membership in the NAD.[1] The Seventh-day Adventist Church in the TED has grown in absolute terms, but its relative position in the denomination worldwide has diminished.

In wider society, the NED came into being as Communism and Fascism were challenging traditional Christianity for ideological dominance in Europe. Ideology itself became passé, however, and individualism, materialism, and postmodernism are predominant today in the Trans-European Division, as across Europe as a whole.

In 1929, European empires ruled or dominated most of Africa and Asia, and Adventist Church structure reflected the Age of Imperialism. The three divisions with 'European' in their titles incorporated much of Africa, the whole of the Middle East, and parts of the Far East, with colonial territories assigned generally to the division of the respective imperial powers. For example, the Southern European Division (SED) had as its core the Latin or Romance-speaking countries, and so it included the Italian, Belgian, and many, though not all, of the French colonies (see Map 1.1). The Northern European Division included Britain, and so British East and West Africa were

---

[1] *ASR*, 66 (1928), 10; *YB 1929*, pp. 3, 120, 126, 157; *ASR* 67 (1929), 12, 14; *ASR Advance Release 2018* (2019), p. 19. To extend the comparison with 1928, the church's 370,000 members on the European continent are 1.8 per cent of the reported world membership and 30 per cent of the NAD membership: *ASR*, 154 (2018 for 2016–2017), 20, 95.

assigned to the NED, along with those parts of French West Africa that adjoined Ghana and Nigeria (see Map 1.2). The attachment of mission fields, especially in Africa, to nominally European divisions continued well into the twenty-first century (see Map 1.3). Meanwhile, the passing decades brought independence to what had once been colonies – and recurrent surges of emigration from them into the countries to whose empires they had once belonged. Thus, ethnic

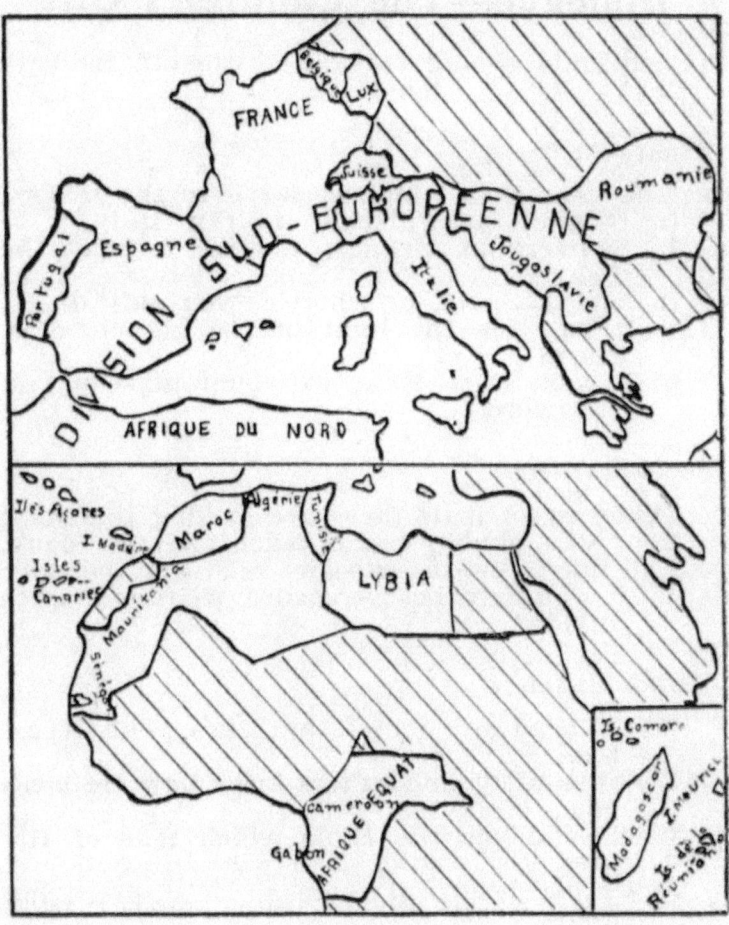

Map 1.1: The Southern European Division in 1929

diversity was created in what once were largely monochrome societies. Despite that influx, population growth in Europe has slowed in the last ninety years; one result is that whereas in 1929 Europeans were one in three of the global population, they now are one in ten.

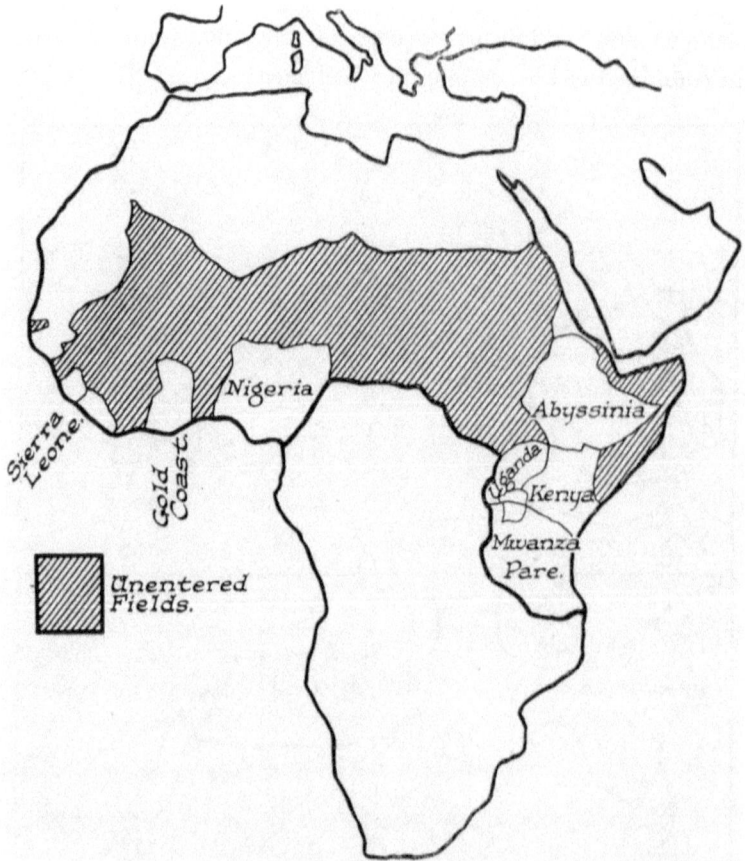

Map 1.2: The Northern European Division's African Mission Fields in 1929

Perhaps most significantly, the last nine decades also witnessed a world war that was disproportionately destructive in Europe; a decades-long 'cold war' during which it experienced no combat but was divided and polarised as never before; and the creation, for the first time in centuries, of a supranational authority over much of the continent. The European Union has brought economic unity to much of Europe (including most of the current territory of the TED), yet has not erased all the social, cultural, and economic fault lines created by sixty years of ideological conflict.

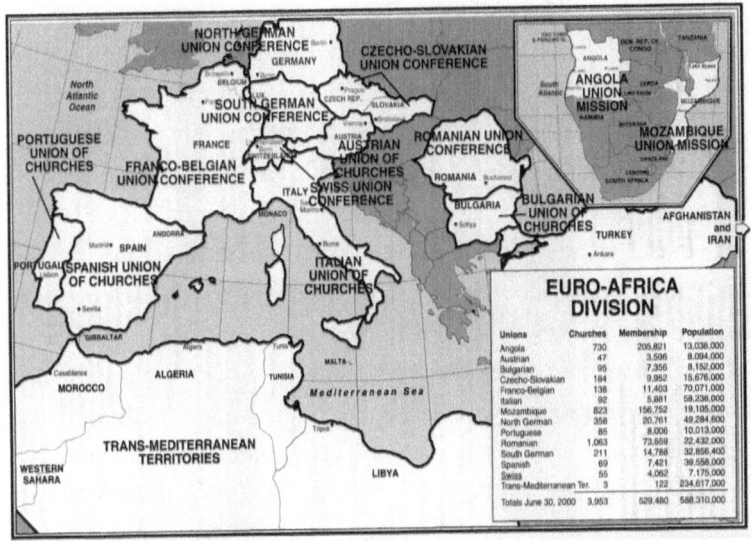

Map 1.3: The Euro-Africa Division in 2001

The world into which the TED was born has altered immensely. As conditions change, church structure changes; two of the four divisions born in 1929 merged in 1971. The Soviet Russian division had already, in the early 1930s, ceased to exist in any meaningful sense, while the limited overarching structure in the USSR was dissolved in 1960; the Euro-Asia Division was established in 1990, covering the former territory of the Soviet Union, but as a new creation. And yet, the NED (now TED) lives on in spite of seismic shifts in its social, cultural, economic, political, and ecclesiastical contexts – and despite a number of changes, too, in its title and territory. It has been known as the Northern European Division, North Atlantic Division, Northern Europe-West Africa Division (NEWAD), and Trans-European Division (see Figure 1, p. 7). Its geographic boundaries

5

have been redrawn frequently; and yet there has been considerable continuity.

The same headquarters, located in England for eighty of the ninety years, has guided Adventist mission and ministry in Northern, East-Central, and South-Eastern Europe, the large islands and smaller archipelagos of the North Atlantic, and associated vast African and Asian mission fields. The work done in the TED's territory and under its direction has, quite literally, been for a 'great multitude [...] of nations, and kindreds, and people, and tongues'.[2] While its territories have fluctuated, there has been a core group of seven countries (as discussed later in this chapter). As of 2019, the division headquarters provides leadership, strategic direction, and resources to 88,000 Seventh-day Adventists, worshipping in 1,400 congregations, organised in eleven unions and three attached fields. The division encompasses twenty-two sovereign nations and six autonomous polities.[3] Their populations amount to some 206 million people, mostly living in the littorals of five seas: the Adriatic, Aegean, Baltic, North, and Norwegian.

Despite an extraordinary degree of diversity, church members in the TED have much in common. They are bound together by their shared devotion to distinctive Adventist doctrines, in the face of indifference, apathy, antagonism, or outright hostility; and European Adventists share, too, a passion for proclaiming the 'everlasting gospel' to those who have not heard it (Rev. 14:6). Their passion for mission – their fervent desire to share Adventism's distinctive, prophetic message of wholeness and hope, both in Europe and beyond – has profoundly shaped the division and Adventists living in it, from church leaders to church members, throughout the last ninety years. The history of the Trans-European Division is a history of passion for mission.

---

2   Rev. 7:9 (KJV), cf. 5:9, 10:11, 14:6.
3   See Appendix I, Tables A.2 and A.3.

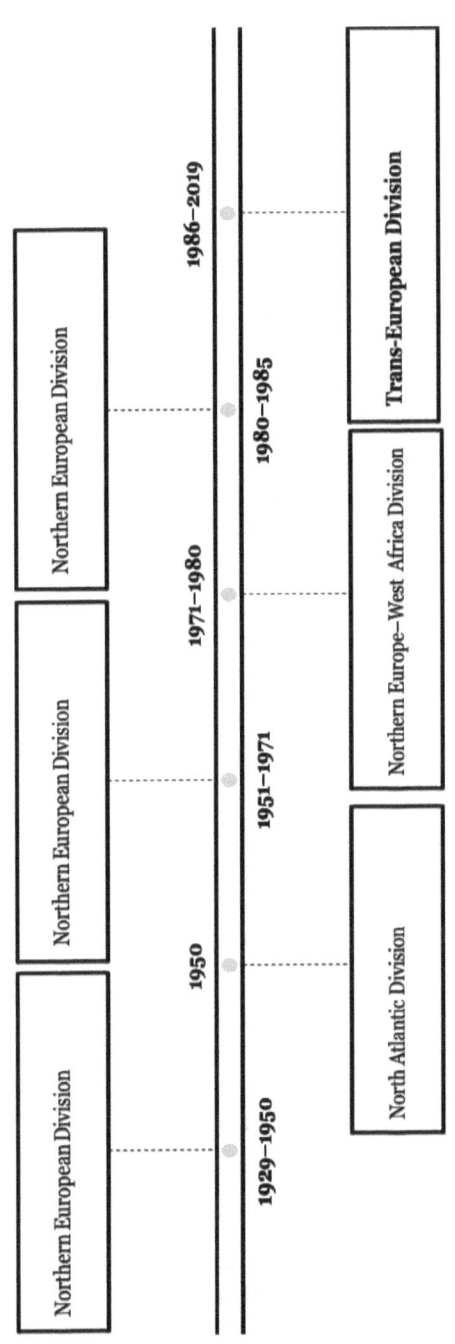

Figure 1: Division Nomenclature, 1929–2019

Commemoration and Evaluation

Why mark this anniversary? After all, 1929 is not the first significant year in the history of the Seventh-day Adventist Church in Northern and Eastern Europe: the General Conference sent missionaries to the continent for the first time in 1874; Adventist work in the territory of what is now the TED began in 1877. Yet both of these events are temporally distant and can seem even more remote because the church's situation in the 1870s was so dissimilar to today. In contrast, the Northern European church in 1929, notwithstanding the transformation of Europe outlined above and in spite of changes in the church, is recognisable to Seventh-day Adventists in 2019. How church leaders tried to shape the development of Adventist mission and ministry in the last ninety years is relevant to church leaders of the twenty-first century and lessons can be learned, despite some obvious differences between then and now.

Ninety years after the founding of the NED is a natural moment to pause and take stock of the TED's history. It is the anniversary not merely of an organisation, but of a major shift in the church's approach to working in and beyond Europe. It represents nine decades of sustained and common effort, by Adventists in a common core of European countries, to uplift Jesus Christ as seen through the lens of distinctive Adventist doctrines. It is a moment for thanksgiving and reflection.

The ninetieth anniversary is, furthermore, an opportunity. In the Holy Scriptures, understanding the past is always a potential springboard to success in the future; the same is true in the writings of Ellen G. White (a corpus that Adventists traditionally have familiarly referred to as the 'Spirit of Prophecy').[4] In words that church leaders and church members alike have often quoted, she affirmed: 'We

---

[4] See D. J. B. Trim, 'Stones of Meaning', part 1, 'Why History Matters: Sacred History', part 2, 'Why Our History Matters: Seventh-day Adventists and History', *ARH*, 188 (9 and 16 June 2011), 500–02, 527–29.

have nothing to fear for the future, except as we shall forget the way the Lord has led us, and His teaching in our past history.'[5] Here she makes explicit the potential to learn lessons from history. At times, however, it is as though Seventh-day Adventists feel that, by quoting her words, they have done all that is required – that there is no need to invest financial or intellectual resources in recovering and understanding their collective past. A distinguished Adventist historian, Floyd Greenleaf, observes: 'The urgency and the momentum of today often encourage us to neglect the meaning of what happened yesterday. [...] It is easier than we think to overlook how we have arrived at our juncture in history.'[6] Greenleaf is too charitable to observe that this propensity is particularly true of his own faith community. Yet on the whole, Adventists, by inaction and ignorance, in fact *do* 'forget the way the Lord has led' and, in practice, learn from 'our past history' only intermittently.[7]

The situation is changing, and this book, commissioned by the TED officers, is an example.[8] Yet in light of the lack of scholarly engagement with many aspects of Seventh-day Adventist history, it is perhaps worth stressing that Ellen White's well-known statement about 'nothing to fear' was not an outlier, but typical of her thought. To cite just two striking examples, which could be multiplied, in a text

---

5 Ellen G. White, *Life Sketches* (Mountain View, Calif.: Pacific Press, 1943), p. 196.
6 Floyd Greenleaf, *A Land of Hope: The Growth of the Seventh-day Adventist Church in South America* (Tatuí, Brazil: Casa Publicadora Brasileira, 2011), pp. 9–10.
7 See D. J. B. Trim, '"Nothing to fear ... except": Understanding the Past and Applying it to the Future', *College and University Dialogue*, 30.2 (2018), 21–23 (p. 21).
8 Other examples: the GC held historical conferences as part of the Spring Meeting of the GC Executive Committee in 2013 (which marked the 150th anniversary of the church's founding) and the 2018 Annual Council; both meetings were held at Battle Creek, MI, the church's historic centre (1863–1903). The proceedings of the 2013 conference have been published: *Lessons from Battle Creek: Reflections after 150 Years of Church Organization*, ed. by Alberto R. Timm and James R. Nix (Silver Spring, MD: Review & Herald, 2018).

first published in 1900 she declared: 'The past history of the cause of God needs to be often brought before the people young and old.'[9] In 1901 she wrote to the then GC president, Arthur G. Daniells: 'Again and again I have been shown that the past experiences of God's people are not to be counted as dead facts.'[10] Ellen White also was clear that histories of God's people should not be hagiographies (lives of saints) nor should they whitewash unfortunate facts. In 1876 she argued that 'one of the best evidences of the authenticity of the Scriptures' is that in its narrative 'the truth is not glossed over nor the sins of its chief characters suppressed'.[11] She returned to this theme near the end of her life: Biblical narratives, she wrote, give a rounded picture of God's people, because they recount 'the struggles, the defeats, and the victories'.[12]

The ninetieth anniversary of the TED is an ideal occasion for Adventists in the division (and beyond) to look back and honour those who came before; honouring them, however, can and should include applying Ellen White's counsel. We should be realists, rather than triumphalist, about the TED's nine decades, acknowledging the struggles and setbacks, as well as celebrating the successes. Only with knowledge in the round of the Adventist Church's past will church members and church leaders in the TED fully comprehend its current position and future prospects. Seventh-day Adventists in South-Eastern, East-Central, and Northern Europe can and should be inspired by their heritage, but at the same time they can analyse

---

9   Ellen G. White, *Testimonies for the Church*, 9 vols. (Mountain View, Calif.: Pacific Press, 1948), vi, p. 365. This formulation first appears in a letter of 4 Dec. 1890, to 'Brothers and Sisters in Norwich': Ellen G. White Estate, Lt. 33, 1890. She did not use it in published form until the publication of *Testimony* no. 34 in 1900.
10 White to A. G. Daniells, Nov. 1, 1903, Ellen G. White Estate, Lt. 238, 1903.
11 White, *Testimonies*, iv, 9 (this is from *Testimony* no. 26, first printed 1876).
12 Ellen G. White, *Patriarchs and Prophets* (Mountain View, Calif: Pacific Press, 1913), p. 596.

it, applying the lessons learned from 'past history' to the present and future of the Trans-European Division.

A Divisional History

We have seen the potential value *of* a history and the need *for* a history, in theological, intellectual, and moral terms. What, though, does it mean that it is a history of the Trans-European Division?

First, let me be clear about what this book is *not*. Firstly, it is not a history of the church in the territory of the TED, for that is a longer history, chronologically: Adventist mission in Northern Europe began five decades before the NED was founded.[13] Further, Adventist history *in* the division (as opposed to a history *of* the division) would be broader and deeper as well as longer, because it would include the history of the church from the perspective of conference, institution, and union leaders. And it would tell the story of 'ordinary' Adventists – the actually extraordinary, faithful, rank-and-file, local church members who are the foundation of everything the organised church does. Ideally, it would not only narrate their experiences, but also analyse their attitudes and actions, situating them in the wider social history of their respective places and times. And it should do all this for every country currently in the TED and cover those that once were but are not, now, telling their collective stories during the years they were in the NED/TED. Such a far-reaching history is desirable and achievable, but a formidable amount of research would be required and the result would be a weighty tome.[14]

13　The beginnings of such a history can be found in the short chapters on the countries currently in the TED found in *HRSDAE*, which in each case trace the Adventist history in the country from its origins; most of these essays are heavily reliant on *SDAE* for the narratives of early years in the respective countries.

14　Cf. Greenleaf, *A Land of Hope*, a remarkable achievement, but 783 pages long and the culmination of decades of work (being a development of idem, *The Seventh-day Adventist Church in Latin America and the Caribbean*, 2 vols [Berrien Springs, Mich.: Andrews University Press, 1992]).

Secondly, then, while this book is not an all-inclusive and wide-ranging history of Seventh-day Adventists in the nations and regions encompassed by the TED, other, more focused histories can also help Adventists in its territory to understand 'how the Lord has led *us* and His teaching in *our* past history' [emphasis mine]. This book has the more modest goal of analysing the higher levels of Adventist Church structure.[15] It is a history of how church leaders acted and reacted, directing the component parts of the division, distributing its collective resources, and shaping activities and initiatives at other levels of denominational organisation. It is written largely from the perspective of the division office and the executive committee.

This history therefore tends to be the view from twenty-thousand feet, rather than ground level.[16] Yet this is not entirely the case: firstly, union presidents always sat on the division executive committee and over time they were joined by other union officers and by conference presidents, whose perspective is at times represented. Secondly, all kinds of matters came before the division administration and executive committee. Requests were received for financial assistance, counsel, new workers, support in disputes with secular authorities, mediation in disputes within Adventism. Sometimes protests were made and heard (if not always actioned). Thirdly, both the organisational culture of each union and the distinctive characteristics of Adventism in each country of the division are felt more widely. They create issues that the division must address and they influence the decisions made by church administrators. So too do political

---

The longer history of the church in the TED and the division's own vast and ever-changing territory would make for a more difficult task and a still-longer book.

15 I use 'higher levels' of structure as in GC and TED *Working Policy*, in which 'References […] to higher level, higher organisation, lower level, lower organisation, or similar terms referring to Church structure, or references to levels of the Church are for descriptive purposes' (*General Conference Working Policy 2018–2019*, B 05, 9).

16 Cf. the very short overview history in the article *sub* 'Trans-European Division', *SDAE*, II, 789–92 (p. 789).

circumstances, of course, and one result of the TED's geographical range was social and political diversity, so that the headquarters and executive committee had to deal concurrently with very different situations as regards religious liberty and relations with wider society. The political situation in a given country often narrowed the options open to church leaders, yet at times also created remarkable opportunities.

For all these reasons, this is not just a history of the headquarters – indeed, the history of any division organisation will inevitably include some coverage of issues at levels other than the division administration. Still, the reader should be aware that this book is not a social history of church members living in the division, but a history of the issues, challenges, and opportunities that faced church leaders at the division level; of how they responded to them; and the initiatives they took to advance the goals and objectives of the division administration.

Even thus focused, ninety years of history would make for a large volume. I have written a concise history of the TED, one that I hope will be read, rather than a comprehensive history 'for the record'. As a result, this book is a selective account: an interpretation, not an all-inclusive narrative.[17] Most of the chapters in Parts One–Three are chronological, but none are strictly diachronic, which is to say, specific themes are explored and chapters are structured around those themes rather than the sequence of events. In Part One, Chapter 1 is focused on the foundation of the division in 1928, though with some looking back. Chapter 2 deals with how the division headquarters was created; it largely focuses on 1929, but it examines some aspects that were still being worked out in the early 1930s. Part Two is structured purely chronologically: Chapters 4–6 each deal with sequential periods of history, though Chapter 4 and Chapter 6, in particular,

---

17 Cf. Eric Hobsbawm's comments in the preface to his justly celebrated *The Age of Revolution 1789–1848* (orig. edn, 1962; New York: Vintage Books, 1996), p. ix. I share almost none of Hobsbawm's presuppositions, but admire his genius, and resonate with his approach.

are thematic within the period each covers. In Part Three, there is overlap, chronologically, between Chapters 7 and 8, though Chapter 9 covers a discrete time period. In Part Four, Chapters 10–12 are all thematic and address particular topics across the whole era, though much of Chapter 11 is focused on the late 1940s, used as a case study to illustrate its particular theme. In sum, each of the next eight chapters includes a narrative of events, but in each case the narrative frames analysis of influential personalities, moments, decisions, and developments. Significant insights into these are afforded by statistics, which allow us to measure success (or lack of success) and trends.

This history focuses on events and episodes that established or exemplify long-lasting trends and patterns of collective thought and action. This approach means that the balance of this book tilts towards the early years, especially in Part One. It is hard to achieve a detached perspective on recent events – difficult to distinguish long-term from short-term trends. Yet it is also the case that, in any national (or, we might add, denominational) community, what we believe and what we do today is governed at least as much by the habits of mind we formed in the relatively remote past as by what we did and thought yesterday. The relatively remote past is apt to constrain our thought and actions more, because we understand it less well than we do our recent past … and it has cut deeper grooves of custom in our minds.[18]

When it comes to the events that occurred within readers' own lifetimes, they will be able to identify for themselves the influence of the patterns of thought and action established in the first decades – but for that to happen, those patterns need first to be expounded, because the older history is misremembered or entirely forgotten. More fully apprehending the earlier, formative period of the TED's history will provide a foundation for understanding the 'grooves of

---

18 Russell F. Weigley, *The American Way of War: A History of United States Military Strategy and Policy* (Bloomington: Indiana University Press, 1977), p. xx.

custom' – and of belief – that moulded this division's organisational culture and shaped how the TED 'does business'.

This is, then, a partial, perhaps partisan, book, and some of the questions posed will be seen by some people as provocative. It is intended, however, to do more than provoke. I seek to prompt reflection not just about this division's history but about its trajectory. The 'past experiences of God's people' *can* be made more than 'dead facts'; they can inspire, edify, and chasten. If we learn from those experiences and facts – if in fact we *do* allow ourselves to be taught by the events 'in our past history' – then the Seventh-day Adventist Church in the Trans-European Division will be more effective in carrying out the mission entrusted to it by our Lord and Saviour (Matt. 24:14, 28:19–20, Luke 10:2, Rev. 14:6–15).

Themes

Having set out the parameters of this history, what of its theme? The Adventist Church in the TED has for most of its history been characterised, among church leaders and church members alike, by passionate enthusiasm for evangelising the world – a fervour that gives this book its title. But what does a passion for mission entail? What arises from it? What are its sub-themes?

Mission is susceptible to different interpretations, but in Christian history generally (and particularly in Adventist history) mission has tended to connote what Seventh-day Adventists for the first century of their history usually referred to as 'foreign' or 'overseas' mission. This requires people who go on a mission, so thinking about the implications of a 'passion for 'mission' ineluctably gives rise to thinking about 'missionaries'. The problem is that the words missionary and missionaries are no longer well understood. There simply aren't as many missionaries as there used to be and neither are mission boards or mission societies as prominent as they once were. When the term 'missionary' crosses many people's mental horizons, it comes heavily freighted with ambiguities, assumptions, insinuations. It comes shrouded in myths.

'The Missionary': A Modern Myth

There is a cliché in modern Europe and America of the missionary as a white man, clad in khaki drill or white linen and a white pith helmet, cutting his way through the jungle with a machete, suffering malarial fevers, fighting off crocodiles or the odd hippo, before finally arriving at a native village. Assured of his personal superiority, supremely confident in his own abilities, and certain of Western moral, theological, and technological rectitude, the missionary confronts the natives with the gospel of Western culture, condemning their pagan behaviours and beliefs. He is a figure of terrible anger and smug hypocrisy, of awful self-righteousness and sweeping self-confidence, seeking to abolish traditional attitudes and ancient customs, thanks to a formidable range of ingrained cultural assumptions and powerful biases, all disguised by the rhetoric of Christianising and civilising. This missionary never doubts that he has nothing to learn and everything to teach. He is there to get the natives to abandon nakedness, to make the women put on blouses, and the men, trousers; most ominously, he's really there to get the savages to accept imperial government and economic exploitation.

The truth is, this purportedly unbiased view of the missionary is fruit of a prejudice as powerful as any held by supposedly bigoted missionaries – a prejudice arising partly from ignorance, since most Europeans now have only the merest acquaintance with Christianity and few know any missionaries. To ignorance can be added deeply felt suspicion of organised religion and a postmodern scepticism of 'conversion'. If past generations constructed heroic myths around Christian missionaries, creating distorted pictures of fallible men and women, in the twenty-first century, myths are still being fashioned

– it's just that now they are negative. But the end result is still a caricature, not an accurate picture.

There were unquestionably some missionaries who equated the gospel with western culture or commerce (or for that matter with male and female fashion). There were others, however, who actively resisted imperialism on behalf of the people they were missionising, educating them and enabling them to improve their lot and cast off colonial rule.[19] This was, moreover, particularly true of Seventh-day Adventist missionaries, due to their characteristic emphasis on education and public health, typically paired with considerable sympathy for the people they worked for and with. The work ethic, agricultural techniques, and technical skills Adventist missionaries imparted were often empowering.[20] As to the pith helmets, the machetes, and the crocodiles, there is a certain degree of truth to this perception, including for Adventist missionaries to Africa (see Illustrations 1.1 and 1.2). But as to the rest, it simply is not a recognisable picture of most Adventist missionaries, especially those from Europe and Australasia. There have been times and places where some Americans

---

19   Neil Parsons, *King Khama and the Great White Queen: Victorian Britain through African Eyes* (Chicago & London: University of Chicago Press, 1998) is an engaging historical case study. Robert D. Woodberry, 'The Missionary Roots of Liberal Democracy', *American Political Science Review*, 106 (2012), 244–74, is a provocative overview of the impact of Protestant missionizing, assessed in terms of present-day outcomes.

20   These points are particularly well documented for Adventist mission in the Andes and the western Amazon basin, but similar approaches were used elsewhere, including in Africa. For South America, see John H. Bodley, 'A Transformative Movement among the Campa of Eastern Peru', *Anthropos*, 67 (1972), 220–28; Charles Teel, 'Fernando and Ana Stahl – Mediators of Personal and Social Transformation', in *Adventist Mission in the 21st Century*, ed. by Jon L. Dybdahl (Hagerstown, MD: RHPA, 1999), pp. 278–85; Fernando Santos-Granero, 'The Enemy Within: Child Sorcery, Revolution, and the Evils of Modernisation in Eastern Peru', in *Darkness and Secrecy: Witchcraft and Sorcery in Native South America*, ed. by Neil L. Whitehead and Robin M. Wright (Durham, NC: Duke University Press, 2004), pp. 272–305 (pp. 283–89); Elena Mihas, *Upper Perené Arawak Narratives of History, Landscape, and Ritual* (Lincoln: University of Nebraska Press, 2014), pp. 20–21.

working overseas have been, or appeared, too self-confident in their cultural superiority – a point made by experienced and successful American Adventist veterans of mission service. Of course, missionaries from other regions, including some, unquestionably, from the NED, have fallen into the same trap, which is always ready to ensnare the unwary. Among the Adventist missionaries from the TED have been a few bigots, and some fools and knaves, but to fixate on them is to distort the reality. What is striking is how many Adventist missionaries who went out to serve from countries in this division were forward-looking, open-minded, and well aware that they could learn from their local hosts, the people with whom they lived, and for whom they laboured.

Mission and Missionaries

Those who spread the myths and misconceptions have one thing right, however, which is that mission ultimately is about people. It is about the people who hear the proclamation of truth and listen to the teaching; it is also about the proclaimers and the teachers. A passion for mission is not a theoretical construct; what it has typically meant in the last ninety years was the regular, personal engagement of Seventh-day Adventist Christians in the Trans-European Division's territory and especially in what I will suggest below are its core countries, its mission homelands, with fulfilling the Great Commission – often in countries far from their own.

Furthermore, as a theme in Northern and Trans-European Adventist history, it really is about the missionaries more than the missionised. There are two chief reasons for this: one general to Adventist history, the other particular to the history of the TED.

1) Foreign Missions vs Home Missions

There has always been a tendency to see 'mission' and 'missions' as things that happen or exist in a foreign land. Today the understanding of mission as something done far away is perhaps becoming problematic (not least in the TED, a point to which we'll return). But why has 'mission' tended to mean 'foreign mission'? Historically, Seventh-day Adventists used terms like 'foreign' or 'overseas' missions partly to distinguish them from 'home missions' – the title given to one of the church's earliest general departments. But they also did not ascribe the same priority to home mission as they did to foreign mission. Indeed, prioritising the latter was seen as a good way of aiding the former. Ellen White wrote:

> *The home missionary work will be farther advanced in every way when a more liberal, self-denying, self-sacrificing spirit is manifested for the prosperity of foreign missions; for the prosperity of the home work depends largely, under God, upon the reflex influence of the evangelistic work in countries afar off.*[21]

But such statements implicitly assumed that 'home' (wherever it was – initially the United States, but later including some countries in Europe, Australasia, and southern Africa) was already Christian in essence; there was need to proclaim prophetic truth and the 'landmark doctrines', because it was presumed that many of the audience would already have some kind of relationship with Christ.

The foreign fields, in contrast, were inhabited by 'pagans',[22] 'heathens',[23] and, in some areas, 'Mohammedans'[24] – terms Adventists regularly used at the time the NED was created. These were people who probably had no hope of salvation if a Christian did not go to their lands and tell them about Christ. Their need was therefore the greater, and hence the priority given to mission fields over

---

21 *Testimonies for the Church*, VI, p. 27.
22 Examples from minutes of NEDCOM meetings: 5–7 Sept. 1928, NEDCOM mins., 1928, GC Ar., RG NE 1, p. 4.
23 NED Winter Council, 4 Dec. 1928, NEDCOM-WCM, GC Ar., RG NE 1, p. 64.
24 NEDCOM Winter Meeting, 19 Nov. 1965, NEDCOM mins., 1965, GC Ar., RG NE 1, p. 260.

(presumably) Christian homelands. That priority could take many forms – financial, organisational, intellectual. But all those really were important only if they delivered a Christian (or Christians) into the mission field to witness about Jesus. Without such a person carrying out mission – a missionary in fact – little would be achieved. Adventists, more than other Christians, might hope that literature would win some souls. In practice, though, Adventist tracts and papers won people over to Adventism who were already some form of Christian. In any case, as Ellen White identified as early as December 1871:

> *Much can be done through the medium of the press, but still more can be accomplished if the influence of the labors of the living preacher goes with our publications. Missionaries are needed to go to other nations to preach the truth in a guarded, careful manner.*[25]

So, for Seventh-day Adventists, there was an order of precedence; home mission was not unimportant, but it was less important than missionaries who went 'to other nations'. That was the ideal: 'a passion for mission' meant, in particular, mission, missions, and missionaries 'overseas' (as the TED's historic mission fields in Africa literally were). That passion was manifested, literally embodied perhaps, by the missionaries from the territory of the TED who accepted 'a call' and were 'appointed' (in the language the church officially used up to the early 1970s) to serve as foreign and, typically, as cross-cultural missionaries. Their number is uncertain but would be around the thousand mark over the last century: a thousand men and women who left their homes, who forsook family and friends to go to faraway places.[26] That figure alone is extraordinary. To that number, however, we have to add the many more who returned tithe faithfully, gave to missions generously, and staunchly collected donations from their

---

25   *Testimonies for the Church*, III, p. 204.
26   See Appendix IV.

local communities, thereby making a crucial contribution to the mission enterprise of the Seventh-day Adventist Church.

In the Europe of post-postmodernity and hyperreality, a culture in which ironic detachment is a cardinal virtue, the sacrifices made by missionaries (especially in the TED's first thirty years or so) are easily misrepresented or misunderstood. One reason is that, as discussed above, Christian mission has become deeply unfashionable and is a subject of ignorance in Western society in general. Yet, even among European Seventh-day Adventists in particular, awareness of exactly what it is that missionaries do, even personal knowledge of actual missionaries, is less common than ever before, because the numbers of Adventists going as foreign missionaries has been in decline since c.1970; the numbers going from countries of the TED to serve as cross-cultural missionaries are also fewer than before.

2) Faraway Places

The other reasons that mission as a theme in the TED's history is largely about missionaries are specific to the TED's history and both relate to distance. First, the far away places to which missionaries went really were very far away indeed, especially before the introduction of affordable long-haul airline flights. The Middle East was relatively close, especially to the Eastern European territories of the TED, in the period 1995–2011. But otherwise, for the seventy-two years in which the TED or its unions had a strong connection to foreign mission fields, they were distant and mysterious lands, in which to serve as a missionary seemed romantic, even glamourous – more so at any rate than literature evangelism in Linköping, Bible studies in Belfast, or temperance meetings in Tampere.

In addition, there is the fact that the faraway places, once evangelised, were dropped from the division. The countries in the Great Lakes region of East Africa went first, and other divisions went on to reap where the NED had sown. In 1970, the Horn of Africa went its own way. Then, in 1980, West Africa. Then, in 2011, the Middle East and Pakistan, though there had been rather less success in those unions than in the East African, Ethiopian, Nigerian, or West African Unions. This isn't to suggest that a division with its centre of gravity in the north of Europe should be controlling territories in Africa or Asia, not any longer. But the point is that, for church members in the TED, the people in mission fields with whom missionaries had the strongest connections kept leaving the division.

Mission for the TED has, historically, been about what 'we' from the TED are doing to amorphous and ill-defined 'people'. It has been about us, not about the people won to Christ in Eritrea, Ethiopia, Ghana, Liberia, Nigeria. They are now just a distant memory (though as we will see in Chapter 7, they remember the TED better than it remembers them), but more recent converts in Sudan and Pakistan are still largely unknown. If the mission fields had been closer, then a larger proportion of the membership in the division might have had encounters with real people from the mission field (as now happens for many North American Adventists via mission trips to Africa and Latin America). Instead they were *always* afar off. This history keeps coming back to those who went out from the territory of the TED, more than those they worked closely with and for, because that has been the reality of the TED's historic experience with mission. It is something 'we' went and did, then came home, and 'they' went their own way; they were always the 'other'.

But here is a question: What about when the other is us? Europe has not been Christian for a long time. Now the urgency is with 'home mission'. There are many more Seventh-day Adventists in Ghana than Great Britain. The priorities have to shift. How will we adjust to the missionised being not afar off, but just down the street? Or to missionaries no longer being a small group of heroic individuals who screw their courage to the sticking place, but being (or needing to be) many of us?

Still Passionate about Mission?

In telling the story of a longstanding, historical 'passion for mission' and thinking about what that means, these are some of the ideas that arise. Here is a last one: as I noted above, the number of Adventists going from the TED is much lower now than in the past – for example, in the late 1950s, twenty new missionaries or more were going out every year on average.[27] The problem of ignorance and incomprehension is not limited to the secular world. There is a question, or rather a set of questions, that arise from this point.

Is the decline of foreign mission service a symptom of a different, larger problem? Is it possible that the long-burning flame of mission is now just smouldering in the twenty-first century? Do the embers need to be stirred and reignited? If the passion for mission has waned, then, once the flames have been fanned, to where should they be directed? After the TED's long engagement with mission fields in East Africa, West Africa, and West Asia, should it now focus primarily on mission in its own territory? Ought that now to be its only concern? Or might turning entirely inward stifle a 'liberal, self-denying, self-sacrificing spirit […] for the prosperity of foreign missions'? Might there be a synergistic relationship between 'the home work […] and the evangelistic work in countries afar off'?[28] What is the ideal balance?

By the end of this book, I will have answered some of these questions, implicitly where not explicitly. Others are left for the reader to ponder and draw conclusions for themselves.

---

27 See below, Chapter 6.
28 Ellen G. White, *General Conference Bulletin*, 1 Oct. 1901; repr. in *Testimonies for the Church*, vi, p. 27.

Mission Homelands

In addition to passion for mission, a second theme is the dynamic interrelationship between the core countries of the TED, the mission homelands, and the mission fields. In considering the TED's history, more than the histories of some divisions, I have found it useful to identify mission homelands and mission fields. This is terminology I use later so it will be helpful to define it here.

To conceptualise the division's composition this way, as 'homeland and mission' fields, is not an imposition in hindsight. It was one used by church leaders of the mid-twentieth century. For example, L. K. Dickson, the GC vice-president who chaired the business meeting at the 1950 GC Session that reunited the British Isles and West Africa with the NED (under the short-lived name 'North Atlantic Division'), visited the division's territory later that year. At a meeting with Adventist students, Dickson answered questions about what had been done and observed, 'regarding the benefits that will accrue because of this organisation', that he believed

> one of the leading benefits will be the strong promotion and enthusiasm that will be awakened throughout Great Britain and throughout Northern Europe in connection with much mission territory that is attached to the division. It seems to be a very well balanced territory from the standpoint of homeland and mission field.[29]

Nine nations, all washed by the North Atlantic and the Baltic have been part of the division for all, or almost all, of its ninety-year history: Denmark, Finland, Iceland, Ireland, the Netherlands, Norway, Poland, Sweden, and the United Kingdom. All have been part of the division since the start (with the exception of the Netherlands), and in 1946 it replaced the Baltic republics, separated in 1940, and they have thus been part of the division for just over four-fifths of its

---

29 'The British Union and the North Atlantic Division', *British Advent Messenger* (Union Session Bulletin no. 5), 13 Oct. 1950, pp. 13–14.

lifetime.[30] The British Union's (BUC) status was anomalous between 1946–1950, but probably the most precisely accurate description is that it was never fully detached from the Northern European Division – that both the BUC and the provisional NED briefly had atypical relations with the General Conference before their status was clarified.

Two of these countries, Iceland and the Republic of Ireland, have never contributed significantly to the wider division budget; in geographical terms they are (literally) peripheral (as they arguably are in financial terms). There have, then, been seven core countries of the Trans-European Division six of these are, I suggest, the division's historical 'mission homelands': Denmark, Finland, Great Britain, the Netherlands, Norway, and Sweden.

Instinctively many would think of the United States as being *the* Adventist homeland but, as the church spread in the nineteenth century, others emerged. Why can these six nations be called 'homelands'?

First, Scandinavia and Britain received Adventist missionaries as early as the 1870s. The church in those four countries has deeper roots than anywhere except the United States, Canada, and Switzerland. Not only is Adventism of longstanding in each of the six homelands, but church organisation also developed early there. The Denmark Conference was the first conference organised outside North America (1880) and the Swedish Conference the third (1882). There were conferences in Scandinavia, then, before there were ones in any of the US states of the Deep South, or even in Maryland, where today the world headquarters is located. The Scandinavian Union Conference (ScUC,

---

30 As noted in Chapter 9, the Baltic Union returned in 1994, but the three Baltic republics have thus been part of the division for 36 years (interrupted by a gap of more than half a century), whereas in the Dutch case it is 73 years: the Baltic Union's share of the TED's history is 40 per cent, for the Netherlands Union it is 81 per cent.

founded 1901) and British Union Conference (founded 1902) were among the first sixteen unions.

Furthermore, the BUC and ScUC achieved self-dependence relatively quickly. They were essentially self-sustaining, financially, by the 1920s. To be sure, their capacity to support themselves was sorely tried during the Great Depression, as we will see in Chapter 4, but in the post-war European economy, the finances of the BUC, East Nordic Union Conference (ENUC), West Nordic Union Conference (WNUC), and the Netherlands Union Conference (NUC) were able, from 1946, to provide the funds necessary to sustain the church at home, and to support missionaries and institutions abroad. Appropriations from the GC and its contributions to the expenses of missionaries were also important for the TED, then as now, but the tithes and offerings from the division's six core countries were the essential basis for its outreach, whether in the mission fields or within Europe. There is another form of self-reliance: the ability to provide workers properly prepared for pastoral ministry and outreach, in numbers adequate for the work to be done. This is a matter both of enough candidates and of a capacity to train them. In this sphere, too, these six 'homelands' were, from an early stage, largely self-sufficient: each of them provided some training, in their own country, for those who felt the call to ministry; there were sufficient men and women who felt called to become pastors and Bible workers; and there were enough also to supply missionaries for foreign service.

Second, the six homeland countries are the historic hotbeds of Protestantism, and, until relatively recently, each was a Christian stronghold. Here we come back to my earlier point, about the perceived difference between 'home' and mission field, one of which was, indeed, that homeland was already Christian. This was a reasonable assumption up to World War II and even beyond; the process of desacralisation really picked up pace in the last quarter of the twentieth century. Today none of the six is a Christian stronghold.

Third, in the most literal sense, it was in these countries that the homes of missionaries were found; from them, missionaries were recruited, resourced, sent forth, and sustained in the mission fields. In contrast, while the Polish Union Conference (PUC) redoubtably resisted the influence of a Communist government for more than forty years, the church in Poland was somewhat isolated from the rest of the division from 1940–1990 and historically has not been a source of missionaries (and only a limited source of money for foreign missions since, for understandable reasons, mission offerings have been modest). A case might be made that Estonia and Latvia were mission homelands in the early 1930s, because they provided a number of missionaries. However, in comparison to the six homelands, their contributions (in terms both of missionary recruits and of financial contributions) were modest; in any case, because of *force majeure*, even their limited role in division affairs stopped nearly eighty years ago. While church workers have gone to serve internationally from the Adriatic, Hungarian, and South-East European Unions, they have not yet supplied large numbers of missionaries to other divisions and other continents, though if one were to include workers serving in other parts of the TED (and the Euro-Africa Division [EAD]), then anecdotally the South-East European Union Conference would be more significant. Nevertheless, over the ninety years, there is no doubt that the six mission homelands have been pre-eminent in the TED's history.

It was these homelands that supplied the missionaries and the money for the far larger mission fields. Yet homeland and mission field always had a complex interrelationship; they constitute a classic sociological dyad. They were not dichotomies – the mission fields, for most of their history in the TED, definitely needed the homelands – yet when one reads minutes of committees and correspondence of homeland church leaders, it often seems that they felt, in their turn, that they needed the mission fields. After all, for its first fourteen years the NED administered Uganda and Kenya; it was responsible for Ethiopia, Eritrea and Somalia for thirty years in all; it had oversight of Sudan for another thirty, though in two widely separated chronological tranches; most significantly, it supervised Adventist mission in almost the whole of West Africa for just over half a century, well over half the division's lifetime.

Further, even though power was usually in the hand of the homelands, the needs and wants of the mission fields tended to set the agenda. It would be easy to conclude, on the face of it, that the mission fields, to adopt another sociological concept, were the periphery to the homelands' core; yet in practice, as we will see, the former increasingly set the priorities of the latter. As we will also see, the mission fields exercised what almost seems a magnetic attraction to the homelands – because of the overwhelming imperative of mission. The complex interrelationship of the homelands and the mission fields is a crucial part of the TED's history.

* * *

The history of the Seventh-day Adventist Church in the territory of the Trans-European Division has been about mission in two senses. First, it has been a history of reaching out, in general – of outreach to people who knew little or nothing of Jesus or of biblical truth. Second, though, it has also been a history of a particular kind of outreach and of the kind of mission that many people think of when they hear the word 'missionary': cross-cultural mission. For many decades this was done in Africa or Asia, reaching out to Muslims and adherents of African traditional religions. Outreach in Europe, the region once known as 'Christendom', meant sharing a fuller understanding of Christ, of the Holy Scriptures, and especially of prophetic truths, with people who were usually members of churches, but often only nominally Christians.

In recent years, with the TED's responsibility restricted to Europe, the significance of cross-cultural mission has changed – and yet it is no less. Although the TED headquarters no longer oversees mission in Africa and Asia, the TED remains a disproportionate source of cross-cultural missionaries around the world,[31] partly because the membership has had more education, is more professional, and has greater technological expertise, than Adventists in many parts of the world.[32] But cross-cultural mission continues to be important in the TED in another way, reflecting a more profound shift than changes in ecclesiastical boundaries.

European Baby Boomers, Gen Xers, and Millennials can hardly be called Christian anymore, even in terms of their culture (except in the most generic sense), much less of belief or practice. The different societies of Western and Central Europe (including virtually all those currently under the TED) have embraced materialism and irreligion. The 'term secularisation is a contested concept' and the enduring affinity for spirituality over religion ('I'm spiritual but not religious') is at odds with certain definitions of secularism; but if we use 'the less loaded' term 'religious decline', which is also more empirically measurable, then the evidence is discouraging. Recent sociological analysis

---

31 Analysis of the annual reports on International Service Employees (ISEs) in service each year, prepared by International Personnel Resources & Services at the GC, shows that, over the last twenty years, the average annual number of ISEs in service has been 61 from TED, as opposed to 963 ISEs from the world, i.e., the TED on average supplied 6 per cent of ISEs per annum; but TED's membership (as noted earlier) is 0.4 per cent, so that TED's share of ISEs is 1500 per cent of its share of reported membership.

32 The 2017–2018 Global Survey of Church Members showed that 52 per cent of church members in the TED are university graduates as opposed to 30 per cent of members worldwide: see D. J. B. Trim, 'Church Member Survey 2017–18: Trans-European Division in the Context of the World Church', presented at TEDEC Midyear Meeting, 21 May 2019: <https://www.adventistresearch.org/sites/default/files/CompressedGCMS%202017-18%20TED%20in%20Context%20edited-compressed.pdf>.

of very large data sets 'find[s] evidence of generational decline in both participation and belief' in God, Christ, and revealed Christian religion, in ten 'Western European societies'. These include Britain, Denmark, Iceland, the Netherlands, Norway, and Sweden, which were also among the earliest to witness notable decline, while other studies have demonstrated a similar trend of dwindling participation in Christianity and 'replacement of the Christian worldview' in the Baltic states. A range of data seem to show long-term, seemingly inexorable 'trajectories of decline' in Great Britain.[33]

The core territories of the TED are now not so much postmodern as post-Christian. An appeal to common scriptural knowledge, even to common cultural values, increasingly means little, which poses profound challenges to Adventism's tried, tested, and trusted modes of evangelisation. At the same time, Adventist church members in Europe are themselves becoming increasingly postmodern and have become, to a great extent, multi-ethnic and multi-cultural.[34] In the twenty-first century, then, Adventist mission is increasingly cross-cultural *within* the territory of the TED. There needs to be the same commitment as in the past to sharing the distinctive Adventist message of wholeness and hope in Christ.

As a result of that commitment, exhibited over nine decades, the Seventh-day Adventist Church is well established in Europe. It has been present in some countries of the TED for more than fourteen

---

33 Eric Kaufmann, Anne Goujon, and Vegard Skirbekk, 'The End of Secularization in Europe? A Socio-Demographic Perspective', *Sociology of Religion*, 73 (2012), 69–91 (pp. 71, 85, cf. esp. pp. 77, 87); Jaanus Plaat, 'Religious Change in Estonia and the Baltic States during the Soviet Period in Comparative Perspective', *Journal of Baltic Studies*, 34.1 (2003), 52–73 (p. 67); Steve Bruce and David Voas, 'Do Social Crises Cause Religious Revivals? What British Church Adherence Rates Show', *Journal of Religion in Europe*, 9 (2016), 26–43 (p. 41).

34 See D. J. B. Trim, 'Modernism and Post-Modernism in Western Thought and Culture: From "Buttoned-Up Tight" to "ad hoc Tattooed"', in *Journeys to Wisdom: Festschrift in Honour of Michael Pearson*, ed. by Andreas Bochmann, Manuela Casti Yeagley, and Jean-Claude Verrecchia (Bracknell: Newbold Academic Press, 2015), pp. 45–72.

decades; nowhere in the current territory has it been present less than a century; and the division itself has existed now for ninety years. In that time, it has made mistakes, of omission and of commission, but it has also achieved remarkable things, on three continents. As the Seventh-day Adventist Church in the northwest and southeast of Europe looks to the future, the TED will doubtless continue to play a major role, in supporting sound administration, in strategic planning, and in providing resources, but above all (one hopes), in mobilising the historic passion for mission of Seventh-day Adventists in the Trans-European Division.

Chapter 2
Foundations

We pledge ourselves under God to make every effort to carry the Advent Message to the [...] unwarned millions.
– Church leaders in Northern Europe, November 1928

Where were you when I laid the foundations [...]? Declare, if you have understanding. – Job 38:4

In the summer of 1928, Adventist church leaders from around the world gathered near Darmstadt, Germany, to discuss and make vital decisions about the future of the church in Europe. They came because they cared about the Seventh-day Adventist Church in Europe and knew that a strong European church was essential for the continued expansion of Adventist mission and growth of the church globally (Illustration 2.1).

The deliberations of middle-aged and elderly men (and the leaders who made decisions in 1928 were exclusively male), about apparently abstruse questions of ecclesiastical organisation, might seem inherently uninteresting to many church members. However, the decisions taken in 1928 had a major impact on Adventism across the world. Among the outcomes was the foundation of the Northern European Division.

This chapter examines the founding of the NED. It explores the who, when, where, and why of the new division. The decision-making process that culminated in the creation of the NED is of more than academic interest, because it was affected by considerations that continue to shape the Adventist experience in Europe today and thus are of enduring significance.

The End of the European Division

In August 1928, the Summer Council of the European Division was held at a German mission training school, Marienhoehe Seminary, near Darmstadt. It was no ordinary council, however: the four representatives from the General Conference included the president, W. A. Spicer, and the treasurer, J. L. Shaw, as well as Oliver Montgomery, a general vice-president, and an associate secretary, B. L. Beddoe. In addition, five more vice-presidents were present: E. E. Andross, W. H. Branson, A. W. Cormack, I. H. Evans, and C. B. Haynes, the presidents, respectively, of the Inter-American, African, Southern Asia, Far Eastern, and South American Divisions. Only the GC vice-presidents for the North American and Australasian Divisions were absent. This was a remarkably heavyweight delegation which points to purpose rather than coincidence – all the more because Montgomery (Illustration 2.2), a former division president, was the church's acknowledged expert on organisation, while Spicer had been for many years the church's chief proponent of worldwide mission and had served as a missionary in Europe.[1]

These church leaders from around the world travelled to Darmstadt because the principal item on the agenda was dividing the European Division, which would affect the whole world church. But, in a deeper sense, they came to Marienhoehe because they knew that if European Adventism were strong, it would benefit the whole world church. They came from around the world because they wanted to help the European church to grow.

---

1   *YB 1928*, pp. 5, 143; European Division Committee Summer Council, 13–21 Aug. 1928, mins. in GC Ar., RG EP 1, box 6599, 1926–1928, pp. 252–89; *sub* 'Montgomery, Oliver', *SDAE*, ii, 119; Godfrey Anderson, *Spicer: Leader with the Common Touch* (Washington, DC: RHPA, 1983). Montgomery later published *Principles of Church Organization and Administration* (Washington, DC: RHPA, 1942). In addition to hundreds of articles, Spicer's writings on mission up to this point included the books *Our Story of Missions for Colleges and Academies* (Mountain View, Calif.: Pacific Press, 1921) and *Miracles of Modern Missions: Gathered Out of Mission Records* (Washington, DC: RHPA, 1926).

Challenges Within Europe and Without

By 1928, the European Division was top-heavy; its 87,000 members were nearly a third of the world membership of 274,000, and while there were more church members in the NAD, the European Division membership was larger than all the other six divisions combined. In addition, the geographical area for which it was responsible was the largest of any division: it was supposed to direct church work in the whole of Europe, most of Africa, all the Middle East, most of Central Asia, and parts of North Asia. As a result, it was meant to manage twenty unions, far more than any other division (there were only twelve in the NAD).[2]

All this was simply too much for one headquarters to administer efficiently. Partly as a result, a degree of restlessness had developed among the various national church leaders in Europe. Some denominational administrators desired to have their territories linked more closely and formally to mission fields with which they had an historic connection.

There were other factors that worked against having one headquarters for the whole of Europe. Pronounced practical difficulties arose from the complex and still-evolving regulatory and governmental situation in the Europe created by the treaties of Versailles: a post-imperial Europe, full of newly independent, ethno-nationalist nation-states, many with a tendency to authoritarianism. The sheer diversity of Europe could be bewildering to American visitors, including Adventist church leaders, some (but not all) of whom took time to learn and adapt. These conditions greatly complicated the task of providing direction to a church that spanned borders. Furthermore, across much of the continent, political leaders of various ideological stripes were instinctively suspicious both of religious movements perceived as alien and of transnational organisations. The Jehovah's Witnesses were to suffer as a result, but so, too, did

2   *YB 1928*, p. 3.

Seventh-day Adventists, who on both organisational and cultural grounds appeared particularly dubious to parochial European elites. In most European nations, Adventists acknowledged the authority of a headquarters across a frontier, often in a distant country, and Adventists regularly moved money and personnel across borders. All this made the Seventh-day Adventist Church as a whole an object of deep suspicion to political elites on both the Right (who embraced authoritarian nationalism) and the Left (who tended towards socialist internationalism). If all this were not enough, in most European countries cultural and religious particularism occasioned prejudice against what was perceived as an invasive American weed disturbing the beauty of the European ecclesiastical garden.

The political and cultural European situation in the late 1920s is very different in some ways to that of the late 2010s, but there are striking similarities and continuities. Europe's diversity makes it a deeply complex operating environment. In relatively confined areas, sometimes living cheek by jowl, are many politically self-aware nations and ethnic groups, each of which has a long, rich history that often includes protracted conflict with neighbours and sometimes subjugation by other ethnicities, nationalities, and religious denominations. Across the continent, state churches moulded national characteristics, with religious loyalty an essential ingredient of certain national identities. The cultural manifestations of confessional allegiance, not least the instinctive prejudices, persist even when adherence to doctrines has dissolved. While pluralist attitudes to faith predominate in Western Europe and are spreading into Eastern Europe, ethnic and ecclesiastical chauvinism endures across the continent; parochialism subsists alongside postmodernism.[3] Although it manifests itself in different ways in different regions, it remains widely influential, in

---

3   D. J. B. Trim, 'Adventist Mission in Europe in Historical Perspective', in *Parochialism, Pluralism, and Contextualization: Challenges to Adventist Mission in Europe (19th–21st Centuries)*, ed. idem and Daniel Heinz (Oxford, Bern, Berlin, Brussels, Frankfurt am Main, New York & Vienna: Peter Lang, 2010), pp. 9–29 (pp. 12–13).

spite of increasing commercial, financial, and regulatory harmonisation emanating from the European Union (EU). Indeed, some prejudices that had apparently disappeared have recently resurfaced. If authoritarianism is far less common than ninety years ago, it, too, has reappeared, including in nations now part of the TED.

Here, then, is an example of continuity across the last ninety years: Europe's diversity and complexity continue to affect the church's work on the continent. Furthermore, that is even truer of the Trans-European Division than of the Euro-Africa Division. To be Greek means to be Orthodox, while to be Polish or Croatian means to be Catholic – rejecting these religions means rejecting one's entire community to an extent not true of any other European country. Prejudices arising from histories of religious conflict are also marked in Hungary, Northern Ireland, and Serbia. All this partly reflects the fact that the TED encompasses countries ruled by, or bordering on, the old Ottoman Empire; the particular historical development of religious adherence and nationalism in these regions turned the dominant religion in the respective countries into 'a national religion [that] left no space for the kind of anti-church secularism that emerged in Western Europe' and that 'became a marker of national identity'. This has made evangelisation in the TED's Eastern European territories particularly difficult.[4]

Europe as a whole, however, is characterised by ethno-cultural, social, religious, and political intricacy and multiplicity, affecting attitudes right across the continent, north and south, east and west. Local and regional aspects differ, but there is a common overarching reality. Despite the apparent homogenisation engendered by the EU, heterogeneity endures. There are still significant boundaries Adventists have to cross, and many of them are not national borders; the figurative frontiers, those of the imagination, are perhaps more potent than those of countries or states and give greater rise to provincialism

---

4   Mark Mazower, *The Balkans: A Short History* (New York: Modern Library, pb edn, 2002), p. 76.

and prejudice. The decisions taken in Darmstadt in 1928, and in Washington DC and New Orleans in 1985, have thus had a lasting impact on the TED, precisely because although the particular facets of the circumstances faced in 1928 or 1984–1985 have altered, the fundamental nature of the challenge is the same. The continent's complexity and diversity are not as well recognised by Adventist world-church leaders now as in the 1920s, yet they continue to shape the church's work in ways in ways not appreciated by those who assume Europe is monocultural.[5]

The Darmstadt Council

At the 1928 European Division council, the first substantive item on the agenda was a proposal from the Inter-Union Association of Seventh-day Adventists in Germany, a confederation of unions with church members in Germany, which occupied an irregular position between union and division levels, helping to facilitate cooperation between unions that had much in common. The Inter-Union Association's very existence spoke to the extent to which the European Division's responsibilities had become too much for one division. Its proposal also directly addressed the issue of diversity: 'Europe is composed of many nations, some smaller, some larger. National spirit runs high throughout Europe. Sometimes it is difficult to secure co-operation'. The association's document, which had been reviewed in advance by the GC representatives and division presidents, also highlighted the political and regulatory realities of nationalist Europe in an era of totalitarian ideologies, and it acknowledged the reality that the Adventist Church in the Soviet Union was already, 'by force of circumstances, an organisation operating practically as a Division'.[6]

---

5 On the decisions taken in 1984–1985 to add Albania, Greece, Hungary, and (former) Yugoslavia to the TED, see Chapter 8.

6 'An Appeal to the European and General Conference Executive Committees in Council', 14 Aug. 1928, text in European Division Committee mins., 14 Aug. (morning) 1928, in GC Ar., RG EP 1, box 6599, 1926–1928, pp. 254–255 (p. 255).

In pushing for restructuring, German Adventist leaders were not immune from national prejudices themselves; they sought a role commensurate, in their eyes, with the fact that Germans were four out of ten of the European Division's members and one in eight of all members worldwide. They wanted to be responsible once more for missions in the former German colonies in Africa, appropriated by the Allies in 1919 (and consequently assigned to Adventist Church organisations in Britain and France). Yet the German church leaders were also genuinely concerned about church growth. By 'dividing Europe', the Inter-Union Association's leaders argued, 'the cause would be much better served'. Each division would 'come nearer' the church member and the constituencies of unions, and thus could 'secure fuller co-operation' in the plans made. 'Larger funds could be gathered for the promotion of mission work. Closer supervision could be given to mission territory and increased returns in soul-winning would result.'[7] The German proposal was supported by Adventist leaders from across the continent and sympathetically received by world-church leaders. Although the Germans suggested 'dividing Europe into two Divisions', almost immediately 'the discussion leaned towards the plan of creating three Divisions apart from the one practically existing in Russia'.[8]

Although Lewis Christian, the president of the European Division, was nominally still chairing, it was the world president, William Spicer, who moderated the discussion that followed (Illustrations 2.3 and 2.4). The council delegates swiftly agreed, 'unanimously', to recommend to the GC Executive Committee, 'that the present European Division be organised into four Divisions, Russia operating as one of them in its present form'. They also settled on a tripartite partition of Europe outside the Soviet Union as follows:

7 Ibid., p. 255.
8 Ibid.; European Division Committee Summer Council, meetings of morning and afternoon, 14 Aug. 1928, GC Ar., RG EP 1, box 6599, 1926–1928, pp. 255–56.

- Northern European Division: four unions, with 18,762 members, population 106 million.

- Central European Division: five unions, with 40,055 members, population 101 million.

- Southern European Division: four unions, with 12,980 members, population 180 million.

This trifurcation achieved something close to a balance in the distribution of organisational units, members to be served, and population to be reached – at least within Europe.[9]

Soon, however, church leaders turned from consideration of Europe alone, to the large portions of the globe governed by Europeans. Both imperial and missiological impulses are evident in the formal, voted action: 'That each of these three Divisions be assigned such mission territory as can appropriately be worked by each Division from a political viewpoint, and also in proportion to the resources that will be available.'[10] Moving swiftly, the world was carved up and assigned to the three European divisions, based partly on 'the Budget figures of the various mission fields' and the income of the European mission homelands. Much of the territory apportioned to the three prospective divisions was then unentered and thus the territorial allocation was aspirational – missionally, as much as administratively, motivated.[11]

Restructuring the World Church

All of these actions of the European Division council were in fact recommendations to the GC Executive Committee. The proposal to reorganise then went to the 1928 Autumn Council.

General Conference President Spicer presented the recommendations and affirmed that 'post-war conditions had made it necessary

---

9   Afternoon, 14 Aug. 1928, ibid., pp. 256–58.
10 Evening, 14 Aug. 1928, ibid., p. 258.
11 Idem, ibid., pp. 258–59.

[…] to give serious consideration to the creation of smaller divisions within the boundaries of the European Division'. L. H. Christian explained that 'encouraging figures concerning the post-war increase in membership and institutional expansion in Europe' were part of the rationale, but church leaders from Europe also referred to the evolving political and regulatory situation that, they affirmed, 'made these changes essential'. They expressed their 'confidence that the new divisions suggested would lend strength to the ever-increasing and developing work in the European Division and its missions'.[12] The end result was that the General Conference Committee voted to approve 'the reorganisation of the European Division field into four divisions […] to take effect January 1, 1929': the four were the Central, Northern and Southern European Divisions and what was initially designated 'the Russian Division' and then as the 'United Socialist Soviet Republics Division (Russian Division)', although, reflecting the sensitivities of Communist authorities, the GC soon referred to it not as a division but as the 'Federation of Seventh-day Adventists in the Union of Socialist Soviet Republics' (evidently Adventists, always conservative, took time to adjust to the formal title of the Union of Socialist Soviet Republics).[13]

The 1928 Autumn Council also elected officers and departmental secretaries for all the new divisions, but in fact it simply endorsed a slate of nominations that had been made at Marienhoehe. The president and treasurer of the European Division were both elected to those offices in the new NED. Lewis H. Christian, an American missionary, had been division president since 1922 and could, no doubt, have become president of any of the successor divisions, but from 1902 to 1904 he had been a missionary to Denmark, where he was ordained,

---

12 GCC Autumn Council, 25 Sept. 1928, GCC Proc., xiii, ii, 630.
13 Idem and 1 Oct. 1928, ibid., pp. 630–31, 661. Its name is inconsistently presented in the *YB*, even in the same edition: *YB 1929*, pp. 4–5, 161; see also, e.g., *YB 1930*, p. 266; GC Officers' Meetings, 23 Mar. and 1 Aug. 1932, and Home and Foreign Officers' Council, 12 Oct. 1932, GCOM, GC Ar., RG 2, vol. i, pp. 401, 501, vol. ii, p. 50.

followed by eight years as secretary of the Danish-Norwegian bureau of the North American Foreign Department. It was natural, then, that he inclined towards the new NED. Christian Pedersen had been treasurer of the European Division since 1920 (Illustration 2.5), but, as a native of Denmark, was not going to be elected an officer of any other division. Walter E. Read, an Englishman (Illustration 2.6), had been foreign mission secretary of the European Division, having previously served as BUC secretary; he became the first NED secretary.[14]

This re-formation of the Adventist Church in Europe and its empires affected the entire Adventist ecclesiastical polity as it then existed, for it significantly increased European influence at the General Conference. This was intensified by the fact that African and Asian church members would not have real influence for many years to come. Europe's weighting in the higher councils of the church went up, from one among eight, to four among eleven. The renewal of rigorous persecution in the Soviet Union, soon after the founding of the new federation or division, was followed by the suppression of Seventh-day Adventist structure and, in L. H. Christian's words, the loss to 'the church [of] this entire Division'.[15] Yet that still left three 'European' divisions among ten by 1932 – rather greater sway than in 1928.

What, then, can we say about the restructuring of 1928–1929? It was the most consequential reform of Adventist organisation after the epochal reforms of 1901–03, a quarter century earlier, and was not equalled for another four to five decades, until the more gradual

---

14 European Division Summer Council, 15 Aug. 1928, GC Ar., RG EP 1, box 6599, 1926–1928, pp. 261–62; GCC Autumn Council, 25 Sept. 1928, GCC Proc., XIII, ii, 659–61 (p. 660); *YB 1904*, p. 64; *YB 1920*, p. 8; *sub* 'Christian, Lewis Harrison' and 'Read, Walter E.', *SDAE*, I, 347 and II, 420; L. H. Christian, 'Change in the Division Treasury', *Advent Survey*, 7.6 (June 1935), 8.

15 See the summary of discussions at meetings of the Home and Foreign Officers' Council, 11 and 12 Oct. 1932, GCOM, GC Ar., RG 2, II, pp. 47–48 (Christian quotation at p.47), 50; *YB 1931*, p. 276; *YB 1932*, p. 275; see also *SDAE*, *sub* 'Russia'.

reforms of 1969–1980 ended with three independent African divisions and two European divisions (discussed in Chapters 7 and 8). The 1929 structure ended up making European Adventist leaders more influential; arguably there was some justification, because at the time Europe was home to three out of ten church members worldwide and, while America probably supplied more missionaries, European missionaries may have been working in more countries. But what is striking is that American church leaders were willing to see American influence lessened somewhat because first and foremost they wanted the church to expand. The reforms were undertaken (to quote one of the voted actions of the 1928 council), 'in view of the magnitude of the field, the large membership, the many diverse nationalities, and the great number of extremely difficult problems that arise under existing economic and political conditions.' The new structure would, they believed, enable 'the proclamation of the message [to] be more successfully carried forward'.[16]

With hindsight, it is clear they were right. As we will see in Chapter 4, the reorganisation did have a measurable impact on growth.

Embracing the Challenge

The Territory of the Northern European Division

We have considered not only why reforms were mooted in Europe, but also why they were embraced by the wider Seventh-day Adventist Church. What is striking, however, is how much of the former European Division's territory ended up with Northern, rather than either Central or Southern, Europe. This disparity was in geography, in square miles, and in ethnic complexity, rather than in other aspects of church organisation. The initial partition of Europe was, as noted earlier, roughly balanced. But by the time the mission-field territory had been carved up and added into the mix, although all three divisions

---

16   14 Aug. 1928, GC Ar., RG EP 1, box 6599, 1926–1928, p. 258.

were responsible for supervising similar numbers of organisations, the NED ended up with the smallest share of both population and congregations; in contrast, while it had always been clear that the CED would have the most members, because it had the buoyant German church as its core, the NED had half as many members again as the SED (see Table 2.1). In 1929, of the eleven world divisions, the NED was the third largest in terms of membership.

Table 2.1: Distribution of European Division Components in Three New Division

	Unions	Conferences	Missions	Total Organisations	Churches	Membership	Population (millions)
Central Europe	6	24	17	47	1,076	41,317	223
Northern Europe	6	12	18	36	441	22,402	165
Southern Europe	7	17	11	35	490	14,569	180

The Netherlands was assigned to the Central European Division (CED). The Netherlands was at this time, as it had been since before World War I, a conference in the West German Union. This arrangement reflected the fact that it was German and German-American missionaries who first worked in the Netherlands so that the Dutch Adventist Church looked east to Germany. During World War I this began to change. In the twenties and thirties, while Germany was the Netherlands' largest trading partner and the two had significant financial relations, Great Britain was its biggest export market and the Dutch had longstanding cultural and political, as well as commercial, connections to Great Britain. Nevertheless, on the trifurcation of the European Division, Dutch ties to Britain were ignored and the Netherlands remained with the CED. This was in part because of the enduring significance of Dutch Adventists' connections to the German church, but in part because the CED's German leaders deeply desired their own mission fields (partly, it has to be said, on grounds of prestige) yet faced the reality that the German colonies had been appropriated by the Allied powers after World War I.[17]

The Germans therefore successfully requested responsibility for the Arabic Union, but the inclusion of the Netherlands in the CED allowed its leaders to lay claim to the vast Dutch colony in Southeast Asia (what is now Indonesia). In an ill-advised action, the world church assented, even though the Netherlands East Indies Union Mission was much further from its parent division than any other mission field. To be sure, German missionaries were sent to the Dutch East Indies and worked there successfully, alongside missionaries from the Netherlands (and other countries). But the transfer of the Netherlands East Indies Union to the CED cut it off from the countries to which it had historically been culturally and commercially connected. It was cut off, too, from the Far East Division, its ecclesiastical parent for the preceding decade; in contrast, the CED was unfamiliar with local conditions and much slower to respond to challenges and opportunities in a very faraway field. At the 1936 GC Session, the unwisdom of the decision was silently acknowledged and the assignment to CED reversed. If the Dutch East Indies and its 50 million inhabitants had simply remained with the Far East Division from the first, the NED in 1929 would have had the largest population of any European division (as it did after the 1936 GC Session). Of the new divisions, the NED had, moreover, been allocated 'by far the largest share' of the old division's territory and mission responsibilities. Its

---

17 Hein A. M. Klemann, 'The "Tommies" or the "Jerries": Dutch Trade Problems in the Inter-War Period', in *Unspoken Allies: Anglo-Dutch Relations Since 1780*, ed. by Nigel John Ashton and Duco Hellema (Amsterdam University Press, 2001), pp. 101–20; H. G. van Rijn, *Advent Exposé. 100 Jaar Adventkerk in Nederland* (Bosch en Duin: Uitgeverij 'Veritas', 1987), pp. 79–80. The bibliography of works on Anglo-Dutch relations, from the late Middle Ages to the present day, is too extensive to cite here.

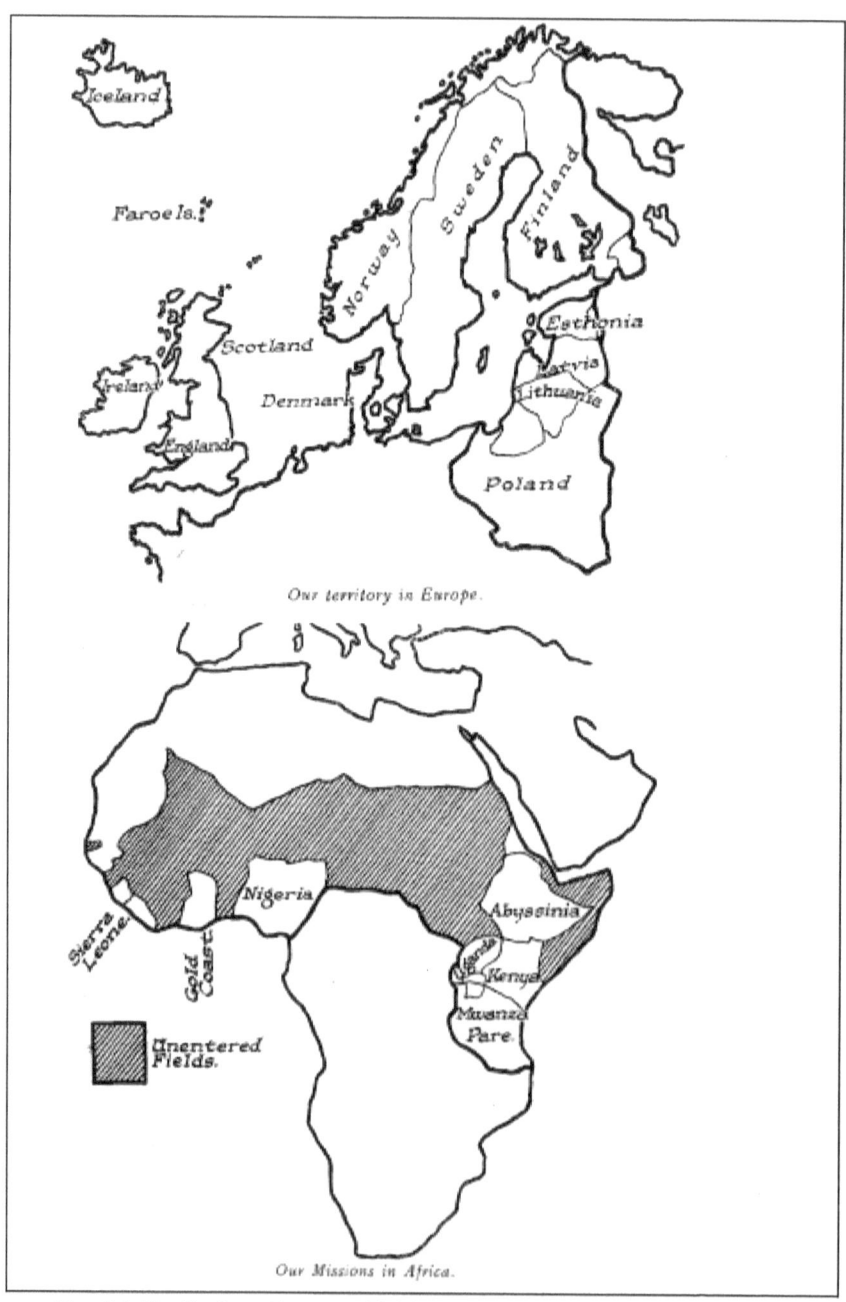

Map 2.1: The Northern European Division in 1929

'mission interests' in Africa were dispersed 'over a territory [...] fully 5,000 miles from east to west and 2,000 miles from north to south'.[18] In the European Division, just 4071 of the division's 90,631 baptised members (4.5 per cent) were in the mission fields in Africa.

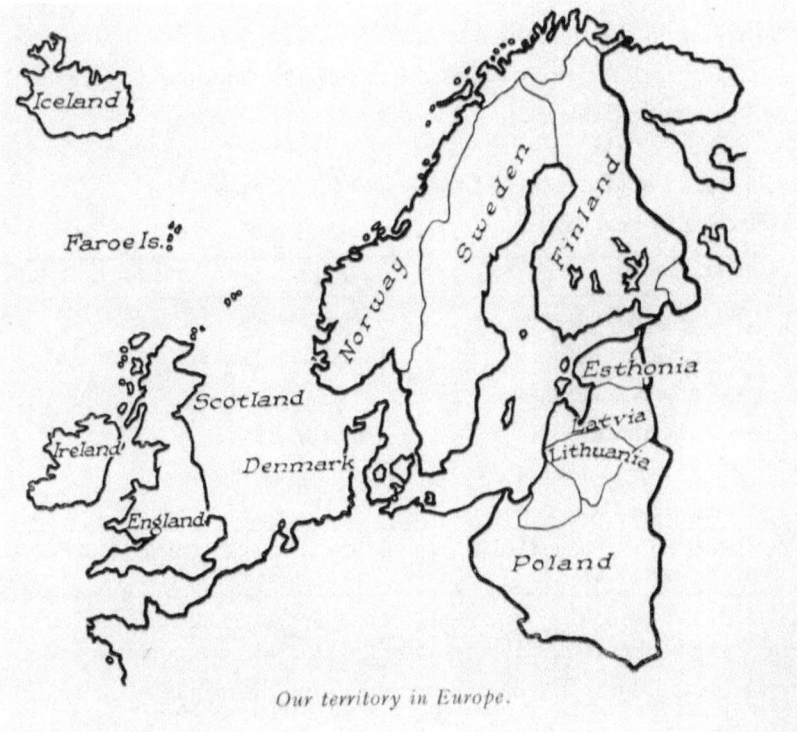

Our territory in Europe.

Map 2.2: The NED's European Territory in 1929

The equivalent figures for the new NED were 3202 of 24,228 baptised members (13.2 per cent), which illustrates the extent to which it had been given responsibility for evangelising Africa north of the Zambesi and south of the Sahara.[19] It was the homelands, however,

---

18 NED Winter Council, 29 Nov. 1928, NEDCOM-WCM 1928, p. 6.
19 W. E. Read, 'Report of the Foreign Missions in the European Division' (Aug. 1928), p. 10, GC Ar., RG EP 31, box 5646–5717, doc. no. 5658; *ASR*, 66 (1928), 8; *ASR*, 67 (1929), 12, 14.

that were most represented in terms of denominational organisation, rather than the vast mission fields – church structure thus initially reflected populations of existing members, not the populations yet to be reached. In addition to four unions in Europe, there were two in Africa, plus five 'detached missions', that is, attached directly to the division (in current church terminology): three were British colonies in West Africa; two embraced the three insular autonomous regions of Denmark (Table 2.2).

Table 2.2: Major Ecclesiastical Organisational Units in the Northern European Division, 1929

Union	*Attached*
Baltic Union Conference	Faroes Mission
British Union Conference	Gold Coast Mission
East African Union Mission	Nigeria Mission
Ethiopian Union Mission	Iceland Mission
Polish Union Conference	Sierra Leone Mission
Scandinavian Union Conference	

Source: GCC Autumn Council, 25 Sept. 1928, GCC Proc., XIII, ii, 630; *YB* 1929, pp. 127–44

The NED's responsibilities in geographic and demographic terms were astonishing. The division spanned from the tropics to the arctic circle.

Empires, Missions, and Missionaries

All this prompts an obvious question. Why did the NED gain responsibility for so much of the world?

There were two main underlying factors influencing the outcome. First, for several reasons relating both to worldly power politics and to longstanding British trade links with Scandinavia, the NED was a better fit for Britain than either the CED or SED; but this meant in turn that Britain's vast stretch of colonies and protectorates in East and West Africa naturally were assigned to the NED (the even more expansive array of British colonies in southern Africa remained part of the African Division). Large portions of these territories were fertile and thickly populated and therefore a focus for missionary activity. Because France and Italy were in the SUD, Italian colonies in Africa went to the SED, as did some French colonies in West Africa. Some, but not all, because church leaders believed that mission could be more effectively launched into parts of France's African empire from Britain's three West African colonies.[20] Thus, the NED was additionally assigned the whole of French West Africa and the northern part of French Equatorial Africa, creating a contiguous belt across the continent between the equator and the Sahara. These were immense territories but large parts were arid or semi-arid, they were underpopulated, and Islam was the dominant religion. For all these reasons, there had been no Adventist mission activity in these regions, unlike Ethiopia, Kenya, Uganda, Nigeria, Gold Coast, and Sierra Leone. But the net effect was that forty-one nations, colonies, or dependent territories became part of the NED (see Appendix I).

The responsibilities entrusted to Northern Europe reflected more than geopolitics, however, and here we come to the second factor underlying the assignment of so vast a mission territory to the NED. The region's Adventists already had a track record of both remarkable passion for and successful management of foreign mission. The new division homelands, especially Britain, Denmark, Norway, and Sweden, had already shown generous financial support for work around the world; many church members from those countries had already gone as missionaries to the countries that were assigned to the NED; and, crucially, church leaders in those countries had taken responsibility for mission in the previous decades, not waiting on the brethren in America.

In 1906, for example, when the Scandinavian Union Conference

---

20 E.g., see summary of discussion at NEDCOM, 5–7 Sept. 1928, NEDCOM Mins., GC Ar., RG NE 1, box 6630, 1928 Mins., p. 3.

was only five years old, its leaders undertook to evangelise Abyssinia (as Ethiopia was then known in the Western world), developed plans to send two missionaries there, and raised the necessary funds. The British Union Conference, which had only been formed in 1902, took responsibility for mission in British East Africa. In October 1906, the BUC sent Arthur Carscallen, Canadian born but trained at Duncombe Park (later Newbold College) and then pastoring in Britain, to Africa; he opened a mission station at Gendia, on Victoria Nyanza in what is now western Kenya. In 1907, two Swedes, Per Lindegren and Julius Persson, sent by the ScUC, opened a mission station in Eritrea, an Italian colony on the Red Sea coast which had been carved out of the Abyssinian empire, and the population of which was, in part, ethnically Ethiopian; Western missionaries were permitted in the colony of Eritrea, unlike in Ethiopia proper, which was independent. Abyssinia and British East Africa had been part of the Oriental Union Mission, but in 1907 were transferred: East Africa became the fourth mission in the British Union, alongside the Ireland, Scotland and Wales Missions; Abyssinia became the fourth mission in the Scandinavian Union, joining the Finland, Iceland and Greenland, and Northland Missions (the latter consisting of the northern half of Norway and Sweden). Today these may seem like mismatches and certainly it has not been typical for either of these two unions to include territories in Africa! But these were the precedents for attaching much of Africa to the NED in 1929.[21]

---

21 GCC meeting, 6 Aug. 1906, GCC Proc., VII, 168; GC Committee in Europe, meeting of 12 Aug. 1906, mins. in GCC Proc., ibid., p. 172; *YB 1907*, pp. 86–88; *YB 1908*, pp. 114–17. See Baldur Ed. Pfeiffer, 'The Coming of the Mission to East Africa', in *Seventh-day Adventist Contributions to East Africa, 1903–1983*, ed. idem (Frankfurt am Main, Bern and New York: Peter Lang, 1985), pp. 27–32; Yvonne Oster, *Till jordens yttersta gräns: Svenska adventistmissionärers liv och verksamhet*, Historisk Arkiv för Sjundedags Adventistsamfundet serien, 5 (Stockholm: Skandinaviska Bokförlaget, 2018), pp. 209–14; Brian Phillips, 'British Adventists Overseas', in *The Story of Seventh-day Adventists in the British Isles 1902–1992*, ed. By D. N. Marshall (Grantham, UK: Stanborough Press,

Church members from Northern Europe had, moreover, eagerly volunteered for overseas mission. Statistics on the origins of missionaries are not always available, but such evidence as we have is striking. In this book, when discussing numbers of missionaries, I have included spouses in the statistics, since they served together, faced the same challenges, and endured the same trials; in contrast, official statistics up to the late twentieth century distinguish 'missionaries' and 'wives' (though single women counted as missionaries), when they give numbers of spouses at all.

From the British Isles, sixty-four missionaries had gone overseas in the period 1907–1927, a fact of which British Adventists were rightly proud, as witnessed by the photographic celebration commissioned in 1927 or 1928 (see Illustration 2.7). Twenty-six missionaries went from Sweden to foreign lands between 1892 and the creation of the NED.[22] From the 1922 GC Session until the autumn of 1929, 122 missionaries went out from the countries that became the NED's homelands: eighty went to mission fields that would come under the NED, forty-two went to other divisions (and fourteen missionaries came to NED missions from other divisions: four from North America, eight from the other two European divisions, and two from South Africa). Of the 122 missionaries sent in the twenties, the overwhelming majority came from Britain and Denmark: sixty were British and Irish, thirty-six were Danes, plus fourteen Swedes, ten Norwegians, and two Latvians.[23]

1992), pp. 22–23; Jack Mahon, 'What Happened in 1906?', in *Messenger*, Souvenir Special, ed. by David Marshall, *100 Years of Mission 1906–2006* (2006), pp. 3–6.

22 See the summaries in Oster, *Till jordens yttersta gräns*, pp. 18, 34, 138, 158.

23 'Some Statistics and Information Concerning Our Missions in Africa', 12pp. (unnumbered), n.d., presented to NED Winter Council, 31 Oct.–6 Nov. 1929, appended at end of NEDCOM-WCM, 1929.

Willing 'To Make Every Effort'

This eagerness on the part of church members in Northern Europe to be engaged in mission leads to the most important reason why the world church assigned to the NED the most expansive and far-flung territory of any of the new divisions: despite the immensity of the territory and thus of the task facing them, the NED administrators regarded the challenge with enthusiasm. They wanted the assignment. They were eager to push back the frontiers of Seventh-day Adventist mission.

Even before the new division had officially begun its life, its leaders had met and affirmed that 'we feel deeply the great and solemn task committed to us'. They pledged themselves 'to make every effort to carry the Advent Message to the many millions in the countries of the Northern European Division, including its large mission fields'. Accepting the 'solemn responsibility to carry the message as quickly as possible to the many millions in our large fields', they acknowledged that for this to happen 'call[ed] for a larger and more extensive work in evangelism, not only on the part of our regular workers, but by all our church members'. This issue of lay involvement was one of vital importance, one that perhaps did not always subsequently receive the attention from NED and TED administrations that it was given ninety years ago. Northern Europe's assembled church leaders concluded with a clarion call on behalf of the 'many millions in the fields where our work is represented. The unwarned millions make their pathetic appeal and in view of the nearness of the coming of Jesus we must certainly lay plans for a larger work'.[24]

I have quoted at length from this statement because it was more than noble rhetoric. It reflected real sentiments and resulted in real action. The language of 'unwarned millions' kept being used in reports to the NED Committee and Winter Council for the next

---

24 NED Winter Council, 28 and 29 Nov. 1928, NEDCOM-WCM 1928, pp. 3-4, 6-7.

decade – indicative of the impact it had on church leaders who had heard and solemnly undertaken 'to make every effort to carry the [...] message as quickly as possible'. Throughout the thirties, moreover, division leaders kept on 'laying plans for a larger work' – at times perhaps too large. But it is plain that they preferred to err on the side of ambition rather than caution. Here they are surely an example to church leaders in the TED today. In sum, fine words led to vigorous deeds; the statement voted in the autumn of 1928 shaped the division's endeavours for decades.

To return to the question asked earlier, as to why the NED *gained* responsibility for so much of the world, the answer is this: Because the NED's leaders *took* responsibility for much of the world.

A Heritage of Mission-Mindedness

What we see, then, is that passion for mission has been present in the TED literally its entire life. It was present among both those elected to serve as leaders and the rank-and-file church members. It was present across the division. Here we come, if not to another example of continuity across the ninety years, then to an aspect where continuity is devoutly to be wished. Were the desire to make disciples diminished or gone; or little or no passion for proclaiming the gospel and prophetic truth; were there no eagerness to engage in the healing, preaching, and teaching ministry of Jesus Christ; no willingness to sacrifice so that others might share in the blessings we have received: then Adventists living in the TED in the twenty-first century would have forsaken the principles and values on which the division was founded, nine decades ago.

Chapter 3
Beginnings

Behold, I am doing a new thing;
* now it springs forth, do you not perceive it?*
I will make a way in the wilderness
* and rivers in the desert.* – Isaiah 43.19 (RSV)

Well begun is half done. – English proverb

First Steps

One of the first tasks for the new division was to find a base for its operations, which involved choosing a location and then creating a new headquarters organisation. All the financial and logistical arrangements attendant on the creation of three divisions out of one had to be negotiated. There were also important matters that had to be addressed following the founding, in order to achieve smooth functioning. Among the issues to resolve were questions about communication: how would the division relate to and share information with its component units and their leaders? How would it communicate to church members, making them feel part of the division's goals and plans, and mobilising them for mission?

Creating a Headquarters

Agreeing a location for the main office could easily have taken considerable time, as different conferences and unions vied for the honour of hosting the headquarters (and the potential advantages of proximity to leadership). Instead, the decision had been made in Darmstadt just three days after the plan to restructure the European Division was approved. A meeting of the Northern European church leaders in attendance voted: 'That we locate in London or neighbourhood'.[1] Even though the meeting had no formal standing to decide anything, the ad hoc group's swiftly made decision has stood the test of time. The headquarters of the TED has been in Britain for all but nine years of its ninety, and those were in the 1940s as a result of World War II.

Veteran British missionary William Bartlett and new division secretary, Walter Read, were tasked with finding a suitable location and, by the end of the year, the new division officers had accepted their recommendation of the northwest London suburb of Edgware. Thereafter, Read, who had 'for [...] seven years worked in the vicinity of London' when secretary of the BUC and president of the South England Conference, oversaw the purchase and renovation of eight properties, seven to provide homes for NED workers, plus a larger house 'for our office building' (Illustration 3.1). Initially, NED leaders hoped that they would move into their own dedicated office building on 1 March but, perhaps inevitably, the necessary building work took longer than expected.[2]

For several months, the NED skeleton headquarters continued to be based in the old European Division office in the Swiss city of Berne, though this had become the headquarters of the Southern European Division. In contrast, the new Central European Division was able to begin an independent existence immediately by virtue of taking over the office of the old Germany Inter-Union Association (now replaced, in effect, by the CED). The NED was thus the only one of the three new European divisions lacking its own home. While waiting for a headquarters to be located, agreed on, purchased,

---

[1] 'Minutes of Meeting held at Darmstadt', 17–18 Aug. 1928, in NEDCOM mins., 1928, p. 1.

[2] NEDCOM meetings of 5–7 Sept. 1928, NEDCOM Minority Committee meeting, 8 Dec. 1928, and NED Winter Council, 4 Dec. 1928, NEDCOM mins., 1928, pp. 5, 16–17, and NEDCOM-WCM, p. 43; *YB 1929*, p. 127. See Nigel G. Barham, 'Walter E. Read and the British Union Conference', *Adventist Heritage*, 5.1 (Summer 1978), 16–24 (pp. 19–21).

modernised, and modified, the first NED Winter Council was hosted by Skodsborg; the first regular meeting of the Northern European Division Committee (NEDCOM) took place in January, in Berne.[3] Finally, in April 1929, the division proudly cabled the other division headquarters around the world:

> *At the end of April we shall be moving our headquarters from Switzerland to England, and we are asking you to take note of our new address, which from May 1, 1929, will be 41 Manor Gardens, Edgware, Middlesex, England.*[4]

This was to be the division headquarters for the next twelve years (during which the street was renamed Hazel Gardens) and then again for another fifteen years in the fifties and sixties.[5] (Illustration 3.2)

We know little about exactly why they settled on Edgware, but a major factor must have been ease of access to the British government. This was helpful when religious liberty and church-state issues became significant, as they could and did in a division, most of whose countries had a state church (including England and Scotland). In 1931, for example, NED President Christian and Secretary Read joined three BUC officials in delivering a petition to abolish Sunday laws to the door of No. 10, Downing Street (the official residence of the British Prime Minister) (Illustration 3.3). Such moments were infrequent, whereas the NED headquarters regularly had to approach the Colonial Office and India Office, to obtain authorisations for entry to and work in the many and far-flung dominions, colonies, and protectorates of the British Empire, then at its zenith. Part of a division's role was to liaise between the GC and other divisions and so the NED had to help missionaries obtain the documentation necessary to work in British imperial territories outside the NED as well as

---

3   See *YB 1929*, pp. 104–05, 127, 145, with which cf. *YB 1928*, pp. 99, 102, 109. NED Winter Council, NEDCOM-WCM, 1928, p. 1; NEDCOM meeting, 6 Jan. 1929, NEDCOM mins., 1929, p. 1.
4   Message printed in *Far Eastern Division Outlook*, 18.5 (May 1929), 16.
5   See Appendix III.

within it. Access to imperial authorities in London was thus doubly valuable for the new division. Sweden had possessed no overseas colonies since the early nineteenth century, while Denmark had divested itself of its colonies in Asia, West Africa, and the West Indies in the late nineteenth and early twentieth centuries; consequently, neither Copenhagen nor Stockholm offered these kinds of advantages.

The General Conference already had an office in London: for thirty years, one of six GC 'transportation agents' (and the only one outside North America) had been located in London. In the era when 'Britannia ruled the waves', British ports were crucial nodes in global shipping networks, linking the distant outposts of empire, but additionally connecting them to countries beyond the British Empire's bounds. Church workers traveling all around the world might transit through London, Liverpool, and Southampton in particular.[6] This centrality was another reason for locating the NED headquarters in Britain – but even though the transportation agent came under the new division, the expense was subsidised by the GC, and his office remained at Oxford Street until 1939, before moving to the division office.[7] The division had carved out an independent existence for itself.

Taking Care of Business

Establishing the headquarters came at a price, however, especially when purchasing property in the London area. Moving into the new office did not end the expense. In the summer of 1929, the Northern European Division Committee was obliged to request $11,700 'as a special appropriation towards the expenses of our headquarters in Edgware'. The expenses incurred would have been in pounds sterling

---

6   E.g., D. J. B. Trim, *A Living Sacrifice: Unsung Heroes of Adventist Mission* (Nampa, ID: Pacific Press, 2019), pp. 53, 76–77. This remained the case into the second half of the twentieth century: e.g., 'From Home Base to Front Line', *ARH*, 137.26 (30 June 1960), 22.

7   NEDCOM meeting, 11 Sept. 1928, NEDCOM mins., 1928, p. 11; *YB 1929*, pp. 23, 127; *YB 1939*, pp. 21, 157; *YB 1940*, pp. 21, 158.

and $11,700 converted to £2340, the equivalent of some £140,000 in 2018 values. By the end of the year they had to ask for another $11,825 to pay off a loan of £2356 sterling.[8]

The creation of a new division required the NED officers to take care of a range of business. Sometimes major undertakings were involved, such as setting up a corporation to legally own and administer properties, World Wide Advent Missions Ltd (see Chapter 10). Even more minor actions, such as setting up a new bank account for the division in London, was time consuming for a foreign business or organisation.[9] Making arrangements for the transfer of funds to and from the United States was not straightforward in the 1920s and would become less so after the Great Depression and the institution of foreign-exchange controls in the United Kingdom, even though these were not rigorously enforced. The NED kept a US bank account to help streamline financial transactions with denominational organisations in America.[10]

One of the major tasks for the new division was recruiting a capable Treasury staff in the new headquarters. The NED Treasury had to hit the ground running because the new division began its life with the major and urgent task of working with other divisions to divide the financial resources of the European Division. Just in the first week of January 1929, £948 19s. 9d. (equivalent to more than US$4750) was transferred from the Central and Southern European Divisions to the NED or its unions. By the end of the month, the NED was already sending significant funds to its unions: for example, £310 to the BUC alone for education and the division's English-language

8   NEDCOM actions, 19 July and 1 Dec. 1929, NEDCOM mins., 1929, pp. 38, 67. Conversions of past sums to 2018 values used the *Measuring Worth* website: https://www.measuringworth.com/.
9   NEDCOM meetings, 28 May and 19 July 1929, NEDCOM mins., 1929, pp. 27, 37.
10   See the 'check' books in RGL, NED Collection; John Atkin, *The Foreign Exchange Market of London: Development Since 1900* (New York: Routledge, 2005), pp. 58–60.

publishing house, Stanborough Press. The division was also, however, receiving funds from its unions. In a typical transaction in 1929, the BUC transmitted £311 6s. 4d. to the NED, the total of a variety of offerings received: Annual Offering, Harvest Ingathering, Sabbath School Offering, Thirteenth Sabbath Offering, Week of Sacrifice; the division remitted back £77 16s. 7d. as 25 per cent of the offerings received.[11]

What was the character of the division office? The NED subscribed to the *National Geographic* magazine from the start; by the mid-1930s it had added subscriptions to the *Literary Digest* and *Chicago Daily Tribune*. Not far from Edgware, in the BUC headquarters, Arthur Maxwell, editor of the church's British paper (which was read in other parts of the division territory) was a subscriber (or regular reader) of *The English Review*.[12] Meanwhile, NED President Christian quoted the widely read British historian, journalist, and novelist, Sir Philip Gibbs, when addressing the GC Executive Committee.[13] The picture that emerges is of church leaders who were outward-looking and wanted to be well informed.

---

11 BUC Cash Journal 1929, pp. 143–45, 147, in RGL, BUC Papers.
12 Cheques in US dollars to National Geographic Society and Literary Digest, 9 Oct. 1929 and 17 Jan. 1935, RGL, NED Collection, 'Checks: 1–501', nos. 3, 202; NED Committee, 7 Mar. 1933, NEDCOM mins., 1933–1934, p. 16; A. S. Maxwell, "The March of Events', *Present Truth*, 10 Sept. 1936, p. 2. At L. H. Christian's request, the GC officers later paid for a subscription to *National Geographic* for a Latvian official: GC Officers' meeting, 1 May 1940, GCOM, second series, p. 3892.
13 Devotional, Autumn Council, 21 Oct. 1932, GCC Proc., xiv, iii, 778. Either Christian or the stenographer attributed a quotation to 'Sir Arthur Gibbs', but the summary in the minutes can be identified as coming from Philip Gibbs' 1928 book, *The Day After Tomorrow*. See Reginald Pound and A. J. A. Morris, 'Gibbs, Sir Philip Armand Hamilton (1877–1962), writer and journalist', *Oxford Dictionary of National Biography* (Oxford: Oxford University Press, 2004): <https://doi.org/10.1093/ref:odnb/33387>.

Mobilising for Mission

It was one thing for church leaders to commit themselves to 'making every effort' to reach 'the many millions' in the NED's 'large mission fields', but they could not, by themselves, 'carry the message as quickly as possible to the many millions in our large fields'. As we saw in Chapter 2, they recognised the need to motivate active participation in mission 'not only on the part of our regular workers, but by all our church members'.

If that was to happen, NED leaders needed to be able to connect with the rank and file of the church across Northern Europe and in the North Atlantic. It had to have clear lines of communication to leaders at the union, conference, and mission headquarters, so that they knew what had been determined at the division level and understood what was expected of them. The NED needed to communicate efficiently and emotively to all levels of the church in order to mobilise all Adventists in the division for mission.

Communication Channels

At the first full meeting of the division executive committee it was decided that there should be a monthly 'division paper', which initially was to be four pages, though in fact this was exceeded in the new *Advent Survey*.[14] The decision indicates that the new division administrators wanted to ensure that church members were aware of the new denominational organisational model and that they had a common sense of purpose as to the NED's goals. *Advent Survey* was published until 1941 when the NED itself was suspended (see Chapter 4). But the journal was valued by church members and when the NED was, in effect, refounded in 1950, one of the first actions of the new officers was to reinstate a division paper, given a new title, *Northern Light* (see Chapter 6). Despite its dry title, *Advent Survey* was important for the NED's communication plans and is the ultimate

---

14 NEDCOM, 11 Jan. 1929, NEDCOM mins, 1929, p. 5.

predecessor of https://ted.adventist.org/, of the Trans-European Division Facebook page and YouTube channel, of @Trans_European and @TEDHealth on Twitter, and of an active TED presence on whatever social media platforms emerge in the future.

In complex organisations, part of effective communication is having what the military would call clear 'lines of command and control', to ensure that leadership at different levels is fully seized of strategies and action plans. *Advent Survey* helped the NED to communicate to church leaders at the various union and conference offices, as well as to the members in the pew. But, of course, the NED communicated more directly with church administrators and this raised interesting practical questions that had to be resolved. One was: What would the official languages of the division be? When church leaders wrote to each other, composed position papers and memorials for higher levels of church structure, or prepared and circulated agendas and minutes, what languages were they to use?

In practice, the NED administration settled on two. It was inevitable that English would be the premier language of the division. It was the language of the second-largest union, of the country where the division headquarters was located, and (of course) of the General Conference headquarters. The second language adopted by the division, though, in which copies of documents would be prepared and circulated during meetings to those with poor English, was German, rather than one of the Scandinavian languages. German was used in commerce and widely understood in Denmark and Sweden. In addition to being a common second language across the Baltic region, there were significant ethnic German communities, in which German was the first language, in Estonia, Finland, Latvia, Lithuania, and Poland. In these countries, moreover, the first Adventist converts had been won in German-speaking communities.[15] Their significance for

---

15 See Edward C. Thaden, 'Finland and the Baltic Provinces: Elite Roles and Social and Economic Conditions and Structures', *Journal of Baltic Studies*, 15 (1984), 216–27 (pp. 219–21); Baiba Metuzāle-Kangere and Uldis

the church in the NED was tacitly acknowledged in the election, in 1928, of John Schilling, a German-American missionary and veteran of work in Latvia and Germany, as the first field secretary of the NED – and in his fellow officers' anxious and successful attempt to prevent him retiring early, due to 'our special needs in this Division'.[16] The importance of German-speaking Adventists was explicitly recognised in the decision in 1931 that reports 'of the Winter Councils' should be translated 'into German for us in the Baltic and Polish fields' (it is also notable that German was one of the languages used in both the Baltic Union session in 1932 and the Polish Union session in 1936).[17]

There was, though, another reason for the initial adoption of German as the division's second language (which did not outlast World War II): it avoided the need of preferring one of Danish, Norwegian, or Swedish over the other two. It is notable that even when NED meetings were held in one of the three Scandinavian countries, copies of the agendas and minutes were prepared in German as an alternative to English, rather than using the local language.[18] This hints at a degree of national pride which may help explain the division

---

Ozolins, 'The Language Situation in Latvia 1850–2004', *Journal of Baltic Studies*, 36 (2005), 317–44 (pp. 318–20); James E. Casteel, 'The Russian Germans in the Interwar German National Imaginary', *Central European History*, 40 (2007), 436n.; and, on German Adventists in the region, e.g., Voldemar Viirsalu, 'Estonia', *HRSDAE*, p. 79; *sub* 'Latvia' and 'Lithuania', *SDAE*, I, 906, 933.

16 NEDCOM Minority Committee, 12 Mar. 1929, NEDCOM mins., 1929, p. 10; *sub* 'Schilling, John H.', *SDAE*, II, 549.

17 NEDCOM Minority Committee, 21 Apr. 1931, NEDCOM mins., 1931, p. 9; see Clarence V. Anderson, 'Meetings in the Baltic Union', *Advent Survey*, 4.8 (Aug. 1932), 7; W. Czembor, 'The Polish Union Meetings', *Advent Survey*, 8.11 (Nov. 1936), 3.

18 There is limited evidence for this, because the main copy of division committees' minutes were always in English and these are what was archived. However, the agenda for the first Division Summer Council, held at Vejlefjord, the Adventist school in Denmark in 1934, was issued in English and German (and not in Danish): 'Agenda | Summer Council | [...] Daugaard, Denmark | August 1–7, 1934' and 'Agenda | Sommersitzung | [...] Daugaard, Dänemark | 1–7. August 1934', both 6 pp., inserted in NEDCOM Mins. 1934, between pp. 57–58.

of the ScUC into the East Nordic Union Conference (ENUC) and West Nordic Union Conference (WNUC) in 1931, which was the first major restructuring of its territory that the NED carried out.

The NED structure was of course a legacy; the new headquarters and administration, being closer to the ground level, was always likely to see things differently than had the old European Division leadership. In the winter of 1930/31, the division officers gave 'careful thought' to a suggestion 'that the interests of the field could better be served by having two Unions instead of one'. This had emerged from discussions held during 1930 by 'members of the Division committee together with the brethren from Scandinavia'. Size mattered, in the age before high-speed trains and commercial air travel. However, it is notable that the point that 'considerable time is of necessity taken up in travelling in such a large field' is listed as an 'added fact', subsidiary to the ScUC's 'widely scattered interests'. This language hints that it was not only the 'large areas to be covered' that motivated a subdivision of the ScUC but also its diversity of languages and sub-cultures even within Norway and Sweden, much less all four Nordic countries. In the end, the NED approved the creation of the two new unions (and for the moment 'the Iceland-Faroes Conference [was] included in the West Nordic Union').[19]

What was the effect? Travel was made easier and cheaper and the introduction of two unions where there had been one made administration more responsive to local needs (part of the reason for splitting the European Division). In addition, it made for better communications. At the very least, the similarity of Danish and Norwegian made internal communications in the WNUC relatively straightforward and it is notable that, for much of its history, the WNUC was marked by Danish-Norwegian cooperation. In the east, even though Finnish and Swedish belong to entirely different linguistic families, the importance of the Swedish-speaking minority in Finland (reflected

---

19 NEDCOM meeting, 21 Apr. 1931, NEDCOM mins. 1931, p. 9.

in the existence of separate 'Finland Finnish' and 'Finland Swedish' conferences) meant that the union, with its headquarters in Stockholm, was to find managing its two Finnish conferences relatively straightforward in the 1930s (in contrast to the situation twenty years later, when the influence of ethnic Swedes in Finland and in the Finnish Seventh-day Adventist Church was less: see Chapter 6). The twofold division of the ScUC was thus the fruit of the need for clearer communications and more effective management of different levels. The NED was happy to facilitate organisational reform intended to improve mission effectiveness.

Meanwhile, the financial, institutional, and membership strength in the Scandinavian countries were so crucial to the NED that, even though German became its official second language, one of the division administration's first decisions was 'to secure an office helper from Scandinavia', albeit 'one who can also do work in English'. The NED officers plainly (and wisely) wanted to be able to communicate clearly and directly with the leaders of what was their largest union (and, after 1931, their largest and third-largest unions).[20]

Money and Mission

Simply managing divisional finances was not straightforward and taxed the abilities of the newly created Treasury staff at Edgware. In theory there were forty separate countries or dependencies in the division; the church did not yet have a presence in all the African colonies, but relating with the different unions in Europe required constant international financial transactions. In the 1930s this became more difficult by the collapse of some banks and by government restrictions on foreign exchange in some countries. As a result of concerns both about loss of funds and the ability to send and receive money across borders, in 1931 the NED agreed to establish bank accounts

---

20 NEDCOM, meetings of 5–7 Sept. 1928, NEDCOM mins., 1928, p. 6. On the significance of the ScUC and its component conferences in the NED, see Chapter 11.

in London for both the Baltic Union and the Polish Union. At some point the NED set up its own bank accounts in Copenhagen, Helsinki, Oslo, and Stockholm, in addition to its account in Washington, DC.[21]

The NED Treasury managed regular transfers of funds to and from the various union headquarters. From the unions, a proportion of tithes were sent to the NED headquarters; so, too, from the unions in Europe in particular, were the fruit of the various mission offerings (see Chapter 4). From the NED, on the first of each month, instalments of 'general appropriations' were transmitted to its unions. In the case of the BUC, the monthly figure was initially £623 6s. 8d., nearly £7500 per annum (US$37,500), though by the mid-thirties, as the Depression continued to hit the United States hard, affecting tithe in North America, it was down to half that (£3616).[22] For other unions the schedule was different. On the second and fourth Fridays of every month, the Baltic Union, with headquarters in Riga, Latvia (and with a smaller ecclesiastical footprint and lower cost of living) received sums that initially ranged, depending on exchange rates, between 3400 and 3700 lats (£140–£150), although NED's appropriation for the Baltic, too, reduced greatly as the 1930s went on. When the Nigerian Union was created, total appropriations for its first year amounted to £3560 and the base appropriation remained above £3000 even in the mid-thirties, because the NED was determined to keep supporting the frontline mission fields.[23] These funds were essential for carrying out public evangelism, supporting literature evangelism, establishing mission stations, and maintaining

---

21 NED Minority Committee meeting, 17 July 1931, NEDCOM mins., 1931, p. 50; and see NEDCOM meeting, 18 July 1934, NEDCOM mins, 1934, p. 56.
22 BUC Cash Journal 1929, RGL, BUC Papers; NED Winter Council, 21 Dec. 1935, NEDCOM-WCM 1935, p. 44.
23 'Baltische Union' accounts book, RGL, NED Collection; NED Winter Councils, 27 Dec. 1931 and 21 Dec. 1935, NEDCOM-WCM, 1931, p. 20; 1934, pp. 33–34; 1935, pp. 44–45. (Baltic Union appropriations were, in 1932, 87,314 *lats* ($16,740), and, in 1934, 59,183 *lats* (£3,219).

schools and treatment rooms. Money mattered for mission.

As we saw in Chapter 2, for almost thirty years, missionaries had been going overseas from Scandinavia and Britain (countries that had themselves been Adventist mission fields until the turn of the century). The strong tradition of foreign mission service was heightened by the creation of the NED with its vast African mission fields – literally, now, not just figuratively, East Africa and West Africa were the responsibilities of Adventists in Northern Europe and the North Atlantic. And they responded. In just three months in the late summer of 1929, fourteen missionaries (ten Britons, two Danes, and two Norwegians) sailed from the NED for ports like Freetown and Mombasa: eight were returning from furlough and six were 'new recruits'.[24] At the end of the year, the division officially counted 104 missionaries serving overseas. These included the first Latvian Adventist missionaries, who were called and went even though conditions in the Baltic states meant that the call documents had to be hand delivered.[25] Before the end of 1929, the new division put through its own first call to Latvians, when Dr John Schneider and Dr W. Purmal were called to serve in Ethiopia; in 1931, the first Estonian foreign missionary, Amanda Nuka, was called to West Africa. The Baltic Union Conference was thus firmly on the missionary map.[26]

---

24 W. E. Read, 'Missionary Sailings', *Advent Survey*, 1.3 (Sept. 1929), 3–4 (p. 3). The nationality of most is stated, but one couple is not, the Gudmundsens: for their Norwegian origins see Gunnar and Marit Gudmundsen's completed 'Information on Returning Missionaries' forms, 18 June and 9 July 1946, in GC Ar., RG 21, Secretariat Appointee Files, box no. 2043, fld. 'Gudmundsen, G.'.

25 'Some Statistics and Information concerning Our Missions in Africa', 12pp. (unpaginated), n.d., presented to NED Winter Council, 31 Oct.–6 Nov. 1929, appended at end of NEDCOM-WCM, 1929. GC Secretariat to D. N. Wall, June 23, 1926, in GC Ar., RG 21, Secretariat Appointee Files, Box 9822, fld. 'Baar, Marie'.

26 NED Winter Council, 31 Oct. 1929, NEDCOM-WCM 1929, p. 3; 'Gleanings from the Winter Council held in Warsaw', *Advent Survey*, 2.1 (Jan. 1930), 8; on Nuka, see below, Chapter 12.

For missionaries to be called, sent, sustained, furloughed, and eventually returned home (or buried), there had to be church members willing to serve, but there also had to be a global infrastructure. One crucial part of the latter was a well-staffed division headquarters, able to deal efficiently with banks, government officials, and church officials on at least three continents, in order to transfer funds internationally, obtain the necessary visas and permits, and manage the Adventist Church bureaucracy, which was inherent to a global 'missionary enterprise'. All these things had to happen – and for ninety years they have happened. Mistakes have been made along the way. But the NED was well begun in 1929.

Chapter 4
'A Solemn Responsibility':
Depression and World War, 1929–1946

The TED was born and grew to maturity in tumultuous times. In the seventeen years that are explored in this chapter, the division had to negotiate the Great Depression, the flourishing of Fascism, the rise of Nazism, and the most devastating war in history. This chapter is the longest in the book, because so much happened.

Apart from the immediate impact of the war, which is hard to exaggerate, it profoundly shaped both general European history and European Adventist history thereafter. In the TED there were obvious organisational effects, including the permanent addition of the Netherlands Union to the division and the separation, for more than half a century, of the Baltic Union. There were also manifold subtler influences whose exact nature and implications we are still trying to discern fully. Perhaps most significantly, war and genocide sculpted the scepticism that makes outreach so difficult in the countries of the TED today; they decisively shaped the Northern European turn towards postmodernity and post-Christianity.[1] The events of the seventeen years covered in this chapter cast a shadow over the division's seven subsequent decades.

The Great Depression

It was a highly unpropitious time for a new organisation to begin its life. On Thursday October 31, 1929, L. H. Christian welcomed church leaders from across the division to Warsaw for the first Winter Council of the new Northern European Division, hosted by the Polish Union Conference (PUC). Six weeks earlier the London Stock Exchange had crashed, with investors' losses in the billions. Yet

---

1   Trim, 'Modernism and Post-Modernism', pp. 52–54, 56–57.

this was soon overshadowed by events in New York City. The NED Winter Council opened one week after Black Thursday, October 24, 1929. It is now seen as the start of the Wall Street crash and the Great Depression, yet on Monday the 28th, the situation worsened; the Dow Jones declined 13 per cent. The next day has assumed almost mythical status: on Black Tuesday, October 29, 1929, the Dow Jones average declined another 12 per cent and the stock market lost more than US$14 billion just that day.

At that stage, probably no one was aware of how serious the economic situation would become, but church leaders would have known that the outlook was not good. President Christian 'read a few verses from the fourth chapter of John emphasizing particularly verse thirty-five' ('Say ye not, There are yet four months, and then cometh harvest? behold, I say unto you, Lift up your eyes, and look on the fields; for they are white already to harvest' [John 4:35 KJV]). According to the minutes, Christian then 'called attention to the tremendous task that faced us in the Division with its 162,000,000 millions of people'. He went on to challenge his listeners:

> *God has laid upon us a solemn responsibility to carry the gospel message to the many millions in both our home fields and the fields across the seas in the African continent. We are conscious of our limitation as we face the great task and we certainly need to seek God for power and wisdom in all our plans at this time.*[2]

This was to remain the outlook of church leaders in the NED even as they negotiated the worst economic situation since the Industrial Revolution. They remained determined to carry out the commitment they had made in late 1928, when the division was in embryonic form, now that it was fully formed.

---

2   NED Winter Council, 31 Oct. 1929, NEDCOM-WCM 1929, p. 1.

They continued to embrace the challenge, as two examples indicate. In 1933, the second man to serve as division secretary, Ernest D. Dick (Illustration 4.1), reminded the NED Winter Council: 'The Northern European Division had been given the responsibility of carrying the gospel to approximately one half of Africa's people.' This was not a complaint, but an occasion for sharing how the missionary work force had grown; yet Dick concluded 'that while there are many evidences of God's prosperous care for our missions, there is great need of increasing our mission forces and investment at the earliest possible date'.[3] In 1936, Dick's successor, James I. Robison (Illustration 4.2), 'rendered his report' and initially sounded a little daunted as he

> *set forth the colossal missionary task which the Northern European Division faces in their mission work in Africa. It was revealed that this Division has 40% of Africa's territory under its supervision, with 46% of her population, and [...] that the greater part of its territory is still unentered.*

However, his response was unequivocal: the facts 'constitute a challenge to this Council for a definite advance in our work in the mission fields. [...] surely the time has come for the Northern European Division to do more'.[4]

However, the plain facts were that the Great Depression harmed the church and its mission. Indeed, the following year, in 1937, Robison sounded downhearted, acknowledging that, 'As we look at our resources, our small numbers, and our limited budgets, we are tempted to feel that the task is impossible.' His conclusion, 'that nothing is impossible with God', while a view no church member

---

3 Secretary's Report to NED Winter Council, 22 Nov. 1932, NED-COM-WCM, 1932, p. 3.

4 Secretary's Report to NED Winter Council, 17 Dec. 1936, NED-COM-WCM 1936, p. 17.

would have dissented from, lacks the punch or confidence of a call for increasing numbers of missionaries, or 'definite advance'.[5]

The BUC provides a case study of the impact of the Depression. In the spring of 1931, for example, William H. Meredith, the first British-born president of the BUC, reported dejectedly to the NED Committee that in Britain they had

> *been compelled to lay off several workers and to put others on a basis of part self-support. Several of the workers this year are obliged to earn from $250 to $500 in order to get their salary. The situation is really acute and [...] they hardly know what to do, particularly in view of the fact that they have drawn to the limit on their capital and funds which they have available.*[6]

Between October 1931 and 1 May 1932, the BUC cut the salaries of its workers three times (by 7 per cent, 5 per cent, and a further 5 per cent), then, in 1933, instituted another cut of 8 per cent.[7]

Dramatically, the 1933 GC Spring Council cut the appropriations already voted for 1933 by 15 per cent. The NED cut the base appropriations of the unions in Europe by 10–13 per cent, but those of the African union missions were each cut by only 6 per cent.[8] In the autumn of 1934, the executive committee felt obliged to turn down a series of union requests for extraordinary appropriations, despite being aware of particular, as well as general, problems that would ensue. Annual Council reduced GC appropriations to divisions for 1935 by another 5 per cent and in order not to reduce the base appropriations of the six African unions, the five European unions suffered

---

5   J. I. Robison, 'Items from the Secretary's Report at the Winter Council', *Advent Survey*, 10.1 (Jan. 1938), 4–5 (p. 5).
6   NEDCOM meeting, 24 Apr. 1931, NEDCOM mins., 1931, p. 13.
7   Barham, 'Walter Read and the British Union', pp. 21–22.
8   NEDCOM meeting, 8 May 1933, NEDCOM mins., 1932–1933, p. 89.

cuts of 8–12 per cent.[9]

A detailed history could be written of how the church in Northern Europe survived the Great Depression. These examples are intended to give a sense of the challenges that faced church administrators across the division territory, and the NED headquarters, as it tried to support leaders at union and conference level, when the division's own resources were diminished. Despite everything, the Seventh-day Adventist Church in Northern Europe survived and by mid-decade began to thrive again, at least in some unions. There were three reasons. The first was divine blessing, which Adventist church leaders at every level in the thirties saw at work. The second was an increase in the various mission offerings (not only the Thirteenth Sabbath Offering) in the NED and GC approval for the division to keep a higher proportion of those offerings. This proved to be vital because in North America the various mission offerings all suffered a disastrous collapse and did not recover.[10] The strong focus of division administration on mission offerings (discussed later in this chapter) paid off. The effective mobilisation of church members and their willingness to get involved enabled a strong foreign mission programme to continue; at the same time, the church in the NED also helped other divisions' mission fields make up for the NAD shortfall.

The third reason was leadership. Lewis Christian was an avuncular figure, but had an understated style and sometimes sardonic sense of humour, both more common in Europe than America. He was not an intellectual, but he was insightful, knowledgeable, and spiritual. When, at the 1936 GC Session, Christian became a general vice-president, his successor was Walter Read, who had been the first

---

9 NEDCOM meetings, 25 Sept., 16 and 27 Nov. 1934, NEDCOM mins., 1933–1934, pp. 81–82, 84, 88, 95; NED Winter Council, 10 and 13 Dec. 1934, NEDCOM-WCM, 1934, pp. 11, 33–34.
10 Mission offerings in the NAD fell for four years in a row (1930–1933) before starting to rise again; the total given in 1933 was only 60 per cent of the 1929 total. Not until 1937 was the 1929 total surpassed: see the *ASR* for the respective years.

secretary of the division, until elected president of the British Union in 1932. At the BUC, his leadership and sound financial judgment helped to steer the union into calmer, safer waters, while continuing to prioritise outreach:

> *Although the appropriations received from the General Conference for 1932–35 were down about thirty percent, still a total of 107 public evangelistic campaigns were held during that period.*[11]

It is unsurprising that Read was elected to replace Christian. The first TED national to serve as first officer of the division, Read was a very successful president. He brought together brainpower and spirituality, along with shrewd financial acumen.[12]

The first NED treasurer, Christian Pedersen, accepted a call to Skodsborg in the spring of 1935 (whereas Christian and Dick served until elected to more illustrious posts at the 1936 GC Session) and there are hints he was a little out of his depth. Pedersen was replaced by a Swedish-American missionary, Ellis R. Colson (Illustration 4.3), who, unusually for Adventists of this period, had done postgraduate study at the Universities of Chicago and Uppsala. Robison was then elected secretary in 1936 and he appears to have been a competent administrator, though Read and Colson seem to have been the key figures. Taking the NED officers of the thirties as a group, they undoubtedly made mistakes, but in general, the management of finances was prudent, in desperately difficult circumstances, and the growth achieved in the NED (also discussed below) is suggestive of good leadership and sound planning.[13]

---

11 Barham, 'Walter Read and the British Union', pp. 22–23.
12 For a taste of the way he combined these, see W. E. Read, 'Another New Year', *Advent Survey*, 10.1 (Jan. 1938), 1–2.
13 Christian, 'Change in the Division Treasury', p. 8; cf. W. T. Bartlett, 'The Winter Council', *Advent Survey*, 8.2 (Feb. 1936), 2. Colson obit., 'In Remembrance', *ARH*, 144.44 (2 Nov. 1967), 49.

Organisational Development

Almost immediately after the NED came into being, the division and its unions looked at reorganising church structure within their own territories. In 1929, with division leaders' counsel and approval, the Baltic Union divided the Latvian Conference (which was larger than the Estonian Conference and Lithuanian Mission combined) into three new conferences: Courland, Livonian, and Riga. This meant the union had five local fields instead of three. In the Scandinavian Union Conference, similarly, the existing four conferences (Denmark, Finland, Norway and Sweden) became seven: Finland, Norway, and Sweden each became two conferences.[14] As we saw in the previous chapter, in 1931 the NED instituted a more major restructuring of its own territory, with the ScUC wound up after thirty years and replaced by the ENUC and WNUC.

This was not the end of matters, however, for NED leaders were determined to see progress in Africa and to that end were willing to think big. The year after the ScUC was reorganised, the NED officers initiated an even more radical restructuring of the division's African mission fields. They were prompted partly by knowing that the East African Union Mission (EAUM) was about to lose responsibility for Tanganyika. Until 1919, Tanganyika had been German East Africa and the original Adventist missions established in 1903 had been German. The German leaders had an almost proprietary attitude to Tanganyika and proposed an exchange of territory: Liberia in West Africa for Tanganyika.[15] Here one gets a glimpse of the imperialist attitudes that underpinned Adventist thinking; swapping colonies

---

14 *YB 1930*, pp. 206–09, 218–24; cf. *YB 1929*, pp. 129–31.
15 GC Officers' Meeting, 11 and 13 Oct. 1932, GCOM, second series, pp. 46, 55. See the magisterial study of Stefan Höschele, *Christian Remnant – African Folk Church: Seventh-day Adventism in Tanzania, 1903–1980*, Studies in Christian Mission, 34 (Leiden: Brill, 2007); see also, for revealing insights into how German church leaders regarded Tanganyika, L. H. Christian's report to GC Officers Meeting, 23 July 1939, GCOM, second series, p. 3439b.

was typical of Great Power diplomacy in the late nineteenth and early twentieth centuries. After repeated discussions and review by the GC officers, the GC Executive Committee voted at the 1932 Autumn Council 'to transfer Tanganyika Territory of the East African Union to the Central European Division as from January 1, 1933'. President Christian 'expressed the regret of the Northern European Division in losing Tanganyika', as subsequently did NEDCOM; Christian added that he thought it would be for the best if the CED 'should have the missions they had established before the war'. In exchange, Liberia, which was English-speaking and had NED territory to its east, north and west, became part of the NED, though some German missionaries continued to be under appointment to Liberia.

Table 4.1: Major Ecclesiastical Organisational Units in the Northern European Division, 1933

Europe	*Africa*
Baltic Union Conference	East African Union Mission
British Union Conference	Ethiopian Union Mission
East Nordic Union Conference	Gold Coast Union Mission
Polish Union Conference	Nigeria Union Mission
West Nordic Union Conference	Sierra Leone Union Mission
	Upper Nile Union Mission*
	French Equatorial Africa Mission (attached)

* The Uganda Union Mission's territory was renamed in 1933.

The division secretary, Ernest Dick, visited Liberia almost immediately, typical of the hands-on approach to mission leadership of the NED officers.[16]

---

16 GC Officers' Meeting, 16 Oct. 1932, GCOM, second series, p. 62; GCC Autumn Council, 25 Oct. 1932, GCC Proc., xiv, iii, 800; NED Winter Council, 17 Nov. 1932, NEDCOM-WCM, 1932, pp. 25–26; report in *Advent Survey*, 5.1 (Jan. 1933), 11. See E. D. Dick, 'Visiting Our Missions

This was the first time TED territory was transferred elsewhere, but also the first time new territory was added to the division. It became the occasion for rethinking how the NED was organised in Africa. A committee 'appointed to give study to the reorganisation of our African Mission territory' came back with a bold plan to reorganise the existing two union missions (EAUM and Ethiopian) and three attached missions: the EAUM would consist only of Kenya and Italian Somaliland; a new Uganda Union Mission would be created; the Gold Coast, Nigeria, and Sierra Leone missions would each become a union mission (each of them including adjacent French colonies); and a new French Equatorial Mission would be created which would be the only field attached directly to the division. This wholesale reform, which would see two unions in Africa become six (Table 4.1), and which effectively devolved more authority closer to

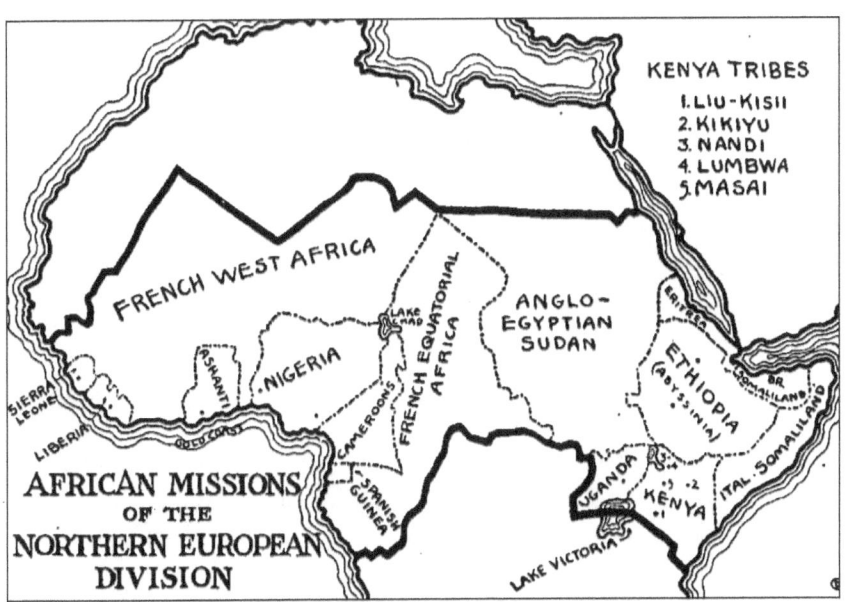

Map 4.1: The NED's African Mission Fields in 1935

in West Africa', *Advent Survey*, 5.6 (June 1933), 1; Chigemezi Nnadozie Wogu, 'Forgotten Trailblazers: Unearthing Stories of Our Mission Pioneers', *Mission 360°*, 7.2 (2019), 20–21.

the actual mission stations, was perhaps ahead of its time, given the actual Adventist presence in the various African territories. It was literally mission-focused in that it was based not on the existing membership but rather on the peoples who needed to be reached. It was adopted by the NED Executive Committee at the end of the year.[17] Church leaders in the NED were neither unimaginative nor timid.

In October 1935, Italian armies invaded Ethiopia. The resulting war caused massive destruction and loss of life in the country as the Italians used poison gas and deployed bomber squadrons against a country that had changed little since the nineteenth century. Adventist institutions and missionaries were among those who suffered at the hands of the Italian air force.[18] Before the end of 1936, Italy had accomplished the conquest of Ethiopia. At that point, the fact that the British government had strongly condemned the invasion made it politically impracticable for the union to come under a headquarters in London (roughly similar circumstances would arise in 1946, 1983, and 1993, though on the latter three occasions the result would be that a union *joined* the TED rather than left it). Late in 1936, 'an agreement [was] entered into the between General Conference and the Northern European Division, whereby the General Conference [would] temporarily supervis[e] the work in the Ethiopian Union Mission'.[19]

The Clash of Ideologies

The brutal Italian subjugation of Ethiopia was only a symptom of a turn to extreme politics in inter-war Europe; it was the first but not the last time that its consequences went beyond national politics

---

17 NED Winter Council, 18 Nov. 1932, NEDCOM-WCM, 1932, pp. 29–30; report printed in *Advent Survey*, 5.1 (Jan. 1933), 11.
18 E. D. Dick, 'Our Losses in Ethiopia', *Advent Survey*, 8.2 (Feb. 1936), 1–2.
19 GCC meeting, 11 Jan. 1937, GCC Proc., xv, i, 231.

and disrupted international order.[20] As well as the Great Depression (and in part because of it), the 1930s in Europe were characterised by political polarisation between Left and Right. This led to a rising tide of civil violence and a turn to authoritarianism in several European countries, in addition to Nazi Germany and Fascist Italy; they included Latvia and Poland, in the NED's territory (and Hungary and Yugoslavia, which would later be in the TED's territory), though in the Scandinavian democracies and the United Kingdom, both Communists and Fascist-inspired movements remained marginal.

The rise of ever more extreme forms of nationalism inevitably affected a transnational movement like the Seventh-day Adventist denomination. By the mid-thirties, for example, the NED reported to the GC that 'the Baltic states [were] following the trend that Germany has taken with reference to restrictions on religious literature sales and transfer of money from their countries for mission purposes'. In 1935, the Latvian government would not permit a German edition of the Week of Prayer readings to be put on sale. Later, it forced the dissolution of the organised church in the country, obliging the Baltic Union to move its union office to Tallinn, in Estonia.[21]

Signs of the Times

Most of all, the decade was overshadowed the increasing likelihood of another major European war.

As was widely understood, any future conflict between the European powers would, even more than the 'Great War', be a contest

---

20 It was followed in the spring of 1936 by the German remilitarisation of the Rhineland, in defiance of international treaties.

21 As summarised by M. E. Kern to GC Officers' Meeting, 1 Jan. 1936, GCOM, GC Ar., RG 2, II, 1619. See 'Report of a Joint Meeting of the Home Committee of the Division and Representatives of the Baltic Union Committee', 21 Jan. 1936, copy in NEDCOM mins., 1935–1936, pp. 6–8a, 10. Some German-speaking Latvian Adventist leaders supported nationalist-authoritarian political groups: see W. H. Williams's report to GC Officers' Meeting, 26 March, 1993, GCOM, second series, p. 3255.

not merely between armies and navies, but between peoples and nations, with combat affecting entire populations, thanks to aerial bombardment, which was experienced first-hand in Spain during the Civil War (1936–1939). There was a silver lining to the gloomy war clouds gathering overhead, which was an openness, in the population at large, to eschatological prophecies in a way that had not been true in Britain, certainly, and probably not in the Netherlands or the Scandinavian countries, since some point in the nineteenth century. In the Low Countries, Britain, and North America there had been, in the 1920s, a resurgent proclamation of the imminent Second Advent. It picked up steam in the 1930s and, while this 'Second Adventist' movement was clearly distinct from Seventh-day Adventists, there were obvious similarities: the former, for example, were also enthusiastic exegetes of the prophecies of Daniel, though they drew different conclusions about the nature of the resurgent Roman power. Notably, moreover, political and cultural heavyweights either were part of or publicly supported the Second Advent movement; their involvement attracted considerable interest in the mainstream press.[22]

This must have made the ground more fertile for Seventh-day Adventists expositing Daniel and Revelation and preaching the Second Coming of Christ. Certainly in Sweden and Britain, and probably elsewhere, the 1930s were years of relative success for public evangelism; indeed, the mid-thirties 'were a golden age for evangelism' in Britain, thanks partly to the powerful preaching of Australian Roy Anderson, who had been brought to the BUC in 1930 and served in the UK until called to the United States in 1936, but not before mentoring a group of talented young British evangelists.[23]

---

22 See Timothy Larsen, *Christabel Pankhurst: Fundamentalism and Feminism in Coalition* (Woodbridge, Suffolk: Boydell Press, 2002), pp. 50–51, 56–58, 61–62, 65, 67–68; Crawford Gribben, *Evangelical Millennialism in the Trans-Atlantic World, 1500–2000* (Basingstoke: Palgrave Macmillan, 2011), pp. 92–93, 95–105.

23 Ingemar Linden, 'Sweden', in *HRSDAE*, pp. 219–20; D. S. Porter, 'The Church in the Age of Dictators', in *Story of Seventh-day Adventists*, ed. by Marshall, pp. 14–15; Nigel Barham, 'British Isles', in *HRSDAE*, p. 35.

As Adventists witnessed the developing crisis, there was perhaps sometimes a sense of anticipation that, as it seemed, the last-day events were about to unfold; but more typically, reading reports in the church's papers, one has a sense of gloom at the likely conflict, and even in Britain there were fears that society might be destabilised by the clash between Right and Left, as had happened in Germany and Spain.[24] Twentieth-century Adventists in most countries of the world have tended to be sympathetic to conservative politics; the German Adventist Church did not take the stance against Hitler that it ought to have, partly seeing Nazism as a defence against atheistic Communism.[25] Yet it is noteworthy that the radical right-wing movements that were so prominent in the Central and the Southern European Divisions were neither as successful in Northern Europe nor viewed positively by Adventists in the British Isles and Scandinavia.

At the NED's 1933 Winter Council, the elder statesman of the world church, William Spicer, referred to the difficulties faced during World War I and how the church had emerged in many places stronger. This makes all the more striking the remarks that followed, made by NED President Christian, 'that never before' had European church leaders 'met in times like these [...] so perilous; times of possibilities and of dangers'.[26] Earlier in the year, the Nazis had taken power in Germany and by late November, when the Winter Council met in Oslo, had already laid the foundations for the Third Reich, which would soon plunge Europe into war and commit genocide. There can be little doubt that this is why Christian thought 1933 more potentially dangerous than 1914–1918.

The following year, A. S. Maxwell (Illustration 4.4), editor of the British church paper, *Present Truth* (but better known to later generations as 'Uncle Arthur'), attended a 1934 rally of the British Union of

---

24 See, e.g., Arthur S. Maxwell, 'Is Britain going Fascist?', *Present Truth*, 5 July 1934, pp. 6–7.
25 Roland Blaich, 'Religion under National Socialism: The Case of the German Adventist Church', *Central European History*, 26 (1993), 255–80.
26 22 Nov. 1933, NEDCOM-WCM 1933, pp. 1–2 (p. 2).

Fascists as an appalled observer. He describes, plainly disturbed, how 'everywhere wild disorder and inexcusable brutality prevailed on a scale never seen in the country before'. With a rhetorical question, he stresses the source of the aggressive ideology: 'Was this [...] Germany or Austria, or Italy?' No, he concludes:

> *It was the Olympia, London, the huge hall where the British Industries Fair is held annually. [...] If I had not seen it with my own eyes I should hardly have believed it possible. But Fascism has come to Britain. And we may well be thankful for Olympia for bringing its fruits so early and abruptly to the public attention.*[27]

Maxwell immediately perceived that Fascism was a would-be rival to Christianity, not its saviour from Communism, concluding that the British Fascist movement 'is as fanatically enthusiastic as a new-born religious community'.[28]

Two years later, reflecting on the Spanish Civil War, which included German, Italian, and Soviet contingents of troops, Maxwell editorialised that 'it would seem that Europe and the world are being sucked deeper and deeper into the vortex of war'. He was far from alone, of course, in drawing similar horrified conclusions, but Maxwell does not end there. Instead, he concludes on a distinctively Adventist note: 'while the "outlook" is ominous, the "up-look" is clear and encouraging, for these solemn portents of universal strife only bring nearer the promise of divine intervention in the coming of the Lord Jesus Himself'.[29]

Maxwell here did not identify any particular events from Daniel or Revelation in what was going on around him. Other church leaders, too, focused on the reality of what was in front of them. In 1939, L. H. Christian, by now a general vice-president of the

---

27 Maxwell, 'Is Britain going Fascist?', p. 6.
28 Ibid., p. 7.
29 Maxwell, 'March of Events', p. 2.

General Conference, visited Germany on behalf of the GC officers. Reporting on his return, he cited with distaste and dismay the prominent German Adventist educator who told a hall full of German church leaders 'that this work [education] should be based on race, that it should have a motto up in the school room "For the people and God," which in its interpretation, of course, meant for Germany and perhaps God'. The anti-Christian nature of Nazism was plain to Christian, and he was probably representative of leaders in the NED.[30]

Yet many other Adventists in the NED tended to look a little too hard for prophetic fulfilments of the type they expected, seeking evidence of the machinations of the Papacy, when the real cause of incipient conflict in Europe lay in secular, indeed atheistic, political movements. In 1938 for instance, even while lamenting the direction taken by the 'regimes in Russia, Italy, and Germany', the new editor of *Present Truth* was still pointing readers to the danger of the 'policy of the Vatican', in which, he averred, 'one cannot but see [...] an ominous warning of the approaching zenith of Antichrist'.[31] A different kind of anti-Christian tyrant was already in power in Germany, who was to usher in events which, though not those foretold in the Apocalypse, seemed apocalyptic indeed to many of those who lived through them.

---

30 GC Officers Meeting, 23 July 1939, GCOM, second series, p. 3439b.
31 W. L. Emmerson, 'The Tide of Time', *Present Truth*, 10 Mar. 1938, pp. 2–3 (p. 3). Possibly Emmerson had in mind the sympathetic views among fellow writers, but Catholic ones, towards Fascism: see Kevin Morris, 'Fascism and British Catholic Writers 1924–1939: Part 2', *New Blackfriars*, 80 (1999), 82–95.

The NED in a World at War

In 1939, of course, Europe was again engulfed in war, which soon became global. World War II posed a myriad of challenges, of different kinds, but almost all of them very considerable, to Adventists across the Northern European Division.

Administrative Adjustments

The exigencies of wartime prompted radical responses. Although the NED maintained operations from Edgware for the first twenty months of the war, its ability to liaise with its unions, both in Europe and in Africa, was compromised by the developing realities of the conflict. In June 1941, immediately following that year's GC Session, the GC Committee met and voted to establish a 'temporary headquarters of the Northern European Division […] in Washington, DC.' A new NED committee was constituted with both GC officials and church leaders from Northern Europe. In addition, the executive committee 'temporarily' assigned 'the Northern European Division territory in East Africa' to the Southern African Division. Although no one knew it then, Uganda and Kenya would never again be part of the TED. Meanwhile, 'the West African territory of the division', along with the SED's 'territory in West Africa [… was to] be administered temporarily' by the temporary NED headquarters in Washington.[32]

The new Division Committee's members from the NED were the division president, Read, who had been re-elected at the 1941 GC Session, and Paul Knudsen, the assistant treasurer, who had attended the Session and stayed on in the United States as acting secretary-treasurer. Subsequently, the 1941 Annual Council formalised his position, electing Knudsen, at just 35 years of age, NED secretary-treasurer (Illustration 4.5). Read returned to the UK after the session and, during the autumn, took steps to ensure some continuity. W. T. Bartlett, a veteran British church official and NED field secretary, who

---

32 GCC meeting, June 8, 1941, GCC Proc., XVI, i, 14; W. E. Read, 'Some Changes at the General Conference', *Advent Survey*, 12.3 (Oct. 1941), 3.

Read had got the NED Committee to appoint effectively as his representative when he travelled to the Session, was assigned to stay at the NED headquarters in Edgeware, in order, as Read wrote in a report in *Advent Survey*, to 'care for our property and other matters as they may develop from time to time'. Almost all the staff at the division headquarters were employed by the BUC, reassigned elsewhere, or laid off. All the NED property in Edgware, except the division office, was leased to new owners and, for a number of years, only four people used the office in Hazel Gardens: Bartlett (Illustration 4.6), who did so, however, in the capacity of company secretary of World Wide Advent Missions Ltd (WWAM), which was the legal owner of the division's properties; the GC transportation agent, C. H. Anscombe, who was also the treasurer of WWAM; a stenographer, Miss Schmidt, who was employed by WWAM; and a retired church worker, a Mr W. James, who served as office caretaker.[33]

In practice, the new NED committee never met. In Takoma Park, Paul Knudsen received requests from the fields (calls for new missionaries, for example) and took them to GC Secretariat for processing. But they were then taken not to the committee nominally set up in June to oversee NED, but rather to a 'Committee on General Conference Missions'.[34] Even this arrangement did not last long. After less than three months in his new office, Knudsen, whose wife and young daughter had been in Denmark when the Germans invaded and had

---

33 Read, 'Some Changes', p. 3; NED Home Committee meeting, 31 Mar. 1941, NEDCOM mins., 1941, pp. 17–18; 'Report of Committee on Edgware Office Matters', [no date, *c*. June 1942], GC Ar., RG 25, Records of Committees, box MIN80, fld. 'E Miscellaneous'; GCC meetings, 8 June and 27 Oct. 1941, 8 June 1942, and 24 May 1943, GCC Proc., xvi, i, 14, 159, ii, 483–84, iv, 957; Paul M. Knudsen service record, in GC Ar., RG 21, GC Secretariat Appointee Files, no. 16828; *YB 1941*, p. 159; *YB 1942*, p. 121.

34 GCC Autumn Council, 21 Oct. 1941, and GCC meeting, 8 June 1942, xvi, i, 121–22, ii, 484; Knudsen to Dick, 25 July 1941, to T. J. Michael, 12 and 18 Aug. 1941, and to A. W. Cormack, 17 Aug. 1941, in GC Ar., RG 21, box 9871, fld. 'Knudsen, Paul'; Committee on GC Missions, minutes in GC Ar., RG DF 1, box 6595, fld. 'Committee on General Conference Missions: 1941'.

been unable to leave, resigned and travelled via neutral Sweden to take up a position at the Danish publishing house.[35] This, along with the US entry into the war (so that it was no longer neutral), was the occasion for further action at the world headquarters. The GC secretary, E. D. Dick, noted that even the reformed NED Committee 'was so scattered' that it was 'impossible for them to get together for counsel at such a time as this'. Accordingly, it was decided that 'the administration of the work of the Northern European Division, in toto, should now be under the direction of the General Conference Committee'. This also led church leaders to dissolve the GC Missions Committee and place all missions unable to relate to a division committee or headquarters directly under the GC Executive Committee. Read was initially appointed a general field secretary of the General Conference in early 1942, with responsibility to advise regarding the NED and its mission fields, but later that year he was elected president of the Caribbean Union Conference, a position he held for four years, until the 1946 GC Session.[36]

Late in 1943, the Executive Committee took an action to rescind all previous plans 'for the temporary administration of the Detached Mission Fields' and instead created a provisional division committee,

---

35 The separation helped lead to the breakdown of the Knudsens' marriage and, despite Paul Knudsen's return to Scandinavia, he and his wife divorced in 1946; his employment became an ongoing sore point among Northern European church leaders. See NED Winter Council, 16 Dec. 1940, NEDCOM-WCM 1940, p. 1; Knudsen to Dick, 16 Dec. 1941, Dick to Knudsen, 12 Feb. 1942, Knudsen to P. G. Nelson, 31 May 1942, Robison to Dick, 26 Dec. 1946, and Axel Varmer to Dick and Robison, 12 Sept. 1947, GC Ar., RG 21, box 9871, fld. 'Knudsen, Paul'; Knudsen's service record, and P. M. Knudsen, 'Observations', 4 Sept. 1972, in his file, GC Ar., RG 21, GC Secretariat Appointee Files, no. 16828.
36 Dick to Knudsen, 12 Feb. 1942, GC Ar., RG 21, box 9871, fld. 'Knudsen, Paul'; GCC meeting, 30 Mar. 1942, xvi, ii, 348–49; *YB 1942*, p. 7; *YB 1943*, pp. 9, 120. On Read's career after 1946, see below, Chapter 6.

> to administer the work in the fields whose regular division committee is not able to function during the present emergency, it being understood that as soon as circumstances permit, these fields will be returned to their former divisional connections.

The new Provisional Division Committee for Detached Missions (PDC) was chaired by a GC vice-president, W. H. Branson (Illustration 4.7), and had GC Secretary Dick as its vice-chair.[37] The BUC, ENUC, and WNUC continued to relate directly to the GC headquarters, but West Africa was withdrawn from the temporary administration of the Southern African Division and placed under the PDC which became responsible for the whole of West Africa (including the Portuguese, Spanish, British, and French colonies), as well as Ethiopia, Eritrea, and Somaliland, which had been under the NED up to the Italian invasion and had by now been liberated by British forces.[38]

The net result of all these administrative developments was that the NED Executive Committee did not meet from 1 April 1941 up to 10 February 1947. The division at least continued to exist, in theory, but the division organisation and its operations had been entirely suspended.

Managing Mission

The mission fields still had to be staffed and resourced during the war. Managing the complex processes involved fell on the PDC and the local unions. Even from Washington, the longstanding connection between Ethiopia and Scandinavia was maintained, despite the wartime exigencies. In July 1941, for example, after the British had defeated the Italian occupying armies and liberated the country, new calls were processed as a result of which three missionary couples went to 'Abyssinia', including two Norwegians, Gunnar and Marit

---

37 GCC meeting, Dec. 16, 1943, GCC Proc., xvi, iv, 1190.
38 Ibid., p. 1191.

Gudmundsen, who had served in the country in the thirties, while another Norwegian, N. B. Nielsen, was appointed secretary-treasurer of the union.[39]

West Africa was never occupied, but sending and furloughing missionaries was restricted by limits on numbers of civilian passengers on shipping and the dangers of being attacked by German submarines. Nevertheless, in 1942, a new British doctor was called to 'the Nigerian Union Mission for medical missionary work' and a Danish missionary, Svend Aage Broberg, was given a furlough from Sierra Leone (which he took in the United States).[40] In December 1943, the PDC was liaising with British missionaries in Ghana, Nigeria, and Iraq.[41] By the late spring of 1944, it processed furloughs back to Britain and (more remarkably) to Sweden, while new missionaries were sent to the Cameroons. All this partly reflected the improved war situation for the Allies and partly the greater safety of sea transport.[42] The PDC continued its oversight role for detached missions after the war ended, right up to the 1946 GC Session (see Chapter 5). In the year after the war in Europe ended, the PDC dealt increasingly with the French West African colonies where there had been limited activity during the war; with the advent of peace, missionaries were sent to the area and funding assigned for new mission projects. But new missionaries were also sent to the British colonies in West Africa, where there had been less interruption to missional efforts.[43]

39 Committee on GC Missions, meeting of 20 July 1941, minutes p. 1, in GC Ar., RG DF 1, box 6595, fld. 'Committee on General Conference Missions: 1941'.
40 GCC meeting, 3 Sept. 1942, GCC Proc., XVI, ii, 563. Broberg was a veteran of Sierra Leone: see obit., 'Deaths', *ARH*, 152.3 (16 Jan. 1975), 31.
41 PDC meetings, 20 and 23 Dec. 1943, mins. in GC Ar., RG DF 1, box 6595, fld. '1943–44', pp. 1–3.
42 PDC meeting, 24 April 1944, ibid., p. 26; E. D. Dick, 'African West Coast Union Mission', *ARH*, 123.3 (17 Jan. 1946), 17.
43 See mins. of PDC meetings in 1946, GC Ar., RG DF 1, box 6595, fld. '1946', pp. 136–64; Dick, 'African West Coast Union Mission', pp. 16–17; V. Clifford Brown, 'Twentieth-Century Adventure', *The Youth's Instructor*, 94.17 (23 Apr. 1946), 1, 17–18.

All these territories now constituted the West African Union Mission (WAUM). The General Conference had exercised vigorous oversight; in addition to managing missionaries, it also undertook restructuring. In 1943, the Gold Coast and Nigerian Unions (both of which included French colonies), and the detached missions in Liberia, Sierra Leone, French Equatorial Africa, and Spanish Guinea were provisionally recombined into what was initially called the African West Coast Union Mission, but was soon formalised under the title West African Union Mission. The WAUM would be the only union in the region for thirty years.[44] Given the limits imposed by wartime, it made sense to consolidate the organisation. The expansion in number of unions by the NED in the thirties had been intended to help effect growth – but that was in peacetime and the ambitious pre-war plans had to be postponed.

The Experience of War

Every European country was affected by the war, even neutral nations like the Republic of Ireland and Sweden, though the countries of the TED experienced different levels of destruction and dislocation. The war's impact was particularly terrible in the Baltic republics, Greece, Hungary, and the states that formed Yugoslavia; it was very bad in Norway and the Netherlands, especially late in the war (see Chapter 5). But the stresses of war were also felt in Denmark, where the occupying Nazi forces were very restrained, and in the United Kingdom and Iceland, which were never occupied by hostile forces. The damage and disruption affected the Adventist Church institutionally, and individual Seventh-day Adventists shared in the suffering.

What stance were church members to take in a war which involved the entire populations of countries caught up in the conflict? Refusing to bear arms in the army had been a straightforward church

---

44 *YB 1944*, pp. 204–08 (p. 240); *YB 1946*, p. 218ff.; cf. *YB 1942*, pp. 130–32.

position in the mid-nineteenth century, but no longer fully addressed the issues of twentieth-century wars and how citizens should comport themselves and what contribution they should make, if any, to national war efforts. Seventh-day Adventists wanted to be good citizens of their countries. Most probably identified Nazi Germany, with its militarism, social Darwinism, and anti-Semitism, as being not just an earthly rival of their own nation but as espousing truly evil policies. The traditional Adventist position was that the denomination was a 'peace church'. This position was largely officially abandoned in Germany and the territory of what became Central European Division during the First World War, while at the same time it was being maintained by the church and church members in the British Isles and Scandinavia. Thus, Seventh-day Adventists had to live up to a pacifist stance, while wanting, even so, to be seen as good citizens and desiring the defeat of the Nazis and their Fascist allies.

Some warlike preparations were essentially defensive in nature and aimed at preserving life, so church officials had little incentive to avoid them, though it did mean the church was contributing to the war effort. By late 1938, war clouds were already looming and Adventist institutions began to make preparations; at Newbold College, for example, working parties of students and church members were set up to dig trenches (and provided with tools and materials at church expense). In 1939, the division committee took an action authorising 'arrangements for the erection of two air-raid shelters [...] in Edgware', 'one to accommodate 26 to 30 people' on Hazel Gardens, 'the other to accommodate 10 to 12 people to be built' two streets over where the church also owned property.[45]

In Great Britain, the Adventist commitment to conscientious objection had been a major problem for the church during World War I. While the British government had become more willing to make allowances for conscientious pacifism by 1939, the Adventist

---

45 BAM Board Meeting, Sept. 26, 1938, RGL, BMB 1938–47, fol. 26ʳ. NEDCOM meeting, 31 Aug. 1939, NEDCOM mins., 1939, p. 64.

stance would have made the church stand out, as would the international connections of the NED. There was concern in the British government about the loyalty of Seventh-day Adventists, which resulted in an investigation by the Home Office. While British church leaders might not have been aware of the investigation, they must have known that Adventist refusal to bear arms made them an object of suspicion, and could not have known that the Home Office would conclude that Adventists were not a threat.[46] How, then, were Adventists to comport themselves?

In the summer of 1940, as the United Kingdom prepared to fight the air-defence campaign against Germany that became known as the Battle of Britain, ordinary citizens joined together to help raise funds to build more Spitfire fighter planes. The British church's headquarters and some of its institutions were in Watford, a town just north of London, and the Mayor of the borough of Watford went around the town's businesses and organisations, including the British Union, requesting that each 'participate in helping to raise funds for the Watford Spitfire Fund'. Apart from any feelings of patriotism, this was not a cause in which Adventists could be disinterested, for during the course of the war, thirty church members 'were killed in air raids, and over fifty were injured'. The BUC, having counselled with the NED officers (at that point still in Edgware), took an action to donate £100 'towards a Borough Ambulance or their medical services'. Thus, church leaders showed themselves good citizens, contributed towards civil defence and healing, and yet avoided contributing actively to military efforts.[47] In Norway and Denmark, in contrast, which largely escaped Allied bombing and where there was limited fighting, only three church members were killed.[48]

---

46 The resulting Home Office file is NAUK, HO 144/21481/1.
47 BAM Board Meeting, Aug. 22, 1940, RGL-SC, BMB 1938–47, fol. 92ʳ. Casualties from German bombing are in H. W. Lowe, 'The British Union Conference', report to 1946 GC Session, *ARH*, 123.24, General Conference Report, no. 2 (7 June 1946), 41.
48 P. G. Nelson, 'The West Nordic Union', report to 1946 GC Session, *ARH*, 123.24, General Conference Report, no. 2 (7 June 1946), 44.

Casualties must have been worse in Poland, which probably experienced greater destruction and certainly suffered a higher proportion of civilian casualties (more than one in six) than any other European country during World War II.[49] It also experienced very significant population displacement. There are no certain statistics for Seventh-day Adventist casualties but there are indications. The membership of the PUC in 1939 was 4268, but at 'the close of the war [was] nearly a thousand'. These figures were made lower by the Soviet annexation of much of eastern Poland and the expulsion of ethnic Germans from western Poland, for many members of the PUC had, pre-war, been from or Ukrainian- or German-speaking communities in the country's east and west.[50] In addition, large numbers of Polish citizens fled the war-torn country in the last months of the conflict, swelling the multitudinous ranks of refugees and 'Displaced Persons' (DPs), in the parlance of the time. Many (though not all) of those who fled west were forcibly repatriated after the war ended and their return helped to increase Adventist membership; but forced repatriation also applied to ethnic German and Ukrainian citizens of Poland, expulsion of whom continued for at least three years, to the detriment of the Adventist Church. At the same time, numbers of church members from the Baltic states (whose border with Poland was porous and kept changing), now separated from the NED, were also caught up as DPs.[51] Less is known about the former Baltic Union, but by mid-1948 there were 'about twenty-five hundred church members

---

49 Just over one million Polish servicemen were killed, wounded, or taken prisoner; approximately 5.3 million civilians, out of a pre-war population of 34.8 million were killed: John Ellis, *The World War II Databook* (London: BCA, 1993), table 51, pp. 253–54.
50 *YB 1940*, p. 170; G. A. Lindsay, 'The Light of the Advent Shines in Northern Europe', *ARH*, 125.32 (5 Aug. 1948), 8–9, 19 (p. 8).
51 PUC report, NED Winter Council, 1 Dec. 1948, NEDCOM mins., 1947–1950, p. 165; GC Officers' Meeting, 22 Feb. 1950, GCOM, p. 50–36. A sense of Polish wartime sufferings, the experience of displacement, and fear of forced repatriation can be gained from Ian Serraillier's classic novel, *The Silver Sword* (London: Jonathan Cape, 1956 and many subsequent editions and reprints).

in Poland'.⁵² Even if many of the 1800 balance were now regarded as citizens of Germany or the Soviet Union, or had been granted asylum in Western countries, it still suggests a terrible death toll.

Yet the church felt there were beneficial as well as injurious effects; during the war, Adventists and members of other denominations perceived a turn back to Christianity in many European countries. Interesting insights emerge from the report of the Home Office investigation into the Seventh-day Adventist Church in the United Kingdom: in 1940 in Britain, Adventist colporteurs (who had mostly not been conscripted) achieved sales totalling £13,248 – an astonishing sum for such a small group. After the first three quarters of 1941, sales had already surpassed 1940, totalling £16,837. A year later, by request from the BUC, the GC Executive Committee voted a special appropriation of £500 ($2500), via the NED, 'to the British Union Conference, to enable them to take advantage of special openings for evangelistic work'.⁵³ In Croatia and Hungary, not then part of the division but later to come under the TED, numbers of baptisms increased during the war. Likewise, in Denmark and Norway the WNUC president later reported that during the war years, 'Every winter our ministers held their efforts and advertised their subjects, although they had to be more careful with their advertisement.' The West Nordic Union averaged 360 baptisms per year from a pre-war membership of just over 7000, thus increasing by one-fourth during the war.⁵⁴

---

52 Lindsay, 'Light of the Advent', p. 8.
53 Report of 24 Oct. 1941, NAUK, HO 144/21481/1; H. W. Lowe, BUC report, NED Winter Council, 16 Dec. 1940, NEDCOM-WCM 1940, p. 5; GCC meeting, 21 Sept. 1942, GCC Proc., XVI, ii, 580. It has recently been argued that there was no wartime revival in Britain: Bruce and David Voas, 'Social Crises', pp. 32–39. However, their analysis particularly focused on adherence and attendance in the Church of England and the mainstream dissenting denominations (Methodists and Presbyterians). Adventism's apocalyptic focus may well have lent it particular appeal during the war years.
54 A. V. Olson, 'First Detailed Postwar Report from Southern Europe', *ARH*, 123.3 (17 Jan. 1946), 18; Nelson, 'West Nordic Union', p. 43.

Mission Focus

Thus far, this chapter has provided an overview of the main lines of development of the NED from the time it came into existence until 1946, when the world began to draw breath again. It has also briefly explored the ways in which the war could have an impact on church members. With that we start to get beyond voted actions, official pronouncements, and administrative matters. In this final section of the chapter, we go further: What was the NED like? What was its collective character?

The new division was highly focused on soul winning. The unions in Europe were encouraged to mount public evangelistic campaigns wherever political conditions permitted, and the NED provided subsidies especially for evangelism where financial circumstances would otherwise have made such initiatives impossible. Division administration also liaised with the GC and other divisions to bring in financial resources and capable workers to conduct evangelism in key locations. For example, the Northern European Division Committee recognised that 'Great Britain occupies a strategic position in the world, both politically and from the standpoint of missionary enterprise' and noted that Ellen G. White had called for major efforts in London and British cities. However, 'the present small membership in the British Isles, though willing [...] to sacrifice to the utmost to advance the cause', simply could not 'supply the constantly increasing demands made upon it from the mission fields'. The need for growth in Britain was especially marked and so the NED appealed to the GC:

> *[To] arrange for a number of successful soul-winning evangelists in the United States, Australia, or other English-speaking countries, to undertake city evangelistic work in the British Isles, the General Conference bearing*

the cost of their transportation, salary, and expenses for the first year.[55]

As time went by, however, the gaze of the division more and more was fixed on its mission fields.

Raising Money for Foreign Missions

This focus on Africa partly was a result of history. As described in Chapter 2, there was a heritage of commitment to mission countries of the division and, even in 1929, a tradition of missionary service. As we saw in Chapter 3, the NED promptly built on those foundations; it immediately increased the numbers of missionaries in its fields. With extended family connections, there must have been many church members in Northern Europe who had a relative serving overseas, and few who did not personally know a missionary. This helps to explain the willingness of this generation of European Adventists to serve overseas themselves and, for the many who did not receive a call, their readiness to actively fundraise for mission in their wider communities, an enthusiasm that the NED skilfully encouraged and coordinated.

The NED led from the top in ensuring that the church at all levels emphasised offerings such as Week of Sacrifice, Big Week, and Thirteenth Sabbath Offering, but above all else was Harvest Ingathering. The division officers consistently took a personal interest in Ingathering and ensured that their union counterparts made it a priority. The division committee set goals, which were reviewed in subsequent meetings, and also spent much time and energy in planning; as NED

---

55 'Memorial on Evangelism in the British Isles', approved NEDCOM meeting, 10 Sept. 1929, NEDCOM mins., 1929, pp. 49–50. For Ellen White's counsels about London and Britain, see E. G. White, 'Our Missions in Europe', *ARH*, 64 (6 Dec. 1887), 753; *Testimonies*, vi, 25–26; and her comments made during devotional meetings at the Thirty-Fourth GC Session, 19 Apr. 1901, published as 'The Work in England. W. W. Prescott and Mrs. E. G. White', *General Conference Bulletin*, 4 (1901–2), 396–98.

administrators travelled, they ensured that progress in meeting the goals was on the agenda of union executive committees. Only by mobilising members, however, could goals be met. Accordingly, the division and union papers highlighted each year's goal and encouraged church members to be involved. The NED closely supervised the production not only of leaflets aimed at the public, but also of promotional materials to foster participation, and it provided subsidies to some unions to produce their own materials. Division officers and departmental directors put personal time and effort when traveling into inspiring members to take part. The result was very successful Ingathering efforts, despite the terrible circumstances of the thirties and forties. Even at the height of the Great Depression, division-wide goals, along with goals set by unions, conferences, missions, and individual institutions, were regularly not merely met but exceeded.[56] During the war, the annual collection was not halted, though domestic medical or social programs were stressed in some countries, alongside missions in Africa.[57]

---

56 The pattern was set early on. The following references are not exhaustive but illustrative of points made in the text and of the priorities of church leaders: NEDCOM meetings of 11 Jan., 27 Nov., and 1 and 2 Dec. 1929, and NEDCOM Winter Council 4 and 6 Nov. 1929, NEDCOM mins., 1929, pp. 5–6, 38–39, 63–64, 66, 68–69, and NEDCOM-WCM 1929, pp. 25–26, 37–38; 'Statement of Greeting to Our Believers', 5 Nov. 1929, NEDCOM-WCM 1929, pp. 28–29 (curiously not printed in *Advent Survey* vol. 1, no. 1); L. F. Oswald, 'Our God is Able', *Advent Survey*, 2.3 (Sept. 1930), 1; NEDCOM meetings, 27 and 29 Apr., 1, 10 and 13 May, and 14 and 15 July 1931, NED Winter Council, 23, 25 and 30 Dec. 1931, NEDCOM mins., pp. 20, 22, 24, 27, 34, 49–50, and NEDCOM-WCM 1931, pp. 2, 4, 12, 34, 36; untitled newsnote, *Advent Survey*, 4.1 (Jan. 1932), 8; W. G. C. Murdoch, 'News from Stanborough College', *Missionary Worker*, 9 Jan. 1931, p. 6; H. L. Rudy, 'Our Foreign Missions Campaigns in 1931', *Advent Survey*, 4.2 (Feb. 1932), 2–3; S. G. Joyce, 'Ireland: Great Britain's Neediest Mission Field', *Missionary Worker*, 6 Feb. 1931, p. 1; NEDCOM meetings, 5 July, 4 and 12 Aug., and 19 Dec. 1932, NED Winter Council, 20–22 Nov. 1932, NEDCOM mins., 1932–1933, pp. 28–29, 35, 40, 71, NEDCOM-WCM 1932, pp. 45–46, 53–54, 59–60.

57 E.g., BAM Board Meetings, 2 July 1940, 23 Apr. 1941, RGL, BMB 1938–47, fols. 113ʳ, 120ʳ; Nelson, 'West Nordic Union', p. 43.

Ingathering was a big deal for Adventists in the NED – and not just in one country or union. From the British Isles in the west to the Polish borders with Prussia and Russia in the east, from Norway in the north to Sierra Leone in the south, and throughout the period covered in this chapter, there was a major commitment by church members. In Poland in 1929, 'the great poverty' in the villages on the Soviet Russian frontier meant 'one can gather but a little from each. This makes the work much harder.' Yet Polish members were inspired rather than daunted, as John Isaac, the union superintendent, reported. 'Two sisters and some of the brethren went from village to village for over two weeks [...] so that they might reach their goal', while another 'sister walked 500 kilometres before returning home to her family'. In Sierra Leone in 1931, the Depression was having an impact on the European settlers from whom Adventists normally collected. Accordingly, the mission superintendent, H. J. Gronert reported:

> *I have been up to the bush to collect. This is the first time a European has solicited up-country, but I must say that the Lord helped me greatly [...]. There is not as much money up there as in Freetown [the capital], and one has to do quite a lot of travelling.*

Given the lack of good roads and transportation, this was undoubtedly an understatement.[58]

Meanwhile, British church members were known for their dedication to 'Ingathering work', which was 'their specialty', so much so that, regularly, 'the British Union [...] outstripped every other union in the world in per capita returns.' In 1941, when World War II was going badly for the Allies, the total collected in Britain exceeded £12,000, setting a new record. In Norway, during the war, '[o]ne of our sisters in Bergen' who had 'home and children to take care of,

---

58 Letter from H. J. Gronert in *Advent Survey*, 3.2 (Feb. 1931), 7; J. Isaac, 'Success in Spite of Difficulties', *Advent Survey*, 2.3 (Sept. 1930), 5, 8.

went out in her spare time'. She did not walk 500 kilometres but she did collect assiduously and in one campaign gathered in the equivalent of $3000.[59]

The burden of mission was thus shared by the rank-and-file church members right across the territory of the TED. But this prompts an obvious question: To what end? What effect or impact did the huge commitment of Adventists in the division's homelands have in its mission fields?

Mission Impact

Before 1929, the African continent, from roughly 5° south of the Equator northwards, had been the responsibility of one of the Adventist Church's world divisions. The very fact of there being three divisions responsible for mission in that vast region, which had previously competed for attention and resources from one headquarters, helped the church to grow across the three divisions' territories as a whole. This is suggested by statistical, or what we might call quantitative, analysis, but it is also suggested by a more qualitative analysis of actions that helped to effect numerical growth.

Expansion in the NED's First Decade

The European Division's territory did not exactly equate to the new Central, Northern, and Southern European Divisions, for it had included the Soviet Union (constituted a separate division in 1929), but had not included the Dutch East Indies, which became part of the Central European Division in 1929, having previously been part of the Far East Division (to which the colony reverted in 1936). Apart from these two exceptions, however, other differences were minor, so

---

[59] Arthur S. Maxwell, 'European Council', *ARH*, 100.36 (Sept. 6, 1923), 8; untitled news note, *Advent Survey*, 12.3 (Oct. 1941), 2; Secretary's Report, NED Winter Council, 16 Dec. 1940, NEDCOM-WCM 1940, p. 4; cf. photograph and caption in *Story of Seventh-day Adventists*, ed. by Marshall, p. 32; Nelson, 'West Nordic Union', p. 43.

that the three new divisions with 'European' in their title, together, were essentially the same as the old European Division. This allows for relatively straightforward comparative statistical analysis.[60]

Table 4.2: Membership in European Division(s), 1928–1938.

	1928	1932	1938
European Divisions	90,631		
Europe (less Soviet Union)	76,860		
European Divisions (less East Indies)		96,508	
Three European Divisions		99,365	116,232
NED's territories	22,603		
NED		29,523	37,873

In its last year, the European Division had a total of 90,631 church members, but 13,771 of those were in the 'Russian Unions'. By the end of 1932, there were 99,365 members in the three successor divisions (not including the USSR Federation/Division), but 2857 were in the Netherlands East Indies Union Mission. The adjusted membership of 96,508 members meant growth of 25.5 per cent in the four years, an improvement on the 20.17 per cent growth in the European Division in its final four years. That growth was sustained and actually increased, in spite of the Great Depression, suggests that the new tripartite administrative arrangement facilitated mission. Six years later, a decade after the European Division was divided, and in Europe's last year of peace, the three European divisions totalled 116,232 church members. Their aggregate decadal growth rate of 51.2 per cent was significantly lower than that achieved by the European Division (approximately 120 per cent) in the preceding ten years, but

---

60 The statistics in the next four paragraphs (and Tables 4.2 and 4.3) are from the denomination's *Annual Statistical Report* [*ASR*] for relevant years: see *ASR*, 66 (1928), 3, 8, 10; *ASR*, 70 (1932), 8, 10, 16; and *ASR*, 76 (1938), 10, 12, 16. See also *YB 1928*, pp. 99, 134, 160, 172; *YB 1932*, pp. 87, 111, 122; *YB 1938*, p. 153.

these had largely been characterised by relative prosperity. In contrast, in the thirties the Depression devastated the whole continent, while the rise of the Nazis caused considerable administrative and financial instability in the Central European Division, which must have affected growth.

Furthermore, while there had been 2219 workers in the European Division (less Russia) in 1928, by 1932, the Central, Northern and Southern European Divisions (less the East Indies) had a total workforce of 2745: an increase of 526 despite the Depression. By 1938, the three European divisions had 3143 workers between them, an increase of 42 per cent. Growth rates can never be determined by church leaders alone, no matter how determined they may be, because so many factors affect church growth, and individuals may choose not to convert despite every effort. The work force, however, is more in the hands of church administrators, though church finances will strongly influence decisions; the fact that the total work force increased across an extraordinarily difficult decade speaks to the commitment of European Adventist leaders.

In the first decade after the trifurcation of the European Division, of all the successor divisions, it was the NED that made the most of the new opportunities, and it was the church in its territories that felt the greatest benefit of the new tripartite organisation. In 1928, church membership in the unions and miscellaneous missions that were to be placed under the NED was 22,152. Four years later there were 29,523 members in the NED, a growth rate of 33.3 per cent; NED membership increased by exactly one-third, exceeding the one-quarter increase in the three divisions as a whole in those four years. By the end of its first decade, the NED had 37,873 members. The growth rate of 71 per cent in the ten years thus significantly exceeded the growth in the three European divisions as a whole during the decade 1929–1938. This was not a coincidence; in 1928 there were 127 pastors (ordained and licensed) in what would become the

NED's territories; in 1938, that number had increased to 294, more than doubling.

Table 4.3: Membership in Europe and Attached Mission Fields, 1928–1938

	1928	1938	Decadal Growth Rate
Baltic Union Conference	3,768	5,304	41%
British Union Conference	4,473	5,921	30%
Polish Union Conference	2,260	4,268	89%
Scandinavian Union/East & West Nordic Unions/Faroes/Iceland	8,730	12,278	41%
European/N. Atlantic unions/missions (total)	19,231	27,771	44%
African missions and unions (combined)	3,372	10,102	200%

This is not the whole story, however, for while growth in the division's homelands in Northern Europe was good during the division's first decade, it was not as strong as in the NED's territories in East and West Africa (see Table 4.3). Membership in the various African missions and unions, diversely organised and grouped in the thirties, as a percentage of the division membership, increased from 14.9 per cent to 26.7 per cent. The fact that growth in the NED in its first decade improved even more than in the other two successor divisions, but did so disproportionately in the mission fields, suggests that the Scandinavian and British leaders of the TED in its early years made mission in Africa their top priority.

Targeting Unreached Areas and Peoples

The statistics mask human stories and also say little about how the statistical trends came into being. Two case studies follow, which exemplify the way the division officers prioritised foreign mission, but also give a sense of what that meant, how it was done, and some of the implications.

(1) Northern Cameroon

The German West African protectorate of Kamerun had been occupied by the British and French during World War I. The League of Nations mandated the territory both to France, which took the greatest part, and to Great Britain. Most of the French mandate, 'Cameroun', was assigned to the SED, but 'British Cameroons' and the northernmost part of French Cameroun were assigned to the NED. These were notional because at the start of 1929 neither British nor French mandate had been entered. Under the NED, that was to change.

Cameroun had become subject to what was known as a 'comity agreement'. Western mission boards and missionary societies would divide mission field territories into spheres of influence, assigning one region to one mission board, another to a different society, and so on. Adventists, as a matter of official policy, declined to enter into comity agreements, but in practice they did make informal arrangements with other missionary societies in some places. In Tanganyika, for example, comity agreements were put in place by agreement between different missionary societies, some of which reached a mutual understanding with the German Adventist missionaries. Alternatively, not all of a country was carved up by the prominent (often politically well-connected) mission societies and the comity agreements left some regions untaken. This was the case in the Cameroons, where Seventh-day Adventists were effectively subject to French and British mission society comity agreements to which they had not been party, because Adventist missionaries were only authorised by the colonial officials to work in a region that had been left open.[61]

Reporting to the 1946 GC Session, William McClements (illustration 4.8), a pioneer missionary to Nigeria and long-serving mission leader in West Africa, declared: 'Away up in the northern Cameroons is found what I think is the most lonely station we have in all Africa.' This was Dogba Mission, where missionaries were, according to NED Secretary Dick, writing in 1933, '900 miles from Yaonde [Yaounde, the capital], the rail terminus where they buy their supplies'. So remote was the region (in the far north of Cameroun), so far from the centre of government, and so fierce and hostile to Europeans were its inhabitants, that they seemed unreachable by missionaries; government officials were even opposed to missionaries trying to reach them. Presumably for this reason, Northern Cameroon had not been claimed by a European missionary organisation – but Adventists were willing to go where others would not. As so often, it was through medical ministry that contact was made with them: Ruben and Hanna Bergström (Illustrations 4.9 and 4.10), a Swedish missionary couple, treated their sick and subsequently were able to treat their souls. By the end of World War II, there were 120 church members among the tribe that seemed impossible to reach. According to McClements, the colonial authorities 'acknowledged that our mission work there [did] something that they with their soldiers and their armies couldn't do'.[62]

But why were the Bergströms in that inaccessible and dangerous region? Why was there a dispensary there, at which the sick could be treated, and so introduced to the Great Physician? It was because in

---

61 See Stefan Höschele, *Christian Remnant – African Folk Church: Seventh-day Adventism in Tanzania, 1903–1980*, Studies in Christian Mission, 34 (Leiden: Brill, 2007); and Eyezo'o Salvador, 'Un paramètre de l'histoire du Cameroun: La Mission Adventiste (1926–1949), MA thesis (University of Yaoundé, 1985) – I am indebted for this reference to Reinder Bruinsma.

62 McClements report, Forty-Fifth GC Session, 10 June 1946, proceedings published as 'An Afternoon With the Provisional Division', *ARH*, 123.29, General Conference Report, no. 7 (13 June 1946), 147; Dick, 'Visiting Our Missions in West Africa', 3–4.

1930, the NED president and secretary, Lewis Christian and Walter Read, had visited British Cameroons and Cameroun, travelled into the interior of both, identified that there was a significant unreached people group, subject to no comity agreements, and decided that a mission station had to be planted in northern Cameroun. As a result, by 1945 that mission station had seven outstations. Much credit was due to the Bergströms (Ruben remained until 1966, even after Hanna's death in 1953) – but they were only there because of the vision of the NED officers.[63] Without that vision, the support of local leaders like McClements, and the courage of people from Northern Europe, like Ruben and Hanna, willing to risk death in order to share good news, none of those seven stations would have existed.

(2) Uganda and the Upper Nile Region

The East African country of Uganda, then a British protectorate, provides an example of this prioritisation in practice and exemplifies the positive outcomes that could result. In the early 1900s, General Conference leaders had repeatedly urged that an Adventist presence be established in Uganda.[64] The Uganda Mission was organised within the East African Union Mission (EAUM) during 1926, with two ministers assigned, but they were based in neighbouring Kenya for a year and very little happened in the mission's first three years.[65] At the beginning of 1929, when the NED took responsibility, there were only fifteen Ugandan Seventh-day Adventists. Things changed

63 Ella M. Eastcott, 'North Cameroons Mission', *Advent Survey*, 3.1 (Jan. 1931), 5–6; McClements report, in 'An Afternoon with the Provisional Division', 147. On the Bergströms, see Oster, *Till jordens yttersta gräns*, pp. 254–66.
64 A. G. Daniells, presidential address to 1905 GC Session, in *ARH*, 82.19 (11 May 1905), 9; idem, 'Chairman's Report' to GCC Council, Gland, Switzerland, 7 May 1907, GC Ar., RG 1, GCC Proc. vii, 276.
65 European Division Committee, meeting of 18 Nov. 1926, GC Ar., RG EP 1, box 6599, 1923–1926 mins., p. 236; W. T. Bartlett, 'East Africa Union Mission', *Quarterly Review of the European Division of the General Conference of Seventh-Day Adventists*, 12.1 (1926), 5; W. E. Read, 'Off to the Far-Away Fields', ibid.,12.3 (1926), 4; and see *YB 1925*, p. 124; *YB 1926*, p. 136; *YB 1927*, pp. 148–49; *YB 1929*, p. 142.

quickly; even though the stock-market crash and coming of the Great Depression meant finances were tight, the NED officers were determined to advance mission. This led the division committee to counsel the EAUM officers to reduce the union's administrative expenditure, even as it approved special appropriations for missionaries and mission stations in Uganda, as well as other parts of the East African Union. In 1931, Gustav Lindsay, the YPMV and Sabbath School secretary of the NED, visited Uganda. He reported the founding of a new station and that

> *over 100 souls have already been added to the church. There are still about another hundred adults who are studying the truth and are diligent Sabbath-school members. Fresh calls for workers are coming in from various parts of the country.*[66]

Furthermore, church leaders back at the division headquarters in Britain shaped mission decision making so as to ensure that 'calls' could be answered by local people, as well as by expats. Church leaders, recognising the capabilities of many African converts, were keen to develop indigenous (or 'national') workers. They also recognised that a missionary was someone who left their home and cultural context to go to a foreign country and alien culture; this could be a church worker from Tanganyika as much as from Estonia (though there was as yet no thought that an African missionary might go to Europe rather than to another part of Africa).

Growth was far from being solely due to the work of missionaries from the NED's mission homelands. Lindsay also wrote:

---

66 G. A. Lindsay, 'The Advent Message in Uganda', *Advent Survey* 3.8 (August 1931): 6; *ASR 1929*, 12; *YB 1930*, p. 214; *YB 1931*, p. 219; NED Minority Committee, 27 Apr. and 14 May 1931, NEDCOM Mins, 1931, pp. 20, 30–31. *Note*: the indigenous membership of 15 is deduced from the 1929 *ASR*'s end-of-year membership figure of 42, 24 of whom had been added that year, and three of whom, according to the *YB*, were missionaries.

> *It is only fair to state [...] that the missionaries from Europe are not the only ones who have volunteered for service in Uganda. Several evangelists and teachers, together with their families, are natives of East Tanganyika [...]. They have done noble service in a field foreign to them, among a people who speak an altogether different language. One of these families has paid the supreme price, for shortly before our visit, the evangelist died from blood-poisoning [...]. He left a wife and several children to go back alone and sorrowful to their people in Pare, East Tanganyika.*[67]

The division officers already, in 1931, believed 'that the time has come when larger responsibilities can be carried by our African workers', and therefore voted to approve 'opening two new stations [...] one in Tanganyika and the other in Uganda', that were to be largely 'manned by workers [local to] the East African Union'.[68]

Uganda was constituted as its own union in 1932, which meant it received its own appropriation direct from the division – a key point.[69] With funding, with intentional planning, and with the aid of African missionaries, Adventist mission began to take root in Uganda. Soon after, though, in the summer of 1933, the new union mission had the southern provinces of Sudan (taken from the Arabic Union Mission of the Central European Division) added and therefore was renamed the Upper Nile Union Mission in 1933.[70] Sudan was subject, however, to a comity agreement brokered by British colonial officials, so that there was no prospect of an informal agreement with other missionary organisations to work in their territories.[71] In the 1930s, Adventist church leaders in East Africa were not able to find a way for the church to enter Sudan – a reminder that missional plans

---

67 Lindsay, 'Advent Message', 7.
68 NED Minority Committee, 14 May 1931, NEDCOM Mins, 1931, p. 30.
69 E.g., NED Committee, 28 Apr. 1933, NEDC Mins. 1933, p. 86.
70 NEDCOM meetings, 12 and 14 July 1933, NEDCOM mins., 1932–1933, pp. 93, 96–97.
71 Sudan Government, 'Mission Spheres', 1926, DUL, SAD/PF 26/5/1.

do not exist in a political vacuum but are shaped by circumstances. In the end, war intervened before the Upper Nile Union Mission could encompass more than Uganda. Then, under the pressure of war, the GC's Provisional Division Committee and the Southern Africa Division agreed to consolidate it with Kenya and Tanganyika into one large union. Not until 1987 would a separate Uganda Union be created again. It may seem as if the NED had been too ambitious in 1932–1933, but by 1946, there were nearly a thousand Seventh-day Adventists in Uganda where, on 1 January 1929, there had been fifteen. In mission, ambition is often no bad thing.

Growth to 1946

If the proof of the pudding is in the eating, one proof of mission impact is church growth. At the end of 1946 – the end of the period covered by this chapter but also the first year of statistical reports from some parts of Africa, due to the war – the membership in the African unions and missions that had been part of the NED in the 1930s, some of which now were part of the Southern African Division, came to a total of 20,815 – double the 10,102 total at the end of 1938 and six times the membership in those territories when the NED came into existence (see above, Table 4.3). The majority of that was in the EAUM (now Kenya, Tanganyika, and Uganda), which had been part of the Southern African Division since 1941, and which had enjoyed remarkable growth. But membership in the Ethiopian Union Mission and West African Union Mission (WAUM) totalled 8372; eighteen years before, there had been 1236 church members in the Ethiopian Union and the several union missions in West Africa (consolidated in the WAUM). The growth rate actually exceeded that in the EAUM.

Statistics alone can never be the whole story, but in addition to numerical growth were the establishment of an Adventist presence for the first time in the Cameroons and French Equatorial Africa, the opening of multiple new mission stations in Ethiopia, Liberia, and Uganda (expanding into previously unentered areas of those countries), the founding of new hospitals and clinics, and the successful operation of the Nigerian Adventist publishing house. In Africa, from the Gulf of Guinea to the Gulf of Aden, the NED had done well.

Conclusion

In much of East Africa, the NED had planted the seed and the Southern African Division watered it and would see the harvest; in the Horn of Africa and in West Africa, the NED both planted and watered the seed (and the Northern Europe-West Africa Division [NEWAD] would see the harvest). Of course, 'God gave the increase' (cf. 1 Cor. 3:6 KJV), but much of the groundwork – the ploughing, harrowing, manuring and weeding, to extend the agricultural metaphor – was done by the Trans-European Division, in its earliest iteration. It pushed forward the work of mission in Africa despite the Great Depression and the most destructive war in history. The 'solemn responsibility' that church leaders from across the division felt 'to carry the gospel message to the many millions' who had not heard it, was one that the headquarters staff took seriously and on which they acted. But part of the reason for success was that they were able to motivate church leaders at other levels and the proverbial man and woman in the pew to get up out of their pews and make a contribution.

Chapter 5
'A Passion to Win Men and Women to God': The Refoundation, 1946–1950

This chapter examines only five years, but they were crucial ones in the TED's history. The knock-on effects and ramifications of World War II included dramatic shifts in the division's territorial responsibilities, among them the expatriation of the headquarters for half a decade to Stockholm – the only time in the division's history it has been outside the United Kingdom.

The NED's structure of the fifties and sixties was the product, in the late forties, of political manoeuvring within the church, something that Adventists tend to regard as appalling, but that Seventh-day Adventists in the TED put out of their minds long ago. In the face, though, of uncertainty about how best to structure the world church for mission in the post-war world, the world of an emerging Cold War and the beginnings of decolonisation, there was bound to be organisational politics about the best way forward. It seemed entirely possible, in the four years between the 1946 and 1950 GC Sessions, that the Northern European Division might be replaced by two divisions, with two headquarters in Britain and Sweden, responsible for various countries on the North Sea/Baltic Sea littoral and guiding mission in different parts of Africa and perhaps the Middle East. We might easily not be celebrating a ninetieth anniversary. These few years were the hinge on which the TED's history turned.

In the end, however, instead of going down different paths, the British Union Conference and the Ethiopian and West African Union Missions were reunited with the remnant of the NED. Church leaders, both in those territories and at the General Conference, recognised that the mission homelands still had much to give to the African mission fields. In 1950, the NED was restored to virtually its pre-war configuration. It was in effect a re-foundation of the division. But this outcome came about neither by accident nor by grand design, but through prolonged discussion and debate about what would be best for the church in Europe and Africa.

Organisational Development

In June 1946, the Forty-Fifth General Conference Session, meeting near the church's world headquarters in Takoma Park, took major decisions regarding the world field, but with particular impact on the NED. The Provisional Divisions Committee was wound up, but the *status quo ante bellum* was not restored. Poland did remain with the NED, despite the incipient Cold War, while the Netherlands was added. Yet the separation from the NED of the BUC and the WAUM, effected in 1941 by wartime exigencies but intended as a temporary measure, was formalised and continued, with the prospect of it becoming permanent.

Post-War Realignment

In 1946, the loss of the Baltic Union was formally recognised but the Netherlands was added to the NED. This was the consequence of brutal wartime experience.

As we saw in Chapter 2, the Netherlands had been originally placed with the CED, for a variety of reasons, which probably made more sense in Berlin and Washington, DC than in Den Haag, London, or Stockholm. The Netherlands East Indies Union Mission was returned to the Far East Division by the 1936 GC Session and the Netherlands was separated from the West German Union and created as a separate union conference in 1938, yet no serious thought seems to have been given to moving it to the NED, despite the strong historic and contemporary Anglo-Dutch economic and cultural connections noted in Chapter 3.

In the event, during World War II, the Netherlands was not only occupied by the German army; it also suffered worse than perhaps any other occupied country in Western Europe, especially in the last twelve months of the war. The winter of 1944/45 was unusually harsh and followed sustained extraction by the Germans of agricultural produce from the Netherlands, sent east to Germany; war conditions meant food and fuel could not easily be imported into the Netherlands and the Germans, vindictively, prevented internal redistribution. The result was the notorious *Hongerwinter*, the last famine in Europe and largely manmade; at least ten thousand Netherlanders died as a result, but the death toll probably exceeded sixteen thousand. Most died of starvation, but hypothermia, increased incidence of susceptibility to disease, and outbreaks of typhoid and diphtheria epidemics in the weakened population were also factors.[1] Yet the situation could have been worse; 'mass starvation was only averted by the German surrender the week the food reserves gave out.' And while to some extent this was the fruit of circumstance, it was also the result of policy, one of vengeance: to a great extent, the 'German occupiers [...] deliberately allowed [the Dutch] to starve'.[2]

The result was that by the end of the war there was intense anti-German sentiment in the Netherlands, which was to last the next half century. The church is rarely immune from wider cultural currents. The fact that Britain, Canada, Sweden, and the United States were responsible for most of the food and medical supplies delivered to the Netherlands in 1945 shaped post-war Dutch social attitudes, and

---

1   C. Banning, 'Food Shortage and Public Health, First Half of 1945', *Annals of the American Academy of Political and Social Science*, vol. 245, *The Netherlands during German Occupation* (May 1946), 93–110; Nicky Hart, 'Famine, Maternal Nutrition and Infant Mortality: A Re-examination of the Dutch Hunger Winter', *Population Studies*, 47 (1993), 27–46 (pp. 27–29); William I. Hitchcock, T*he Bitter Road to Freedom: A New History of the Liberation of Europe* (New York: Free Press, 2008), pp. 98–122; Anthony Beevor, *The Battle of Arnhem* (New York: Viking, 2018), pp. 372–79.

2   Hart, 'Famine, Maternal Nutrition and Infant Mortality', p. 27; Hitchcock, *Bitter Road to Freedom*, p. 98; and cf. Beevor, *Battle of Arnhem*, pp. 293, 372, 379.

helped to orient Dutch Adventism west and north, rather than east, as had traditionally been the case.³ The profound antipathy to Germany and Germans extended to Dutch Adventists, which had significant consequences for the Adventist Church in Europe. There were some German pastors who had started working in the Netherlands before the war who were still accepted, but Dutch church members and the Netherlands Union refused to be part of an organisation (the CED) the majority of whose church members were German and whose leadership was overwhelmingly German. Dutch Germanophobia has largely disappeared today, as a result of generational change, but it was a long-lasting and potent factor in Dutch Adventism as well as Dutch society.⁴

As a result, the Netherlands Union Conference was removed from the CED by the end of 1945.⁵ At first it was not clear where it would make its home. At the 1946 GC Session, 'the representatives from Holland [were] grouped with Northern Europe' but putatively only 'for the purposes of the session', though later L. H. Christian, chairing a business session, commented 'Holland, too, is part of Northern Europe'. A future direction was strongly foreshadowed but it was left

---

3   See Banning, 'Food Shortage and Public Health', p. 110; Hitchcock, *Bitter Road to Freedom*, pp. 117–19; Van Rijn, *Advent Exposé*, pp. 79–81.
4   Stephen Kinzer, 'For Dutch, It's O.K. to Despise Germans', *New York Times*, 8 Feb. 1995, national edition, p. A0013, available at www.nytimes.com/1995/02/08/world/for-dutch-it-s-ok-to-despise-germans.html, accessed 28 April 2019; David Danelo, 'Germany in the 21st Century: The View from the Netherlands', Foreign Policy Research Institute blog, 5 May 2015: www.fpri.org/article/2015/05/germany-in-the-21st-century-part-ii-the-view-from-the-netherlands/, accessed 28 April 2019. I also draw here on personal experience: I was told by Dutch Adventists in 1985 and 1989 that the Netherlands would never again be in the same division as Germany, because of what happened in the war; in 2003, two veteran pastors stated that this had been attitude in the past but that younger church members felt differently. I am indebted to Reinder Bruinsma for the point about German pastors.
5   See GC Officers' Meeting, 20 Jan. 1946, GCOM, second series, p. 6325.

undecided.⁶ At the GC Executive Committee's first meeting of the new quadrennium, held the day after the Session closed, there was an idea of pairing the NUC with the BUC,⁷ perhaps with an idea of having two sections in the NED, as had been the case in the CED in the thirties. If that had happened, then subsequent events (discussed below) suggest that the Anglo-Dutch section might well have been given responsibility for West Africa and then been hived off into a completely separate division. By October, however, having reviewed the situation, the Home and Foreign officers proposed that 'Holland' should be part of NED 'for the present' and this was approved by the GC Executive Committee.⁸ The provisional became permanent at the 1950 GC Session.

It took a little while to integrate the Netherlands into the NED,⁹ but from the fifties, Dutch Adventists found their brethren in the Nordic countries and the British Isles congenial company. This partly reflected long-established and ever-increasing Anglo-Dutch cultural and commercial connections, manifested not least in the prominence of the English language in the Netherlands; but there were also long-standing and 'important ties' between the Netherlands, Denmark, and Norway.¹⁰ To these factors, anchored in culture and society, can be added a broadly similar approach to theology in the Netherlands, Denmark, and Sweden; and a common passion for foreign mission. Perhaps it was because the Netherlands had a long imperial history

---

6   Forty-Fifth Session, first and third meetings, 5 and 6 (p.m.) June 1946, proceedings, *ARH*, 123.24, General Conference Report no. 2 (7 June 1946), 13, 36.
7   GCC meeting, 16 June 1946, GCC Proc., XVII, ii, 2.
8   GCC Autumn Council, 17 Oct. 1946, GCC Proc., XVII, ii, 211.
9   Cf. 'News Flash', *Northern Light*, 1.1 (March 1951), 12.
10 Matti Klinge, 'Aspects of the Nordic Self', *Daedalus*, 113.2 (1984), 265; and see, e.g., *The North Sea. A Highway of Economic and Cultural Exchange: Character – History*, ed. by Arne Bang-Andersen, Basil Greenhill, and Egil Harald Grude (Stavanger: Norwegian University Press and Oxford: Oxford University Press, 1985); Louis Sicking, *et al.*, *Dutch Light in the 'Norwegian Night': Maritime Relations and Migration across the North Sea* (Hilversum: Verloren, 2004).

and large colonies (though the Dutch empire was to break up quickly after World War II), but whatever the cause, Dutch Adventists looked outwards in ways not always true of Adventists in some other parts of Europe. A number of Dutch Adventists went as missionaries in the next forty years, while the NUC was a steady contributor to division finances. The Netherlands Union was, from the perspective of the division administration, a better than like-for-like replacement for the Baltic Union; and for the last seventy-five years, the Netherlands has been, with Britain, Denmark, Finland, Norway, and Sweden, one of the division's key mission homelands.[11]

Provisional Divisions

Between the 1946 GC Session in Takoma Park and that year's Autumn Council in Grand Rapids, Michigan, the NED was both restored and reduced to the East and West Nordic, Netherlands, and Polish Union Conferences. Exactly how and why this came about is unclear, but this five-month period of uncertainty was the beginning of an almost five-year period which, with hindsight, we can see was the pivot on which the division history turned.

It is unclear what concerns were taken into the GC Session or what outcomes were expected before it convened. On the one hand, the NED had been in suspended animation since December 1943 and its executive committee had not met since April 1941. In the opening business meeting of the session, E. D. Dick, the GC secretary (and former NED secretary) observed, 'It will be understood, I believe, that this division is not functioning as a division at the present time'.[12] However, in session business thereafter the NED was

---

11 Up to 1997, twenty-two Dutch missionaries (*not* including spouses, so probably 30–40 in total) had gone overseas, according to *HRSDAE*, App. A, p. 264: this was fewer than any of the Nordic countries or the UK but more than Poland, Yugoslavia, its successor states, or Hungary.
12 Forty-Fifth Session, first meeting, 5 June 1946: proceedings, *ARH*, 123.23, General Conference Report, no. 1 (6 June 1946), 13; he made the same point in the formal 'Secretary's Report', second meeting, 6 June (a.m.) 1946, *ARH*, 123.24, General Conference Report, no. 2 (7 June 1946), 24,

always distinguished from 'the Provisional Division', which otherwise comprised the territories that had come under the Provisional Division Committee. These territories were treated as a division; they collectively had their own delegation, the division made its own report to the session, and so did its unions, as with every other division.[13] The WAUM, which had been part of the NED, was included, in terms of delegates and of reports, with the Provisional Missions Division. Thus, it was plain that the NED was no longer under the PDC. Its future was still to be defined, yet its African fields (including the Ethiopian Union, which had not been part of the NED since the Italian conquest, as well as the WAUM territories that had been part of NED in 1941) were clearly not thought as being integral to the Northern European Division.[14]

As the session commenced, however, the BUC *was* still thought of as part of the NED. Its representatives were part of the NED delegation. Harry W. Lowe, the BUC president, began his report by referring to himself and his colleagues as 'com[ing] to this important assembly […] from Northern Europe' and in his conclusion declared that 'Northern Europe needs a larger evangelistic program' – so there was little hint of what was to come.[15] Yet, in practice, separation had been foreshadowed since the start of the year, when the GC Executive Committee had increasingly acted in the place of a division committee for the BUC, which it had removed from under the Provisional Division Committee for Detached Missions, though the PDC retained authority over the West African Union Mission until the

---

and text of report ibid., 25–28 (quotation at p. 26).
13 Report of PDC and its unions, ninth meeting, 10 June 1946: proceedings, *ARH*, 123.27, General Conference Report, no. 5 (11 June 1946), 127; text of PDC report published as: W. H. Branson, 'The Provisional Division', ibid., 123–24; Verbal reports of unions published as 'An Afternoon With the Provisional Division', *ARH*, 123.29, General Conference Report, no. 7 (13 June 1946), 147–48.
14 See Branson, 'Provisional Division', p. 123.
15 Forty-Fifth Session, third meeting, 6 June (p.m.) 1946: proceedings, *ARH*, 123.24, General Conference Report, no. 2 (7 June 1946), 36, and text of report: H. W. Lowe, 'The British Union Conference', ibid., 41–42.

committee was itself dissolved at the 1946 session. GC Secretary Dick had visited Britain (where he had lived in the early thirties) early in 1946 and, while there is no record of what might have been said in private, it is likely that Dick informally encouraged any aspirations the British leaders had for continued independence from the NED.[16]

In the end, the PDC was wound up and its unions attached directly to the GC, which meant the WAUM was separated from the NED and the Ethiopian Union not restored. The GC Bylaws regarding 'division sections' were not amended, which meant that the Northern European Division still existed.[17] But a permanent decision about its future was not taken and no officers were elected. Although no GC Session minutes refer to it, the matter was presumably discussed in private and referred for further review. In the run-up to Autumn Council, the Home and Foreign Officers proposed (and the Executive Committee disposed, approvingly):

> *That the Northern European Division be reorganized on a provisional basis and that the following countries and islands comprise its territory for the present: Denmark, Norway, Sweden, Finland, Poland, Holland, Iceland, Greenland, and the Faroe Islands.*

Thenceforth, the NED was regularly referred to in official minutes and church publications as the Provisional Northern European Division. The same Autumn Council action approved relocation of the division headquarters to Stockholm. It also deferred 'consideration of the organisational status of the British Union [...] to a later meeting'.[18]

It is notable, however, that as the session had ended, the GC Executive Committee had begun passing calls from the BUC to divisions

---

16 E.g., GCC meeting, 21 Jan. 1946, GCC Proc., xvii, i, 2259.
17 The post-1946 *Constitution and Bylaws* are in *YB 1947*, pp. 332–37: Bylaws Art. 1, § 3.
18 GCC Autumn Council, 17 Oct. 1946, GCC Proc., xvii, ii, 211.

and vice versa, just as it did for a division (including the NED); it would continue this for the rest of the quadrennium.[19] There must have been a strong lobby in favour of attaching the British Union directly to the GC. This is also evident from the fact that, in practice, a 'later meeting' meant much later – not until 1950. The decision at Autumn Council to defer deciding was a decision by default; by not making other arrangements, the BUC in effect became independent of the NED.

Map 5.1: The NED after the 1946 GC Session

---

19 See, e.g., GCC meetings, 16–17 June, 20 and 22 Oct. 1946, GCC Proc., XVII, ii, 2, 9, 12, 228, 247.

Meanwhile, the last action the 1946 Autumn Council took regarding the NED was to elect officers and departmental leaders. The East Nordic Union Conference (ENUC) president, Gustav A. Lindsay, was elected 'president of the Provisional Northern European Division' (Illustration 5.1). An experienced administrator, he had been born in Sweden in 1895, but emigrated to the United States in 1912, where he was converted. He trained at Broadview Seminary, the church's Swedish-language college in North America and, after just a year of pastoral work in the USA, he and his wife Hildur returned to Sweden as missionaries in 1922. In 1929, Gustav had become one of the NED's first departmental secretaries, leading the Missionary Volunteer and Sabbath School departments, until he was elected ENUC president, a position he held until 1946. Lindsay was the first NED president born in Scandinavia, though not the first Scandinavian, since he was a US citizen.[20] Alf Karlman, a Norwegian, was elected treasurer (Illustration 5.2), but the position of secretary was left unfilled (in 1947 Karlman was made secretary-treasurer) and only three departmental secretaries were elected – all this further highlights the provisional nature of the NED.[21]

The evidence points to disagreement among world-church leaders about future directions for both the former and current territories of the NED. In the budget for 1947, also approved at 1946 Autumn Council, the base appropriations to divisions had separate line items for each division (including the Provisional NED) and for four 'Detached Unions' (listed under that rubric): the British Union Conference, the Ethiopian Union Mission, the Middle East Union Mission (MEUM), and the WAUM. In the special appropriations, the BUC was separately itemised and not under 'Detach [sic] Union Missions' but among the divisions! The 'appropriations from the Church Extension Fund to Overseas and North American

---

20 Obit. 'Deaths', *ARH*, 151.41 (10 Oct. 1974), 31. He and Hildur eventually retired in the United States.
21 GCC Autumn Council, 21 Oct. 1946, GCC Proc., xvii, ii, 214, 237; 'Fall Council Election', *ARH*, 123.52 (7 Nov. 1946), 23.

Divisions', however, had one line item for 'Detached Union Missions', not broken down, and one for 'Northern Europe including British Union'. In a further allocation of 'Church Extension' funds a few weeks later, appropriations for West Africa and Ethiopia were voted separately, but the appropriations for the 'British Union [and] Northern European Division' were voted together, though with separate line items. Administratively, almost every possible future permutation was implied in the different appropriations. If money talks, the GC 1947 budget was saying rather disparate things about the future prospects of the different regions.[22]

Restoring the Breach

Deliberations and Negotiations, 1948–1950

The Forty-Sixth General Conference Session convened in San Francisco on 10 July 1950. Ten days later, two days before it concluded, it voted to approve a recommendation to combine 'the unions of Northern Europe – the two Scandinavian unions and Poland – and also the mission territory of Eritrea and Ethiopia' with 'the British Union [and] the present West African Union […] in one new division to be known as the North Atlantic Division'.[23] How had the rupture of the 1940s come to be healed?

Northern European Division leaders had agitated for an enlargement of the division ever since the 1946 GC Session. In the words of a 'memorial' to the GC officers, drafted by the presidents of the ENUC

---

22 GCC Autumn Council, 23 Oct. 1946, GCC meeting, 11 Nov. 1946, GCC Proc., xvii, ii, 253–58 (pp. 253–54, 256), 296.
23 Forty-Sixth Session, fourteenth meeting, 20 July 1950, in *ARH*, 127.36, *GC Session Bulletin* (21 July 1950), 211–12, quotation from speech in support of the motion by GC President W. H. Branson (p. 212).

and WNUC, then endorsed and referred to the GC by NEDCOM in 1948, there had been 'general satisfaction' when the NED was

> re-established [...] at the Autumn Council in 1946, after an interregnum of about five years due to the disruption caused by the World War. However, at the same time it came as an unpleasant surprise to the field that no mission territory in Africa was assigned to the Division as in former years; and consequently a deep regret was expressed throughout the entire Division.

For two years, the NED officers had been requesting that the old model be reinstituted but kept being told by 'different officers of the General Conference [...] that the time was not yet fully ripe for such a move'.[24]

In 1948, they turned to financial arguments. In drafting the memorial, the Scandinavian leaders highlighted recent record receipts for 'the Week of Sacrifice and the Week of Prayer offering, etc.' and for 'the Harvest Ingathering campaign'. However, they then proceeded to emphasise:

> We have problems when it comes to sending out our mission funds [...] because we are not recognized as mission societies, when we do not direct any mission fields. The authorities contend that if American and British mission organizations employ missionaries from our countries, they must also be responsible for their support.

The NED urged both that it had the resources to support mission fields and that it would find it easier to transmit mission funds from Northern Europe to the world church 'if we have definite mission

---

24 'Memorial to the Officers of the General Conference', n.d. – signed by presidents of the East Nordic and West Nordic Unions; NEDCOM voted to endorse it and send to GC on 1 Sept. 1948: text in NEDCOM mins., 1948, pp. 151–54 (pp. 151–52).

fields under our direction and for which we would be responsible'.[25] Relevant here was that the NED's foreign mission offering was the third-largest of the eleven world divisions (and NED was likewise third-largest both for tithe per capita and foreign mission offering per capita), so that though temporarily reduced in membership, its financial impact remained disproportionate.[26]

Whether or not the potential risk to the flow of funds was the reason, the GC officers clearly concluded that the time was ripe. Citing the 'Northern European Division['s] Memorial to the General Conference', at the 1948 Autumn Council, the GC Executive Committee reassigned the Ethiopian Union Mission (including southern Sudan, Eritrea, and the Somali colonies of Britain, France, and Italy) to the NED, effective 1 January 1949.[27] The return of the West African mission fields by the 1950 GC Session restored almost all of the division's African mission empire as it had existed in 1941 when the NED was suspended; only Uganda was missing.

Finances and disposition of African mission fields may also help to explain British Adventist willingness to be reunited with the NED. By the end of the forties, the GC Executive Committee was looking to the BUC to contribute directly from its funds towards 'the support of the medical, evangelical, educational and other activities in [several] territories'. These included 'Nigeria, Gold Coast, Sierra Leone', and all parts of WAUM which, like the BUC, was no longer under the NED but attached directly to the GC; but BUC support was also sought for 'Nyasaland [Malawi], and the Malay States', in the Southern Africa and Far East Divisions.[28] All were part of the British Empire and British missionaries had pioneered work in West Africa and Malawi (though there was no particular historical connection to

---

25   Ibid., pp. 151, 153.
26   *ASR*, 87 (1949), 18–19.
27   GCC Autumn Council, 21 Oct. 1948, GCC Proc., xvii, iv, 1203. Cf. the report by Gustav Lindsay, the NED president, to the NED Winter Council, NEDCOM-WCM 1948, p. 163.
28   GCC meeting, 19 Apr. 1949, GCC Proc., xvii, v, 1464.

Malaysia). Yet the British church was being asked to shoulder financial responsibility for territories for which they had no administrative responsibility. This must have given pause for thought. Furthermore, by this time the General Conference officers were leaning against prolonging the attachment of the BUC directly to the GC and the BUC president, E. B. Rudge, was well aware of that (Illustration 5.3). Some at the world headquarters wanted to see Britain come under the NED, but others canvassed the possibility of creating a new division based around the BUC and its traditional mission fields in the WAUM.[29] Such a new division would, however, have put a considerable burden on Britain; sharing it with Scandinavia must have seemed attractive.

By the winter of 1950, thanks to the mediation of the GC officers, a meeting of British and Scandinavian church leaders, with GC President McElhany and two GC departmental directors, had been arranged for 20 March 1950. Although no record survives, it must surely have tentatively agreed to a merger of the BUC and NED (and WAUM), for that was the result a few months later. It seems plain that GC administration was pushing that outcome.[30] Yet the Scandinavians had agitated in the late forties only for the return of territories in East Africa with which they had an historic connection; and there is no evidence that the BUC, ENUC, or WNUC were actively seeking reunification. If they had strongly opposed the GC officers' design, there could have been a different outcome. The most likely explanation is that by 1950 there was a consensus among Nordic, Dutch, and British church leaders about the benefits of a return to what was, after all, the *status quo ante bellum*. Further evidence for this hypothesis is, simply, that harmony ensued; whatever manoeuvring had taken place in the late forties, after 1950 the six unions in

29 GC Officers' Meetings, 3 and 18 Apr. and 22 July 1949, GCOM, pp. 49-80, 49-100, 101, 49-176.
30 The travel of the three GC men was approved by the GC Officers' Meeting of 11 Sept. 1949; the minutes of the meeting of 16 Oct. 1949 refer to the 20 March meeting and 'preliminary meetings' involving McElhany and his colleagues 'with the brethren of the British Union' scheduled for 16 March 1950: GCOM, pp. 49-219, 49-248.

question (BUC, ENUC, NUC, PUC, WAUM, and WNUC) worked together effectively and with little or no hint of sectional hostilities.

North Atlantic Division to Northern European Division

If church administrators in Britain and Scandinavia were coming around to the idea of an organisational restoration, there was not yet a wider consensus among church leaders. In early July, a 'special committee [...] of home officers, division presidents, delegates from the British Union, the West African Union, the Middle East Union, and the provisional Northern European Division', worked on 'recommendations to the session' regarding 'territorial adjustments'; a report was reviewed by the Home and Foreign Officers on 5 July, less than a week before the session started. The ad hoc committee agreed that the BUC, WAUM, and MEUM ought to 'be attached to some divisional organisation [...] from which they should receive direction'. Yet the report concluded: 'The way is not clear to deal with this matter at this session'; and its recommendation, which the Home and Foreign Officers accepted, was that the matter be given further study by the newly elected administration and any plans brought to Autumn Council.[31] We know neither the nature of any objections nor who objected at this 5 July meeting. What we do know is that fifteen days later, apparently after work *during* the session by the 'special committee',[32] but without further review by the wider officer group, a major proposal to establish two divisions, the North Atlantic Division and a new Middle East Division, went to the GC Session and, as we have seen already, was approved.

In the absence of documentary evidence, one must speculate, both about how the proposal was brought to the Session after stalemate among the officers, and about the name adopted. It is likely that

---

31 Forty-Sixth Session, proceedings of 20 July 1950 (see fn. 1), p. 211, chairman's introductory comments; Home and Foreign Officers' Meeting, 5 July 1950, GCOM, pp. 50-172, 173.

32 'Winter Council of the Northern European Division', *Northern Light*, 1.1 (March 1951), 5.

'North Atlantic Division' was chosen to imply a merger of the NED, BUC, and WAUM, rather than a takeover of the latter by the former. The only public comment on the name was made by the newly elected GC president, W. H. Branson, in a speech supporting the proposal, in which he observed of the new division: 'Practically all of their territory is on the North Atlantic. That would not be true, of course, of two of their little mission fields in Africa [Ethiopia and Eritrea], but it would be true of the great West African field.' Branson continued: 'I am happy to strongly endorse this recommendation'. This offers an insight into the other issue, too; Branson's strong backing would explain how an idea that could not command the support of the wider officer group suddenly got developed into a proposal and put before the Session delegates. Branson had had been a church leader in both Africa and Europe in the twenties and thirties. By the mid-forties, he had a strong personal interest in the work in the Middle East. It seems probable that he had been pushing for the idea of the two new divisions and that, after his election as president, he worked behind the scenes at San Francisco to break the deadlock.[33]

A hint of the compromises engaged in establishing the North Atlantic Division is that the president elected was A. F. Tarr, a South African serving as a missionary in India (Illustration 5.4). There can be little doubt that Tarr was chosen because candidates from within the NED would not have been politic choices. Gustav Lindsay, the serving division president, born in Sweden and former ENUC president, could not continue, but neither could Edmund Rudge of the BUC replace him. Tarr was an experienced leader, a former union president and serving division secretary; he was knowledgeable about Africa, having spent most of his career there; he was an English-speaker

---

33 Reports in *ARH*, 127.36, *GC Session Bulletin* (21 July 1950), 211–12; *Northern Light*, 1.1 (March 1951), 5–6. For Branson's career and interest, see *sub* 'Branson, William Henry', *SDAE*, I, 227; D. J. B. Trim, *Adventist Mission in the Middle East: A History* (GC Archives Monographs, forthcoming).

but not British.³⁴ In a remarkably gracious gesture, Lindsay agreed to serve as the treasurer. Rudge was elected secretary of the NED. Their election to these positions, with a neutral president, is a further indication of the political influences at work in Tarr's election and the balancing act required to create the North Atlantic Division. All three officers continued to serve in those capacities for several years – serving together for six years, until Rudge retired. In all, Lindsay served eight years as division treasurer and Tarr, twelve as president.

The day after the session concluded, the GC Executive Committee held its first meeting of the new quadrennium and took an action: 'That it be understood that the officers of the two new divisions, the North Atlantic and the East Mediterranean, shall begin to function at once', though 'the divisions as organisations [would] begin to function January 1, 1951.'³⁵ At some point in the two months after the GC Session, however, the officers of the new North Atlantic Division belatedly recognised that the new division title could be seen as provocative in Poland, given that the previous year the North Atlantic Treaty Organisation (NATO) had been created, chiefly to defend Western Europe against attack by the Soviet Union and its Eastern European allies. Given the need for a new name and the simple fact that the new division essentially *was* the old NED, common sense presumably prevailed; at any rate the obvious solution was recommended to the GC officers.³⁶ Subsequently, the GC Executive Committee voted to 'approve of the name of the Division being changed to Northern European Division', which would take effect 1 January 1951 when the restructured division formally came into being.³⁷ The

---

34 Notice under 'Deaths', *ARH*, 157.45 (2 Oct. 1980), 23.
35 GCC Meeting, 23 July 1950, GCC Proc., XVIII, i, 37.
36 GC Officers' Meeting, 24 Sept. 1950, GCOM, p. 50-230. This records the request for a name change as coming from the 'Division Committee', but only three NEDCOM meetings were held in the period between the GC Session and Autumn Council and the issue of the name does not appear in the minutes of any of them. Hence my conclusion that the division officers must have identified the terminological problem.
37 GCC, 2 Oct. 1950, GCC Proc., XVIII, i, 114.

NED had now truly been brought fully back to life.

The Hinge of Fate

With hindsight one can see that the two Nordic union conferences and perhaps the Polish Union might easily have been be merged into one or other of the CED and SED, perhaps as part of a wider reorganisation of the two, with Britain and perhaps the Netherlands forming the core of a new division that could have included the NED's old African mission fields, and perhaps the Middle East (part of which had been attached directly to the BUC immediately after World War I). Much of this history uses a wide-angle lens, whereas this chapter is in close focus, but that is because the episode it describes was absolutely pivotal in the TED's history. The division could conceivably have been directed onto a dramatically different trajectory or even had its organisational life concluded, in which case there would have been no ninetieth anniversary in 2019. These four years are the hinge on which the history of the TED turned.

The final half of this episode overlaps with the gestation period of the fourth part of Winston Churchill's best-selling, six-volume history, *The Second World War*, entitled *The Hinge of Fate*. Serious writing began in the spring and summer of 1948, as the Scandinavian church leaders honed their arguments for recovering East Africa. The British political giant and his assistants continued writing through 1949 and the winter of 1950, as the BUC's leaders confronted the implications and repercussions of autonomy. As Churchill was writing about a victory in the Middle East and Africa, and about 'fighting with allies' as they disagreed about how to win a worldwide conflict, GC leaders were using their influence to shape the future of the residual NED, the BUC, West Africa, and the Middle East in ways that would benefit a worldwide church. As the book went through the press in the summer of 1950, the GC Session was meeting and reaching its conclusions. It is a curious coincidence: Churchill was writing about the turning-point of World War II, hence his evocative title, *The Hinge of Fate*, though he also considered 'The Balance Turns'; but the book was also 'the hinge of his whole work' and one that turned around declining sales.[38] Meanwhile, the years in which it was written and published were a turning point for the TED – perhaps we might say a hinge of faith.

An alternative metaphor is of a pivot. In 1950 the course of events could have taken a quite different turn; instead the division and the world church pivoted in the direction of a reunion of the Ethiopian (northern) region of East Africa, West Africa, the British Isles and islands of the North Atlantic, the Nordic countries, and Poland (with the addition of the Netherlands). The direction taken decisively shaped the next thirty years, or one third of the division's life. But it was not taken by accident, nor simply because the Holy Spirit dictated a direction to church leaders. Some reflections on church decision making follow, which are directly about the course of action agreed in 1950, but implicitly about policy making in the seventy years since then.

Church Politics, Structure, and Mission

This chapter has explored in some detail the protracted negotiations of 1948–1950, in part precisely because of its pivotal nature. But I have also described the jockeying for global and ecclesiastical position by British and Scandinavian church leaders (among others) in part because it is the reality of church administration when humans are involved. What appears awfully like politicking, prompted by ambition and pride, is an authentic part, albeit not the most attractive part, of Adventist history. It is usually ignored in narratives intended to be edifying or inspiring, but when we disregard or discount the human interactions, we run the risk of reaching a distorted understanding of

---

38 See David Reynolds, *In Command of History: Churchill Fighting and Writing the Second World War* (New York: Basic Books, 2007 [2005]), pp. 286-93, 348-49, 368; quotation at p. 286; 'Fighting with Allies – and Colleagues' is the title of chap. 21.

the denominational decision-making process. Seventh-day Adventists prefer to see providence guiding every decision made; and there is no doubt that church leaders, around the world and in the TED throughout its history, have sought the guidance of the Holy Spirit. However, first, God's people have and do sometimes use His gift of free will in ways that do not always conform to His plans. Second, in any case, sometimes there are multiple 'good' choices. The options the organised denomination takes and the decisions it makes, for good or ill, are often affected (or effected) by the church's internal politics.

For many Adventists, the 'P' word is appalling; admitting that politics is at work in the church means conceding a lack of Spirit-filled leadership. We are not talking here, though, of secular, partisan politics, but of organisational politics (or administrative politics, as one student of Adventist history described it).[39] Following the insightful analysis of an historian of ecclesiastical policymaking (though in a rather different period), I understand politics to mean, 'quite simply [...] the art of getting things done.' Politics 'is the art of winning agreement [and] of gaining consensus'. Thus defined, every sphere of human interaction 'has a political dimension' because 'every act of decision making requires political skills'. Church leaders often have different priorities; in seeking or securing the support of others to implement one set of plans rather than another, they are engaging in politics. Church officials are of course sometimes influenced by personal factors such as pride or ambition, but Adventist leaders are often moved primarily by theological or spiritual principles. Yet whatever the source or the character of their ideas and beliefs, in attempting to put them into effect, in trying to turn ideas into policies and actions, leaders move from the intellectual to the practical – hence the political.[40] Consequently, in identifying political factors

---

39 Anthea N. Davis, 'West Indian Immigrants and Administrative Politics in the Seventh-day Adventist Church in Britain c.1950–1980' (MA dissertation, University of London, 2003).

40 H. A. Drake, *Constantine and the Bishops* (Baltimore, MD: Johns Hopkins University Press, 2000), pp. xvi–xvii (quotations at p. xvi).

at work in Adventist decision making, it is not intended as censure of those involved for not being led by the Holy Spirit. Rather I seek to delineate how the Seventh-day Adventist Church in a particular time and place accepted the plans of one Spirit-filled leader over another's.

I have dwelt on this here because 1948–1950 was probably the first time that a major policy shift relating to the NED/TED was subject to sustained debate and political wrangling – although it was not the last. In 1928 there had been near unanimity about the need to decentralise the sclerotic European Division. The significant organisational changes of 1941 were effectively forced on the church by wartime exigencies. Those of 1946, which were the working out of the 1941 actions, were more divisive, but were also generally regarded as provisional, inviting subsequent debate and negotiation. The eventual course the world church charted in 1950 was not inevitable; instead it was the result of church politics, in which clearly conflicting ideas about what organisational arrangements would have the most positive outcome for the Adventist Church, in Europe and more widely, were presented, discussed, nuanced, and eventually conclusions were reached. At times of collective indecision, inertia triumphed (not for the last time in Adventist administrative history), as in the perpetuation, after 1946, of the NUC's status and that of the BUC. But the former really did become permanent, whereas the latter did not. The trump card (not for the last time either) was deep personal engagement with a particular plan by the president of the General Conference. The pattern we see here was to be repeated later in the TED's history.

What must not be lost sight of, however, is that the Great Commission was central to the manoeuvring and negotiating of the late 1940s. What was at stake for the stakeholders in the once and future NED, and for most of the world leaders who perused plans at San Francisco in the summer of 1950, was not primarily power, nor even prestige. The world church did not assign African territories to European divisions merely because their leaders desired them, but only if a division could provide the mission fields with money, missionaries, and leaders who could credibly manage the resources supplied. This concern was manifested in the initial caution about restoring African fields to the provisional NED during 1946–1948. It was evident, too, in a decision made in the summer of 1950, for the Central European Division submitted its own 'requests for mission territory' – in vain.[41] Just five years after the end of the war, the German Adventist Church could not realistically support mission work, nor would German leadership have been accepted in most parts of the world. The CED's yearning appears more reputational than missional. That the new NED finally entered the fifties with responsibility for West Africa and the northern parts of East Africa was because world-church leaders believed their counterparts in the NED were passionate about, and proficient in managing, mission.

Whatever politicking was done by British and Scandinavian church leaders in the second half of the forties, they sought to serve and to do so effectively. That this was their priority is particularly apparent in the compromise choice of the division officers in 1950; whatever Lindsay or Rudge felt in private about Tarr's elevation over them, in practice the three men worked together congenially and capably for six years. Personal feelings were put to one side because, above all else, all three wanted to serve God and His Church. What we have surveyed in this chapter was thus, in a sense, the politics of service.[42] There were different views about the best way forward, debate ensued, various church leaders sought to convince colleagues to support them, and bargains were probably made before they made their collective decision. In the end, hindsight suggests they reached a good resolution. Sustained growth ensued in the NED. Providence

---

41 Home and Foreign Officers' Meeting, 26 June 1950, GCOM, p.50-150.
42 A term I borrow from Bill Knott's important study of the milieu of early Adventism, though I use it in a rather different sense: William M. Knott, 'Foot Soldier of the Empire: Hannah More and the Politics of Service' (PhD dissertation, George Washington University, 2006).

can take the often base metals of human motivations, ambitions, and interactions, and transmute them into the silver and gold of good news shared and souls saved.

Above all, passion for mission continued to be the driving force. In December 1949, the last Winter Council before the old NED was re-founded adopted this resolution:

> *It is imperative that every worker in the cause of God and every church member sensing the inestimable value of a soul, be imbued with the power of the Holy Ghost and a passion to win men and women to God.*[43]

The fervour for mission that had been integral to the division at its conception, twenty years before – the readiness 'to make every effort' to take the Adventist message far and wide – was still strong among church leaders. This would stand them and the division in good stead as a little over five years of organisational volatility was followed by two decades of stability.

---

43 NEDCOM, 1949–1950 mins., p. 312.

Chapter 6
"Evangelism in Every Community': Years of Stability, 1951–1970

The twenty years of the TED's history considered in this chapter seem, to some older church members, like the division's golden age: an era of economic prosperity and flourishing church finances in most of the homelands; of church growth in the mission fields, in particular, but also in Europe. It was also an era of social and political stability, at least in the division's Nordic and North Atlantic homelands, one that mirrored (and was partly a product of) a wider 'stability and uniformity' in Western European society.[1] Overshadowing the fifties and sixties was the threat of cold war turning hot and nuclear destruction, but Adventist apocalyptic understanding meant this was less of a fear for Seventh-day Adventists than for the population at large. The passage of time has lent a glistening patina to the two decades between the restoration of the Ethiopian Union (which included countries around Ethiopia) to the NED in 1949, and its permanent separation from the division in 1970.

Nostalgic perspectives are often misleading, however. It is easy to forget that this era was also one in which white men (and they were mostly men) controlled the church, not only in the homelands, but also in Africa, where the word of the missionary was generally law. The stability of the fifties was perhaps stagnation and was in any case succeeded by the radical social and cultural revolution of the sixties. It was an era in which older perspectives, presumptions, and methodologies still held sway – in the church as well as wider society; yet not for much longer. And that is one reason why, through the gold-tinted lenses of nostalgia, the era has a warm sunny glow: an

---

1   Cf. Martin Conway, 'The Rise and Fall of Western Europe's Democratic Age, 1945-1973', *Contemporary European History*, 13 (2004), 67-88 (pp. 69, 87).

autumnal Indian Summer of certainties, before the wintry onset of postmodernity. Yet the sexual revolution, rock 'n' roll, student uprisings, economic stagnation, American cultural creep, Third World independence and obstructiveness, rejection of organised religion – all were already seen in the sixties. The twenty-five years between the end of World War II and the NED's metamorphosis to NEWAD were not really so straightforward and stable as wistful longing can make them seem.

The full story of the impact of Europe's secular turn on the Seventh-day Adventist Church is still to be written, but from the perspective of church leaders the chief issues that emerged in the sixties were the increasing imbalance between growth in the mission fields, especially those in West Africa, and the core territories – the homelands. This in turn reflected the growing indifference, indeed insouciance, to Christianity in Europe, which made evangelism in the NED's homelands ever more difficult, even as Africans were becoming Christians and members of the Seventh-day Adventist Church in large numbers. This created a dilemma that division leaders did not successfully resolve.

Looking Outwards

These were, in many ways, quiet years, prosperous years, in Europe and for the church. The NED had huge responsibilities. As W. D. Eva, division president in the late sixties described, its territory and the church members living in them ranged 'from Laplanders of the far Arctic north, from true-hearted believers more than 5,000 miles south in the humid jungles of West Africa, from hardy dwellers in "the island of fire and ice" on the western extremity of our division' [Iceland], to, 'on its eastern extremity, [believers] from that great country with its 13 months of sunshine [...], Ethiopia.'[2] There were

---

2   W. Duncan Eva, 'Report of the Northern European Division', Fifty-first GC Session, *ARH*, 147.27, suppt., *GC Session Bulletin* (16 June 1970), 94.

many challenges in enabling concerted action across such distances and such linguistic, cultural, and socio-economic diversity.

To help meet the challenge of keeping church members across the division on the same page, the 1950 Winter Council took an action to create a monthly paper. The NED thus had its own journal again after a ten-year hiatus. The new *Northern Light* was intended to help 'to create a Division-consciousness, making and keeping us acquainted with each other'; throughout this period it actively encouraged church members to 'be Division minded'.[3]

The division administration was aided by the fact that it avoided major restructuring. The years between the epochal shifts of 1949–51 and 1969–1971 were marked by considerable organisational stability – perhaps the greatest of any twenty-year period in the TED's history. The only restructuring took place in 1955, when the East Nordic Union Conference (ENUC), was replaced by two new union conferences: the Finland Union and Swedish Union (SUC). Each new union had two geographical conferences; part of Finland stayed with Sweden, for the tiny Finnish-Swedish Conference, consisting of members from the Swedish-speaking minority in Finland, was included in the SUC as a third conference (it was later to be become part of the Finland Union, before eventually being discontinued in 2014). As the assignment of that conference to Sweden hints, one of the reasons for the separation was tension over the very different languages spoken, along with the maturation of the church in Finland, which had been founded from Sweden.[4] The end of the East Nordic Union affected neither the nomenclature nor the organisation of the West Nordic Union.

3   A. F. Tarr, 'Greetings from the President', *Northern Light*, 1.1 (March 1951), 1; cf. 'Northern Light', ibid., 3; B. E. Seton, 'By the Editor', *Northern Light*, 16.12 (Dec. 1966), 2.
4   NEDCOM meetings, 6 July and 15 Sept. 1955, NEDCOM mins., 1955, pp. 85, 106; GCC meeting, 18 Aug. 1955, GCC Proc., xix, ii, 382; *YB 1956*, pp. 130, 132-33; GCC Spring Meeting, 8 Apr. 2014, GCC mins., 2014, p. 14-40; Kai Arasola, 'Finland', in *HRSDAE*, pp. 90-92.

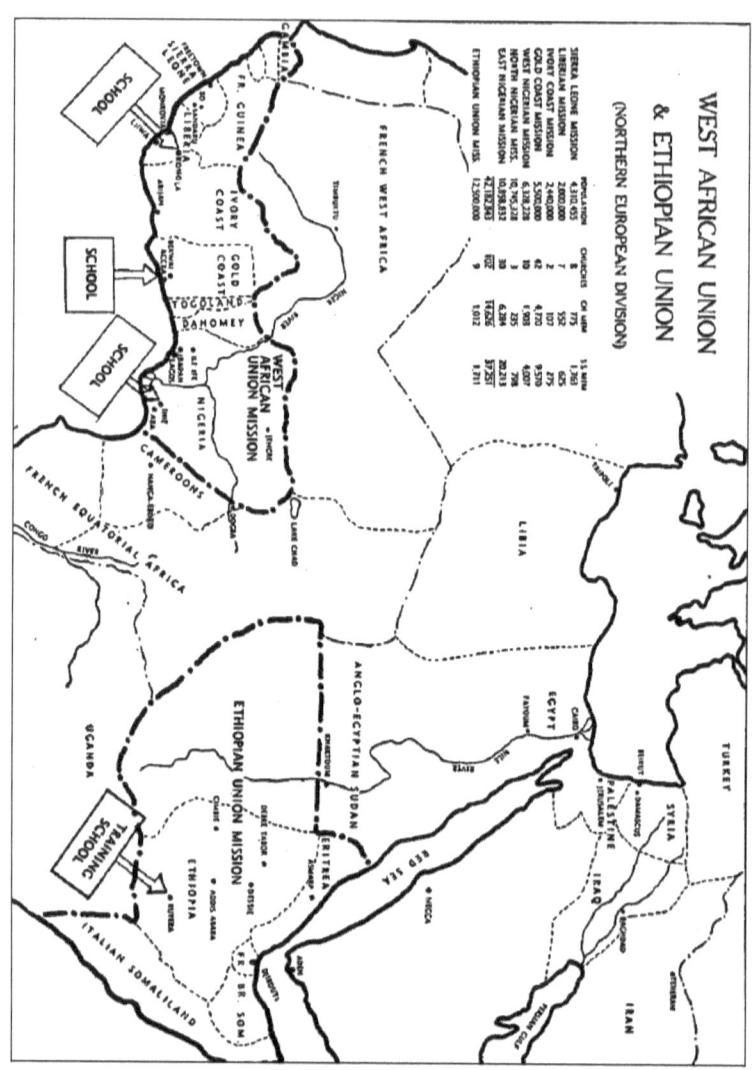

Map 6.1: The NED's African Mission Fields in 1954

There were to be adjustments in the number and territory of conferences and missions but the only other administrative changes that were not localised involved the division office. In the autumn of 1950, the headquarters returned to 41 Hazel Gardens, Edgware. Since 1 May 1965, the division office has been located at 119 St

Peter's Street, St Albans, north of London, where it remains.⁵

Amid the stability and continuity, NED leaders often found it difficult to deal with big-picture issues, because the demands of administering and supervising such a large territory, especially its large mission fields in opposite quadrants of the African continent, regularly left no time to think strategically. The division committee had a regular routine of voting itineraries, budgets, and appropriations; scheduling union meetings and programming division councils; managing its own finances, investments, and properties, including those around Hazel Gardens in Edgware; actively supervising the budgets and plans of the mission unions in Africa; and generally overseeing the plans of the unions in Northern Europe. There was no ADCOM of the NEDCOM – that was an innovation that lay decades ahead; consequently, many matters took up the time of the division committee. The business of managing the division's large force of missionaries also took up the time of NED administration.

This is illustrated by one randomly selected meeting of NEDCOM in October 1958, the business of which included: reviewing and approving the daily schedule for the upcoming Division Biennial Council; setting up a subcommittee to review *Working Policy*; sanctioning two permanent returns of missionaries; authorising another missionary's request to go to the United States for further study; approving an open call for a physician to serve at Kwahu Hospital in Ghana; and calling a cook, Miss Rigmor Knudsen, a Norwegian, to serve at Filwoha Hospital in Ethiopia.⁶ Calling a cook, and on another occasion a 'kitchen supervisor',⁷ as a missionary is a reminder of the obligations incumbent on a division with major mission fields. The NED had to staff eight mission hospitals, ten schools and

---

5   See the mins. of the NEDCOM meetings of 31 Dec. 1950 and 1 Jan. 1951, and of 29 Apr. and 5 May 1965, NEDCOM, 1950–51 mins., pp. 1–6, 1965 mins., pp. 110, 112.
6   NEDCOM meetings of 21 Oct. 1958, NEDCOM mins., 1958, pp. 66–72.
7   NEDCOM meeting, 23 Apr. 1958, ibid., p. 36.

colleges, and two publishing houses in Africa.⁸ This had far-reaching implications. As well as managers, accountants, mission and union departmental directors, schoolteachers, and later college teachers, the NED had to supply sufficient professionals to run hospitals to the highest standards. It found it hard to recruit sufficient 'qualified doctors' and had to institute special measures for 'securing satisfactory medical appointees for the mission field'.⁹ But to staff mission-field hospitals in the 1950s, missionaries were called to fill almost every function. The division recognised that 'doctors, nurses, physiotherapists and cooks' all had a role to play in medical missionary work, along with laboratory and x-ray technicians, engineers, and others.¹⁰

All this placed a heavier burden on the small Adventist population in the homelands than if, as today, only highly qualified professionals were wanted. It was a challenge to the unions as well as the division, for at both levels of church structure, it took time and effort to manage the NED missionary programme: to find potential appointees, persuade them to serve, equip them, send them out, bring them home, and eventually replace them, at which point the cycle began anew. There was a positive side to this, however, for the comprehensive nature of the needs also meant that many more Northern European Adventists experienced missionary service than otherwise would have been the case. The upshot was to ensure that the needs of Africa had a high profile among church members as well as church leaders; yet it also meant that the needs of Africa tended, though not necessarily by design, to be placed above those of the homelands.

Division leaders were justly proud of the level of commitment to foreign mission that the NED demonstrated. In a report given in the autumn of 1956, the division secretary, George D. King (Illustration 6.1), drew particular attention to 'the 43 mission appointees who

---

8   *YB 1958*, pp. 148–49.
9   NEDCOM meetings, 29 May and 15 July 1952, NEDCOM mins., 1952, pp. 49, 53.
10 NEDCOM meeting, 4 Dec. 1951, NEDCOM mins., 1951, p. 123; cf. call voted by NEDCOM, 12 Feb. 1958, NEDCOM mins. 1958, p. 13.

[had] left the home bases of this Division for service overseas' in the two and a half years since the GC Session of May 1954.[11] In 1958, King, who had himself been a missionary in West Africa, highlighted that a further '44 mission appointees [had] left our home base' in the following two years, which, as he justly observed, 'indicates clearly that our home fields continue to make a most worth while [*sic*] contribution both in men and means for the finishing of the work in mission lands.'[12] King's reports both understate the actual numbers, however, because he undoubtedly followed normal practice and did not count the wives of male appointees. Britain continued to be a disproportionate source of missionary recruits, providing half the NED appointees in 1954 and 1955 and a third of those in 1956 and 1957, though it had a fourth of the membership in Europe. In an eight-year period, 1954–1961, seventy-six 'new mission appointees [were] sent out from Britain'.[13] The spirit of thirty years before was still alive and well.

International Influences

The NED during these years was intentionally outward looking and open to influence from the rest of the world. Yet the flow of people and therefore of ideas and practices was not one way. The full history of leaders from the English-speaking world contributing to the church in the British Isles, Scandinavia, and Southeast Europe goes well beyond the twenty years covered in this chapter. An overview of this topic is provided in Chapter 12 but here we survey those who played a role in the fifties and sixties; these years were notable for the number of church leaders from Australia and South Africa, whose leadership in and of the NED was decisive, almost definitive, in the

---

11 Secretary's Report to NED 'Annual Meeting' 'Winter Council', 28 Nov. 1956, NEDCOM Mins., 1956, p. 107.
12 Secretary's Report to NED Biennial Council, 7 Nov. 1958, NEDCOM Mins., 1958, p. 93; see King's obit., *ARH*, 143.41 (1 Sept. 1966), 25-26.
13 See NED Secretariat to J. A. McMillan (BUC president), 31 May 1962, RGL, BUC Papers, 1962 box, fld. 'G. D. King'.

decades considered in this chapter. Yet this era was also remarkable for the extraordinary influence, on the wider Seventh-day Adventist Church, of theologians and administrators from Northern Europe.

From the Southern Cross to the North Star

Albert Floyd Tarr, who went by his middle name, was the dominant figure of the new NED's first decade. Tarr spent much of his career in his native South Africa, including as president of the South African Union, but in middle age he accepted a call to missionary service to India as secretary of the Southern Asia Division. After nine years in this capacity in India, where he was a popular figure and demonstrated 'special abilities in [...] leadership', the 1950 GC Session elected him first president of the reconstituted NED (Illustration 6.2). As discussed in Chapter 5, Tarr was probably a compromise choice. He turned out, however, to be a very good choice. He had a forbidding countenance and was known for being 'dignified always in dress and deportment' (Illustration 6.3); but Floyd Tarr was also known for being 'very friendly' and he became a much-loved figure throughout the NED's far-flung territories (Illustration 6.4). After serving three four-year terms as president, A. F. Tarr ended his career with four years as an associate secretary of the General Conference.[14]

His successor had previously also served as a GC associate secretary. Erwin E. Roenfelt was from the large German-speaking community in South Australia. He entered pastoral ministry at age 19 and worked as an evangelist for sixteen years before moving into administration (Illustration 6.5). He served as conference president, Australasian Union Conference secretary, and Australasian Division vice-president, before being called to the GC in 1946, where he served as an associate secretary for four four-year terms. He then served one term

---

14 S. James, 'A Tribute to Pastor Albert Floyd Tarr', *Southern Asia Tidings*, 1 Oct. 1980, p. 12; cf. anon., 'He Served the World Church', ibid.; and obit. under 'Deaths', *ARH*, 157.45 (2 Oct. 1980), 23.

as president of the NED, from 1962–1966 (Illustration 6.6).[15]

Australians had already influenced the division. As we saw in Chapter 5, Edwin Rudge was BUC president in the late forties and shaped the negotiations that led to the re-emergence of the NED in 1950. Rudge had worked as a colporteur and a nurse, which led to his appointment as manager of Adelaide Sanitarium; this in turn led to church administration. He had served as president of three Australian conferences, of the Fiji Mission, and of the Australasian Union Conference (1938–1944). He had served almost two years as president of the Australasian Division when, in 1946, he was called to the presidency of the BUC, serving one four-year term, before his election as NED secretary at age 64. He served six years as division secretary, retiring in 1956.[16] During his total of ten years in Northern Europe, the church's 'workers learned to love and revere Pastor Rudge'. In addition to the connection to Britain, Rudge was 'intensely interested' in the Ethiopian Union while division secretary.[17]

In 1946, presumably at Rudge's instance, two close friends, T. J. Bradley and E. L. Minchin, were also called from Australia to Britain. Tom Bradley worked as an evangelist in England, enjoying some success, while Len Minchin became departmental secretary of the BUC's Sabbath-School, Young People's Missionary Volunteers (YPMV), and Temperance departments. In 1950, Bradley became secretary of the Ministerial Association of the newly reshaped NED, and Minchin the Sabbath School and YPMV departmental secretary.[18] Bradley's time in the NED and in pastoral ministry ended, sadly, with a transfer

---

15 See Bruce Price, 'Life-Sketch of Pastor Erwin E. Roenfelt', *Record*, 7 Nov. 1987, p. 13. The obit. under 'Deaths' in *ARH*, 165.10 (10 Mar. 1988), 23, is so concise as to be almost useless.
16 Obituary, *ARH*, 137.52 (29 Dec. 1960), 26; this leaves unclear his transition from union to division president, but see *YBs 1944* and *1945*.
17 'Pastor E. B. Rudge', *Northern Light*, 10.12 (Dec. 1960), 8.
18 'News Flash', *Northern Light*, 1.1 (March 1951), 12; Bruce Manners, 'Evangelism and Health Pioneer Dies', *Record*, 16 Aug. 2003, p. 7; 'Life-Sketch of Edwin Lennard Minchin', *South Pacific Record*, 30 May 1987, p. 12; *YB 1946*, pp. 71, 76; *YB 1947*, pp. 211–12.

to health administration in Canada in 1954, as a result of indiscretions twenty years earlier.[19] Minchin was still only 42 when he came to Britain, having served ten years as an inspirational and visionary YPMV secretary at the Australasian Division. In Australia, forty years later, it was recalled of him that 'many of the church's later leaders [in the South Pacific] trace their conversion to Pastor Len's prayerful, loving ministry'; one of them was the young Walter Scragg, later NEWAD and NED (and South Pacific Division [SPD]) president.[20] The tributes paid on his death point to a warm and sympathetic character, but so, too, does an accolade of the time, by a British Adventist, who in 1950, with unusual effusiveness, called Minchin a 'beloved leader' – praise matched nearly twenty-five years later (while he was still alive) by the historian Dennis Porter, who called him 'one of the best-loved youth leaders the British field has ever had'. Minchin's eight years at the BUC and NED headquarters had lasting impact. At the 1954 GC Session he was elected associate secretary of the YPMV department at the GC, a position he held until elected a general field secretary at the 1962 Session, an office he filled until he retired in 1970.[21]

Influencing Global Adventism

As well as providing missionaries to the traditional mission fields, the NED also provided workers for other church 'homelands'. This was true for much of its history, and, in later decades, among their

---

19 See correspondence and memoranda, 1954–1955, GC Ar., RG 21, Secretariat General Correspondence, box 3490, fld. 'T. J. Bradley'.

20 Goldie Down, 'Adventist Youth', in *Seventh-day Adventists in the South Pacific 1885–1985*, ed. by Noel Clapham (Warburton, Vic.: Signs Publishing, 1985), p. 136; see Marye Trim and D. J. B. Trim, 'Revival and the Holy Spirit: The 1939 Australasian Revival', *Ministry*, 89.2 (Feb. 2017), 16–18.

21 K. Gammon, '"For Such a Time as This": Great Conference Youth Rally', *British Advent Messenger* (Union Session Bulletin no. 5), 13 Oct. 1950, pp. 9–10 (p. 9); D. S. Porter, *A Century of Adventism in the British Isles: A Brief History of the British Union Conference of Seventh-day Adventists* (Grantham, UK: Stanborough Press, 1974), p. 36; cf. 'Life-Sketch' (Minchin), p.

number would be church leaders from Scandinavia, but in the fifties it was mostly Britons who played a part on the Adventist world stage and who had influence, especially on theology, that was unprecedented and remained unsurpassed.

Foremost among these missionaries from the NED to the GC, other European divisions, and Australasia, was Walter Read, former NED secretary and president who, at the 1946 GC Session, was elected general field secretary of the General Conference (Illustration 6.7). He served in that capacity until his official retirement in 1958 (aged 73). Theology had increasingly been the burden of his responsibilities as field secretary; from 1952–1958 he served as first chairman of the Committee on Biblical Study and Research, the predecessor of the Biblical Research Institute (BRI). Even before that, he seems to have served as a kind of biblical and theological trouble-shooter for GC administration. After retirement, he retained an office at the GC headquarters and went there daily, continuing to work on biblical and theological scholarship. Almost up to his death in 1976, he continued to provide counsel on knotty theological questions to senior church leaders and to other scholars.[22]

In these capacities and in others, Read was a major though insufficiently acknowledged influence on Adventist theology.[23] His admin-

---

12. See file, 'Minchin, E.', GC Ar., RG 31, Transportation & International Personnel Services Files, no. MR6045; obit., under 'Deaths', *ARH*, 164.16 (16 Apr. 1987), 22.
22 See the brief but vivid biographical sketch by David Marshall, 'W. E. Read (1883–1976): Administrator and Scholar' in *A Century of Adventism in the British Isles*, ed. idem (Grantham, UK: Stanborough Press, 2000), p. 14; cf. *sub* 'Read, Walter E.', *SDAE*, II, 420; and obit., 'Deaths', *ARH*, 153.25 (17 June 1926), 23. Read's papers are in GC Ar., Personal Collection 25, and include his correspondence through the mid-1970s. On the Biblical Study and Research Committee, see Raymond F. Cottrell, 'The Bible Research Fellowship: A Pioneering Seventh-day Adventist Organisation in Retrospect', *Adventist Heritage*, 5.1 (Summer 1978), 39–52; Keld J. Reynolds, 'The Church Under Stress, 1931–1960', in *Adventism in America*, ed. by Gary Land (Grand Rapids, Mich.: Wm. B. Eerdmans, 1986), pp. 182–94; and *sub* 'Biblical Research Institute', *SDAE*, II, 205–06.
23 Marshall, 'Read'. A proper study of Read's career is needed.

istrative skills were used to lay the foundations for what later became BRI. He contributed to the *Seventh-day Adventist Bible Commentary*, a multi-volume work of scholarship, sponsored by the General Conference, the first volume of which appeared in 1953, and was a major step forward in the development of Adventist theology.[24] Even more important was Read's key role in the dialogues Adventists held in 1955–56 with evangelical leaders in the United States; these led *Eternity* magazine to declare in 1956 that, despite doctrinal differences, Seventh-day Adventists were a legitimate Christian denomination, rather than a non-Christian cult; they led, too, to the publication in 1957 of the book usually known simply as *Questions on Doctrine*.[25] This was a collaborative work, presenting a series of well-supported, biblically founded answers to controversial questions about Adventist beliefs, posed by prominent American evangelicals. The answers, which were discussed in the dialogues, had been prepared by a group of scholars and administrators led by Read, L. E. Froom, another general field secretary and long-time secretary of the Ministerial Association, and R. A. Anderson, an Australian evangelist who had worked in the NED for six years in the thirties and was now GC Ministerial Association secretary (Illustration 6.8). Ever since it was published, Adventists have differed about the legacy of the dialogues and of *Questions on Doctrine*. But no one doubts that they were immensely significant in Adventist history.[26]

The group who took part in the dialogues and prepared the answers to the 'questions on doctrine' included Harry W. Lowe, another

---

24 Reynolds, 'Church Under Stress', p. 184.
25 *Seventh-Day Adventists Answer Questions on Doctrine* (Washington, DC: RHPA, 1957).
26 For a concise overview of the episode, based on primary-source research, and without a polemical agenda, see Reynolds, 'Church Under Stress', pp. 185–88. For scholarly analysis of *Questions on Doctrine*'s development, publication, and reactions to it, see Knight's introduction and *apparatus criticus* in the Adventist Classics Library edition, *Questions on Doctrine*, ed. by George Knight (Berrien Springs, MI: Andrews University Press, 2003); Paul McGraw, 'Born in Zion?: The Margins of Fundamentalism and the Definition of Seventh-day Adventism' (PhD dissertation, The George

Briton (Illustration 6.9). Lowe had been president of the BUC from 1936 to 1946, when he was elected associate secretary of the Sabbath School department at the GC, the position he held ten years later when he was brought into the dialogues, presumably by Read. He served at the GC until 1966, for the last four years as general field secretary.[27] Between Read, Lowe, and Anderson, the NED could claim a share in ownership of *Questions on Doctrine* – and though European Adventist theologians at the time had concerns both about parts of the book and about the dialogues from which it emerged, they saw it in a generally positive light.[28] Further, the book was found to be helpful, if indirectly, in outreach in Northern Europe (as discussed in the final section of this chapter).

Other influential 'missionaries' from the NED to the other mission homelands included two former Newbold principals, W. G. C. Murdoch and E. E. White (Illustrations 6.10 and 6.11). William Murdoch had been the boy prodigy of British theology, appointed principal of Stanborough College at age 28 after being talent-spotted by Read. He served sixteen years as principal (1930–1946), the longest term of any Newbold principal, during which he oversaw the

---

Washington University, 2004); Juhyeok Julius Nam, 'Reactions to the Seventh-day Adventist evangelical conferences and *Questions on Doctrine*, 1955–1971' (PhD dissertation, Andrews University, 2005); and idem, '*Questions on Doctrine* and M. L. Andreasen: The Behind-the Scenes Interactions', *Andrews University Seminary Studies*, 46 (2008), 229–44. For an elegant articulation of the negative perspective on the dialogues and book, which includes an historical summary, see Herbert Edgar Douglass, *A Fork in the Road. 'Questions on Doctrine': The Historic Adventist Divide of 1957* (Coldwater, Mich.: Remnant Publications, 2008). Read is depicted as less significant in the dialogues than Froom and Anderson, but for a corrective see Russell Hitt (the then editor of *Eternity*) to Read, 11 Mar. 1969, GC Ar., Personal Collection 25, Box 10826, fld. 'Boyce, J. M.'

27 There is a very short obit., 'Deaths', *ARH*, 168.20 (16 May 1991), 22; his career can be tracked in the annual *Yearbooks*.

28 See, e.g., Heppenstall to Keough, 25 Feb. 1957, CAR, Collection no. 190, box 42, fld. 8; Keough's unsympathetic annotations of M. L. Andreasen, 'Atonement VI', open letter, 5 Jan. 1958, in RGL, Keough Papers, fld. 4, no. 5, at pp. 3, 5, 6; and Keough to GC President R. R. Figuhr, 13 July 1958, GC Ar., RG 11, box 11358–59.

move to Newbold Revel and renaming of Stanborough to Newbold. Murdoch was called from Newbold to Australia, where he served with distinction as president of Avondale for six years (1947–1952), raising academic standards and laying the foundations for external accreditation.[29] E. Edward White had succeeded Murdoch at Newbold.[30] He then replaced him at Avondale, where he, too, served six years (1953–1958); under his leadership the college started awarding bachelor's degrees and introduced, for the first time, postgraduate theological education in the Australasian Division (as it then was), after White successfully negotiated with the Seventh-day Adventist Theological Seminary to provide 'Seminary Training Schools' hosted by Avondale.[31] Both men continued in conspicuous church careers outside the NED: Murdoch served many years at the Seminary, including thirteen years as Dean (and two more, after retirement, at what later became AIIAS), while Eddie White (as he was called by his many friends) was a popular division departmental director for twenty-four years: sixteen at the Australasian Division (1947–1952, 1959–1970) and eight at the Euro-Africa Division (1970–1978).[32]

Another to be called abroad and to exercise considerable influence was Edward Heppenstall (Illustration 6.12). Heppenstall had gone to

---

29 A biography of Murdoch, a significant figure in global, not just European, Adventist history, is needed. I draw here on: E. E. White, 'In Memoriam: William G. C. Murdoch', *Messenger*, 20 Apr. 1984, pp. 13, 16; my parents' recollections of their time as students under Murdoch's presidency at Avondale; the (shamefully short) obit. in *ARH*, 161.16 (19 Apr. 1984), 19; and *SDAE*, *sub* 'Avondale College', I, 144–45, *sub* 'Newbold College', II, 176–77. For Read's connection with Murdoch, see Read to Louise Dederen, 16 Aug. 1972, GC Ar., Personal Collection 25, Box 10826, fld. 'Dederen Mrs Louise'.

30 BUC Committee meeting, 16 Aug. 1946, GC Ar., RG NE 1, fld. 'British Union Conference Minutes 1946', p. 85.

31 John B. Trim, 'Pillars of the Faith Strengthened', *Australasian Record*, 3 Mar. 1958, pp. 1–2; Nalissa Maberly, 'Former Avondale College Principal Dies' (White obit.), *Record*, 5 Apr. 2003, p. 5; *SDAE*, *sub* 'Avondale College', I, 144–45.

32 See their missionary appointee files, GC Ar., RG 21, Secretariat Appointee Files, nos. 44405 (Murdoch) and 12374 (White), though these files do not cover all of either man's career, but these can be traced in the annual

the United States in 1934 and spent the rest of his career in positions there, but it was in the fifties and sixties that he established himself at the forefront of Adventist academic theology. He taught at La Sierra College, the Seminary, and Loma Linda University, retiring from full-time teaching only in 1970, aged 69. Heppenstall did not publish widely, but his teaching was deeply spiritual and he was a popular presenter of devotional series, including at a General Conference Session. His influence derived as much from his inspirational presentations, as from his books; his views on soteriology carried particular weight. As a colleague and senior academic administrator later recalled: 'All who took his courses remember those classes as watershed experiences in their religious growth. His influence reached worldwide. He was really one of the key figures in the history of our denomination's thought leaders.' Many of his students went on to have distinguished careers of their own as religion teachers at Adventist colleges. One was William Johnsson, later the editor of the *Adventist Review*, who characterised Heppenstall as, 'probably one of the greatest thinkers the Adventist Church has produced.' Where Heppenstall led, refuting the possibility of perfection and offering new insights into the implications of righteousness by faith for eschatology and other doctrines, other Adventist theologians followed.[33]

The man who was the connection between the three was George D. Keough (Illustration 6.13). A friend of Read's from college days,

---

editions of the *YB*. Additionally, I draw here on my parents' stories of White, both at Avondale and in his time at the Australasian Division, and on my own knowledge of him in retirement at Newbold.

33 Anon., 'Church Mourns Loss of Theologian' (quoting John Jones), *Record* [South Pacific Division], 17 Sept. 1994, p. 5; anon., 'Adventist Theologian Heppenstall Dies', *ARH*, 171.36 (8 Sept. 1994), 6–7 (p. 7); and see obit., *Lake Union Herald*, Oct. 1994, p. 23; notice under 'Deaths', *ARH*, 171.41 (13 Oct. 1994), 22; David Marshall, 'Dr Edward Heppenstall (1901–1994): Theologian and Thought Leader', in *A Century of Adventism*, ed. idem, p. 20; and Gary Land, 'Coping with Change, 1961–1980', in *Adventism in America*, ed. idem, p. 216. I also draw on correspondence with Louis Venden, Heppenstall's student and later colleague: Venden to Trim, emails, 15 and 22 Feb. and 16 Mar. 2010.

Keough was a pioneer missionary to Egypt and the Middle East for twenty years (1920–1928); he had been present at the Marienhoehe Council in the summer of 1928, representing the Arabic Union. He was a mentor of Heppenstall, Murdoch, and White, who were his colleagues on the staff at Newbold, where Keough taught from 1929–1937. He continued an epistolary mentoring of Heppenstall in the United States and White in Australia into the fifties.[34] Meanwhile, in 1937 Keough had returned to the Arabic Union Mission as president, before in 1942 joining the faculty of the Seventh-day Adventist Theological Seminary, then located next door to the GC headquarters in Takoma Park. In 1947 (aged 65!), he and his wife Mary accepted their third call to the Middle East; he worked there for seven years, as the first director of radio ministry for the Middle East Union and then the Middle East Division.[35] In 1954, he returned to Newbold College and served there for another twelve years, not retiring until 1966, when he was 85.

In the Middle East, Keough was an innovator: his pioneering, trail-blasing approach to contextualisation helped grow a small Arabic-speaking church, although, in the second half of the twentieth century, it was to be sadly forgotten. As an inspiring teacher and original theologian, he shaped the thinking of two generations of European and American theologians and church leaders, at Newbold, the Seminary, then Newbold again. Among his students at the seminary was Neal C. Wilson, later president of the General Conference (Illustration 6.14).[36] Students at Newbold in the 1950s–'60s who acknowledge his influence include a veritable roll call of distinguished Adventist scholars, evangelists, and administrators, from North America and Europe as well as Britain. Meanwhile, colleagues

---

34 RGL, 'Annual Calendar[s]' of Stanborough College/Newbold Missionary College; White to Keough, 4 May 1949 and 1 Mar. 1950, RGL, Keough Papers, fld. 4; Heppenstall to Keough, 28 Feb. 1956, CAR, Heppenstall Papers (Collection no. 190), box 42, fld. 8.
35 Keough appointee file, GC Ar., RG 21, box 9984.
36 CAR, 'Bulletin of the Seventh-day Adventist Theological Seminary', 1943–44.

Keough influenced, who were themselves influential in the fifties, included Denton E. Rebok, later president of the Seminary and secretary of the General Conference, and Leroy E. Froom.[37]

A last figure from the NED to parlay his experience and expertise into global reach in this period was Emanuel W. Pedersen. After nearly sixteen years' service in his native Denmark, he and his wife Esther accepted a call to Upper Nile Union, one of the NED's mission fields; they served in Uganda from 1937–1942, before moving to the EAUM where Emanuel was president of the Kenya Mission for ten years. In 1953 they took permanent return and he served at the NED as Home Missionary departmental secretary for five years. The 1958 GC Session elected Pedersen associate secretary of the Lay Activities department at the GC, where he served one term before, at the 1962 Session, he was elected secretary of the NED (Illustration 6.15). He served only one term in that office, too, because, with his wealth of international experience, including at GC and division level, he was called back to the world headquarters at the 1966 GC Session. He followed in Read and Lowe's footsteps, succeeding Lowe as a General Conference general field secretary, and served in that capacity until his retirement in 1973. He was so well respected by GC President Pierson that in 1969 his name was suggested for president of the SED and thus must undoubtedly have advised on plans for the major restructuring addressed in the next chapter. Pedersen lived into 2006, dying a little short of his 102nd birthday.[38]

These seven – Heppenstall, Keough, Lowe, Murdoch, Pedersen, Read, and White – were all native sons of the NED; six were

---

37 Rebok to R. W. Scarr, n.d., in 'This is Your Life: George Dorkin Keough', 14 Nov. 1959, unpublished MS; Froom to Keough, 30 May/6 June 1968, RGL, Keough Papers, fld. 3 and cf. Froom to Keough, 5 May 1965, Keough Papers, fld. 4.
38 See appointee file, 'Pedersen, Emanuel Warthou', GC Ar., RG 21, Secretariat Appointee Files, no. 13783; GC Officers' Meeting, 6 Nov. 1969, GCOM, p. 69-490; and brief obit. under 'At Rest', *ARH*, 183.24 (24 Aug. 2006), 30.

thoroughly British in upbringing and manner (though Keough and Murdoch were Scots-Irish, not English). Each one had a truly global impact in the fifties and sixties; and to them we could add R. A. Anderson and E. L. Minchin, who had spent fourteen years in NED territory between them. All but Pedersen and White had significant, even extraordinary, theological influence; Read, Lowe, and Pedersen (and Minchin) had administrative impact as officers of the General Conference; Keough and White were departmental directors at divisions. Read, Murdoch, Heppenstall, Pedersen, and White all continued to be influential, though to a lesser degree, past the period covered by this chapter, into the 1970s (and, in Heppenstall's case, the 1980s). The period covered by this chapter, however, was the high point of NED influence on Seventh-day Adventist theology – and of British Adventist influence on the world church.

Challenges

Communism

Living under Communism was to be an ongoing challenge for the NED (and later TED), all the way to the end of the Cold War in 1989, but it was in the early 1950s when the religious liberty situation deteriorated badly in Eastern Europe. In the NED, the PUC found it increasingly difficult to operate. It was easier for church leaders from the western side of the Iron Curtain to travel to Poland than to the Soviet Union or some other Communist countries. Restrictions on contact ebbed and flowed: in 1956, in the aftermath of the Hungarian Rising, NED Treasurer Gustav Lindsay described the Polish Union Conference to NED Executive Committee members as 'a field cut off from us' – so much so that Lindsay thought 'a recent telephone conversation with our denominational leaders in Poland' cause for celebration.[39] Gradually restrictions on communication and even

---

39   NED Winter Council, 27 Nov. 1956, NEDCOM Mins., 1956, p. 102.

travel were eased however. By the spring of 1957, Tarr and Lindsay, division president and treasurer, were able to visit the country and make contact with leaders of the Polish Union.[40]

In the 1960s, leaders from the NED headquarters and occasionally even the General Conference were able to visit. In 1966, for example, GC Secretary Walter Beach and Theodore Carcich, a vice-president, along with NED President Duncan Eva and Bert Beach, Sabbath School departmental secretary (and Walter's son) all attended a worker's meeting and ministerial council in Warsaw in September, hosted by PUC President Stanisław Dabrowski. While the two GC officials were only permitted to be present for one of the four days, the NED officials stayed throughout, speaking frequently.[41] They were joined by 'several of our leaders from Hungary', including the union president and secretary – a signpost to future developments, though no one recognised it at the time.[42]

While the Polish government periodically gave special dispensation to visiting Western dignitaries (doubtless in part to avoid negative publicity), ordinary church members in Poland still endured considerable restrictions. As a result, when church leaders from the West did visit, they faced an unusual response. Bert Beach described how in 1966 'nearly 3,000' Polish church members attended the Sabbath service in September 1966: this was around 75 per cent of the entire membership, but it provided a rare occasion for open celebration and for hearing leaders from outside Poland. Beach wrote: 'The services on Sabbath were literally packed with people, with not even "standing room" left. The seats and aisles were filled with scarf-covered sisters, earnest men, eager youth.'[43]

---

40 NEDCOM, 19 Mar. and 23 Apr. 1957, NEDCOM Mins., 1957, pp. 13, 31.
41 W. Duncan Eva, 'Progress in Poland', *Northern Light*, 16.12 (Dec. 1966), 1.
42 B. B. Beach, 'An Open Bible in Thousand-Year-Old Poland', *Northern Light*, 16.12 (Dec. 1966), 5.
43 Ibid., pp. 5–6; cf. *ASR*, 103 (1965), 12.

In 1968, for example, John Coltheart, the NED evangelist, took J. F. Spangler, editor of *Ministry*, to Poland. Coltheart described his experiences vividly:

> *I was taken to the mountain district of the south. Here it seemed that I was taken back to Adventism of 30 years ago [...]. Youngsters of six, eight and ten years just gazed with full attention as we preached from 9.30 a.m. until 6.30 p.m. It was incredible! The church was located in the midst of an orchard [...].*
>
> *The next day, they said, 'We are opening an Evangelistic Campaign – you will preach for us.' When we arrived at the church, which was picturesquely situated in the woods on the side of a mountain, the brethren said, 'Now we begin at 2.00 p.m. and you will preach first, then [a Polish pastor] and then you will preach twice more.' I said, 'But surely not to the same people – four sermons in a row is too much.' But they had their way and so we went on 'till 7.00 p.m. The church was packed with many standing outside and yet their only permitted advertising had been the band playing in the village and a word-of-mouth invitation.*[44]

The courage and commitment of church members living under a government hostile to Christianity was utterly remarkable.

As the NED leaders were able to spend more time in Poland, the PUC developed a reputation for being well organised and administered. In 1967, Elder Stanisław Dabrowski, the PUC president, was asked to tour Bulgaria, another Eastern European country under Communist rule (Illustration 6.16). As a result of his visit, Dabrowski made a series of recommendations for development of the church in

---

44 Coltheart to 'Fellow Worker' [newsletter], 17 Sept. 1968, pp. 3–4 (emphasis in original), in GC Ar., RG 29, GC Secretariat missionary appointee/IDE/AVS files, no. 13153.

Bulgaria that were prioritised for action by the GC officers.[45]

Ethnic Diversity

The 1950s–'60s saw large-scale immigration from Britain's Caribbean colonies to the United Kingdom. The tensions that arose, as an ethnically similar church rapidly became a diverse one, came to a head in the seventies (discussed in Chapter 8). However, British church leaders began to feel beleaguered over race (never seeming to query the nature of their feelings or to recognise their prejudices) in the late fifties. They tended to perceive immigrants from the Caribbean in negative terms, focusing on the difficulties that arose, and not on the advantages that accrued from having more members, many of whom 'were proficient lay leaders and well trained evangelists'. Many West Indians were poor, as immigrants often are, and they tended, understandably, to appeal to fellow Adventists for help; but this was resented by indigenes who regarded the immigrants as burdensome. In 1957, the first of what were to be increasingly frequent appeals from British leaders to higher levels of church structure for help in dealing with what they increasingly saw as a problem, was a request for financial assistance to help with additional expenses. The NED refused, because it was wary of 'open[ing] the door' to an ongoing commitment.[46]

Soon enough, British church leaders began to raise the issue of race relations, and did so with the General Conference as well as the division. In the early sixties, BUC President John McMillan began

---

45 Robert H. Pierson to Theodore Carcich, 1 Aug. 1967, GC Ar., RG 21, box 10564, fld. 'Correspondence 1967'.
46 Herbert Griffiths, 'The Impact of African Caribbean Settlers on the Seventh-day Adventist Church in Britain 1952–2001' (PhD thesis, University of Leeds, 2003), p. 174; N. H. Knight (BUC secretary-treasurer), circular letter 'To Presidents and Treasurers of the Conferences and Missions', 27 June 1957, RGL, BUC Papers, 1957 box, fld. 'N. H. Knight'.

collecting statistics on 'West Indians' in the BUC.⁴⁷ In the summer of 1963 he wrote to GC President Figuhr, sharing concerns about the changing racial balance in the union, and declaring a need to undertake evangelistic 'campaigns in those parts of the country where we can still depend on a more or less 100% white attendance'.⁴⁸ What was in McMillan's mind is amplified by a letter he wrote the next day to a pastor in the North of England.

> *Unless we have some men left in this Union to carry on campaigns where the white population can be gathered out [sic] and won to the Message, we face the grim prospect of seeing this Union going entirely black in a period of ten to twelve years – a prospect which would bring nothing but sorrow to all our hearts.*⁴⁹

Macmillan was articulating attitudes common to people of his generation in Great Britain, unaccustomed to cultural and ethnic diversity. But to those who embodied the new British Adventist diversity, his views and those of some colleagues were naturally hurtful.

The following year, the president of the North England Conference penned an appeal to Figuhr, pejoratively writing that blacks had 'swarmed' in from the Caribbean. He petitioned the GC for funds for evangelism in 'carefully chosen strategic points', i.e., targeted at whites.⁵⁰ In the end, as we will see in Chapter 8, the GC and division did step in, taking steps that fostered harmony. But as the sixties drew to a close, some, though certainly not all, British church administrators

---

47 'Information re West Indians', n.d., with papers from late Sept. 1960, but in RGL, BUC Papers, 1962 box, fld. 'Miscellaneous'.
48 J. A. McMillan to R. R. Figuhr, 21 Aug. 1963, RGL, BUC Papers, 1963 box, fld. 'General Conference various'.
49 McMillan to Kenneth Lacey, 22 Aug. 1963, RGL, BUC Papers, 1963 box, fld. 'K. Lacey'.
50 J. H. Bayliss to Figuhr, 19 Nov. 1964, quoted in Davis, 'West Indian Immigrants', p. 29.

saw not potential, but a West Indian 'problem'.[51]

Church Growth and Outreach

The fifties and sixties saw steady growth in the division (see Figure 2), from just over 41,000 in 1951 to more than 95,000 in 1970. In each decade, membership increased by 50 per cent.

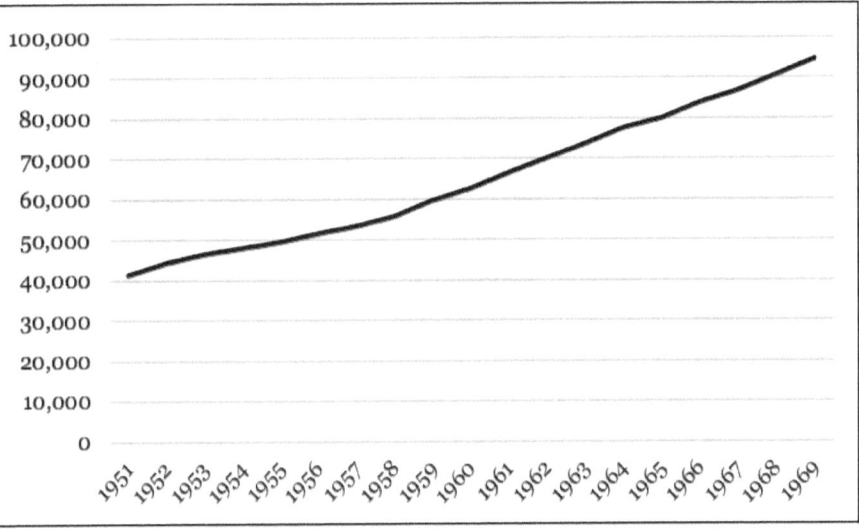

Figure 2: NED Membership, 1951–1969

The increase in membership chiefly depended, however, on Africa. In 1951, at the end of the re-created NED's first year, there were 12,443 church members in the Ethiopian and West African Union Missions and 29,013 in the NED's European territories: almost 60 per cent of the membership was in the homelands. By the end of the last year of the NED (before it became NEWAD), the equivalent figures were 59,985 and 38,845. Total membership had increased on both continents; but by 1970 just over 60 per cent of the division's

---

51 See Davis, ibid. For an example of a relaxed attitude see Ken Elias's response to an evidently concerned McMillan, 8 Nov. 1960, RGL, BUC Papers, in 1962 [*sic*] box, fld. 'Miscellaneous'.

members were in Africa: the proportions had been reversed (see Figure 3).

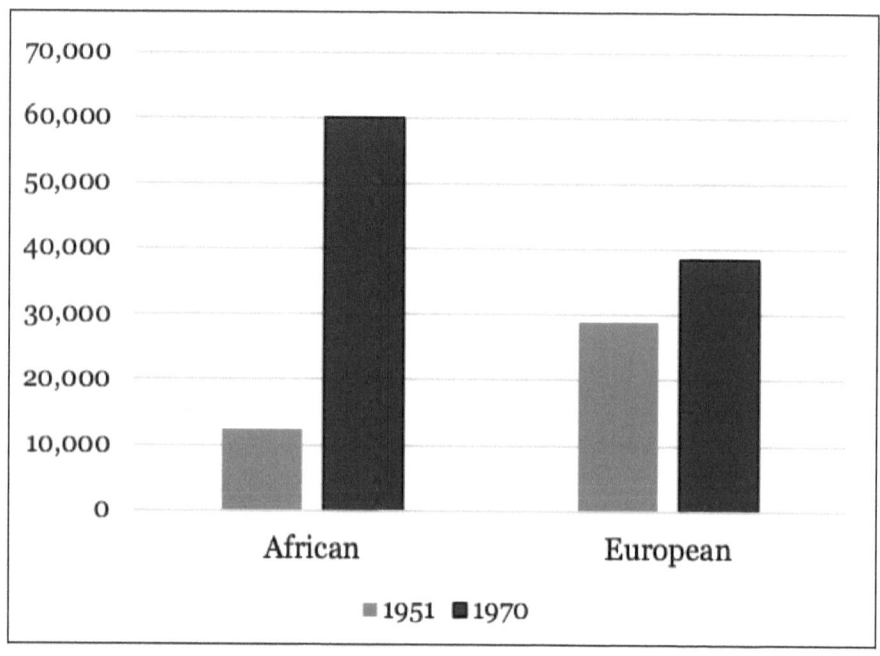

Figure 3: NED Membership in Africa and Europe Contrasted, 1951 and 1970

This shift, moreover, had happened rapidly. As Figure 4 indicates, European membership exceeded African for most of the fifties and sixties. In fact, only at the end of 1963 was the total number of members in the Ethiopian Union and WAUM more than half the NED's membership (51.7 per cent). Having taken thirteen years to rise 11 percentage points, the Africa-based membership then rose another 9 points in just seven years.[52]

The overall statistics mask, moreover, the reality that some conferences and countries, such as the Denmark Conference, started to experience negative growth in the period covered by this chapter.

---

52   *ASR*, 101 (1963), 20.

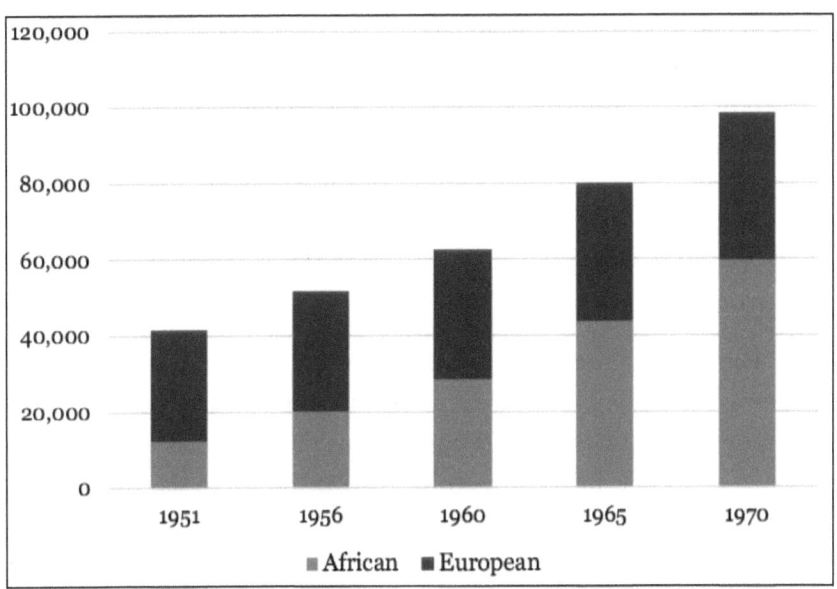

Figure 4: Membership in Africa and Europe, NED, 1951–1970

In Denmark's case, membership peaked in 1965 and there has been almost continual decline ever since.[53] Yet, as the graphs illustrate, there was still growth in this era elsewhere in the TED's European territory, including in the Netherlands and Poland.[54] In the 1950s this owed much to a strong emphasis on outreach in the homelands. Evangelism was particularly encouraged by the South African president of the division for twelve of the twenty years (1950–1962), A. F. Tarr. From the start of his presidency, church members were urged: 'To have EVANGELISM as our constant watchword – Evangelism in every community and [...] in our home conferences' as well as the division's 'vast mission territories'. Particular 'emphasis was placed upon the [...] evangelical [sic] programme in the home fields'.[55] Tarr

---

53 Hans Jorgen Schantz, in 'Denmark', *HRSDAE*, p. 77 (though this states the year as 1955, which must be a misprint).
54 Cf. Reinder Bruinsma, 'The Netherlands', and Zachariasz Lyko and Hugh Dunton, 'Poland', both in *HRSDAE*, pp. 160, 176.
55 Tarr, 'Greetings from the President', p. 1 (capitals in original); President's Report, NED Winter Council, 27 Nov. 1951, NEDCOM-WCM, p. 7.

conceived evangelism broadly and under his leadership the NED fostered a range of initiatives that sought to involve church members. In the Netherlands, for instance, where public campaigns had only had limited success, the NUC adopted a new lay evangelistic programme of personal witnessing; Dutch Adventists also stressed *Weldadigheidswerk* ('Benevolence Work'), in which many church members, including women, through Dorcas Societies, were actively involved.[56]

Public evangelism was, nevertheless, a major factor in the steady growth. Public meetings were a 'regular and tolerably successful' feature of Finnish Adventism throughout 'the late fifties and early sixties', resulting in rapid growth.[57] In Britain, the fifties saw the heyday of public evangelism. In 1952, the BUC and NED brought the American evangelist George Vandeman, then serving as one of the associate secretaries of the Ministerial Association at the GC, to London for a major campaign, along the lines of Billy Graham's successful crusades. Vandeman's initial campaign, which began in September 1952, is still legendary among British Adventists of a certain vintage. 'London was inundated with posters', in addition to a bold advertising campaign, while the supporting music and visual aids were of the highest class, as was Vandeman's preaching. More than ten thousand were 'attracted [...] to the London Coliseum Theatre on the first night' and the regular attendance remained around 2500.[58] A new church, the Central London Church was established from the converts. Its new home served as a permanent evangelistic

---

56 Odd Jordal, 'Glimpses from the Netherlands', *Northern Light*, 10.12 (Dec. 1960), 5; Van Rijn, *Advent Exposé*, pp. 85, 88; G. H. Koning, *Enige markante gebeurtenissen uit de geschiedenis van het Kerkgenootschap der Zevende-dags Adventisten in Groningen* (Groningen: Kerkgenootschap der Zevende-dags Adventisten, 1983), pp. 53, 57.
57 Arasola, 'Finland', p. 92.
58 Nigel Barham, 'British Isles', ed. Hugh Dunton, in *HRSDAE*, p. 36; Martin L. Anthony, 'A Century of Evangelism', in *A Century of Adventism*, ed. Marshall, p. 13. Porter, *Century of Adventism*, pp. 36–38, provides a detailed account.

centre in a fashionable area of central London: in 1953 the NED joined the BUC in purchasing the leasehold on the New Gallery, a former cinema and art gallery, located in the centre of London. The NED paid the bulk of the expense of £167,394 14s. 6d. in creating the new London Evangelistic Centre, though partly with funds made available by the General Conference. Vandeman christened the New Gallery with a new evangelistic campaign, begun in October 1953 that continued well into the following year.[59]

None of this could have been achieved without the backing of the BUC and the enthusiastic support of local church members. But the success also owed much to the vision of NED administration, which took a request from the BUC for counsel about evangelism and saw in it an opportunity for a major push in Britain. Here one sees Tarr's influence. The NED asked the GC to send Vandeman for a major campaign in a large, prestigious theatre in London ('the Festival Hall, the Palladium, or the Coliseum Theatres, or some other large meeting place in the centre of London' were explicitly mentioned in the NEDCOM action), allocated £3500 for the campaign (equivalent to at least £100,000 in 2018) and obtained, too, a special GC appropriation of US$35,000. Without the commitment of NED administration to evangelism and the officers' vision and boldness,

---

59   NEDCOM meeting 26 Aug. 1953, NEDCOM mins., 1953, p. 70; proposal to NEDCOM, 26 Aug. 1953, and MS 'Present Situation with Reference to London Church and Evangelistic Centre', 28 Aug. 1953, separate pagination appended to NEDCOM minutes; and NEDCOM meeting, 19 Sept. 1954, NEDCOM mins. 1954, p. 78; Porter, *Century of Adventism*, pp. 38–39. Note that, *pace* Martin L. Anthony, 'Decades of Change', in *Story of Seventh-day Adventists*, ed. by Marshall, p. 27, and idem, 'Century of Evangelism', p. 13, the purchase price was not £122,000: strictly speaking it was £112,500 but with transfer fees, stamp duty, etc., came to £122,000; however there was considerable additional expense for 'alterations, decorations and refurnishing'. The figure of over £167,000 is what was proposed and approved (Porter's account is almost accurate).

the BUC's great evangelistic leap forward of the fifties would not have happened.[60]

The results were spectacular, by European standards at the time. There were nearly a thousand baptisms in the mid-fifties, which pushed church membership in the British Isles over 8000 for the first time. Vandeman departed, having put his stamp on a new generation of young British pastors, who, enthused by his example, took up public evangelism with zeal. The NED supplemented them with successful American and Australian evangelists as well. The New Gallery remained a base for public evangelism for the rest of the 1950s, still heavily subsidised by the GC; the result was another 310 baptisms in the last four years of the decade.[61]

Literature Evangelism

Across both decades covered in this chapter, 'canvassing', the contemporary term for literature evangelism, enjoyed what seemed at the time like its heyday but, at least in some parts of the division, with hindsight seems like an Indian Summer. Yet it had solid achievements to its credit in the fifties and sixties. Ellen White's books on the life and teachings of Jesus, *The Desire of Ages* and *Steps to Christ*, were particularly successful but other examples of 'truth-filled literature' sold, too, including in countries like Denmark where 'to gather people for religious meetings' was 'very difficult'.[62]

60 NEDCOM meeting, 12 Dec. 1951, NEDCOM mins., 1951, pp. 140–41; cf. NED budget for 1951, Winter Council, 3 Dec. 1951, NEDCOM-WCM 1951, pp. 44–45.
61 See Porter, *Century of Adventism*, p. 39; Barham, 'British Isles', pp. 36–37; Anthony, 'Century of Evangelism', pp. 13, 21; NEDCOM meetings, 19 Sept. and 30 Nov. 1954, NEDCOM mins. 1954, pp. 78, 141; anon., 'Confidential Communication: New Gallery Programme', n.d. [1957], and Russell Kranz, 'Analysis of the New Gallery Evangelistic Centre', n.d. [c.1975/76], both in fld. 'New Gallery (London)', CAR, Roy Allan Anderson Papers (Collection no. 152), box 44, fld. 3.
62 Viggo Thomsen, 'Denmark', *Northern Light*, 7.11 (Nov. 1957), 5–6, 13 (p. 6); and see, e.g., Alf Lohne, 'Phenomenal Booksales in Norway', *Northern Light*, 10.3 (March 1960), 6; J. W. Nixon, 'The Publishing

The successes of literature evangelism included eroding widely held suspicions in Northern Europe and the British Isles. Perceptions of Adventists as 'sheep stealers' seem to have been almost ubiquitous across the NED, but so were claims of heresy. As an Adventist public-relations pioneer wrote in 1960, in Europe Adventism 'face[d] a barrier of prejudice'; whether in the Netherlands, or Sweden, or Finland, it was widely perceived as 'an American sect', 'a sub-Christian cult'.[63] The Anglican Dean of Bedford in Great Britain thus articulated a view common to Protestant clergymen across Northern Europe in a circular he sent to all the parishes in his deanery in the 1950s, which classified '7th day Adventism' with Jehovah's Witnesses, Mormons, Christian Scientists, and British Israelites, and even with Spiritualism, Astrology and Theosophy, as 'Modern Substitutes for Christianity'.[64]

It was this kind of hostility that Adventist literature was able to reduce in the fifties and sixties. The book that had a particularly positive impact on external perceptions of Seventh-day Adventists was *Questions on Doctrine*. In Europe it helped to shape a reassessment of Adventists as being 'within orthodox evangelicalism' so that it was no longer simply dismissed as heterodox and/or 'American' (a term that, in the countries of the TED, has tended to carry as much baggage as 'sect' or 'cult'!). Adventist literature thus had not only a direct impact, but also an indirect influence in breaking down what a British publishing leader, R. D. Vine, shrewdly summed up as 'a prejudice that [was] designedly and deliberately blind'. Books that helped to 'to give the Church a more positive image', included *Questions on Doctrine* and Froom's two-volume *Conditionalist Faith of Our Fathers*,

---

Department' and R. D. Vine, 'The British Union', *Northern Light*, 11.1 (Jan. 1961), 5, 8; Arasola, 'Finland', p. 93.

63 R. D. Vine, 'Disarming Prejudice', *Northern Light*, 10.3 (March 1960), 4–5 (p. 4); Bruinsma, 'The Netherlands', p. 159; Edwin Torkelson, 'Norway', in *HRSDAE*, pp. 162–63; Ingemar Linden, 'Sweden', ibid., p. 220; cf. Arasola, 'Finland', p. 93.

64 Frank Cotton, circular letter, Bedfordshire and Luton Archives and Record Service, P134/28/2.

which the NED, on proposal by the BUC, paid 'to place [...] in strategic libraries and with leading [non-Adventist] church personalities'.[65] Yet, also significant, and more widely distributed or sold, were books by local authors, including Alf Lohne's *Hvem er Syvendedags Adventistene?* ('Who Are the Seventh-day Adventists?'), more than 175,000 copies of which were distributed in Danish and Norwegian, and F. J. Voorthuis's *Vanwaar? Waartoe? Waarheen?* ('Whence? Why? Whither?') in Dutch, which sold 100,000 copies. All helped to cast Adventists in a different, positive, light.[66]

The diminution of some Protestant clergymen's suspicion of Seventh-day Adventists was certainly welcome. Yet in a sense it came too late: from the 1960s onwards, European people paid less and less attention to their pastors and priests. They also became less and less likely to buy religious books – or to attend big public evangelistic meetings.

Public Evangelism in the Sixties

The 1960s was perhaps the last decade when public evangelism could gain large audiences and successfully garner considerable numbers of new Adventist believers. By the mid-sixties there was already a great deal of scepticism about the utility of large public campaigns in the European territories of the NED.[67] From the perspective of the NED headquarters, however, evangelism remained the priority and that did not alter with a change in president. Both Tarr and Roenfelt were on the same page. In a devotional at an NED Winter Council, Roenfelt had challenged assembled administrators: 'In the early days

---

65 Vine, 'Disarming Prejudice', p. 5; idem, 'British Union', p. 8; V. Norskov Olsen, 'The Lord's Day in the Second Century', *ARH*, 139.4 (25 Jan. 1962), 1, 4–5 (p. 1); Bruinsma, 'The Netherlands', p. 159; Linden, 'Sweden', pp. 219–20; NEDCOM meeting, 11 Jan. 1967, NEDCOM mins., 1967, p. 3.

66 Bruinsma, 'The Netherlands', pp. 158–59; Alf Lohne, 'West Nordic Union', *Northern Light*, 11.1 (Jan. 1961), 8.

67 See, e.g., A[lf] L[ohne], 'Big Scale Evangelism in Continental Europe', *Northern Light*, 18.4 (April 1968), 1–2 (p. 1).

of this movement our people had only one passion: to win souls for God. [...] As leaders in this cause we must see to it that the evangelistic purpose of this cause is maintained.'⁶⁸ This could include all forms of outreach, but Erwin Roenfelt had been a successful public evangelist in his time and he wanted to encourage evangelistic boldness.

The NED called J. F. Coltheart from Australia in 1965. He was chosen partly to meet a need, identified by Roenfelt, for 'a well qualified evangelistic worker to take charge of the New Gallery Centre', but also partly in the awareness that eleven years after Vandeman, there was the need to find a new role model for evangelists in Northern Europe. John Coltheart had enjoyed immense success in Australia with what he called 'the "Dead Men Do Tell Tales" approach', using archaeology as a hook and a way to support claims about prophecy. He used it in an evangelistic series at the New Gallery in 1966, where later his fellow countryman, Russell Kranz, continued to use Australian methods, if 'adapted [...] to suit English tastes'.⁶⁹

There was an immediate impact. In most of the NED's European territory, there had been a decline in public evangelism since the heyday of the early 1950s. For example, in the fifties the (post-Vandeman) average annual number of baptisms at the New Gallery was 77.5; for the whole of the sixties, the average number per annum was 38.7. But Coltheart's crusade at the New Gallery in 1966/67 resulted in 121 baptisms, the largest number from a campaign since 1958. Roenfelt had by this time retired at the 1966 GC Session and been succeeded as NED president by W. Duncan Eva, another South

---

68 NED Winter Council, 6 Dec. 1498, NEDCOC-WCM, 1948, p. 222. Roenfelt was a GC associate secretary at this point but was one of the GC delegation to that year's Winter Council.

69 Roenfelt to W. R. Beach, 31 Dec. 1964, GC Ar., RG 21, Secretariat Correspondence; E. W. Pedersen to D. S. Johnson, 6 Jan. 1965, in file 'Coltheart, John F.', GC Ar., RG 21, Secretariat Appointee Files, no. 13153; Porter, *Century of Adventism*, p. 39; Down, 'Adventist Youth', p. 137.

African (Illustration 6.17). Encouraged by Coltheart's success, Eva invested sizeable division resources in a major evangelistic push in 1968. Remarkable successes were achieved right across the division – not just by Coltheart but by others he had trained in his methods and who applied them.[70]

In Stockholm, in the spring, Coltheart conducted a major campaign. According to his custom in Australia, he booked a hall that seated 1200 people and scheduled four meetings a day on successive Sundays – and faced polite disdain from experienced Swedish pastors. But after massive advertising, in the end, the hall was booked out for all four meetings the first Sunday so that Coltheart spoke to five thousand people. There were another thousand at the midweek meeting, then five thousand again the second Sunday. According to a Norwegian church official, reporting for *Northern Light*, cynical Scandinavian pastors dared to hope that rich harvests could be gained from public meetings. Later that year, Coltheart reported, 'Kaj Pedersen opened with 4,000 in attendance – the largest audience ever for Copenhagen'; Pedersen, too, had used the archaeology approach. In Cambridge in the autumn, as Coltheart delightedly described, John Baker, holding 'his first public campaign' with 'no helper and a very small budget' met with success, having 'two crowded sessions' his first evening and 'two more overbooked sessions' on the second. Because he was 'meeting in a fairly small lecture theatre at the university', Baker needed all 'four sessions to pack in his audience of over a thousand'. In the spring of 1969, Coltheart preached to audiences of almost a thousand in Helsinki and baptised 116. In the Netherlands, Coltheart 'trained two pastors' in his methods who enjoyed success. President Eva wrote to a colleague at the GC, reporting some of these successes, anticipating upcoming campaigns in Helsinki and Oslo, and concluding: 'We are daring to hope that we have made a

---

70 Coltheart to 'Fellow Worker' [newsletter], 17 Sept. 1968, p. 2, in Coltheart's appointee file, GC Ar., RG 21, file no. 13153; Kranz, 'Analysis of the New Gallery', CAR, Anderson Papers, box 44, fld. 3.

breakthrough' – that is, in finding a way to make public evangelism work in Britain and Northern Europe.[71]

Church Growth and Evangelism

After growth rates of 6–7 per cent in the early fifties, the annual average for the six-year period 1953–1958 was just 3.9 per cent and in no year did it reach 5 per cent. But in the next six years (1959–1964), the annual growth rate for the division was never below 5 per cent and the six-year annual average was 5.6 per cent; yet for the final six years (1955–1970), the annual average was down to 4 per cent, with (again) no year reaching 5 per cent.

These figures tell us, then, that Duncan Eva's hope proved to be too daring. Indeed, the subsequent decades saw the pace of 'religious decline' quicken as the West of Europe passed from modernity into postmodernity, with increasing and more complete rejection of claims to 'spiritual authority'.[72] This had lasting consequences for the church's preferred approach to outreach. Evangelism in the fifties still yielded rich fruit, if in some places more than others, but the writing was already beginning to appear on the wall. The successes of the late sixties were genuine but localised and any 'breakthrough' was of its time, not of lasting significance. The quest for breakthroughs in public-evangelistic methodology was to continue for the next fifty years.

---

71 Lohne, 'Big Scale Evangelism', pp. 1–2; Eva to R. R. Frame, 29 Feb. 1968, Coltheart to 'Fellow Worker' [newsletter], 17 Sept. 1968, pp. 2 and 5, and Coltheart to Frame, 20 May 1969, in Coltheart's appointee file, GC Ar., RG 29, file no. 13153; G. Henk Koning, 'It Has Been Done', in *Re-visioning Adventist Mission in Europe*, ed. by Erich W. Baumgartner (Berrien Springs: Andrews University Press, 1998), p. 211.

72 Kaufmann, Goujon, and Skirbekk, 'The End of Secularization in Europe?', 71.

Chapter 7
'Saying Goodbye with Heavy Hearts': Separating from Sub-Saharan Africa, 1969–1980

In 1971, in its forty-third year of existence, the Northern European Division's name was changed to Northern Europe-West Africa Division (NEWAD), a change in title that reflected a change in territory enacted by the 1970 GC Session, which placed NED's territory in East Africa under a new division. Less than a decade later, its unions in West Africa also separated and became the core of another new African division. Northern European Adventists no longer had responsibility for any territory in Africa. That had briefly been true in the forties, but this time the separation, at least from sub-Saharan Africa, was to be permanent. North-East Africa would be assigned to TED in 1995, but the vast territories south of the Sahara and their tens of thousands of Seventh-day Adventists would henceforth control their own destiny. Where would this leave a division, much of whose *raison d'être* had historically been conversion of 'the heathen' in Africa?

From NED to NEWAD

In the 1960s, the development of the church in much of Africa, the decline of imperialism on the continent and concomitant spread of self-determination, along with the growing importance of the civil rights movement in the United States, all prompted a sea change in how the Adventist Church was organised in Africa. In 1970, the regime of benevolent European direction that had obtained since 1929 was shaken up, although 1970 marked the beginning (rather than the conclusion) of a process of increasing independence in the church. Political self-government in Africa gave rise to ecclesiastical self-governance in African Adventist entities.

The Winds of Change

Early in 1960, the British Prime Minister Harold Macmillan had given two celebrated speeches in Ghana and South Africa, concerning the 'strength of [...] African national consciousness'. He famously referred in both speeches to the 'winds of change blowing through this continent' – a metaphor for increasing African self-determination and for European decolonisation. The trajectory identified by the prime minister affected Adventists as much as any other white colonisers. In Macmillan's words, regardless of whether Europeans (or white settlers in Africa, or Americans) 'like it or not, this growth of national consciousness' could not be ignored: 'We must all accept it as fact. Our national policies must take account of it.'[1] For Adventists, it was 'denominational policies' that had to 'take account' of national consciousness – and they did.

Northern European Division leaders immediately noted the prime minister's speech. Within weeks, *Northern Light* published an article by NED President Tarr about a recent itinerary through the Ethiopian and West African Unions, which was titled 'Winds of Change Over Africa'. While Tarr praised missionaries, he emphasised the importance of 'national' workers and wrote admiringly of how pastors, 'institutional leaders, colporteurs, teachers, and above all, a great army of lay workers, are bending every energy to the supreme task of proclaiming the advent message.' It was no accident that Macmillan's speech was given first in Ghana, the former Gold Coast and the first British African colony to become independent (and then given again in South Africa, which had instituted apartheid). It was surely no coincidence, either, that Tarr stressed the active role of the 'laymen of Ghana' and wrote at some length about the Ghana Mission president, C. B. Mensah, the only indigenous mission president

---

1   Ph.-J. Salazar and Brett Syndercombe, 'Harold Macmillan, "The Wind of Change"', *African Yearbook of Rhetoric*, 2.3 (2011), 27–39; available at <www.africanrhetoric.org/pdf/J%20%20%20Macmillan%20-%20%20 the%20wind%20of%20change.pdf>, accessed 18 April 2019.

in the WAUM.² A month later, C. D. Henri, an African-American missionary to Ghana and editor of the West African Union paper, wrote in an editorial:

> 'Winds of change are blowing over Africa', said the Hon. Harold Macmillan, Prime Minister of Great Britain, but we [...] suggest 'Winds of progress' would be more descriptive. West Africa is on the march and Seventh-Day [sic] Adventists must keep step.³

This captures how wider political and cultural currents almost inevitably influence how the church thinks and acts, sometimes without Seventh-day Adventists being aware of it, but at other times, as in this case, quite consciously.⁴

Less than a year after the prime minister's speeches, GC President Figuhr began an article, written while on an African itinerary: '"The winds of change are blowing over Africa," is an expression frequently heard as one travels over this great continent.' Referring to the fact that eighteen African nations had gained political independence in 1960, Figuhr declared that such a dramatic and sudden shift, 'taking place within a limited time cannot but affect our mission program and create new problems, making necessary adjustments and modifications in our work.' Figuhr approvingly reported that church organisations had recognised the emerging situation, including 'the Southern African Division' whose executive committee had just 'met in Salisbury, Southern Rhodesia [today Harare, Zimbabwe], and

---

2 A. F. Tarr, 'Winds of Change Over Africa', *Northern Light*, 10.4 (April 1960), 4–5.

3 *West African Advent Messenger*, 8.5 (May 1960), 8.

4 On his return to the United States in the mid-sixties, Henri became important in black Adventist striving for full rights in the North American Division. He may thus have been more conscious of the struggle for independence than many European missionaries, but that he clearly thought his remarks would resonate with his readers suggests a developing 'national consciousness' among Adventists: Henri's obituary is at the *Black SDA History* website: <http://www.blacksdahistory.org/c--dunbar-henri.html>, accessed 4 Feb. 2019.

addressed itself to the study of new problems and urgent challenges'.[5] The president of that division was Robert H. Pierson, a veteran American missionary, who used Macmillan's metaphor himself later that year in his column for the Southern African Division's monthly magazine.[6]

Five years later, Pierson was elected General Conference president by the 1966 GC Session (Illustration 7.1). Pierson had been president of the Southern Africa Division since 1958, having previously spent many years in India and Central America. His colleague as secretary, Walter R. Beach, who had been in office since 1954, had been president of the Southern European Division from 1946–1954, having previously been the SED secretary (Illustration 7.2). Both men had thus been responsible for Adventist mission fields in Africa, while Pierson had lived on the continent for eight years. This personal experience and awareness of the reality underlying the British prime minister's rhetoric was crucial, for they opened Adventist Church doors to the winds of change, which ventilated and refreshed its fusty structure. While Pierson's presidency is remembered today chiefly for his emphasis on revival and reformation, the key emphasis in his first term and beyond was getting the Adventist Church, worldwide, to sail downwind with the gusts of change, rather than tacking against them.

Restructuring Africa, Restructuring Globally

A key difficulty the Seventh-day Adventist Church faced as it sought to engage with the emerging realities on the African continent, which included the maturing of the church in much of Africa, was that any reforms could not be limited only to Africa. The quasi-imperial nature of Adventist church structure and the embedding of African territories into European organisations meant that major

---

5   R. R. Figuhr, 'A Report from Africa', *ARH*, 138.2 (12 Jan. 1961), 1.
6   Robert H. Pierson, 'Heart to Heart', *Southern African Division Outlook*, 59.8 (Aug. 1961), p. 2.

administrative modifications could have far-reaching ramifications. Restructuring to give African church members the self-determination they increasingly enjoyed in the political realm would affect a vast swathe of territories – on two continents, not one. Reforms, furthermore, could potentially affect the church's ecclesiastical polity as a whole, since they might decrease the number of European divisions and increase the number located in Africa. (Indeed, this is what happened, although it would take longer for control of African divisions to pass from missionaries to church leaders from the majority populations.)

Church leaders thus had reason to move carefully, which is the Adventist tendency in any case. But Pierson grasped that limited and piecemeal action would not be sufficient, and he was determined to move as quickly as possible. Within six months of his election, the GC officers appointed a 'committee to study problems affecting West Africa', consisting of GC Treasurer Kenneth Emmerson, Secretary Beach, two associate secretaries and a general vice-president. Three weeks later it established a 'Commission on European Affairs', with two general vice-presidents, Maynard Campbell and Theodore Carcich, as chair and vice chair, and the three executive officers as members, along with representatives of the three European divisions.[7] Conditions in Africa and their relationship to circumstances in Europe were now very much on the agenda at the GC. The commission moved cautiously, however – too cautiously for the GC president's liking. The clock was ticking if changes to church structure were to be made at the 1970 GC Session in Atlantic City, New Jersey.

In early 1969, the process acquired the momentum that would take it through to the 1970 Session, when, at Pierson's urging, the officers appointed a new 'committee [to] study territorial adjustments involving territories of the Trans-Africa Division, Southern European Division, and Northern European Division on the continent of

---

7   GC Officers' Meetings, 4 and 25 Jan. 1967, GCOM, 1967, pp. 4-67 [*sic*, for 67-4), 67-27–28.

Africa'. The committee included the three officers of both European divisions, but none from the Trans-Africa Division, which hinted whose territory would be most affected; and notably its chairman and secretary were Pierson and Beach. The GC president's goal, he wrote later, was that 'National leadership in the countries of Africa be developed and given greater responsibilities'.[8] To achieve that goal, the commission and the new study committee – guided by Pierson – began to develop a vision, one of remarkable range, in which global restructuring would be (as it had to be) undertaken to restructure Africa.

One issue was that the East African Union (part of the NED's original territory) had, for secular political reasons, been detached from the Trans-Africa Division and attached to the GC. The Committee on African Problems convened in Berne in the summer of 1969 and discussed placing the EAUM with the NED again (which it favoured), although the Middle East Division was also suggested as an option.[9] In January 1970, GC officers reviewed a 'Report of [the] Africa-Europe Organisation Commissions' that seems to have been a combined report from the committee appointed in the winter and the commission set up in 1967. The report's major recommendations included: 'A new Afro-Indian Ocean Division to be organized', made up of the EAUM, the Ethiopian Union (which included Somalia and Djibouti as well as Ethiopia), Tanzania, and the Indian Ocean Union Mission.[10]

In May, however, less than a month before the Session in Atlantic City, an *ad hoc* committee, personally chaired by Pierson, suddenly resurrected the idea of a merger of the Middle East Division with the

---

8   GC Officers' Meeting, 13 Jan. 1969, GCOM, p. 69-13. Robert H. Pierson, 'New Division Formed during Autumn Council', *ARH*, 148.44 (4 Nov. 1971), 46.

9   Committee on African Problems, five-page report of meeting of 13–15 July 1969, copy with GCOM, pp. 69-313–314 *et seq.*

10   GC Officers' Meeting, 15 Jan. 1970, GCOM pp. 70-28 *et seq.*, including the Commissions' report.

EAUM and other African unions. It recommended that the Indian Ocean Union be dropped from the new division, but that it should include a new Middle East Union (a transmuted Middle East Division). Pre-empting potential caution at this very major change, the report stressed the 'immediate urgency' of the EAUM's situation. Despite the lateness of the day and the consequent relative lack of scrutiny of what was now proposed, in contrast to the possible organisational models reviewed earlier in 1970, this proposal went forward to the pre-Session officers' council, which approved it, and it then went to the Fifty-First Session.[11] There is little doubt that Pierson used the prestige of the GC presidency to ensure that his preferred organisational scheme was put to a vote at the GC Session, ignoring the option identified by the committees that had spent time considering the issues. Some might see this as a good example of leadership, as a dynamic president cut through the red tape encumbering the church committee system. Others might conclude that, although Pierson's intentions were noble, the process was flawed.

Three division presidents spoke when the proposal was discussed and their words hint at a degree of unhappiness, doubtless at the way things were rushed, although they all were carefully affirming. Duncan Eva, the NED president, made a particularly fine short speech:

> *I belong to a family that is rather emotional at times, and when we say Good-by* [sic] *we shed tears, but we like to shed them where they can't be seen. We are going to greatly regret losing our brethren in Ethiopia from the Northern European Division family. I think we have indicated in the past [...] how much we think of them. [...] Nevertheless, we can see the wisdom of the move that is being made. We say Good-by to them with heavy hearts in one way, but wish them every blessing in their new affiliations*

---

11 GC Officers' Meetings, 13 and 27 May 1970, and Home and Overseas Officers meeting, 1 June 1970, OM Minutes, pp. 70-233–34, 70-261, 70-264.

and associations and pray for the rapid advancement of the work in Ethiopia.

And then the motion to create a new division, including the Ethiopian Union from NED, was put to the vote and passed. The minutes intriguingly note that the vote was not unanimous, and that there were 'a couple of hands' raised to vote against.[12] Whether they were from the Northern European Division, Middle East Division (which was euthanised), or the Trans-Africa Division (which lost Tanzania) is unknown. The Session had approved the most major organisational reforms since 1928.

The same day, the delegates in Atlantic City also voted 'A Call to Repentance, Revival, Reformation, and Evangelism'.[13] It was full of stirring phrases of organisational and spiritual ambition, but much of it was boilerplate Adventist rhetoric that had been voiced at many sessions and councils over the previous century (although no less sincerely meant, or enduringly applicable, for being reiterated). Yet this resolution included an important section, the emphasis of which was novel:

> *The true scope of our message can be seen only through the framework of the cross. God so loved, not just one people or one country, but the WORLD. God so loved, not just the whites or the blacks, but ALL RACES. God so loved, not just the middle class, but ALL CLASSES. Our message is to transcend every barrier – social, political, racial, and geographical.*[14]

This official rejection of prejudice was much more emphatic

---

12 Fifty-First GC Session, Seventh meeting, 15 June 1970 p.m., report in *ARH*, suppt., *GC Session Bulletin* (16 June 1970), 101–02 (p. 102).
13 Text in proceedings of sixth meeting, 15 June 1970, a.m., 'Partial Report of the Plans Committee', *ibid.*, pp. 100–01.
14 Ibid., p. 100 (capitals in original).

than those previously voted by Annual Councils earlier in the sixties.[15] Although it would take time for church members and church administrators in many parts of the world to live up to this vision, nevertheless it laid down an important marker for the Seventh-day Adventist Church. It was in part a response to the great wave of concern in America in the sixties about civil rights; but it also partly reflects Pierson's desire that the Adventist Church in Africa should become authentically African. It provides important context for the 1970 reorganisation.

The restructuring had an immediate impact on the NED and future implications for the SED and Trans-Africa Division. The final configuration of the new Afro-Mideast Division turned out to be ill conceived (doubtless because it was rushed) and, a decade later, East Africa and the Middle East had to be reorganised again.[16] For good or ill, it is plain that all the plans had Pierson's support, expressed his personal opinion of the best way forward, and reflected his desire to make the changes by 1970. Thus, as in 1950, major changes could be made, some at the last minute, when a GC president supported a cause and was personally deeply engaged in a process.

The End of a European Era

As well as removing the Ethiopian Union from the NED, the Africa-Europe Organisation Commissions' recommendations affected the three European divisions in other ways. Quite reasonably, 'the NED and the SED [were to] be structured and named in such a way as to eliminate the inference that "Europe" directs "Africa."'[17] The NED responded promptly to this. With its mission fields now located solely in only one part of Africa it was hard to justify the label *Northern European* as a catchall for the division. West Africa was beginning

---

15 Cf. Arthur L. White, 'Further General Conference Actions on Race Relations', *ARH*, 143.16 (21 Apr. 1966), 6–8.
16 See Trim, *Adventist Mission in the Middle East* (forthcoming).
17 'Report of [the] Africa-Europe Organisation Commissions', p. 1, n.d. [1970], in GCOM, appended after p. 70-28.

to produce articulate, capable leaders; nearly half the NED's church members had been located there before the GC Session action; and it now had more than half the membership of the division. The old title was less accurate than ever. At its Winter Meeting in late 1970 the NED Executive Committee voted to request a change of name so that it would include West Africa. It took several months for the action to be reviewed by the GC officers, but in May they did so and swiftly the GC Executive Committee voted 'that the name of the Northern European Division be changed to Northern Europe-Africa Division'. Strictly speaking it was a recommendation to the 1975 GC Session, but the action was approved on 'the understanding that the terminology be authorized in the meanwhile'.[18] It was a red-letter day.

Meanwhile, although the Commissions' report had proposed that the 'territories of the European Sections of the NED, CEO and SED' were not to be realigned right away, it also recommended that they 'be restudied during the coming quadrennium with a view to reducing the present number of division organisations at an appropriate time'.[19] As it turned out, the 'appropriate time' was little more than a year later. The NED's territory was not trimmed any further, but, dramatically, the CED and SED were merged by vote of the 1971 Annual Council; and in order 'to eliminate the inference that "Europe" directs "Africa"', the new division was to be called the Euro-Africa Division; strictly speaking, this, too, was a recommendation to the 1975 Session, but the new division 'began to function officially' on 1 January 1972.[20] The two remaining European divisions now both had 'Africa' in their titles. They would continue to include territories on the continent of Africa for another forty years (and the Euro-Africa Division retained territories in sub-Saharan Africa for thirty). Yet, thanks to

---

18   NED Winter Meeting, 17 Nov. 1970, NEDCOM mins., 1970, p. 232, action no. 507; GC Officers Meeting, 5 May 1971, GCOM, p. 71-166; GCC meeting, 6 May 1971, GCC Proc., xiii, ii, 71-485.
19   Commissions' report, ibid. (following p. 70-28), p. 1
20   GCC Annual Council, 8 Oct. 1971, GCC Proc., xxiii, iii, 71-627; *sub* 'Euro-Africa Division', *SDAE*, i, 519.

Pierson, the process of rationalising the European divisions' territories and establishing genuinely African divisions had begun. Some in Northern Europe and Britain may have regretted the shift; but it was a step in the right direction.

From NEWAD Back to NED, 1970–1980

The report of the 'Africa-Europe Organisation Commissions' had included another recommendation with implications for the reconfigured division: 'The NED shall adjust its present divisional organisation to accommodate a European Section and an African Section with appropriate committee and officer structuring to care for each and for the whole.'[21] From the start, NEWAD had two separate 'Sections' and three executive committees: a 'Northern European Section Committee' and a 'West African Section Committee', as well as the NEWAD Executive Committee (NEWAEC). At times it is plain from the minutes, members remained in a room and the name of the meeting they were voting in shifted, but at other times section committees met apart from a NEWAEC or other section committee meeting.

The seventies saw further organisational development in the African Section. In 1972, President Eva expressed his pride at the creation of the Ghana Conference, the first 'black conference [...] in Africa',[22] a term he used to distinguish it from longstanding conferences in South Africa and Rhodesia that had always had white-only constituencies. As early as the autumn of 1970 the full division executive committee took an action in principle to make Nigeria a separate union, with the implications to be studied, and the GC was asked for additional financial assistance. In 1971, the GC Executive Committee gave approval for a second union in Africa. In consequence,

---

21 GC Officers' Meeting, 15 Jan. 1970, Commissions' report, p. 1, appended to GCOM, following p. 70-28.
22 President's Report, NEWAD Quadrennial Council, 17 Apr. 1972, NWDM-ECM 1972, § 132, p. 38.

the Nigerian Union was established in 1972. It was a new creation, with no connection to the old Nigerian Union of the thirties.[23]

For all Ghana's financial self-sufficiency and a general maturation of the church in the two African unions, there was still constant need for missionaries from the European Section, especially for institutions. Physicians and teachers were in particular demand, along with some church administrators and dentists, but, as in the past, other workers were needed, too. A random sample of executive committee minutes and other sources show calls for physiotherapists, nurses, and laboratory assistants for Masanga Leprosy Hospital in Sierra Leone; a 'builder' for the Adventist Girls Vocational Institute in Techiman, Ghana; a maintenance engineer for Upper Volta (now Burkina Faso); and the Ghana Conference office called a cashier. These are of course simply illustrative, merely examples that could be multiplied. Some calls were filled by missionaries from other parts of the world, but most were from the countries of NEWAD's European Section, every one of which (except Poland, for obvious reasons), supplied missionaries. So, too, did Ghana: its first workers called to international service went elsewhere in NEWAD's African Section.[24]

Meanwhile, even though no territories in East Africa remained to the TED, this did not mean the historical connection was lost. The leadership of the Afro-Mideast Division in the 1970s was largely drawn from the British Isles and Scandinavia, including veterans of NED service. The 1970 GC Session elected as president Magdalon

---

23 NEWAD Winter Meeting, NEWAEC, 12 Nov. 1970, NWDM-ECM 1970, § 469, p. 175. GCC Annual Council, 8 Oct. 1971, and meeting, 20 July 1972, GCC Proc., xxiii, iii, 71-627, and iv, 72-1024. NEWAD Quadrennial Council, 19 Apr. 1972, NWDM-ECM 1972, § 147, p. 50.

24 See, e.g., list of 1979 appointees in fld. 'Schantz, Børge', GC Ar., RG 21, Missionary Appointee Files, nos. 15514 (Johnson) and 69408 (Schantz); NEWAEC meetings, 13 and 25 June 1979, and NEWAD Winter Meeting, NWDM-ECM 1979, §§ 241, 243, 276, 278, 280, 607, pp. 58. 64, 204, 212–14; and Oster, *Till jordens yttersta gräns*, who lists 31 missionaries just from Sweden who served overseas during the NED/NEWAD years.

E. Lind, a Norwegian, who thus became only the second Scandinavian-born Adventist to serve as president of a world division. He had been called as a missionary to Uganda nearly forty years before when it was under the NED and served in Uganda for twenty years. In 1954, he had been called to the NED headquarters as YPMV and Sabbath School departmental secretary, but in 1965 had returned to Africa as secretary of the Trans-Africa Division (Illustration 7.3). Lind's successor as Afro-Mideast Division president in 1975, the Englishman Charles D. Watson, had been the Temperance department secretary at the NED from 1959–1963, then served as president of the Ethiopian Union from 1965–1968, when he was called to the GC to serve (briefly) as Temperance associate director (Illustration 7.4). John Muderspach, a Dane, had not previously served in East Africa, but had been a mission secretary-treasurer in Sierra Leone in the fifties and Ghana in the sixties, and was called from a position at Skodsborg to the EAUM in 1978 as secretary-treasurer – although not for long, for in 1980 he was elected treasurer of NEWAD, and served through its changes in nomenclature to NED and TED until 1990 (Illustration 7.5).[25]

In the end, NEWAD had a serious problem, which only got worse as the decade drew on: a dramatic double imbalance between the two sections [this is shown in Figure 5]. The Northern Europe Section had the trained and educated personnel, and the money, as had been the case since the division came into being. Yet the West Africa Section now had all the members, a trend that only accelerated through the seventies. At the end of 1970, the division's first complete year without Ethiopia, it had 85,586 members, of which 38,485 were in the unions and attached fields in Europe and the North Atlantic, and 47,101 in the WAUM. By the end of 1980, the division's last year with its historic African territories, the membership of the Northern Europe Section had grown to 41,847: an increase of 3362, or 8.74

---

25 Missionary appointee files, GC Ar., RG 21, Secretariat Appointee Files, nos. 121019 (Lind), 8610 (Muderspach), and 39764 (Watson).

per cent. Yet the membership in the West Africa Section had grown to 96,735: an increase of 49,634, meaning it had more than doubled – net growth was 105.4 per cent.

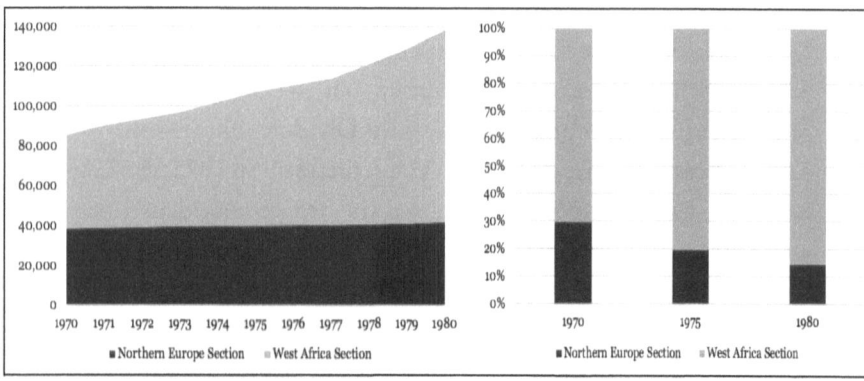

Figure 5: Distribution of Membership and Share of Accessions, Northern Europe and West Africa Sections, 1970–1980

Growth in Europe had plateaued, because growth in accessions had stalled, especially in comparison to Africa. The Northern Europe Section's total of baptisms and professions of faith for 1970 was 1582; in 1980 they totalled 1759. In contrast, WAUM's total accessions for 1970 were 3717 (or twice the number in Europe, although it had six unions), while the total for 1980 in the two African unions was 10,321. Whereas the Northern Europe Section's accessions were 30 per cent of the division total in 1970, in 1980 they were 14.5 per cent, in spite of the small increase in the actual numbers of people joining the church.

All this meant that, whereas the difference between the membership of the two sections was ten percentage points in 1970 (Northern Europe 45 per cent, West Africa 55 per cent), the gap had widened to forty percentage points in 1980. The six unions and attached fields in Europe and the North Atlantic had 30 per cent of the membership and the two African unions, 70 per cent. In contrast, the Nigerian and West African Unions had close to a 50:50 split of the membership in the West Africa Section for the whole decade. And yet, in further contrast, in total tithes and offerings, the sectional shares were more than reversed: in 1980, the Northern Europe Section share of the 'total contributions' was 85.5 per cent, as opposed to the West Africa Section's 14.3 per cent. This created a dichotomy that was neither healthy nor sustainable. When membership, trained personnel, and finances were all on one side, there was not a problem, because it was clear that one section was responsible for the other. When that changed, however, should the division administration reflect where the members were? Or who had the money?

In the seventies, the top echelon of leadership, even most of its middle management, were still European (or whites from elsewhere). As late as 1980, only one-fourth of the West Africa Section Committee members were from West Africa; moreover, when it met in St Albans (the majority of meetings) there would usually be no West African members present.[26] Limited black African input into the division's direction had of course been the case earlier in the TED's history, but it had not been an issue then, both because there were few well-educated or experienced black leaders, and because all parties expected the whites to call the shots throughout the NED's territory. However, the tendency identified by Macmillan in Ghana in 1960 had only intensified. Church members in the two unions of the West Africa Section now expected, given the development of educated and experienced leaders in West Africa, and the distribution of membership in NEWAD, that they would have ecclesiastical, as well as political, self-determination. Yet the established order of things at the division headquarters and on its executive committee remained the same. The best thing for both sections was that the arrangement of half a century before, when Africa was almost entirely ruled by European powers, an

---

26 NWASC, NWDM-WSC, passim.

arrangement that had been put in place to effect the development of Adventism in Africa, should come to an end.

General Conference administration became ever more concerned that church structure in Africa in the era of decolonisation still reflected too much the age of empire. Gradually a consensus emerged around a more radical reorganisation.[27] A lengthy report, which was the basis for the eventual reforms, summarised relevant developments and the decision-making process. Following the reorganisation of 1970–1971, 'our work in Africa has been administered by four', rather than three 'divisions of the General Conference'; and yet, 'all but one […] have headquarters outside the African continent.' The dissatisfaction of the sixties did not disappear; instead, 'continued correspondence came from African fields' to the General Conference.

> *It expressed the viewpoint that our present division organization was not viewed favourably by many Seventh-day Adventist Africans, nor by some African governments since it gives the appearance, at least in some aspects, of holdover colonialism. […] African leaders and constituents also felt that the location of division headquarters in Europe and the Middle East prevented adequate opportunity for Africans to participate in leadership roles in our strongly developing African work.*[28]

President Pierson held a series of consultations in Africa as early as 1973, but there was limited support for substantial restructuring so soon after the 1970 Session.

After the 1975 GC Session, however, Pierson – typically decisive, perhaps imperious – resolved to move things along and 'an Africa Study Committee was appointed'. It made an initial report to the 'President's Executive Advisory' (a select group at the GC headquarters), which endorsed further steps. Pierson's plans were interrupted

---

27 See 'Statement from the General Conference regarding the re-organisation of African Affairs', n.d., reviewed at NEWAEC Winter Meeting, 22 Nov. 1979, in NWDM-ESC 1979, § 511, pp. 127–35 (including 'Exhibits').
28 Ibid., p. 127.

by illness, however, which obliged him to resign at the end of 1978. The new president of the GC, Neal C. Wilson, a former missionary to Africa, was supportive, but had a consensual approach to high-level decision making that contrasted with the executive style Pierson had come to prefer. In the spring of 1979, Wilson chaired a major meeting of the GC officers with 'members of the four division committees [...] in Abidjan, Ivory Coast' attended also by 'the officers of the divisions and representative leaders from various parts of Africa'. This consultation was the basis for developing a proposal that was reviewed by the President's Administrative Council at the GC headquarters. It reached the conclusion 'that the time has now arrived for our Seventh-day Adventist work in Africa to be administered from headquarters located in Africa'.[29] The report was reviewed by the 1979 Annual Council, which formally recommended the proposed series of actions to the 1980 GC Session. In the winter–spring of 1980, at the GC and NEWAD (and doubtless other divisions too), working groups were set up, to address the practical details required by restructuring again.[30]

So it was that the NEWAD configuration and title lasted only ten years. The WAUM and the Nigerian Union Mission were both assigned to the new Africa-Indian Ocean Division by the GC Session in Dallas in April 1980.[31] As a result, for a second time, the title 'Northern European Division' was restored. But now the division really was just the north of Europe and the North Atlantic. Given the importance of the mission fields, many church members must have wondered what the future had in store.

29 Ibid., pp. 127–28.
30 Ibid., p. 133; 'Reorganization of African Affairs', report to Annual Council, 16 Oct. 1979, GCC Mins., pp. 79-390–398; NWASC meeting, Ikeja, Nigeria, 15 Jan. 1980, NWDM-WSC 1980, p. 1; Home and Overseas Officers Meeting, 16 Apr. 1980, GCOM, pp. 80-8, 9.
31 Fifty-Third Session, first meeting, 17 Apr. 1980, 'Reorganisation of African Affairs', *ARH*, 157.17, GC Session Bulletin, no. 2 (20 Apr. 1980), 27–28.

The African Connection

What, however, of the past, of the history that concluded in 1980? What can we say about the TED's historic association with sub-Saharan Africa?

It was Britons and Scandinavians who pioneered the work in both East and West Africa, more than a quarter-century before the NED was founded. Having established the first missions, then, for decades, British, Danish, Dutch, Estonian, Finnish, Icelandic, Irish, Latvian, Norwegian, and Swedish missionaries served in Eritrea, Ethiopia, Ghana, Kenya, Liberia, Nigeria, Sierra Leone, Sudan, Tanzania, Uganda, and other African countries. By the 1960s, the connections between the African mission fields and the NED homelands ran deep: there were many church schools, MV/Pathfinder clubs, and local churches in the British Isles, for example, that had created their own direct ties to counterparts in West Africa, received news from them, did fundraising for them (including but not limited to Ingathering), and at times sent them money directly.[32]

This was a connection of people and therefore of sentiment and emotion. Lives were lost and blood shed, literally, to establish the Adventist Church in Africa between the Equator and the Tropic of Cancer, and especially in the countries around the Gulf of Guinea, which, in the words of William H. Lewis, an early missionary to the region, 'had been properly termed "The white man's grave".'[33] As well as deaths, though, there were long careers spent in Africa: the years lived by missionaries from NED in Africa innumerable. For many, their relationship with Africa and its people was truly a love affair. In 1933, the Bergströms in Northern Cameroon asked Ernest Dick, the

---

32 E.g., A. C. Vine, 'Opportunity Knocks Again', *British Advent Messenger*, 27 Mar. 1964, pp. 1–2; Edgar A. Warren, 'More Wheelchairs', *West African Adventist Messenger*, 25.1 (Jan. 1971), 5.

33 William H. Lewis, 'True Adventures in Africa: A Story of the Pioneer Days of the Advent Movement in Sierra Leone and Ghana West Africa' (1971), p. 17, GC Ar., RG 509, box 12983.

NED secretary who was visiting them, about a furlough, but then Hanna Bergström, 'who had well-nigh lost her health, replied: "If we go can we come back? for if we cannot come back then we don't want, to go." British missionary Albert Watson, for example, having taken permanent return to Britain after twenty-seven years of service in Africa, petitioned the NED officers in 1931 to 'be permitted to go back to his field and labour for at least one more term in the East African Union Mission'.[34]

The reversion of NEWAD to NED was not the end of an African connection in the TED's history. First, because of the history, many missionaries from Northern Europe continued to serve in West Africa, among them a future secretary of the TED, Reinder Bruinsma (Illustration 7.6). Nevertheless, the number gradually diminished and the number of new calls after 1980 was fewer than in the 1960s–1970s. Second, in 1995 the TED would once again be made responsible for substantial territory in Africa, although an area it had previously had little contact with (see Chapter 8). The largest administrative and missional connection, however, a hugely significant one historically, had come to a close; large parts of sub-Saharan Africa had been part of the division for literally half a century. And then the connection was no more. Forty years later, memory of this extraordinary historic association is probably now in danger of disappearing, as time passes, and missionaries pass away.

In Africa, especially West Africa, the missionaries are far from forgotten. Remembrance can take curious forms, such as the remarkable demand received in 2018 for thirty-nine years of back rent for property in Nigeria that had long since become the responsibility first of the Africa-Indian Ocean Division and then of the West-Central Africa Division (WAD).[35] More typically – and more profoundly –

---

34 Dick, 'Visiting Our Missionaries in West Africa', p. 3. NED Minority Committee meeting, 27 Apr. 1931, NEDCOM mins., 1931, p. 21.

35 Yomi Olukolu to 'Managing Director' of WWAM, 14 Feb. 2018, and WWAM, Board of Directors meeting, 28 Feb. 2018, Minutes § 18-1, TEDArc., WWAM Files.

there is a powerful and longstanding interest in and attachment to the church's history, which local church leaders and church members recognise as beginning with the Britons and Scandinavians – and Americans and Jamaicans, too – who brought the Adventist message to the region, often at great personal cost. Adventist universities in Nigeria have been named after pioneer missionaries David Babcock and Jesse Clifford; in recent commemorations of historic Adventist anniversaries in Nigeria, the role of missionaries was highlighted.[36] Yet this is not a recent development: in the mid-1960s, as Ghanaians and Nigerians took leadership positions, they wanted to ensure that sacrifice was not forgotten. In 1965, for example, soon after the capable I. K. Ansong became the first 'national' principal of Agona Adventist Teacher Training College in Ghana, he guided the institution's board to a decision 'to name [...] Houses after [...] veteran Missionar[ies] to the Gold Coast', placed photographs of them in the respective buildings, and made an effort to contact those honoured, some of whom had left fifty years before. Ansong wrote to W. H. Lewis, who was one of them, that his career 'is of very great historical interest to us'.[37] There has been less formal commemoration in East Africa but Adventists there, too, recall with appreciation and affection a century of engagement with the region: the founders of the first mission stations; later missionaries who mentored grandparents, parents and current church leaders; the scholarships granted to East

---

36 Trim, *A Living Sacrifice*, pp. 31–33, 38–40; Onaolapo Ajibade (WAD executive secretary) to Trim (director GC ASTR), emails, 28 Nov. 2013 and 22 Aug. 2014, and Chimezie Omeonu (vice-chancellor of Clifford University) to Trim, emails, 3 Feb. 2014 and 9 Feb. 2015.

37 See Ansong to W. H. Lewis, 2 May 1968, and Lewis to Ansong, 29 May 1968 and 20 Jan. 1971, GC Ar., RG 509, box 12983; *YB 1965–1966*, p. 273. Church leaders recognised Ansong as talented, granting him a year's study leave at Andrews University in 1968/69 where he took an MA in Education: NEDCOM, 10 Apr. 1968, NEDCOM Mins, 1968, § 207, p. 84; Lewis to Ansong, 20 Jan. 1971, *loc. cit.*

African students even after there was no formal connection.[38]

In spite of remembrance of individual missionaries, institutional memory of the larger role of NED/NEWAD is fading, even more so in the division itself than in Africa. There is only limited awareness in the TED today of the division's past responsibility for immense territories in Africa, north of the equator and south of the Sahara, and its historic role in building up Adventism in much of that region. It is simply not part of the history of the TED's Eastern European countries which only became part of the division after it had finally separated from sub-Saharan Africa. In the countries of Northern Europe and the North Atlantic, in which church members for so long looked south to Africa, knowledge of the African mission history is limited mostly to older members – or, ironically enough, among the increasing numbers of immigrants from Africa. There is no point hankering after past glories, but there is much in the TED's mission history of which to be proud, many lessons to be learned, and much that could be inspirational to church members, especially youth and young adults.[39] The passion for mission in Africa that characterised the TED's past can arouse a similar passion for mission, but in Europe, in the present and future.

---

38 E.g., Eric Nyankanga Maangi, 'The Contribution and Influence of the Seventh-day Adventist Church in the Development of Post-Secondary Education in South Nyanza, 1971–2000' (EdD dissertation, University of South Africa, 2014); Geoffrey Mbwana, 'Like a Mustard Seed: Adventism in the East-Central Africa Division', *Adventist World–NAD*, 10.4 (April 2014), 40–41; Mbwana, sermon at the TED Yearend Meeting, 18 Nov. 2017.

39 Cf. Reinder Bruinsma, 'Past Patterns of European Mission Involvement', in *Re-Visioning Adventist Mission in Europe*, ed. by Baumgartner, pp. 32–37.

Chapter 8
'A Caring Community':
Unity and Diversity, 1976–1991

Territorial Expansion

In 1980, the TED had shrunk to its smallest geographic extent since 1 January 1949 when the Ethiopian Union Mission re-joined the NED. Only during the years from June 1946 to December 1948 has the division been smaller than it was during 1980–1985. But, by the end of 1985, it had expanded dramatically, in geographic and demographic terms.

End of 'NED'

With no African territory, the NEWAD title had plainly become inapt, yet at the 1980 Session it had been left in place, though a name change required the emendation of the GC Bylaws, which only a Session could approve. Five months later, the pre-Annual Council officers' council gave its support to a proposal from GC ADCOM to adopt the pre-1971 title along with the necessary amendments to the Bylaws. At the 1980 Annual Council, the title 'Northern European Division' was reinstated (to be used as a working title until the 1985 Session), as was a formal recommendation to the Fifty-Fourth Session in 1985 to amend the Bylaws, and an amendment to *GC Working Policy* to redistribute the territories of the various divisions affected by the realignment of Africa that had been begun (but not formally completed) at the Fifty-Third Session in Dallas.[1] For the next four years, as from 1946–1948, the title was a truly accurate description. But by 1985, the proposed amendment of the Bylaws to adopt the NED

---

1 Meeting of the Home and Overseas Officers and Union Presidents, 5 Oct. 1980, mins., in GCOM, pp. 80-42, 43, 44; GCC Annual Council, 9 Oct. 1980, a.m. and p.m., GC mins., pp. 80-291, 298, 299.

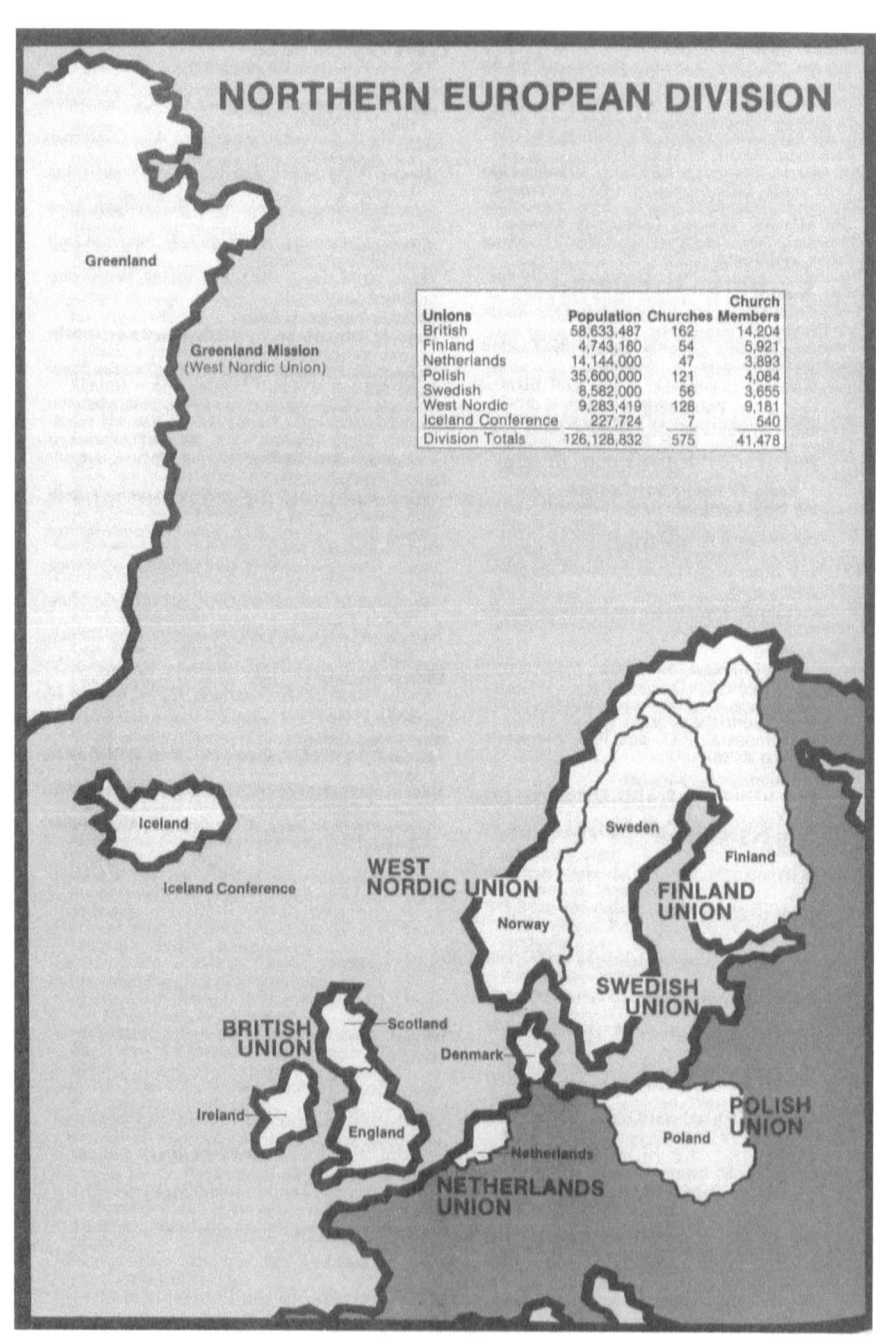

Map 8.1: The End of NEWAD: The NED after the 1980 GC Session

nomenclature was overtaken by events and dropped, as the result of a process by which the TED finally became, in a very literal sense, the *Trans-European* Division.

After West Africa was hived off to become the core of the Africa-Indian Ocean Division, the Northern European Division had 41,478 members.[2] This was the smallest membership of any of the eleven active world divisions; in terms of square miles, too, NED was almost certainly the smallest.[3] We will touch later in this chapter and in Chapter 9 on the increasing difficulties in winning converts in this materialistic and irreligious area, but they were evident in the division's numbers in the next quinquennium. The growth rate of the whole division was 4 per cent – not even 1 per cent per annum. Growth was so slight that, if graphed with the vertical axis showing between nought and 45,000, the membership shows as a straight line; accordingly, Figure 6 shows the base as 40,000 instead. Given its small size to start with, the NED's fortunes in the early eighties had significant implications for its future after 1985.

The NED simply was not viable as one of the world divisions. By 1985, its membership was equivalent to only 28 per cent of the second-smallest division (Southern Asia). It became clear that either the Northern European Division would have to be wound up (not a simple matter, for a number of reasons), or new territories would have to be assigned to it.

Becoming Trans-European

From the point of view of NED leaders in St Albans, there was a fortunate confluence of events. Secular political considerations made it impracticable for Pakistan to continue as part of the Southern Asia Division when the division had its headquarters in India – hostility between the two countries was too great. Meanwhile, in the

2   *YB 1981*, p. 249.
3   Ibid., *passim*. China and the USSR were still nominally listed as divisions at this point.

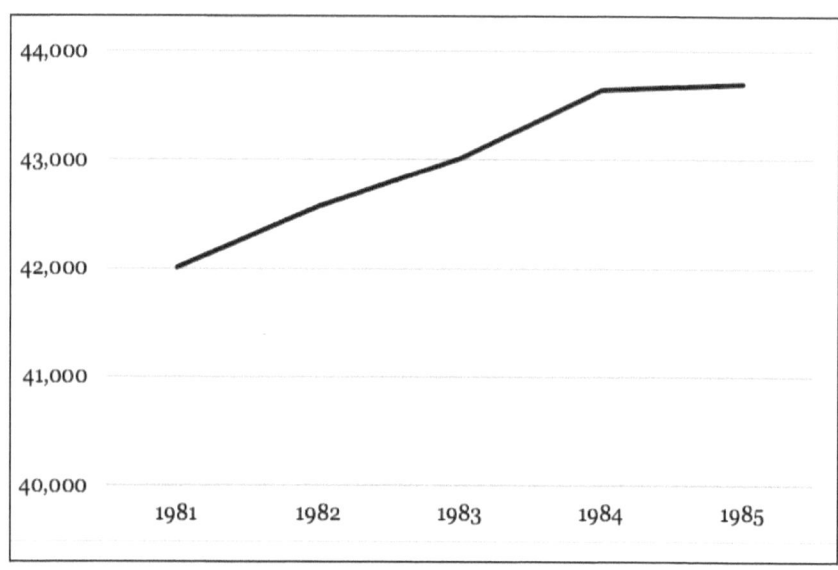

Figure 6: NED Membership, 1981–1985

Netherlands and Norway, longstanding antipathy to German church leaders, dating back to the German occupation of the countries during World War II, meant that the many church members who remembered the war were strongly opposed to becoming part of the Euro-Africa Division (EAD). There was a kind of symmetry. Further, at this point, the idea of attaching mission fields to European divisions still seemed, to some world-church leaders, an appropriate one: the EAD still had responsibility for large African mission fields and the Trans-Africa Division had recently tried to transfer to the NED two insular Atlantic missions off the African coast.[4] Why could not part of Asia become a mission field for a European division?

Church leaders considered making the Middle East Union part of the Southern Asia Division and moving the division headquarters to Lebanon, or making Pakistan part of the Middle East Union, but there many problems with either course of action. An alternative was to place Pakistan in the NED. Meanwhile, church leaders had

---

4   GC Officers' Meeting, 11 Jan. 1983, GCOM, p. 83-10.

known before the 1980 Session that the NED was not large enough to be viable, but they were aware of the various factors (socio-cultural, financial, secular-political, and church-political) that made a merger of the two European divisions infeasible and hence left things as they were in Dallas – except that among the series of actions restructuring African territory was one mandating a 'review [of] the organisation of the Seventh-day Adventist work in Europe at the 1984 Annual Council'. The GC did not leave it so long; by 1983, several possible options 'had been discussed extensively by the organisations affected and [...] by the officers of the General Conference and the European divisions'. The sensible conclusion was that, while the church would 'continue operating two division sections in Europe', the GC would 'confer' with the EAD and NED, the intention being 'to bring about a realignment of territory for the purpose of equalising to some degree the distribution of subsidiary administrative units between, and church membership in, the two divisions'. The second part of a convergence of events was that the question of what to do about Pakistan was being dealt with at the same time that the future of Adventist organisation in Europe was being discussed by the GC officers, just before the 1983 Annual Council.[5]

By the spring of 1985, a proposal for 'territorial realignment' had been developed that would 'balance the responsibilities' of the two divisions in Europe, and would result in the transfer to the NED not only of the Pakistan Union Section but also of two unions and two attached missions from the Euro-Africa Division: the Hungarian Union Conference (HUC), the Yugoslavian Union Conference, the Greek Mission, and the Israel Field. The papers of the study committee do not survive and so why these unions and missions were chosen to move from EAD to NED remains uncertain. However, the Hungarian Union had, since the mid-seventies, faced an unfortunate

---

5   GC Officers Steering Committee, 6 Oct. 1983, mins. in GCOM, pp. 83-261, 262. Session action: Fifty-Third Session, first meeting, 17 Apr. 1980, 'Reorganization of African Affairs', action no. 7.

and damaging schism arising from the stresses of dealing with Communist rule. In the end, it was not to be resolved until the 2010s (and for that reason the history is analysed in Chapter 9). But the key point for this chapter is that by 1985, a decade had passed with the Euro-Africa Division unable to restore the breach. Church leaders with knowledge of events in the mid-eighties recall that this rift in the Hungarian Church was one reason for transferring the HUC to the TED. It was hoped that the TED might have more success in healing the wounds.

The GC Executive Committee adopted the proposal as a recommendation to the 1985 GC Session but during the discussions the inaccuracy of 'Northern European Division' as a title for the new division was highlighted and the action provided for a 'change [of] the name of the [...] Division at an early date'.[6] Within the next five weeks the NED officers met with representatives of the three unions 'proposed for transfer and considered possible new nomenclature'. Whose idea it was is not recorded, but in May 1985 NEDCOM voted 'to recommend to the General Conference that should the GC Session approve the [...] recommendations on territorial realignment [...] the new name for the Northern European Division be Trans-European Division'. This was then approved by the GC Executive Committee four weeks later, 'subject to approval by the 1985 General Conference Session'.[7]

Three weeks later, in New Orleans, the whole package realigning much of Europe and part of Asia, and renaming the transformed NED, was approved by the Session, to take effect on New Year's Day 1986. A week later, 'the first Trans-European Division Executive Committee meeting' was held in the Superdome at New Orleans; as TED President Jan Paulsen (Illustration 8.1) remarked, although 'the new fields' would not 'be part of the Division [until January 1986

6   GCC Spring Meeting, 4 Apr. 1985, GCC mins. pp. 85-118, 119, 120.
7   NEDCOM meeting, 9 May 1985, NEDCOM mins., 1985, § 238, p. 65. GCC meeting, 6 June 1985, GCC mins. p. 85-208.

[...] close co-operation and planning' would needed 'before that time'.[8] Thus it was that, fifty-seven years after the NED came into existence, it adopted the title it would retain for the next thirty-three years. Apart from its mission fields in Asia, it now covered large parts of East-Central Europe as well as its traditional Northern Europe and North Atlantic core (see Map 8.2). As in 1970, the title 'Northern European' had become a misnomer; the division had always included Poland, which has historically been classified as part of Eastern Europe but, with a Baltic coast, it could quite reasonably be regarded as part of Northern Europe too. Now that, for the first time, Central and Southeast Europe were represented in the division, the name had to change. The 'Trans-European Division' was the result.

There had never been any hint in the preceding sixty-five years of European Adventist history that Hungary or the western and southern Balkans might be assigned to the division associated with Northern Europe. As we will see in Chapter 11, after World War II the NED had overseen relief efforts that supplied food and clothing to Hungary – but aid had also been provided to Czechoslovakia. Furthermore, over the years the Polish Union had periodically cooperated with the Czechoslovakian Union, its neighbour to the south. Yet the Czechs and Slovaks remained in the Euro-Africa Division. The TED has included territories in Central and Southeast Europe for more than a third of its history and it is easy to forget that it used to be no easy matter for pastors or church administrators from what are now the south-eastern and north-western sections of the TED to visit the other area. In the seventies, for example, when the SUC wanted the president of the Yugoslavian Union Conference 'to visit Sweden' for a number of speaking appointments, and the Yugoslavian Union in its turn wanted Newbold's principal, Jan Paulsen, to lecture at Maruševec, the union's college, in Croatia, the invitations

---

8   Fifty-Fourth Session, first meeting, 27 June 1985, GC Session mins., 1985, § 245, p. 85-1009. TEDEC meeting, 4 July 1985, NEDCOM/TEDMC-EC 1985, p. 87.

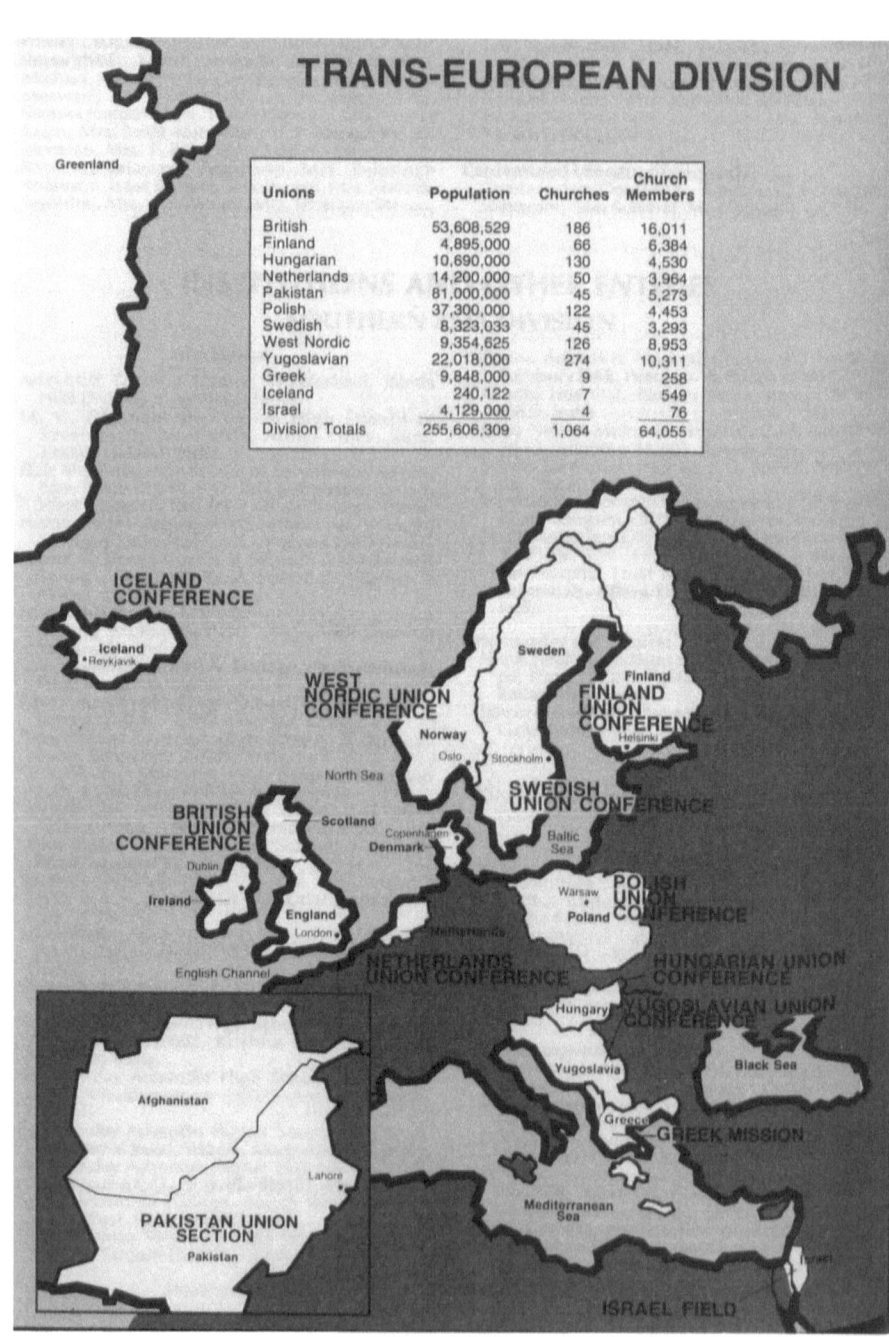

Map 8.2: The Trans-European Division in 1986

had to be channelled through the respective divisions, approved by their officers, and put to both executive committees for formal voted approval.[9]

Responsibility for the Pakistan Union Section meant that the division once again had a very large and heavily populated overseas mission field (as well as the rather smaller Israel Field). The NED had never previously included territory in Southern Asia (or the Middle East). However, because of Britain's centuries-old imperial association with India, many Adventist missionaries from the NED had served in the Southern Asia Division over the decades: mostly Britons (including the Pakistan Union's president at the time of the merger, Derek Clothier), but also a fair proportion from Scandinavia. The numbers of these NED-origin missionaries had gradually declined after British India became independent in 1948, but never disappeared. With the assignment of the Pakistan Union to the TED, a steady trickle of British missionaries to Asia increased, joined by others from Scandinavia.[10]

Theological and Missiological Issues

Issues become issues as and when they arise, without regard for GC Sessions (or years ending in nought). This chapter's chronological scope is from 1976 to 1991 because some themes, some challenges to unity and community in the TED, emerged in the second half of the seventies and were particularly contentious during the eighties, but

---

9   NNESC meeting, 31 Mar. 1976, NWDM-ESC 1976, § 20, p. 8; NEWAEC meeting, 2 Feb. 1977, NWDM-ECM 1977, § 25, p. 5.
10 See, e.g., report of World Wide Advent Missions for 1945, made to BUC Committee, 11 July 1946, in GC Ar., RG NE 1, fld. 'British Union Conference Minutes 1946', pp. 55–59 (pp. 55–56); Oster, *Till jordens yttersta gräns*, pp. 34, 138, who lists nine Swedish missionaries to Southern Asia, though none to Pakistan; and *HRSDAE*, App. A. The first Scandinavian Adventist workers sent to India had been four Danish missionaries, Niels and Edith Nielsen and Christian and Ani Jensen; the documents relating to their applications for passports are in British Library, India Office Records, IOR/L/E/7/1379, File 743.

became less so in the nineties and noughties. The rest of this chapter briefly highlights the issues that emerged in this period, in the area of doctrines and of mission, as regards unity and disunity in the body of believers.

Inspiration and Revelation

For a decade or so after 1976, belief in Ellen White's prophetic ministry and the Adventist 'landmarks' seemed to be under attack. Although the wave of criticism gathered and crested in North America, it swept over Adventists in Australasia and Europe as well. Yet it is difficult to know exactly how it affected Adventists in Northern Europe.

Matters began with the publication in 1976 of a deeply researched but highly tendentious study of Ellen White's thought and writings on health by Ronald Numbers, an historian of science who had been a practicing Adventist.[11] In 1980, the *Los Angeles Times* published a major article alleging that Ellen White was a plagiarist; it drew partly on research by a pastor in California, Walter Rea, who published his claims at length in 1982.[12] Partly as a result, later in 1980 the GC commissioned Fred Veltman of Pacific Union College, to lead the 'Life of Christ Research Project' into *The Desire of Ages* and its sources; in 1986 the massive study Veltman completed was summarised in church periodicals; many church members were reassured but some were left more disillusioned. Meanwhile, in 1979–1980, Desmond Ford had attacked the traditional Adventist understanding of the Sanctuary Doctrine and venerable apocalyptic interpretations, and, as part of his wider theological critique, also made observations that undermined a conservative understanding of Ellen White's inspiration and ministry (even though Ford himself maintained belief in White as exercising a prophetic ministry).

---

11   Ronald L. Numbers, *Prophetess of Health: A Study of Ellen G. White and the Origins of Seventh-day Adventist Health Reform,* rev. 2nd edn. (Knoxville: University of Tennessee Press, 1991 [1976]).

12   Walter L. Rea, *The White Lie* (Turlock, Calif.: M & R Publications, 1982).

In the 1960s, division administration had actively sought to strengthen belief in the prophetic ministry of Ellen White.[13] In the 1970s, division leaders continued to be strongly supportive of 'the Spirit of Prophecy'. In 1973 they had taken the initiative to create the Ellen G. White Seventh-day Adventist Research Centre, Europe, at Newbold College to undertake research on Ellen White and on European Adventist history. The NEWAD officers obtained the support of the EAD leadership, then that of the Ellen G. White Estate, and subsequently the backing of the GC officers. Working with the White Estate and the General Conference Archives, the centre took shape and then NEWAD secured GC funding.[14] The White Research Centre at Newbold was the first of what has now increased to twenty research centres around the world – but the archetype was in the TED at the division institution, Newbold. It became the model for all the other centres and for the creation of world-church policies relating to them.

What this does not tell us is what the members in the pew thought of Ellen White up to the point that Numbers published his polemic against Ellen White and the health message. Nor do we have a clear sense of how that might have changed in the following decade. In the absence of hard data, one is left to speculate as to what most church members thought and what regional differences there might have been. One Swedish Adventist scholar argued in the mid-seventies, writing in the aftermath of Numbers, that Ellen White's writings were 'much read in Norway and in Finland', but that 'her importance

---

13 E.g., a three-part series by a scientist comparing the health counsels of Ellen White to the (then) latest findings of modern science, Karstrom, Henning, 'God's Precious Gift', *Northern Light*, 16.6 (June 1966), 1–3, 7.
14 Annual Council, 18 Oct. 1973, GCC Proc., xxiii, vi, 73-1798, 1799; President's Administrative Council, meetings of 24 and 31 Oct. 1973, PRADCO mins., pp. 73-55, 56, 57, and 73-65, 66; Annual Council, 15 Oct. 1974, GCC Proc., xxiii, vii, 74-356; James R. Nix, *Memorable Dates from our Adventist Past* (Silver Spring, Md.: North American Division Office of Education, 1989), p. 84.

[was] less evident in Sweden and Denmark'.¹⁵ If belief in the Spirit of Prophecy was already diminished by this time, then the impact of the criticisms of Numbers, Rea, and Ford may have been less in Northern Europe than elsewhere – but only because scepticism was pre-existing.

Church leaders feared that scepticism was gathering among rank-and-file church members. The fact that NED President Scragg expressed concern about Ford and Rea to the division Spring Meeting in 1981 suggests that their criticisms were felt to be taking a toll.¹⁶ As a result, the division invested resources in countering the criticisms, such as regularly bringing in two or three scholars at a time from the Ellen G. White Estate and/or the world headquarters in Washington, DC, to conduct seminars in Britain, Finland, the Netherlands, and Sweden, in 1980, 1984, and the spring of 1987.¹⁷ The TED committed substantial resources to planning over two years, and then holding a series of centennial commemorations of Ellen White's epochal sojourn in Europe, a hundred years after its conclusion in 1887. Celebrations were held from 5 September to 12 December 1987 in the eight countries she visited while in Europe, including Britain, Denmark, Norway, and Sweden of the TED countries; workshops were held in Finland, Hungary, the Netherlands, Poland, and Yugoslavia. Thousands of church members attended these events. In addition, the TED provided the funding for a major academic

---

15 Ingemar Lindén, *The Last Trump: An Historico-Genetical Study of Some Important Chapters in the Making and Development of the Seventh-day Adventist Church*, Studien zur interkulturellen Geschichte des Christentums / Studies in the Intercultural History of Christianity, 17 (Frankfurt am Main, Bern & Las Vegas, NV: Peter Lang, 1978), p. 291.
16 See minutes of NEDCOM Spring Meeting, 13 May, p.m., 1981, NEDCOM mins., 1981, p. 45.
17 E.g., NNESC meeting, 26 Nov. 1978, NWDM-ESC 1978, § 59, p. 25; NEDCOM meeting, 8 Sept. 1983, NEDCOM mins., 1983, § 414, p. 111; TEDEC Spring Meeting, 12 May 1986, TDC-EC 1986, §§ 327–28, p. 102.

conference, held at the Dutch seminary at Oud Zandbergen, near Utrecht.[18]

Despite having limited data from the period of peak controversy, there is evidence that suggests the controversies of the seventies and eighties did ultimately have an effect on how Adventists from the TED regard Ellen White and her prophetic ministry. In a global survey of church members in 2018, more than 55,000 Adventists answered questions about Ellen White. It is notable that, when asked to indicate agreement with the statement 'Ellen White's writings are the result of the spiritual gift of prophecy', 69 per cent of church members worldwide agreed strongly; whereas in the TED the proportion was 62 per cent. It is not a huge difference, but was outside the margin of error and was the third-lowest result in any of the thirteen world divisions. On the other hand, when asked to whether they accepted 'that Ellen White was a prophet', 75 per cent answered that they 'embraced it wholeheartedly', a fraction higher than the global average of 72 per cent. Thus, the division's efforts to provide members with a nuanced but faithful understanding of Ellen White and her ministry may have borne some fruit.

Christ Our Righteousness

Another area of controversy in the mid-to-late eighties and early nineties was soteriology – the doctrine of salvation. Without wishing to open old wounds that are now mostly healed, it is important, in a history of the TED, both to acknowledge this extended episode and to recognise the division's role in bringing accord and in helping

---

18   Pierre Winandy, 'After 100 Years, Europe Still Finds Ellen White Relevant', *ARH*, 165.12 (24 Mar. 1988), 17–18 (p. 17); TEDEC meeting, 19 Feb. 1986, and TED Quinquennial Council, 8 May 1986, TDC-EC 1986, §§ 112, 120, 294, pp. 32, 34, 92; see also Pierre Winandy, et al., *Centennial Symposium: Ellen G. White and Europe, 1885/1887–1987* (Bracknell, Berks., UK: Ellen G. White Research Centre, Europe, 1987).

Adventists in its territory to navigate successfully between the Scylla of legalism and literalism and the Charybdis of liberal theology.

Adventist disagreements about how exactly righteousness by faith operates to save men and women underlaid some of the serious theological divides of the late seventies and early eighties, but was masked to some extent by disagreements about the ministry of Ellen G. White and interpretation of biblical prophecy. The differences of opinion had not gone away, however, and controversy emerged into the open in several regions of the TED, especially England, where there was considerable sympathy for Desmond Ford and support for some, at least, of his positions.[19] Adherents of his views started discussion groups modelled on the Adventist Forums that had a longer history in the United States and Australia, invited him to speak, ensured that audiocassettes of his lectures circulated reasonably widely, and founded journals to explore Adventist doctrines and practice. One of the latter was to function for thirty years, operated by a group of laity in the South England Conference; another, shorter lived, but with perhaps greater intellectual influence, was edited by students at Newbold. The subjects examined in these journals went beyond Ford's particular preoccupations; articles could range widely in topics and could be stimulating, but there was a particular focus on issues challenged by Ford. There was also, perhaps, a sense that anything could be questioned.[20]

All this prompted a reaction from their polar opposites: men (and they were mostly men) who had often served in leadership positions in the NED and who felt that what they saw as the traditional Adventist position was being undermined. Some of them styled

---

19 W. J. Arthur, 'Profile of the Present-Day Church: 1981–1992', in *Seventh-day Adventists in the British Isles*, ed. by Marshall, p. 36.

20 Respectively *Opinion* and *Newbold Forum*: Vol. 1 of *Opinion* appeared in 1987; it apparently moved to web publication in the mid-2010s but may have ceased publication in 2016: see www.opinionsda.info/. Vol. 1, no. 1 of *Newbold Forum* was dated Oct.–Nov. 1987; the last issue was vol. 2, no. 4, Winter 1989.

themselves as 'concerned brethren', adopting (ironically) terminology from Australia used by those who opposed Ford's influence there. The pronouncements of the concerned brethren and their ilk in the TED were often not pastoral but polemical; they were perhaps most articulately expressed by men who, like Ford, were from outside the TED (though in one case working there under the aegis of the division), but they found support in the BUC and parts of Scandinavia, while drawing financial support from independent ministries in the United States. While their spokesmen drew on precedents in early twentieth-century Adventist history, their views seemed to many other British and Scandinavian church members to be verging on legalism and perfectionism. These labels were, unfortunately, applied pejoratively to their 'concerned' fellow believers, who indignantly rejected them and, in their turn, hurled accusations of dishonesty, heterodoxy, even heresy, at their opponents.[21]

Yet those they branded heretics were often not Ford adherents and in many cases their goal was to ensure a proper emphasis on the imbued and imparted Righteousness of Christ – itself a venerable Adventist position. On the whole, more heat than light was generated, as both sides talked past each other, misunderstanding the actual grounds of disagreement, and at times exaggerating them – the result of heated rhetoric, of which all parties were guilty. But the bitterest rhetoric came from those concerned to defend historic Adventist doctrinal positions.[22] As a result, 'Church members, ministers and

---

21 Russell R. Standish and Colin D. Standish, *Adventism Challenged*, 2 vols. (Rapidan, Va.: Hartland Institute, n.d. [c.1985]) and Colin D. Standish and Russell R. Standish, *Deceptions of the New Theology* (N.p.: Hartland Publications, 1989) are representative of their body of writings. Russell Standish directed Enton Hall clinic in the UK in the mid-1980s and was BUC Health and Temperance director: NEDCOM meeting, 9 Nov. 1983, NEDCOM mins., 1983, § 492, pp. 129–30. For perspectives, see Arthur, 'Profile of the Church 1981–1992', pp. 35–36; William G. Johnsson, 'Britain – the Church Changes', *ARH*, 13 July 1989), 13–15 (p. 15).

22 Cf. Arthur, 'Profile of the Church 1981–1992', p. 36; D. W. McFarlane, 'The Past and the Future', in *Seventh-day Adventists in the British Isles*, ed. by Marshall, p. 45.

administrators were obliged to expend time and energy resolving internal disputes to the detriment of evangelistic outreach.'[23]

In this atmosphere of controversy, successive division administrations unsurprisingly tried to hold the centre ground, but they also tried to shepherd church members in the division away from those positions that verged on perfectionism and legalism. In the eighties, two division presidents, Walter Scragg and Jan Paulsen, played an important part in preventing Adventist theology in the TED from veering towards one end of the Adventist theological spectrum or the other, and instead in keeping it in the middle of the Adventist road. For example, at his last Winter Council as NED president, Scragg gave the opening devotional on the Sermon on the Mount and pointedly declared: 'The emphasis in the Beatitudes is on God's action, not man's condition. When the total picture is seen it is the scene of salvation. It is God's response to man's situation.'[24]

Under Paulsen's presidency, the theme for devotional speakers at the Quinquennial Council in 1986 was 'peace', a pointed gesture. Nor were presentations only implicit. On the second day, David Marshall, addressing 'shalom', observed: '"Peace" is on many peoples' lips but not in many peoples' plans.' He averred: 'There are two kinds of lives being lived in our congregations. One is built on the spiritual life that is in the control of Christ. The other is lived in bitterness', before observing: 'The term "peacemaker" is sometimes misunderstood. Some feel they should be "all things to all men" [...]. The greatest threat to the church is the factions that live within it.' The implicit message was against the bitterness of the ultra-conservatives and that those maintaining the middle ground were not obliged to compromise.[25]

At the 1988 Winter Meetings, Paulsen adopted Righteousness by Faith as the theme for all the devotionals. On the first morning,

---

23 Ibid.
24 NED Winter Meetings, 21 Nov. 1983, NEDCOM Mins., 1983, p. 132.
25 TED Quinquennial Council, 6 May 1986, TDC-EC 1986, p. 73.

the Newbold-based historian of Adventism, Dr Andrew Mustard, spoke on 'Righteousness by Faith in the Early History of the Church'. According to the minutes:

> *He concluded by suggesting that for the gospel to be accepted among Seventh-day Adventists today, the image of the church as a caring community must shine through so that there is no contradiction between the love of the church which hears the message and the gospel of love itself.*[26]

The next morning, Mustard's Newbold colleague, the Dutch theologian Peter van Bemmelen, 'gave a biblical study of Righteousness by Faith' in the Old Testament and the Pauline epistles. In his conclusion, Van Bemmelen emphasised: 'No one should put any trust in human works or merits […] but only and exclusively in the merits of Jesus Christ.'[27]

Subsequently, Ron Surridge, president of the North British Conference and a former missionary in the WAUM, 'covered the subject of "The Impact of Righteousness by Faith on the Adventist Life-style".' In contrast to those Adventists who put as much weight on Christ's example in 'overcoming' sin as on His sacrifice, Surridge stressed:

> *Righteousness by Faith is not a mere formula which describes the method of salvation and determines the Christian life-style. It is the actual participation in the death and resurrection of our Lord by faith. […] The purpose of the Holy Spirit is to reveal all that Christ is and all that He has done (John 16:13, 14) on behalf of*

---

26 TEDEC Winter Meetings, 15 Nov. 1988, TDC-EX 1988, p. 145.
27 Ibid., 16 Nov. 1988, p. 156.

me the sinner. My response to that revelation is to take up my cross.[28]

Thanks in no small part to the efforts of, and the example set by, the division officers, any trend towards legalism was arrested. Adventists continue to debate the fine points of righteousness by faith and the wider issues of soteriology, but these are far less divisive today than they were, or threatened to become, thirty and forty years ago.

The Decline of Public Evangelism

Meanwhile, the heavily archaeological approach to public evangelism that had been introduced to the NED by John F. Coltheart in the second half of the sixties became less and less successful in the seventies. Coltheart's fellow Australian, Russell Kranz, continued to employ it but with ever decreasing impact, (for example, at the New Gallery in London, the average number of baptisms per year dropped from 39 to 3). Dr Jens Henriksen, a Danish health and wellness expert based at Skodsborg Sanitarium, tried to integrate archaeology and health but without conspicuous success.[29]

Church leaders were divided about missional methodologies. Many were reluctant to accept that the church's trusty, tried-and-true methods for evangelising were no longer very effective in Northern Europe and the British Isles. In the seventies it was masked by the growth rates in the unions of the West Africa Section, which may well have allowed church leaders at NEWAD and probably elsewhere to avoid unpleasant truths about the Northern Europe Section by pointing to increasing numbers of members in the division as a whole.

---

28 Ibid., 17 Nov. 1988, p. 201.
29 Russell Kranz, 'Analysis of the New Gallery Evangelistic Centre', n.d. [1976]; anon. [Kranz?]; 'New Gallery: General Background Information', n.d. [1976 or 1977]; and evangelistic handbills, c.1977: all in CAR, Roy Allan Anderson Papers (Collection no. 152), box 44, fld. 3. Henriksen was briefly NEWAD departmental secretary for the Medical and Temperance departments: *YB 1971*, pp. 15, 199.

At the same time, it led the division to pour more resources into its remaining African mission fields, where impressive results could be obtained, but at the expense of investing in what had always been 'tough territory' (the term of a distinguished Adventist historian) but which became, in the period covered by this chapter, utterly unreceptive.[30]

Growth almost stalled during the 1980s. Traditional evangelism could claim some success among immigrant communities,[31] yet this did not significantly affect overall church growth. To show each year's total membership on a graph for the period 1976–1991 would be meaningless because of the transfer of unions out of NEWAD and into NED/TED in 1980 and 1985; the membership increased from 43,700 in 1985 to 63,825 in 1986 but this was the result of the accretion of territories from EAD and Southern Asia. If one looks not at

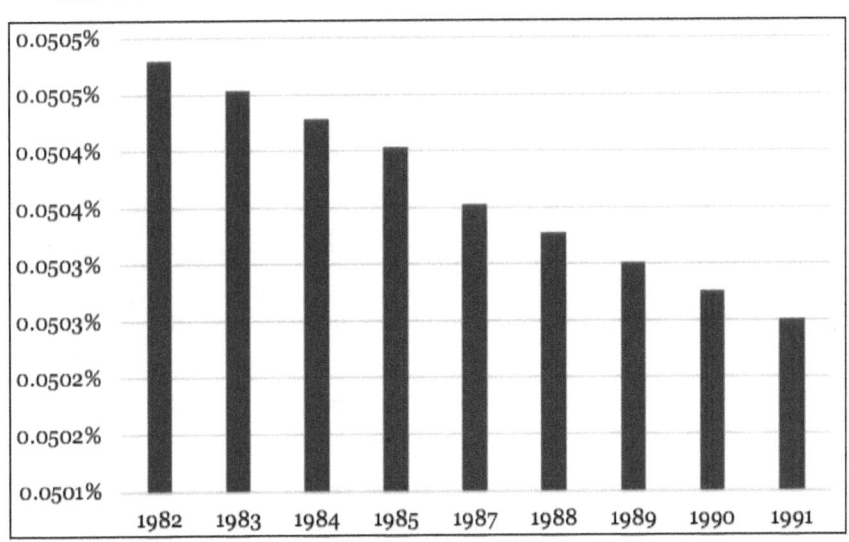

Figure 7: Growth Rate, NED-TED, 1982–1991

---

30 Harry Leonard, 'Evangelising in Tough Territory', in *Story of Seventh-day Adventists*, ed. by Marshall, p. 2.
31 Cf. Don McFarlane, 'Evangelism in the British Union During the Last 25 Years', *Messenger*, Souvenir Special, *100 Years of Mission 1906–2006*, ed. by D. N. Marshall (2006), p. 22.

total membership but at percentage growth rate, a graph only shows the trend over the decade if the vertical axis is shown in increments of one one-hundredth of one per cent – a typical graph would show a straight line, given the fractional variations. Still, not only was growth minuscule, but the trend was still downwards.

The GC continued to subsidise the NED's flagship, the New Gallery and its associated evangelistic campaigns, throughout the seventies, on top of NEWAD appropriations to the BUC and other unions for evangelism; but maintaining a major centre 'in the heart of London's West End' was very expensive.[32] By the mid-eighties, with church growth stalled, church administrators at the BUC and the NED saw the New Gallery as a burden and they were determined to sell or lease it. The GC, which had invested so much over thirty years, accepted the view of local leaders.[33] There was both internal opposition to overcome and then a buyer to be found, but finally, in 1990, the New Gallery Centre was sold for £3 million. This was rather more than the outlay of £167,395 to create the centre in 1953, but that would have been worth roughly £2,056,000 in 1990 and, as £500,000 was spent in 1990 to buy a London property for the Country Life vegetarian restaurant, the profit was not as great as it appeared.[34]

Regardless of issues of financial profit and loss, the forfeiture of a base in the centre of London was a retrograde step. To purchase an equivalent property in a similar location now would be much more expensive than £3 million, even adjusted for inflation. The sale of the New Gallery, at a time of lack of collective self-confidence, prevented the next generation using it as a base for 'Mission to the Cities'. The failure of public evangelism, certainly among the majority population,

---

32 E.g., NED Winter Meetings, NNESC, 25 Nov. 1977, NWDM-ESC, pp. 39, 42; 'New Gallery: General Background Information', p. 1.
33 GC Officers' Meeting, 15 Sept. 1981, GCOM, p. 81-74.
34 TEDEC meeting, 31 Oct. 1990, TDC-EC, 1990, § 267, p. 132. For conversion of 1953 sterling values to 1990: <https://www.measuringworth.com/calculators/ukcompare/relativevalue.php>.

had resulted in discouragement and perhaps a mindset that could not see the New Gallery's potential for rather different kinds of witnessing, based on being part of the community; that *had* been part of the original vision for the centre, but it had been lost sight of in the heady days of the late fifties and late sixties.[35] Twenty years later, there was no memory of a gradualist, genuinely community-based approach to outreach. And so, seeing evangelism as public campaigns or nothing, the New Gallery was sold and its enormous potential forfeited. As church leaders at the TED and in Britain endeavour to meet the world church's steadfast call to prioritise the big cities and to establish 'centres of influence' in the heart of big cities, the lack of vision of their predecessors in Britain thirty to forty years can only be regretted.

The question of methodologies was to be an ongoing matter of debate and heartache; although the accomplishments of the 1950s would be nostalgically cited by some church members and church leaders into the early twenty-first century, public evangelism was never again to have anything like that kind of impact on the majority of people in the nations of the Trans-European Division.

Ethnic Diversity

The NEWAD years witnessed considerable divisions in the ranks of British Adventism. Race was the fault line. While largely restricted to Britain (indeed to England) in this period, racial and ethnic tensions were brewing both in the Netherlands Union (discussed in Chapter 9) and, though along rather different lines, in Yugoslavia. Events in the BUC therefore had a significance beyond the shores of Great Britain.

As we saw in Chapter 6, racial tensions arising from large-scale immigration into Britain, largely from Britain's former and current

---

35   See above, Chapter 6.

colonies in the Caribbean, had been gradually building in the fifties and sixties. In the seventies, however, things came to a head. The politics of race was at the time, and remained for many years after, a highly sensitive issue, which still has not received proper historical study.[36] Polemic was more common than analysis, and even scholarly enquiries, by black and white alike, tended to be partisan: they are tendentious at worst, lacking in empathy at best.[37] Because the details are a matter of *British* Adventist history they will not concern us here, but like the 'contention [that] was so sharp between' Paul and Barnabas (Acts 15:39), the division between white British Adventists and their black West Indian brethren was so sharp that it had wider ramifications, ultimately involving first division and then world-church leaders.

What happened in the BUC was of wider concern for several reasons, some personal, others structural and missiological. First, many American Adventists had British ancestors and were well aware that the roots of Seventh-day Adventism lay with the Puritans, Baptists, and Methodists, all of which arose in England. There was therefore

  36 Studies have mostly been from the disciplinary perspectives of Missiology, Religious Studies, Sociology, and Critical Race Studies, and have been based to a great extent on personal reminiscences. There is some primary-source research in Herbert Griffiths, 'The Impact of African Caribbean Settlers on the Seventh-day Adventist Church in Britain 1952–2001' (PhD thesis, University of Leeds, 2003) and Porter, *Century of Adventism*, Chapter 13. The only history based on research in church archives is Anthea N. Davis, 'West Indian immigrants and administrative politics in the Seventh-day Adventist Church in Britain c.1950–1980' (MA dissertation, University of London, 2003).
  37 These points are illustrated in, e.g., Griffiths, 'Impact of African Caribbean Settlers', pp. 165–66, 183–84 (which also includes significant errors of fact), 200–02; and Porter, *Century of Adventism*, pp. 40–44. To be fair to Porter, his analysis includes 'many acute historical and sociological insights' but it is undermined by his lack of empathy for his subjects (e.g., the title of his Chapter 13 is 'The West Indies' – not West Indians, in effect disembodying them) and his negative tone about them, though these are points of which the author himself was apparently unaware: see Robin Theobald, 'The Politicisation of a Religious Movement: British Adventism under the Impact of West Indian Migration', *British Journal of Sociology*, 32 (1981), 207–08.

a strong sense of spiritual as well as literal kinship, which led white American church leaders to be personally interested in developments in British Adventism. Second, Black church leaders in the United States and the Caribbean often had relatives in the UK, which meant they were well aware of developments there, and which they tended to see through the lens of the African American struggle for equality in the Adventist Church. They, too, thus had a strong personal interest in race relations in the BUC.[38] Third, Britain had been the largest single source of missionaries in Northern Europe before NED was founded and the British church was important for NEWAD's African mission fields (and potentially for other divisions' mission fields). Fourth, it was also vital for Adventist work in Europe. During the first half of the seventies, the BUC was the fourth-largest union in the three European divisions, the largest of any of NEWAD's European unions, and had around a third more members than the West Nordic Union Conference, the second largest in Europe. In terms of tithe returned, it was second in NEWAD behind the WNUC, but these two were far ahead of any others in the division and the BUC's tithe was a quarter of NEWAD's total.[39] Furthermore, as NEWAD and world-church leaders became increasingly aware, church growth in Britain was largely due to high accessions from among the African-Caribbean migrant communities.[40]

The discontent of black British Adventists was warranted. Many native British pastors and local church members had, to be sure, been welcoming to West Indian immigrants.[41] Others were ambivalent at

---

38 Griffiths, 'Impact of African Caribbean Settlers', p. 189.
39 *ASR*, 108 (1970), 10, 14, 20, and *ASR*, 113 (1975), 12, 16.
40 See, e.g., R. S. Watts to J. A. McMillan, 8 Oct. 1962, RGL, BUC Papers, box 1962, fld. 'General Conference – Secretarial [sic]'; M. L. Anthony, 'A Survey of Church Growth Among Seventh-day Adventists in the United Kingdom and Eire During the Period 1940–1980', unpublished MS (Report for the British Union Executive Committee, 1980), RGL, pp. 15–17, 32–33.
41 E.g., Keith Davidson, 'The British Experience in Britain: *Windrush* 2000', in *A Century of Adventism*, ed. by Marshall, p. 23; Davis, 'West Indian Immigrants and Administrative Politics', pp. 21–22; Griffiths, 'Impact of

best, while many were (or became) openly antagonistic. African-Caribbean church members repeatedly experienced incidents of prejudice, ranging from thoughtlessness to deliberate discrimination.[42] There was also a good deal of mutual miscomprehension which gave rise to statements and actions, by church members of all ethnic groups, that were wounding to those of a different ethnicity. With hindsight, it seems clear that not enough was done by leaders, whether ordained or lay, regardless of race, to break down misunderstandings, at least up to the late seventies.

In the end, after agitation for creating 'regional' (i.e., racial) conferences in England, the division and GC were brought in. The end result was what soon became known as the 'Pierson Package', because the concord was brokered by GC President Robert Pierson. In essence, it was agreed to bring ten experienced and talented, 'top-drawer' pastors from the Caribbean, two of whom, it was expected, would very swiftly be placed at the South England Conference headquarters (one as officer) with another to be elected to departmental leadership in the North British Conference.[43]

The NEWAD officers involved themselves carefully and cautiously in the situation in the British Isles (or more accurately in England), partly because the BUC had its own constituency and division interference could well be resented. With hindsight it could perhaps be argued that NEWAD should have intervened sooner and more forcefully. Yet in the end the BUC avoided the potential fragmentation of racial conferences and helped the church in England move towards a New Testament model in which there is no Jew nor Greek, no white

---

African Caribbean Settlers', p. 162.
42   Many examples could be adduced, but the fact is conceded by scholars of different ethnic groups. See Dennis S. Porter, 'Crisis in the British Union', *Spectrum*, 11.4 (1981), 2; Griffiths, 'Impact of African Caribbean Settlers', pp. 162–64.
43   Griffiths, 'Impact of African Caribbean Settlers', pp. 193–94; Orville Woolford, 'The 70s Struggle: A Black Perspective', in *Seventh-day Adventists in the British Isles 1902–1992*, ed. by Marshall, pp. 34–35; Davidson, 'Black Experience', p. 24.

nor black, for all are one in Christ Jesus (Gal. 3:28). And the division helped to mould this conclusion, which was its preferred outcome.[44]

A decisive meeting was held at the New Gallery on 8 March 1978, attended by Pierson, two GC vice-presidents, Duncan Eva and G. Ralph Thompson (a Barbadian and later GC secretary), the GC Undertreasurer M. E. Kemmerer (crucial, as it turned out), the three officers of NEWAD, and the three officers of the BUC, as well as representatives from black-majority churches in England. A close reading of the proceedings – both the transcribed words and between the lines – reveals that Scragg carefully led the discussions in desired directions without closing down discussion, which was probably indispensable to the successful resolution.[45] Pierson's willingness to involve himself and the General Conference so closely in the controversy has puzzled previous writers and been attributed in the past to various church-political factors. But this overlooks the context that we have seen in Chapters 7 and 8: Pierson's deep concern since the late sixties, to empower the African church, and his push not once, but twice, for global restructuring of church organisation to allow black African leadership to emerge and flourish.

At the New Gallery, Eva played a critical role, as a well-respected former president of NED/NEWAD, and as a white South African. He gave a powerful speech, with a remarkable beginning:

---

44 Cf. Walter R. L. Scragg, 'Consultative Group in Britain Opts for Integration', *Northern Light*, 28.5 (May 1978), 7.
45 The proceedings are in an untitled document, rubric: '10:00 a.m., 8th March, 1978 – New Gallery', GC Ar., RG NW 25.

> *Perhaps I stand in a position where I can speak about the colour question. I was born in a country which is the worst in the world [...]. I was born in a situation where I just accepted what I found in life. It took me quite a while to realise there was something wrong about that. [...] I had to make a decision as to what Christianity is and what it teaches. [...] What does the Gospel of Jesus Christ require us to do at a time like this? What is God's ideal? Must the church in Britain settle for less than the ideal?*[46]

Eva set out an anti-racist foundation for the argument against racial conferences.[47]

The dialogue gave the many African-Caribbean representatives a chance to share their hurt and their pain; white church officials shared their frustrations. Scragg and Pierson, supported by Eva and Thompson, then skilfully guided all present towards reconciliation. Of course, without the willingness of Pierson to underwrite the solution – to put, as it were, the GC's money where his mouth was – all might have come to naught. But had the money been offered without the prolonged discussions, and without the shape that was subtly put on the discussions, the financial inducements might have achieved nothing. When, at the end, a black representative exclaimed 'Probably we have found a Moses' (i.e., in Pierson), it was a recognition not just of the money the GC brought to the table, but of high-calibre leadership (Illustration 8.2).[48]

The Pierson Package was not a solution to ethnic disharmony – but it laid the foundations for the eventual resolution of racial tensions in the nineties. The pastors brought from the Caribbean were crucial in helping the division leadership to ensure the plan for accord was implemented fully, that wounds were healed, and that the church

---

46 Ibid., pp. 17–18.
47 Ibid., pp. 18–19.
48 Ibid., p. 27, cf. p. 13.

began to reach for unity in diversity. Silburn M. Reid became the first black conference president in the European territories of the NED when elected by the South England Conference in 1981; it set an important precedent, and thereafter the church in the British Isles moved steadily towards a fully integrated leadership; but as well as achieving a racial first, Reid also 'did much to heal any remaining rift[s]'.[49] Cecil Perry followed Reid as South England Conference president, while Don McFarlane became the first black union officer in the TED, when elected secretary of the BUC. Orville Woolford became the first black departmental director at the division in 1985; he eventually served four terms, until 2005 (Illustration 8.3).[50]

Perry's election as BUC president in 1991 was an important milestone (Illustration 8.4). Perry served a decade and a half as a widely loved union president and helped to build a new, largely harmonious and integrated British church.

* * *

---

49 [David Marshall], 'Top Stories of the Century', in *A Century of Adventism*, ed. idem, p. 2; McFarlane, 'Past and Future', p. 43.
50 See vote of thanks, TED ADCOM, 3 Aug. 2005, TEDMC-AC 2005, § 166, p. 74; and the appreciation by David Marshall, 'Orville Woolford: Headmaster, Motivator, Church Leader', in *A Century of Adventism*, ed. idem, p. 31.

It is possible that all the challenges addressed in this chapter, including the limited growth and difficulties winning new converts, as well as the internal divisions, had a common solution, whether in whole or in part. It is to be found in Andrew Mustard's words to the TED Executive Committee in 1988. They are worth coming back to, as we reflect on the challenges of a generation ago, and those that still face the Adventist Church in the territory of the Trans-European Division today.

> *The image of the church as a caring community must shine through so that there is no contradiction between the love of the church which hears the message and the gospel of love itself.*

Chapter 9
Organising for Mission: 1991–2015

The quarter-century covered in this chapter was one of considerable volatility for the Trans-European Division. After the Iron Curtain was rung down, new opportunities arose for mission in Eastern Europe, but new challenges also resulted from the political fallout of the end of the Cold War. In the mid-nineties it was a case of 'back to the future', as suddenly the TED acquired mission fields in Africa again, as well as expanding its footprint in Western Asia. In the southernmost part of the division, in the Upper Nile region of Africa, growth was dramatic; in Pakistan and the Middle East, deceptive; and in the division's European territories, declining. Indeed, in this era many countries of the TED experienced persistent 'negative growth'. Yet, in the face of the most irreligious society that has perhaps ever existed, some local church leaders, encouraged by their division counterparts, started to innovate. The passion for mission that characterised the TED in its NED and NEWAD guises led down some interesting bypaths during the 1990s and the 2000s. There is reason to fear that many church members are no longer as passionate about mission as they once were, and that it is no longer quite the administrative priority it once was. In the TED's tenth decade, the zeal its founders had for reaching the division's millions of people with the Adventist message needs to be nursed and nurtured.

Realigning Within the Division

At the end of 1991, the TED comprised nine unions and a total of twenty-eight conferences and missions (with the geographical configuration the same as shown in Map 8.2).[1] Probably no one foresaw that two of the three most significant unions in terms of church structure would soon be broken up. The West Nordic Union Conference

---

1   See Appendix I, Table A.8.

had five conferences (three in Norway, two in Denmark) and one mission (Greenland), while the Yugoslavian Union Conference had four conferences (North, South, Southwest, and West). The WNUC had the most organisational units, at six, of any of the TED's eight unions, and between them the WNUC had the third-largest membership. The Yugoslavian Union had the third-largest number of component units (the BUC was second, with two conferences and three missions), but the second-highest number of conferences (after the WNUC), and the second-largest membership (after the BUC). Although there were quite different causes, the clock was ticking for these two large unions that lay on the west coasts of the Scandinavian and Balkan peninsulas.[2] While two large unions were both to break up, each into two smaller unions, one of the NED'S original unions, long lost due to World War II and the Cold War, was to be reunited with what was now called the TED.

Western Scandinavia Divided

In the WNUC, a cluster of health and wellness institutions (broadly defined) developed around Skodsborg Sanitarium, including health-food industries in both Denmark and Norway. In the late 1980s, a combination of overexpansion, poor marketing, unwise management decisions, and imprudent borrowing, resulted in the loss, to the denomination, of most WNUC institutions. This painful episode is considered in Chapter 10, which focuses on institutions in the TED, but it had significant consequences in terms of church structure, which are addressed here. As it became clear that historic and important institutions would close or be sold, and the West Nordic Union took on considerable debt of its own, the TED and GC appointed a commission of enquiry, which reported in January 1992. It recommended not only a series of reforms in the union's management of financial matters and the consolidation of some of the WNUC's conferences as a cost-saving measure, but also that a

---

2   Data from *ASR*, 129 (1991), 25, and *YB 1992*, pp. 325–38.

joint Danish-Norwegian committee 'be appointed to look at the long term reconstruction situation in terms of [...] the identity crisis' among Danish church members, who faced 'the loss of both their major institutions'.[3]

The deliberations that followed were (understandably) complicated by recriminations about the loss of multiple institutions and evident failings in church governance. Relations between church leaders from Denmark and Norway were increasingly marked by mutual mistrust and, by April, it had become necessary for the TED officers to mediate. The upshot, after four months of negotiations, was the merger of both Danish conferences and the Greenland mission and, more dramatically, the end of the WNUC. The Annual Council of 1992 approved the TED Executive Committee's proposal to partition the West Nordic Union Conference and create the Danish Union of Churches and the Norwegian Union Conference (which preserved its three conferences). Whether this was the optimal organisational model for the territories in question, with a total of not even ten thousand church members between them, was an open question. The circumstances from which it emerged had been far from conducive to reflective, strategic decision making. But, by the summer of 1992, the fault lines between Danish and Norwegian church leaders were such that institutionalising their differences seemed the best solution.[4]

After sixty-four years of the TED's history, the fissuring of the Scandinavian Union – the first union conference in the TED's territory and one of the division's founding unions – along national lines was finally finished. One union had become four. The original 1931 split into East and West Nordic unions had been motivated by factors relating to ease or expense of travel and to political divisions.

3   Report to TEDEC meeting, 27 Jan. 1992, and included in the mins., TEDMC-EC 1992, § 18, pp. 11–16 (p. 16).
4   TEDEC meetings, 15 Apr. and 2 Sept. 1992, TEDMC-EC 1992, §§ 59, 2019, pp. 39, 117; Annual Council, 7 Oct. 1992, GCC mins., p. 92-129; Edwin Torkelson, 'Norway', in *HRSDAE*, pp. 166; *YB 1993*, pp. 312, 315-16.

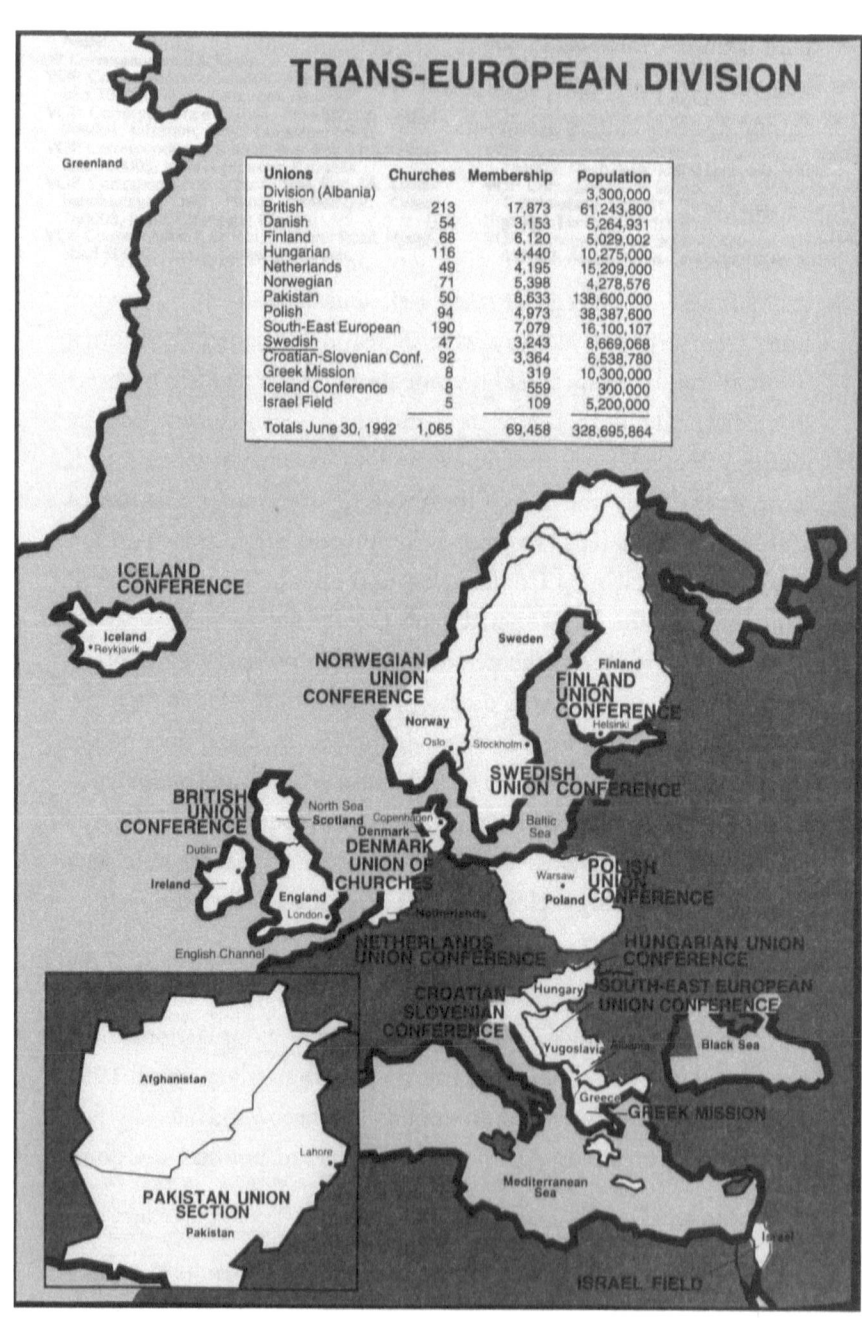

Map 9.1: The TED in 1993

These were largely irrelevant by 1990. It would have been feasible to reinstate the ScUC, resulting in a union with larger membership and more robust finances. Instead there was further fragmentation with the end of the WNUC. A case could be made that it was a good outcome, by allowing for local leadership and quicker responses to local situations. But that was not the rationale for the final split in 1992.

Map 9.1 shows the TED as it was at the end of 1992. It shows the new configuration in Denmark and Norway, resulting from the winding up of West Nordic Union. But it also shows a new configuration in south-eastern Europe, the result of restructuring that was carried out rapidly, probably unavoidably, as a result of the first war in Europe since 1945.

War and Restructuring in the Balkans

In Eastern Europe, the Yugoslavian Union became the second major union to fragment in the 1990s, though for rather different reasons – collateral damage in what one historian calls 'one of the greatest [...] tragedies of recent times'.[5] As we have already seen, war and political turmoil could have consequences for church organisation as well for individual church members. World War II reshaped the Netherlands Union's place in European Adventist church structure; European decolonisation in Africa had a major impact on the organisation of the world divisions based in Europe; and the wars between India, Pakistan, and Bangladesh impelled the Pakistan Union out of one division and towards the TED. The wars in former Yugoslavia resulted in changes to church structure within the Balkans and thus to the way the TED was organised.

Hostilities began in 1991, after Croatia and Slovenia both declared independence from Yugoslavia. In Slovenia, fighting was restricted to the summer of 1991. In the case of Croatia, however, the hostilities

---

5   Alastair Finlan, *The Collapse of Yugoslavia 1991–1999* (Oxford: Osprey, 2004), 7.

that began in the autumn of 1991 were not concluded until Croatian victories in the summer of 1995. Bosnia and Herzegovina declared independence in the spring of 1992, which gave rise to a conflict that continued until the late autumn of 1995.

None of the four conferences of the Yugoslavian Union Conference bore the names of the Yugoslav constituent republics, but all four were in fact defined by ethnic and quasi-national identities. The North Yugoslavian Conference was coextensive with Vojvodina, an autonomous province of Serbia (to the north of Serbia proper). The South Yugoslavian Conference was made up of Macedonia and the rest of Serbia. The Southwest Yugoslavian Conference embraced Bosnia, Herzegovina, and Montenegro. Finally, the West Yugoslavian Conference comprised Croatia and Slovenia. None of the conference boundaries crossed the borders of Yugoslavia's constituent republics, which meant church structure was inevitably affected by the breakup of the country. This was the case even though the Yugoslavian Union as a whole was quite integrated: the union had made strong statements against ethnic divisions; the boarding school and seminary at Maruševec attracted students from all four conferences, though it was in Croatia; and no one ethnic group dominated church leadership positions.[6] Nonetheless, war swiftly took a toll on Adventist identity. Conference leaders fell out with the union leadership and with each other. By the summer of 1992, students from three of the four conferences could no longer attend Maruševec Adventist Seminary. Moreover, as Branislav Mirilov's study shows, many church members quickly identified with their new countries and regarded other conferences of the old Yugoslavian Union through the lens of national conflict. If especially true of Croatian and Serbian church members, this identification with nation also affected Slovenian and Macedonian

---

6   Branislav Mirilov, 'An Examination of the Response of the Seventh-day Adventist Church to some Contemporary Socio-Political Issues in the Light of Two Distinctive Adventist Doctrines: A Comparison of North America and Former Yugoslavia' (PhD thesis, University of Birmingham, 1994), pp. 236–37, 254–56, 259–60.

Adventists to some extent.[7]

In 1992, the TED officers were obliged to travel frequently to the Yugoslavian Union. In his introductory remarks at that year's Spring Meetings, President Paulsen 'commented briefly on the [...] many challenges facing the Division, both financial and political in the West Nordic Union [and] war-torn Yugoslavia'. The TED Executive Committee authorised ministerial training in Belgrade – the origins of today's separate Belgrade Seminary.[8] In May and June it changed 'the name of the former Yugoslavian Union Conference [...] to South-East European Union Conference' (SEEUC) and then that of the West Yugoslavian Conference to 'Croatian-Slovenian Conference', and attached it directly to the division until political considerations made it 'feasible to consider alternative permanent arrangements'. The following year, Macedonia (now known as North Macedonia), which had also declared independence from Yugoslavia, was removed from the South Conference. The war had not spread, but tensions were such that the TED officers felt obliged to attach the Macedonian Mission to the division. Furthermore, during and after the war it proved impossible for the SEEUC headquarters, in Serbia, to administer Adventist churches in Bosnia-Herzegovina. At the TED's request, the Croatian-Slovenian Conference took 'responsibility for the church in this territory', an arrangement that was continued in 1996 (after the Macedonian Mission returned to the SEEUC), and concluded only in 1997.[9]

All this meant that in early 1995 there were no fewer than six missions or conferences attached directly to the TED, while, following

---

7 Ibid., pp. 256–59, 263–64.
8 TEDEC meeting, 15 Apr. 1992 and TED Spring Meetings, 27 Apr. 1992, TEDMC-EC 1992, § 59, pp. 39, 50, and § 83, p. 51.
9 TEDEC meetings, 27 May and 17 June 1992, 14 July 1993, Spring Meeting, 6 May 1996, and Winter Meetings, 28 Nov. 1996, TED-MC-EC: 1992, §§ 146, 163, pp. 82, 96; 1993, §§ 153–54, p. 84; 1996, §§ 5, 159–60, 163, pp. 9, 209–10. Cf. *YB 1996*, p. 345 and *YB 1997*, p. 355.

the addition in 1994 of the Baltic Union (as described in the next section in this chapter) there were also eleven unions (the resulting structure is summarised in Table A.8, in Appendix I).

In the end, it took more than six years before the 'alternative permanent arrangements' hoped for in June 1992 finally were in place. In the spring of 1995, the Croatian-Slovenian Conference requested union conference status. The TED was sympathetic, but hostilities were then still continuing and the TED also had reservations about a number of practical issues.[10] In December 1997, with peace restored to the region, the Croatian-Slovenian Conference again asked to become a union. This time a survey commission gave strong support and Annual Council 1998 recommended to the TED Executive Committee that it create a new 'Adriatic Union Conference'. At its end-of-year meeting, the division Executive Committee formally established the new union, which had separate Croatian and Slovenian Conferences, and the Albanian Mission (previously attached to the division). The Adriatic Union Conference came into existence on 1 January 1999 and the following year's GC Session duly voted to accept it 'into the world sisterhood of unions of the Seventh-day Adventist Church'. Politically, Yugoslavia had been defunct since the autumn of 1995. The Yugoslavian Union was now buried as well.[11]

The organisational pattern put in place twenty years ago still obtains in the western Balkans, which are divided between two unions. The Adriatic Union continues to comprise Croatia, Slovenia, and Albania. The South-East European Union is still made up of Bosnia-Herzegovina, Montenegro, North Macedonia, and Serbia. The existence of these two small unions, both of which arguably lack

---

10 TEDEC meeting, 7 Mar. 1995, TEDMC-EC 1995, § 1, p. 1.
11 TED ADCOM meeting, 7 Jan. 1998, TEDMC-AC 1998, § 6, p. 4; 'Croatian-Slovenian Conference Survey Report', 1–14 Sept. 1998, GC Ar., RG 9, box 12119, fld. 'TED Conference Constitutions'; Annual Council, 30 Sept. 1998, GCC mins., p. 98-82; TED Winter Meeting, 18 Nov. 1998, TEDMC-EC 1998, § 84, pp. 125–27; Fifty-Seventh Session, first meeting, 29 June 2000, GC Session mins. (with GCC mins.), p. 00-1006.

critical mass, where once there was one stronger union, is an enduring legacy of the bitter conflict in the former Yugoslavia.

Territorial Expansion

As well as reorganisations of church structure within the existing bounds of the Trans-European Division, in the mid-nineties, territorial realignment in the wider world church led to the TED's expansion.

Baltic States Restored

The initial enlargement was also a reinstatement. Estonia, Latvia, and Lithuania had come under the recently formed Euro-Asia Division. They had, with Belarus, formed part of a new Baltic Union constituted in 1989, but the legacy of a half-century of occupation and oppression made it difficult for a church entity in the Baltic states to be associated with (and inferior to) an entity headquartered in Moscow. The situation was similar to that which obtained in Ethiopia, the Netherlands, and Pakistan. Recognising this reality, the GC set up a 'Baltic Union Study Commission', whose report was discussed and actioned by the 1993 Annual Council. It voted to separate Belarus from the three Baltic republics, to retain the former under the Euro-Asia Division, and to place the Baltic Union (then comprising two conferences, with Lithuania part of the Latvian Conference) 'under the administration of the Trans-European Division, effective January 1, 1994'.[12]

This was an important development, but not an innovative one. Rather, it was a return to the fold of a lost sheep that had not wandered, but, as it were, been stolen away. As we saw in Chapter 2, the Baltic Union had (like the ScUC) been part of the original NED in 1929, but Estonia, Latvia, and Lithuania had not been part of the division for decades – formally, not since 1946, and practically

---

12 Annual Council, 8 Oct. 1993, GCC Mins., pp. 93-111, 112.

not since the Soviet invasion and occupation of all three nations in 1940. January 1994 was a homecoming of the Baltic Union, after a half-century hiatus, to its original parent division and sister unions. Its restoration extended the division's footprint in Eastern Europe. Today, the Baltic Union Conference continues in the TED, with each country a conference: almost exactly as it was ninety years ago. Its total of thirty-six years of history in the TED is only a little longer than the thirty-three years of the Hungarian Union, Southeast European Union, and Greek Mission, but the Baltic Union can claim precedence as one of the original unions in the division.

Adding West Asia and North Africa

The Middle East Union Mission (MEUM) was a vast, sprawling field, large enough in square kilometres and population to be a division until 1970. Then, as we saw in Chapter 7, it was merged with Ethiopia and the EAUM to create the Afro-Mideast Division: in geographic terms, this was a solid block of countries, but in cultural terms it was utterly diverse, and in missional terms the idea, though well intentioned, was unsound. The new arrangements did little for mission in the Middle East, as opposed to the unions in East Africa, and from 1 January 1982, they formed a new Eastern Africa Division, while the MEUM was attached directly to the GC, as it had been in the late forties (see Chapter 5). At that time, there had been discussion of making it part of the NED, though nothing came of it. But it was an idea that was to be revisited nearly fifty years later. The absence of a supporting division meant there was lack of oversight and support, while the MEUM was isolated from the church in other unions and countries.

In February 1992, GC ADCOM appointed a Middle East Study Commission, which in April 1993 recommended that Libya, Turkey, and Iran be allocated to the EAD, but the rest of the MEUM be made part of the TED. In the winter of 1994, firm proposals were developed to go to Annual Council, which duly approved them. The next year the GC session voted the necessary amendment of the Bylaws, and endorsed dividing the Middle East region between the two European divisions. The Middle East Union (with fourteen countries remaining after three had been assigned to the EAD) became part

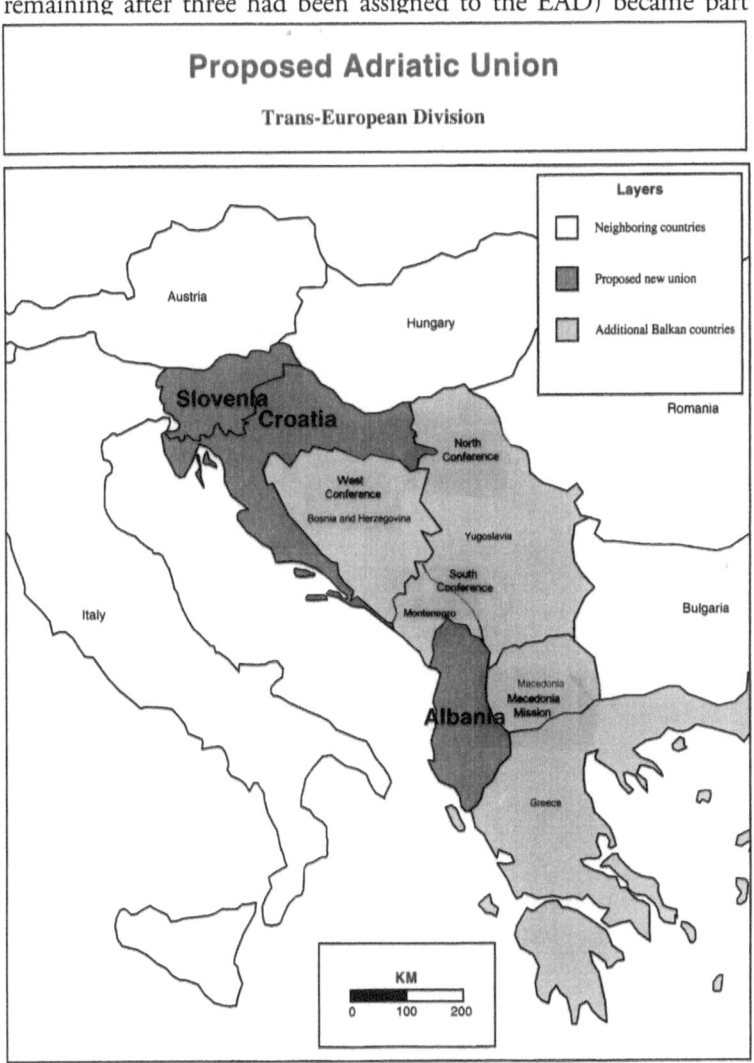

Map 9.2: The Creation of Two Unions in Former Yugoslavia, 1998

of the TED. The new configuration of the TED can be seen in Map 9.3, which shows the territories added to the division (and realigned within it) in 1994 and 1995. The designation 'Trans-European' had never truly taken account of Pakistan (though of course TED was more reflective of the division territory than NED) and, after it was made the parent of the MEUM, the division's title still hardly did justice to its territory. However, 'Northern and Southeast European, Northeast African, and West Asian Division' would have been a rather longer title than typically allowed. So 'Trans-European' the division remained. By 1999, then, with the creation of the Adriatic Union Conference as well as the acquisition of the Baltic Union Conference and MEUM, the unions in the Trans-European Division numbered thirteen, along with three attached fields.[13]

The Middle East was the responsibility of the TED until a new Greater Middle East Union Mission came into existence on 1 January 2012.[14] At the same time, as part of a wider reorganisation, the Pakistan Union Section was transferred to the Southern Asia-Pacific Division. Pakistan had been with the TED for twenty-six years, a quarter century, but the MEUM for just sixteen years, which now seems ephemeral. Only the EAUM and the Upper Nile Union Mission have had shorter periods as part of the division. As things turned out, however, the events of 1995 had lasting significance: in 2012, Cyprus (part of the MEUM) remained with the TED as a mission attached directly to the division. Thus, in 1995, all the countries encompassed by the TED as it marked it its ninetieth anniversary were part of the division for the first time. While with hindsight the

---

13 Middle East Union Study Commission, report (Apr. 1993), pp. 1, 5–6; GC–TED–MEUM Consultation, 28 Feb.–4 Mar. 1994, minutes in TEDArc., 'Middle East – Folder 1'; GCC Annual Council, 7 Oct. 7 1994, GCC mins., pp. 94-315, 316. Fifty-Sixth Session, first meeting, 29 June 1995: proceedings, *ARH*, 172.27 (2 July 1995), 754. See Appendix I, Table A.9.

14 It included the EAD's Trans-Mediterranean Territories as well as the old MEUM; its title was subsequently changed to the Middle East and North Africa Union.

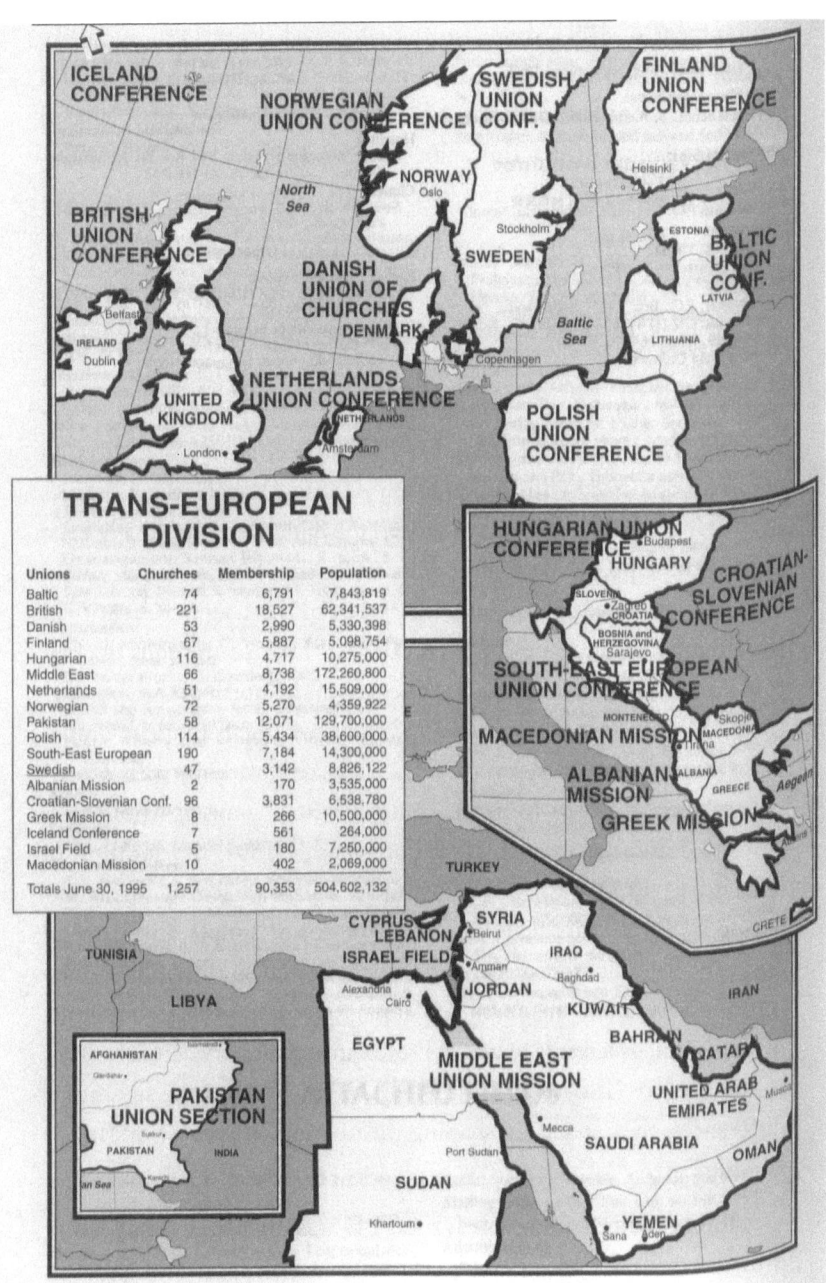

Map 9.3: The TED in 1996

realignment of 1995 seems to point forward, it can also seem like a case of back to the future. Fifteen years after making the painful separation from sub-Saharan Africa, the TED once again included African mission fields. Thus, the division during 1995–2011 harkened back to 1929–1942 and 1949–1980.

In another sense, too, there was a connection to an earlier period, because the MEUM's territory included the Sudan. Geographically, it is usually classed as North Africa, not sub-Saharan Africa; culturally the north of the country looks north and east to the rest of the Arabic world. It is part of the Middle East. In contrast, the south of the country (which in 2011 gained independence) always had more in common culturally with sub-Saharan Africa, especially the countries of the Upper Nile region – and indeed the Sudan had nominally been part of the Upper Nile Union Mission in the thirties (as we saw in Chapter 4), while subsequently it was part of the assigned territory of the Ethiopian Union until the end of the fifties. In the end, the first mission station in the Sudan was opened (in the north of the country) by the Middle East Division in 1953; however, the Ethiopian Union, with funding provided by the NED, started working with Christian refugees expelled from the south in 1964, some of whom later converted and returned to their homeland.[15] Thus, the addition of MEUM to TED was, for the southern Sudan, a return to the situation of forty years before. This point is not simply an historical curiosity. The differences between northern and southern Sudan are profound. Whereas the north is Islamic, the south was largely animist or Christian, as a result of active Protestant missionary activity earlier in the century. The leaders of the TED were aware of the significant differences: they ended up shaping the division's mission work in the Middle East.

During the period in which the TED was not solely European, it provided considerable resources, of time, people, and money, to its

---

15   NEDCOM meeting, 22 Jan. 1964, NEDCOM mins., 1964, p. 16.

mission territories in North Africa and West Asia. At least twenty-seven missionaries from TED served in Pakistan in the first half of that period alone. In its first year as part of the TED, Pakistan's appropriations were £414,347, though a decade later they had fallen to £346,752, whereas the MEUM received £505,703. Neither of these unions generated much tithe income of its own; each received several million pounds sterling in funding from the TED over the years they were part of the division.[16]

Mission Field Membership: Rise, Decline, and Fall

What was the effect of all the resources invested in the TED's two union missions? Context is everything in making such judgments and one must recognise how formidably difficult it was and is to proselytise in Pakistan, the north-eastern littoral of Africa, the Arabian Peninsula, and the Levant. Here Islam holds sway; the sociocultural penalties for conversion to Christianity are as draconian as those imposed by governments. Under the TED's stewardship, the church in Pakistan probably developed as well as could be expected; in contrast, in the Middle East there was a fatal flaw in the approach to church growth.

As Figure 8 illustrates, growth in Pakistan was, as it seemed, steady, but one has to look below the surface. The Pakistan Union was plagued by major inaccuracies in membership records. These probably pre-dated the transfer of Pakistan to the TED but given that membership rose, nominally, from 5428 at the end of 1985 to an alleged 12,852 at the end of 1995, a supposed growth of 137 per cent, plainly, faulty reporting must have been a feature during the union's first decade under the TED. Division administration became aware in 1996 that membership records were deeply flawed and that many

---

16 See *HRSDAE*, Appendix A; and, e.g., the division budgets voted in TEDEC Winter Meetings, 21 Nov. 1986 and 27 Nov. 1996, TED-MC-EC: 1986, § 805, pp. 306, 308, 311–12; 1996, § 138, pp. 183, 185–86.

231

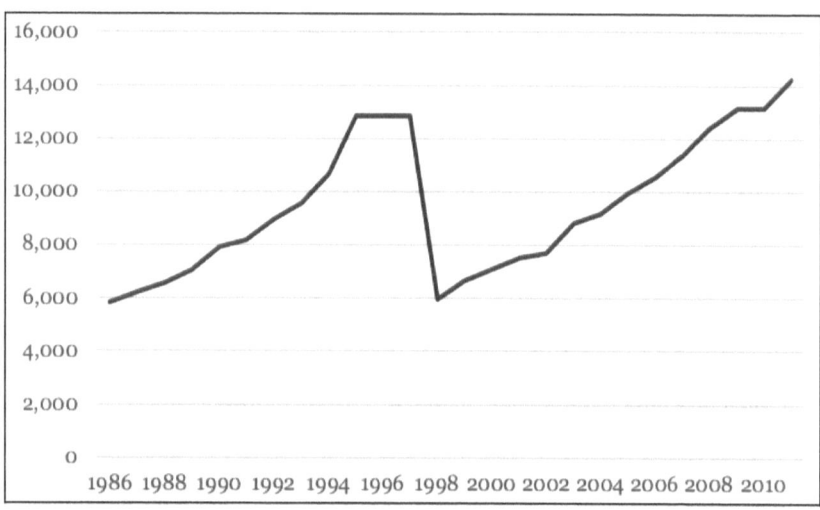

Figure 8: Pakistan Union Section Membership, 1986–2010

reported baptisms probably never took place. It is to the credit of the TED officers that they decided to freeze the official membership statistics until a thorough audit could be made across the country. This took time but, by the end of 1998, 8341 members were identified as missing, along with 421 previously unreported deaths. The result was that the year-end membership was 5968 – only 45 per cent of the 1995 figure.[17]

To audit Pakistan properly was a courageous decision with wider ramifications. It also prompted other audits, which identified another 4500 members as having left the church during the 1995–1998 period. As a result, even with baptisms taking place, total TED membership fell by 741 in 1997 – and by 6253 (7 per cent of the 1997 reported membership) in 1998. The TED's annual growth rate had been around the 3.8 per cent mark in the early nineties but fell to 1.4 per cent in 1996, while in 1997 and 1998, the TED had negative

---

17 Data from the *ASRs* for 1996–1998.

growth, experiencing a net loss in membership.[18] Because prestige and representation are bound up with membership totals, to implement the division-wide audits demonstrated bravery as well as integrity. In the dozen years that Pakistan remained with the TED, its membership had a net increase of 8239 – by a curious coincidence a gain of 137 per cent, the same as in the union's first decade in the TED. There is reason to believe that inaccuracies crept in again, probably due to under-reporting of those leaving, though the total baptisms reported for the year in 2003 and 2008 both look high; but no further audits took place before Pakistan was transferred to the Southern Asia-Pacific Division.

Around the time the Pakistan Union's membership was found to be greatly exaggerated, the Middle East Union joined the Trans-European Division. When one considers how the MEUM fared under the TED, again, on the face of it, growth looks very good; but, again, statistical appearances can be deceiving, and one has to dig deeper into the numbers to find the real trends. As Figure 9 shows, the MEUM enjoyed sustained growth while a part of the TED, despite also having to deduct members after a membership audit in 2002. Because net membership figures were affected by tardy reporting and membership audits, this graph uses two-year moving averages to give a clearer picture of the trend. What it does not show is which parts of the Middle East Union Mission were enjoying growth.

During the MEUM's seventeen years as part of the TED, just 8 per cent of accessions were in the Levant, the Arabian Peninsula, or the Gulf, while 92 per cent were in the Sudan. Of total accessions in the union in that period, 43 per cent were from the north, another 49 per cent in southern Sudan. Yet the Sudan is generally not included as part of the Middle East and certainly South Sudan is not. The nature of 'Middle Eastern' church growth in the last twenty years is brought

---

18 ASTR, Statistical Report, presented to Annual Council, 29 Sept. 1999: see GCC mins., p. 99-87, and full report available at: <http://documents.adventistarchives.org/Statistics/Other/ACRep1999.pdf>.

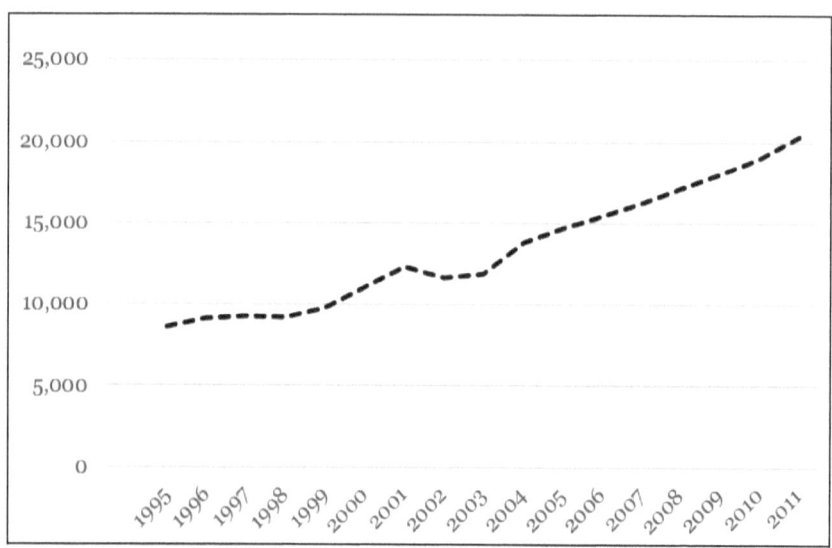

Figure 9. MEUM Membership under the TED (two-year moving averages)

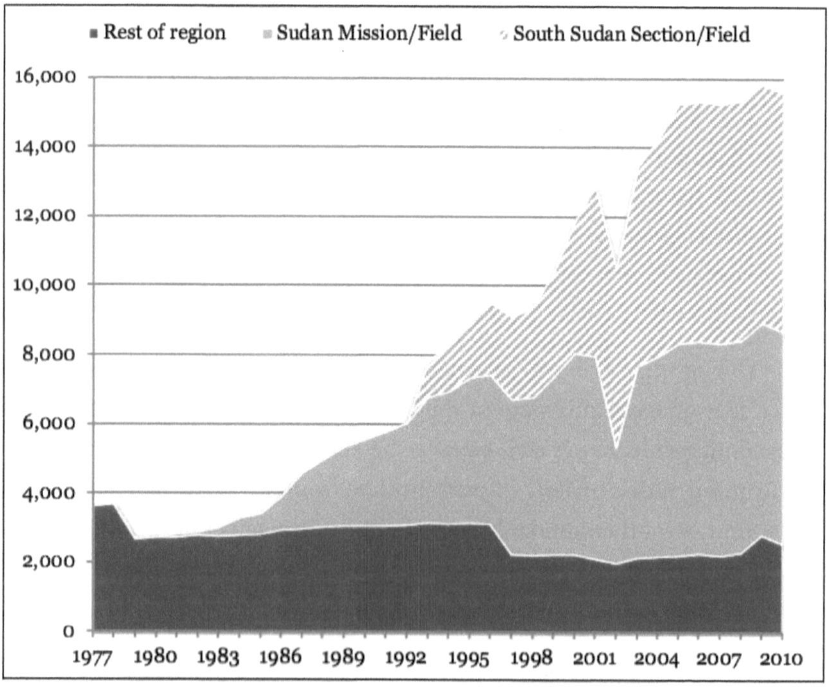

Figure 10. Sudanese Membership in Relation to Membership Across the Middle East

out in Figure 10, which shows the share of members in the MEUM from northern and southern Sudan since the first members were baptised in the Sudan in 1977, after the re-formation of the Sudan Mission. Even in the Sudan Field (i.e., the north of the country), moreover, many conversions were *not* made in Muslim communities, but rather were drawn from Christian minorities in that half of the country. Figure 10 shows a longer-term trend, beginning before the Middle East Union was made part of the TED, but the trend certainly continued while under its direction: in 1995, 65 per cent of the MEUM's church members were in the Sudan; by 2011 the figure was 88 per cent.

If the Sudan is taken out of the picture, the trend in MEUM membership after it was placed under the Trans-European Division is one of stagnation, notwithstanding some good years. Figure 11 shows net membership in the Middle East Union Mission, *excluding* members

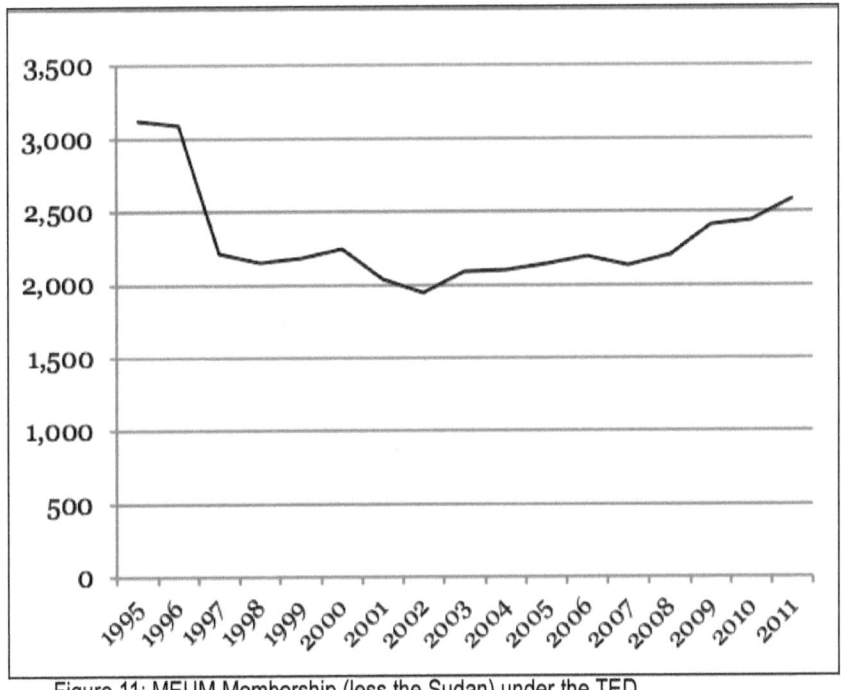

Figure 11: MEUM Membership (less the Sudan) under the TED

in the Sudan, while the MEUM was part of the TED. Now, a valid perspective is that thousands of Sudanese were brought to Christ; moreover, much of the credit for this is due to the TED, for growth in the Sudan had been slow in the late 1970s and throughout the 1980s, while it accelerated after 1995. What would be a faulty perspective would be to look only at net membership figures for the MEUM in the late 1990s and the 2000s. It might appear that, under the TED, mission in the Middle East had been transformed, or that there had been a major missiological breakthrough in outreach to Muslims, but neither was true (albeit both are impressions that some European church leaders sometimes liked to foster). While the MEUM was part of the TED, the membership of the Middle East *Union* grew; the number of church members in the Middle East declined, overall, though recently it started to rebound.

There is a final point. The growth in the Sudan, especially in the south of the country, is significant as one attempts to discern growth trends not only for the MEUM but for the TED as a whole. In 2012, after the realignment of 2011, the TED membership shrank from almost 119,000 to just under 84,000: 70 per cent of the end-of-year total for 2011. In 2011, reported membership in Pakistan was just over 14,000, while there were another 21,000 members in the MEUM – and of those, approximately 18,500 were in the Sudan. Without the Sudanese, the TED's 2011 membership would have been 100,230 instead of 118,712. There was thus every reason for the TED to prioritise mission in the Sudan in the late nineties and the noughties because here, alone in the whole division, dynamic growth could be achieved. It was exactly the same situation that had existed in the sixties and seventies with membership in Africa *vis-à-vis* membership in the rest of the division: slowing growth (indeed decline) in the European territories was masked by growth in Africa. The parts of Africa in question were different. The pattern was the same.

Ultimately, GC administration took a different view to TED administration about what church structure would have the greatest positive impact on mission in the Middle East – *all* of the Middle East. There were sustained negotiations about the future of the Middle East and North Africa but in the end, as in 1949–1950 and again in 1969–70, a plan that had the personal support of the GC president was likely to be adopted. The future of the MEUM was raised by the new GC administration after the 2010 GC Session. The following twelve months saw research (including analysis of missional trends in the MEUM), extensive consultations, and organisational politics. Despite sustaining debate right up to the start of the 2012 Annual Council, in the end, the TED officers' view of the best way forward was not that adopted by the world church. The GC Executive Committee voted to approve the most substantial restructuring in the world church for a decade; the Middle East Union Mission, with the minor exception of Cyprus, ceased to be the TED's responsibility, as did Pakistan (while the Middle Eastern and North African territories of EAD were also realigned). For the first time since 1985, the Trans-European Division would be solely European, with the offshore island (and EU member state) of Cyprus the last vestige of the connection with the Middle East. The TED was once again solely European.

At the Division Office

Mission is affected by many factors. The way an organisation headquarters is managed is one of the more important (and we will return to this point in Chapter 10).

One significant reform was in 1991 when, for the first time in the division's history, it appointed an Administrative Committee (ADCOM). The General Conference had created an Administrative Committee in 1973, but it had been reconstituted with a significantly enhanced area of responsibility in 1991.[19] It is likely that this latter development is what prompted the creation of the TED Administrative Committee. Its original terms of reference were the processing of routine calls and service requests (and related matters such as medical clearances and the various allowances provided for by *Working Policy*), travel itineraries, and contractual, construction, and budgetary items under a certain value. Unusually for such committees around the world, it initially was chaired not by the TED president but by the division treasurer, Anna-Liisa Halonen, with the secretary, Karel van Oosannen, as ADCOM secretary and the president, Jan Paulsen, as a permanent member, plus five other members, four of whom were to be reviewed by the Executive Committee annually. Presumably there was an intention to ease the president's workload but by the following year the decision had been taken to have President Paulsen chair TED ADCOM, which was in line with practice in other divisions. It may have been because Halonen had accepted a call back to Finland, but it must surely also have reflected functional realities in that first year. By the mid-nineties, the regular membership had been expanded to include 'All TED Elected/appointed staff'.[20]

The introduction of an ADCOM doubtless explains why in the twenty-first century the TED Executive Committee has almost always met only during its Spring and Winter Meetings, whereas in the twentieth century it convened throughout the year. It certainly helped to ease the volume of business by removing many of the matters relating to property that had previously had to go through the Division Executive Committee, though the expansion in TED ADCOM's membership might mean that division departmental directors did not see a notable decline in time spent on major committees. Nevertheless,

---

19 D. J. B. Trim, 'Officers' Meetings: History and Character', ASTR Research Report (March 2019), p. 1.
20 TED Winter Meetings, 19 and 21 Nov. 1991, TEDEC meeting, 17 June 1992, and, e.g., TED Winter Meetings, 23 Nov. 1995, TEDMC-EC: 1991, §§ 355, 370, pp. 176, 195; 1992, § 165, p. 93; and 1995, § 147, p. 231.

the practical benefits seem clear.

The TED headquarters also had to grapple with significant financial challenges as the twenty-first century wore on. Some related to institutions, most of which had never been in the most robust of financial health (see Chapter 10). But another, more systemic challenge, arose from the advantages the Adventist lifestyle confers. The result has been an ever-increasing pool of retired church workers at the same time that, in several unions, membership was persistently declining, with implications for general church finances. One result was a need to make new arrangements to ensure retirement schemes were able to support those who relied on them for their autumnal years. Because union resources are, in most cases, limited, the TED played a significant part in reforming pension arrangements to ensure appropriate level of resources.[21]

Early in 2015, division administration sponsored a major strategic visioning exercise in St Albans. Present were church administrators from every level of structure in the division, frontline workers, institutional leaders, and laypeople, all drawn from across the TED's territory. The laypeople included prominent professionals, artists, young adults, and leaders of independent, supporting ministries. All who attended were made to feel valued, were given every opportunity to speak, and were heard. Over the five days, a wide range of ideas emerged, which the TED administration integrated into strategic planning. Concepts of the division's primary functions shifted: away from governance, management of organisations, and resource conservation; towards aggregating collective wisdom, experiences, and talents; dynamically reallocating resources (of all kinds); amplifying human trust and imagination; and a greater stress on equipping, enabling, and energising church members.[22] Whether or to what extent

---

21 See, e.g., TED ADCOM meeting, 16 Jan. 2008, TEDMC-AC 2008, § 14, p. 7.
22 Raafat Kamal, 'Ecclesiology and Mission Barriers–What Barriers?', presentation to the Global Mission Issues Committee, Silver Spring, MD, 3 Apr. 2018.

these concepts will be transferred into ecclesiastical practice, and affect the TED as a whole, is a matter for future historians of the division to judge. However, simply to take part in the 2015 visioning exercise and to be listened to by senior church leaders was a positive experience for many, a transformative experience for some, and was very valuable for all the church leaders present. The level of appreciation among those taking part in this unprecedented event, and the quality of ideas that emerged, indicated that it should not be a one-off.

Mission Challenges and Opportunities

Post-Cold War Opportunities

The foothold in Eastern Europe meant new challenges and new opportunities when the Cold War ended and the Iron Curtain came down. Loosening of restrictions on religion began earlier in Yugoslavia than in Warsaw Pact countries. The division's Spring Meetings were held at Maruševec in 1988 and that year Mark Finley, then the TED Ministerial Association secretary, conducted a public evangelistic campaign in Yugoslavia.[23] Evangelism was a priority of church leaders in the Yugoslavian Union Conference, but in 1990–1991 the ethnic conflict that was soon to result in outright war in the Balkans was already brewing, and soon evangelistic campaigns had to be cancelled – but they were replaced with campaigns in Hungary and Poland, with financial support from the HUC, PUC, and the division.[24]

In April 1991, Ray Dabrowski and John Arthur, respectively Communication and ADRA directors for the TED, arrived in Albania, courtesy of an invitation from the Albanian government's Ministry

---

23 TEDEC Spring Meetings, 1 May 1988 and Winter Meetings, 15 Nov. 1988, TEDMC-EC 1988, p. 51ff., § 347, p. 147.
24 E.g., TED Winter Meetings, 22 Nov. 1990, TEDMC-EC 1990, § 330, p. 237; TED Quinquennial Council, 6 May 1991, TEDMC-EC 1991, § 134, pp. 62–63.

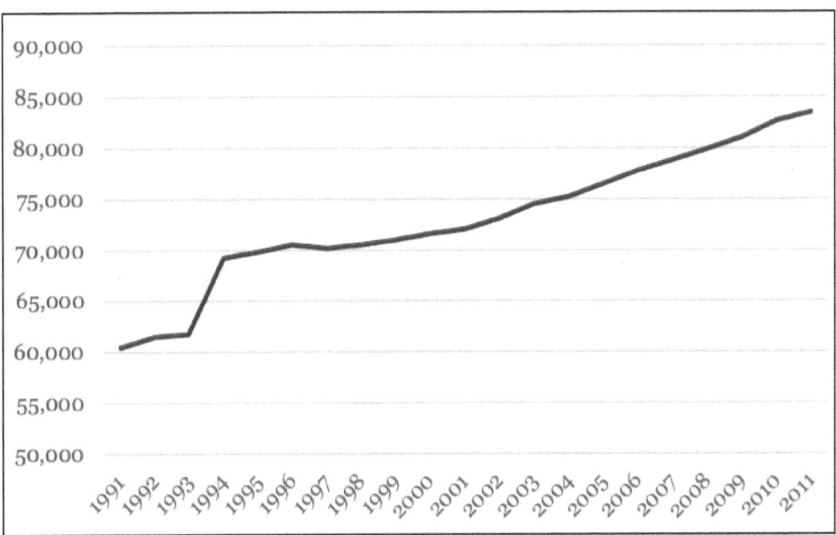

Figure 12. Membership in TED, 1991–2011, Excluding Pakistan and the Middle East

of Health, which was seeking public-health expertise. The two men were 'the first Adventists to visit the country in almost fifty years'.[25] The TED set up an Albania Fund and, in the winter of 1991/92, David Currie, the Australian Ministerial Association secretary at the TED, visited Tirana, identified a handful of believers who had kept their faith secretly since World War II, and made plans for an evangelistic series in the spring. From late March to early May 1992, the series went ahead with two speakers, with Rolf Kvinge of the WNUC supporting Currie. On 18 April 1992, they baptised eight Albanians; they returned for another month of meetings in Tirana in July and August. Later, Robert Folkenberg, Jr spent the winter of 1992/93 conducting further evangelistic meetings in the south of the country. In July 1993, the church employed its first two full-time Albanian workers: Julian Kastrati and Alban Matohiti, both of whom went on to study at Newbold and become the first Albanians ordained to

---

25 Ray Dabrowski, 'Albania', in *HRSDAE*, p. 17; cf. Arthur and Dabrowski, report to TEDEC Quinquennial Council, 7 May 1991, TEDMC-EC 1991, p. 70.

gospel ministry. And in June 1994, TED President Paulsen was in Korça for the dedication of the first Adventist church in Albania.[26]

A strong foundation had been laid; growth was to be slow but, by 2010, church membership was just over 350. None of this could have happened before the fall of the Communist dictatorship. But without the vision of leaders from the TED headquarters and TED funds, none of this would have happened, even given the end of the Cold War.

When the Baltic republics regained their independence, the world church moved to support the church there. In the spring of 1992, for example, the General Conference sent vice-president Kenneth Mittleider to Latvia to conduct evangelistic meetings in Latvia. Despite local scepticism, he rented an auditorium that seated 1300, ran his series for a month, and regularly saw capacity audiences. In the end, 341 people were baptised into the Seventh-day Adventist Church and three new congregations were formed after the meetings ended. In Lithuania, evangelistic programmes supported by the TED resulted in more than five hundred baptisms in the first two years after the Baltic Union returned to the TED, more than doubling the Lithuanian membership. These results were doubtless due in part to the novelty of American and Western preachers, their unaccustomed methods, and the aura of affluence and glamour that inevitably surrounded them. The hundreds of baptisms were also, however, the fruits of continual faithful work by lay members and church leaders in Latvia in the previous decades of oppression.[27]

---

26 TEDEC meeting, 15 Jan. 1992, Currie report to TEDEC, 27 Jan. 1992, TEDEC meetings, 11 Mar. and 15 Apr. 1992, and TED Spring Meetings, 27 Apr. 1992, TEDMC-EC 1992, §§ 8, 21, 38, 69 and 80, pp. 4–5, 17–18, 30, 46, 50–51; Global Mission Report for 1991–1995, TED Winter Meetings, 20 Nov. 1995, TEDMC-EC 1995, § 60, p. 151. This paragraph also draws on information provided by Julian Kastrati and Bob Folkenberg, Jr.

27 Mittleider's report to GCC, meeting of 30 July 1992, GCC mins., p. 92-71. President's Report for 1991–1995, TED Winter Meetings, 20 Nov. 1995, TEDMC-EC 1995, § 51, p. 114; *ASR*, 131 (1993), 42, and 133

Albania, Latvia, and Lithuania were manifestations of a wider openness to public evangelism in former Communist countries. In the early and mid-nineties, church leaders at the TED put resources into the East because they recognised the possibilities of winning more people more quickly than in the core countries. David Currie explicitly urged leaders from across the division's territory at its quinquennial council: 'Plan even more aggressive programmes for Eastern Europe'. This contrasted with his counsel that they should: 'Continue to seek new ways of reaching the secular societies of Western Europe. Aim for an increase in membership.'[28] In many parts of the world, an increase would have been taken for granted; the questions would have been by what percentage, and how many baptisms should be targeted. That the goal of evangelism could be a simple increase, of any kind, speaks volumes about the situation in Western Europe by the late twentieth century.

Sadly, after the freedom, excitement, and successes of the immediate post-Cold War period, the late 1990s and the 2000s saw the novelty of Western-style public evangelism wear off in Eastern Europe.[29] Countries like Croatia, Hungary, Latvia, and Poland, became more affluent and started to emulate Western values as well as material prosperity. There was a window of opportunity in the early nineties and the TED probably made the most of it while it was open.

Slow Growth and Negative Growth

As we saw earlier, in Pakistan, the Gulf, the Levant, the Arabian Peninsula, and Egypt, where Islam was utterly dominant, mission was desperately difficult. In Europe, too, church growth was slow, though

---

(1995), 28. See Børge Schantz, 'Adventism in a New Eastern Europe', in *Adventist Mission in the 21st Century*, ed. by Jon L. Dybdahl (Hagerstown, Md.: RHPA, 1999), pp. 298–99, 302–03.

28 Report to TED Quinquennial Council, 6 May 1991, TEDMC-EC 1991, p. 61.

29 Cf. Schantz, 'Adventism in a New Eastern Europe', pp. 300–01, 303–05.

here it was not Islam but materialism and postmodernism that were the competing 'belief systems'.

The problem is revealed by Figure 12, which shows year-end membership in the TED's European territories (i.e., excluding the Pakistan Union Section and MEUM) for the period 1991–2011. Growth was sufficiently slow in this period that Figure 12 shows the data with 50,000 as the base line, instead of zero. In these twenty years, the TED's membership in Europe rose from 60,553 to 82,643. That was an increase of 30 per cent, but over a twenty-year period and for the whole division; in the same period, world membership grew by 153 per cent. Meanwhile, during the period 2001–2011, seven of the TED's unions (the Adriatic, Baltic, Danish, Finland, Norwegian, South-East European, and Swedish unions) experienced a net decline in membership and had four or more years of negative growth.

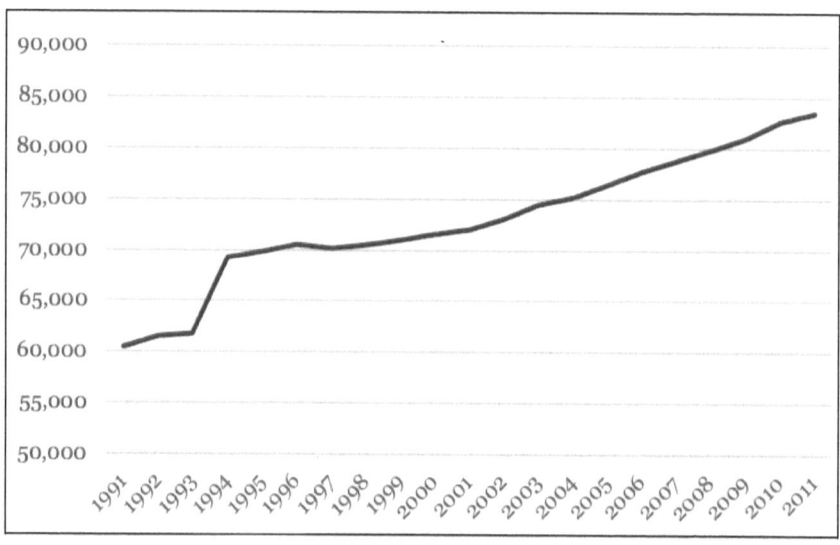

Figure 12. Membership in TED, 1991–2011, Excluding Pakistan and the Middle East

In the face of the slow growth, declining growth, and negative growth, the organised church seemed, to many church members in

Northern Europe, to be like a patient suffering a long-drawn-out illness; there were fears it might be terminal. It was easy to give way to defeatism – easy, in the face of complete disinterest and disdain, to stop trying to reach out, and instead to turn inwards. The Netherlands Union president articulated the concerns in 1998: 'Church members and pastors alike at times feel imprisoned due to the many challenges and problems which the church faces: lack of personnel, financial restrictions, very limited church growth [...], etc.'[30]

New Missional Methodologies in Europe

By the end of the twentieth century, senior church leaders increasingly acknowledged that 'in several countries [...] Adventists [were] declining in numbers under the impact of rampant materialism and secularism'. They were also prepared to admit publicly that: 'Adventism [was] attracting a response among those who migrate, come to study, or are just passing through.'[31] It even began to be acknowledged, publicly, that it was possible for talented, experienced, and spirit-filled preachers to conduct public evangelistic meetings aimed at the majority, native-born populations, in which speakers 'gave it our best shot', but had 'results [that] were meager', in contrast to evangelism among ethnic minority populations.[32] It was not only increasingly apparent but also increasingly accepted that, if the church were to enjoy sustained growth in the TED's territories, a different model of outreach and church growth would be needed. The same levels of effort, intelligence, and resources that had been poured into mission in Africa needed to be put into contextualised mission in Europe.

A significant step was taken when the TED worked with the EAD to organise a major symposium on Adventist mission in Europe. The

---
30 Henk Koning, devotional, TED Spring Meetings, 11 May 1998, TEDMC-EC 1998, p. 33.
31 E.g., see William G. Johnsson, 'Changing Times in Great Britain', *Adventist Review*, 178.6 (8 Feb. 2001), 8–13 (pp. 9, 11).
32 Ibid., p. 10 and cf. p. 12; and McFarlane, 'Evangelism', p. 23.

European Mission Conference was held at Hoevelaken, in the Netherlands, during 8–12 January 1997. The proceedings were published and so the papers given at the conference became a resource. Unfortunately, most of the presentations were very short and many of the published papers really only scratched the surface of their topic.[33] If the European Mission Conference had been the first of a series of events, this might not have mattered, since the terrain marked out as significant and in need of being properly surveyed could have been explored in greater depth at subsequent events. Instead, a number of concepts needed further development (including ones mentioned in the next two paragraphs). Where ideas presented at Hoevelaken made their way into missiology and missional practice in the TED, it was thanks to the initiative of departmental directors and officers at the division headquarters and some union headquarters.

Among the speakers at Hoevelaken was Peter Roennfeldt, who in 1996 had succeeded Currie as Ministerial Association secretary. While this was a matter of one Australian replacing another, Roennfeldt was ready and willing to modify methods that had worked elsewhere, adapting them to the European context. He passionately wanted Adventism 'to learn the language of Europe', which he meant more metaphorically than literally.[34] Roennfeldt valued and taught church planting more than public evangelism; he also stressed evangelism as *process* rather than *event*. During his ten years at the TED, through training across the division and teaching at Newbold, he influenced many church leaders across the division and arguably inspired a generation of students to use church planting and 'process evangelism' or 'narrative evangelism' aimed specifically at secular people or

---

33 *Re-Visioning Adventist Mission in Europe*, ed. by Baumgartner.
34 Peter Roennfeldt, 'Can Adventism Learn the Language of Europe?', in *Pluralism, Parochialism and Contextualization: Challenges to Adventist Mission in Europe (19th–21st Centuries)*, ed. by D. J. B. Trim and Daniel Heinz (Oxford, Bern, Berlin, Brussels, Frankfurt am Main, New York & Vienna: Peter Lang, 2010), pp. 199–205.

unchurched people as models for sustained church growth.[35]

In the British Union, a joint initiative between the BUC and TED encouraged use of process evangelism in what was dubbed the 'LIFEdevelopment' approach, as well as of more intentional church planting. By 2006, however, one study concluded of LIFE development that 'the impact that it was designed to have on the Church in the British Isles has not materialised', whereas church planting was regarded as a success.[36] Yet elsewhere, the approaches to church growth being promoted by the TED met with some success. A particular case is the Netherlands. The early to mid-nineties had been marked by stagnation: a membership of 4124 at the start of the decade had increased by the end of 1998 only to 4137, a net increase of thirteen in an eight-year period. This was minuscule growth even for postmodern, *fin de siècle* Europe. Annual new accessions averaged fifty-six, which meant an average of less than two additional members per year; in three years in this period, this was not enough to replace those who had died or left, so that the NUC had a net loss. But then a new emphasis on church planting, based on an understanding of contemporary culture in the Netherlands and analysis of social factors, began to yield results.[37] By the end of the 2005 quinquennium, Dutch church membership had increased to 4520, a net increase of 388 in seven years, thanks in part to four years in which there were than one hundred baptisms. Accessions averaged 106 per year, while the average annual net increase was fifty-six. Accessions averaged more than a hundred annually in the 2006–2010 quinquennium and more than 150 per annum during 2010–2015. In contrast to unions in

---

35 Peter Roennfeldt, 'The Secular Person as a Target for Mission', in *Re-visioning Adventist Mission in Europe*, ed. by Baumgartner, pp. 59–69 (esp. pp. 64–66); cf. D. W. McFarlane, 'Some Challenges Facing the British Church in the Twenty-First Century', in *A Century of Adventism*, ed. by Marshall, pp. 26–28 (p. 28).
36 McFarlane, 'Evangelism', pp. 22–23 (p. 23).
37 See e.g. Wim Altink and Rudolf H. Dingjan, 'Understanding the Dutch Society', in *Re-visioning Adventist Mission in Europe*, ed. by Baumgartner, pp. 221–28.

Scandinavia, the NUC has experienced growth. Membership passed 5000 in 2012 and 6000 in 2017. Stagnation was succeeded by slow but steady and sustained church growth.

Public evangelism is a wonderfully cost-effective way to reach many people at once. That it is so generally unsuccessful in Europe is unfortunate from the point of view of church leaders and church members alike, because it makes evangelising Europe far more difficult than it would otherwise be. But then, the nature of post-Christian Europe is that there will be no easy fixes to church growth. Adventists accept and understand that growth is slow, painful, and painstaking in societies and cultures that are overwhelmingly Buddhist, Hindu, and Muslim. We should add to that list societies and cultures that are post-religious. If Seventh-day Adventists (in the rest of the world as well as in the TED) can adjust expectations away from what obtained in Britain and Finland in the 1950s, or applies in Brazil and Kenya in the 2010s, to the reality in Europe today, that would be a significant step towards more organic and sustainable church growth.

Unity in Diversity

An issue in relation to evangelistic outreach is the cultural diversity arising from ethnic diversity. Different ethnic groups have different ways 'of doing church'; these often relate to liturgy and worship styles, which attract the most attention, but include diverse approaches to organisational matters at the local church level. This is not merely a matter of immigrants versus indigenes, for there are considerable differences between the cultures of, say, Serbia and Sweden, or Poland and the Netherlands. Nevertheless, differences of that kind, though they affect mutual understanding between Adventists from different parts of the division, have less impact on outreach than do the differences between migrants and the majority population, for Adventism tends to be not only a minority faith, but the faith of ethnic minorities. Thus, Seventh-day Adventists are distinguished not only by the church's 'peculiar' doctrines and attendant religio-cultural practices, but also by distinctive ethno-cultural practices. Together, these can constitute a formidable barrier to members of the majority population, especially since, in the TED's territory, such populations are often far from free of religious or racial prejudice.

The Adventist 'worship wars' have tended to be about the propriety or beauty of this or that style of worship. Perhaps the more important question is how important it is to have a worship style that make church members comfortable if it deters the unchurched person from entering an Adventist church. Phrasing it thus may seem to indicate a 'right' answer, but it is a complex question, because worship has several functions, including drawing the church member into a closer union with Christ. Should this purpose, or that of outreach, be privileged? How is one to reach a conclusion? It will require fine judgment and the answer will surely differ according to circumstance; but unfortunately, this is not the question that has been asked or addressed, at least not as much as it might have been.

One reason is that when different ethnic worship styles have been discussed it has been as part of debates about authority and power, rather than mission. Particular approaches to worship have often become the symbol of this or that ethnic group. As a result, what scholars call 'liturgical space' has become contested ground. Liturgical space is both the physical zone used in Sabbath School and divine services, and the chronological period, the 'sacred time' in which worship and the proclamation of the word take place.[38] The use made of both kinds of space, the physical and the temporal, and what takes

---

38 Only recently have Adventist scholars engaged critically with worship. Two fine new theological studies with strong historical perspectives are David A. Williams, 'Worship Music as Theology: An Examination of Music in the Liturgy of Black and White Adventists in the United States from 1894 to 1944' (PhD dissertation, Seventh-day Adventist Theological Seminary, 2018); Alain Coralie, 'Understanding Adventist Worship: A Liturgical Theology' (PhD thesis, Trinity College/University of Bristol, 2018). There has been almost no engagement with concepts of liturgical space and time

place within their bounds, is vastly different across the territory of the TED, and is associated with national cultures. A Serbian Orthodox or High-Church Anglican service are very different to a Norwegian Lutheran or Dutch Reformed service. Among majority populations of the TED's countries, Adventist worship always reflects to some extent the liturgy of the main national church but there are fewer differences between Adventist worship styles in different countries than between those of those major denominations. Church services in Greece, Croatia, the Netherlands, Britain, and Norway are all recognisably similar – but that is in churches that have made limited or no attempt to engage with ethnic Adventist preferences. Refusing to do so (or, alternatively, forcing a preferred style on Adventists of other ethnicities) is in itself a statement of power, even when not intended as such. It is because particular worship styles are often associated with particular ethnicities that liturgical space has become contested ground, part of struggles over which group will have the upper hand in the church as a whole. Such struggles have happened in several of the Adventist Church's world divisions, and in some countries of the TED.[39]

As ethnic tensions ease, however, then perhaps the grounds of discussion can move away from authority and control, and back to where it arguably ought to be: do worship services discourage or encourage European people to enter an Adventist church? To what extent do they make it more likely that they will remain and return?

Sectarian Diversity

In Hungary, the end of the Cold War provided an opportunity to restore a breach that dated back to the mid-seventies. It took a long time to achieve and there is still some distance to be travelled before

but see Michel Sunhae Lee's forthcoming doctoral dissertation, 'Contesting the Sabbath: A History of Sacred Times in America, 1848–1920' (University of Texas at Austin).

[39] Cf. Woolford, 'The 70s Struggle', pp. 33–34; McFarlane, 'Past and Future', p. 46.

full restoration of the Hungarian body of Christ is realised, but in 2015 an important milestone was reached.

Living under Communism created all kinds of problems for Seventh-day Adventists and other zealous Christians across Eastern Europe. In Hungary, many church members felt that the HUC was too willing to work, where possible, with the officially atheistic state. Growing tensions came to a head in 1975, when a group of 'young pastors and other members' protested collaboration by the HUC 'with the Council of Free Churches, a body formed to represent the common interests of small Protestant denominations that later become a tool of the communist state'.[40] This was a substantive dispute, which led to accusations, variously, of apostasy, of obstructing mission, and of rejecting church authority. But to this were added personal differences and some disagreements about theology and culture that probably could have been resolved in a less heated situation. Both sides adopted unfortunately intransigent positions, dialogue was largely rejected for denunciation, and the Hungarian Union leadership eventually took a stand on the issue of church authority instead of substantially addressing the underlying issue. Even before the mass disfellowshipping of the dissident group, anger and resentment had been engendered on both sides.[41] In 2015 the HUC formally acknowledged, in a statement that the TED helped to draft, that the group of 518 church members 'was disfellowshipped, mostly without a valid biblical reason'.[42]

All this happened while the HUC was part of the EAD, but as we saw in Chapter 8, the TED inherited the situation in 1985. The

---

40 Andrew McChesney, 'Adventist Church in Hungary Reconciles with Breakaway Group After 40 Years', *ARH* online, 1 May 2015: <https://www.adventistreview.org/church-news/story2599-adventist-church-in-hungary-reconciles-with-breakaway-group-after-40-years>.

41 József Szilvási, 'Church Policy in East-Central Europe after the Collapse of Communist Regimes', at the conference 'Memory, History and Reconciliation in the Light of the Papal Declaration on "Memory and Reconciliation"', Newbold College, 20 Oct. 2000.

42 Quoted in McChesney, 'Adventist Church in Hungary'.

ejected members had organised themselves into the Christian Advent Community; the passage of time, and the underlying bitterness, led it and the official Adventist Church in Hungary to drift further and further apart. The end of Communism in Hungary, which removed the underlying cause of the fracture, did not immediately end the schism. Through the 1990s there were repeated calls for the HUC to apologise, which it did, but there was no movement towards reconciliation, until 2011, when the Christian Advent Community leaders 'initiated a series of talks with union and conference leadership'.[43] The TED officers encouraged dialogue, supported the HUC officers through what became a process, and helped with the drafting of an agreement signed on 23 April 2015 by TED president, Raafat Kamal, HUC president, Tamás Ócsai, and the Advent Community president, János Cserbik. A statement issued by the TED summarised that the agreement committed both sides 'to build a future together in order to fulfill the mission God entrusted to His church'. President Kamal commented: 'Over the past two years I personally witnessed first-hand genuine expressions of reconciliation by members and leaders alike'.[44]

At the 2015 GC Session, Cserbik joined Kamal and Ócsai on the stage at the end of the first morning of the GC Session, as the world church celebrated the formal end of the schism. There was still practical work to be done, to overcome forty years of antipathy. There is still a parallel church organisation, but it is now much smaller. The events of 2015 showed how unity and community could be built out of disunity.[45]

---

43 Szilvási, 'Church Policy'; McChesney, 'Adventist Church in Hungary'.
44 Quotations from McChesney, 'Adventist Church in Hungary'.
45 Norel Iacob, 'World Church Welcomes Back Hungarian Splinter Group', *ARH* Online, 2 July 2015: <https://www.adventistreview.org/church-news/story2896-world-church-welcomes-back-hungarian-splinter-group>.

Ethnic Diversity

In the British Union Conference, tensions between church members of African-Caribbean ethnicity and white members eased greatly over the course of the 1990s and early 2000s. By this time, immigration from the West Indies had largely ceased. In the twenty-first century it was immigrants from Africa and Eastern Europe who were seen as newcomers and regarded with some suspicion by the children of those who had themselves not been welcomed as they had hoped in the 1960s–'70s. This situation was ironic but also tragic and was to some extent a result of the British church never having fully explored its past history of racial divisions, an approach taken in the interest of easing tensions in the present, but one that meant some crucial lessons were never learned.

In the 2010s, African migrants are drawn from across the continent but largely from Ghana and Nigeria in West Africa, and from Kenya and Tanzania in East Africa. The overlap with the NED's former mission territories is striking. African Adventists started to establish their own ethnic churches in the south of England in the late 1990s and early 2000s. Friction developed between African church members, largely the first generation to enter Britain, and African-Caribbean members, largely the children and grandchildren of immigrants, but it never approached the level of the white-black tensions of the 1970s – some lessons *had* been learned. As the 2010s wore on, there was increasing harmony between the various 'Black, Asian and minority ethnic' church members (BAME Adventists, to adopt the jargon of race relations); those from Eastern Europe; and those from the majority population, whose numbers are not known with certainty, but seem to have declined since the end of World War II.

In the Netherlands Union, ethnic divisions were between white Dutch Adventists from the majority population; immigrants from Surinam; immigrants from the Netherlands' insular territories in the Caribbean; and smaller but vocal and active groups of migrants from

Africa (especially Ghana, Nigeria, and Rwanda). Simple misunderstandings were sometime more to blame for tensions than bigotry. Cultural differences could be interpreted as signifiers of theological heterodoxy, and/or could led to a breakdown in relations within a congregation. Worship styles were (as in Britain) often a touchstone for ethnic tensions but largely a matter of taste and culture, though often cast in more dogmatic terms. Where prejudice was present (as it sometimes was), it could take forms other than racial (e.g., gender).[46] In the late 1990s and early 2000s, Dutch church leaders worked hard to promote harmony and mutual understanding, drawing in part on expertise developed at Newbold College, which in 2002 established a Centre for the Study of Diversity. Importantly, church leaders were intentional about working towards unity in diversity.

Some tensions remained, in both the BUC and the NUC, but the passage of time tended to help rather than hinder progress. All this matters because immigration, whether from outside Europe or from east to west within the European Union, is increasing; even societies (and churches) that were ethnically uniform can expect to become emphatically diverse. And history suggests that migrants' different backgrounds and expectations increases heterogeneity in a church community. The examples of reconciliation described above are, then, very encouraging and worth emulating by church members and church leaders elsewhere.

---

46 I draw here on personal experience of facilitating dialogues at a church in Amsterdam in 2003 and 2005; of discussions with the NUC president and another Dutch delegate to the conference 'Understanding Difference: Building Communities in Diverse Modern Western Societies' (Newbold College, 23–25 July 2003); and on Danielle Koning's insightful study, 'Place, Space, and Authority: The Mission and Reversed Mission of the Ghanaian Seventh-day Church in Amsterdam', *African Diaspora*, 2 (2009), 203–26.

In sum, in the 2010s, relations among the various groups of Seventh-day Adventists in Great Britain, Hungary, and the Netherlands have been largely harmonious. Unity amid diversity in the body of Christ seemed far off at various times, in several countries of the TED, but recent years have shown it can be achieved.

Chapter 10
Institutions

Much of the work of the Adventist Church is done through its institutions; that has been the case since the first were created in Battle Creek, Michigan, in the late 1860s and the 1870s. There have always been fewer of these in Northern Europe than in some other parts of the world, but schools, colleges, sanitariums, and health-food businesses have all existed in the TED, and have been important. This was true in Africa in the division's first fifty years; it has been true in Europe throughout the TED's ninety-year history, though in the twenty-first century there are fewer institutions than in the twentieth century, due in part to changes in society. The TED has formally had only one division institution, Newbold College of Higher Education (Illustration 10.1). However, one health care institution in the division territory, Skodsborg Sanitarium (Illustration 10.2), loomed considerably larger than any others, its tendrils spreading far and wide. This chapter therefore focuses on those two institutions, but it recognises, too, that the TED's unions have had institutions, that the division has always been supportive of them, and has been supported by them.

Education

When the division began, it had seven educational institutions: the Baltic Union, British Union and Polish Union 'schools', and the Danish, Norwegian, Swedish and Finnish 'schools'. The academic levels of these institutions varied but despite the terminology, they roughly speaking provided further as well as secondary education. The NED's seven schools in 1929 had a total of thirty-nine teachers (with twelve teachers, Stanborough College in Britain was the only institution whose number of teachers was in double figures) and 392 students – Stanborough College again had the most, with ninety-four

257

students. Despite the emphasis on training workers, 157 of the students at the seven schools, or 40 per cent, were women – a reminder that women filled all kinds of roles short of that of the ordained pastor. The seven libraries were only modestly provided for, with 5075 volumes between them.[1]

The British and Scandinavian training schools or colleges were of relatively long standing and were also relatively well supported by the church. The Baltic Union school, Advent-Missionsseminar, in Riga (familiarly known to Seventh-day Adventists of the region as *Suschenhof*), had only been founded thanks to the sacrifices of ordinary church members. A veteran church leader graphically described how they had managed to find the resources necessary for a school: '[T]hey gathered pine cones, medicinal herbs, old rags, bones, and iron, and sold them, thus getting money for the school.' Despite its humble origins, it was well resourced: its library was the largest of any of the seven colleges in the NED, with 1500 volumes. Further, whatever prejudices Western Europeans might have had about the East, Advent-Missionsseminar had the highest proportion of female students, who constituted 45 per cent of the student body. It drew 'students from all three Baltic countries'.[2]

The Baltic passion for local Adventist education was further manifested in 1935, in Estonia, where local church members wanted a school that would teach in Estonian. Latvian and Lithuanian are Balto-Slavic languages, but Estonian is related to Finnish (and both are very different to the Balto-Slavic and Nordic languages spoken by neighbouring peoples). The 'Esthonian Training School' [*sic*] opened in Tallinn in 1935. Two years later, operations of the Advent-Missionsseminar were suspended due to government restrictions in Latvia, though the Suschenhof property was maintained and some

---

1 'Closing Report of the Mission Schools', *Advent Survey*, 1.3 (Sept. 1929), 11.
2 Ibid.; Guy Dail, 'At the Baltic Union School', *ARH*, 102.52 (24 Dec. 1925), 20; Isaak Kleimanis, 'Latvia', in *HRSDAE*, p. 144.

low-level training of pastors may have continued. After 1937, the Estonian Adventusuühingute Usuteaduse Kool (the English title now given as 'Estonian Mission School') was the only educational institution in the union.[3] Soon enough the Soviet occupation, German invasion, and Soviet reoccupation would put an end to Adventist education in the Baltic states. In contrast, in Poland (where for various reasons government treatment of Seventh-day Adventists was less rigorous than in the Soviet-occupied Baltic republics), the 'Polish school' which had 'suffered much damage' during the war, reopened in the autumn of 1947, thanks to strong support from the division.[4]

By 1965, the NED was proud of its '37,000 students' in all 'educational institutions' across the division. In fact this was an understatement: there were 35,637 students in primary schools, 2098 in secondary schools and 'junior colleges' (most of whose students were secondary level), 962 in teacher and nurse training colleges, and 326 in higher education colleges; for a total of just over 39,000.[5] Most of the students were, however, in the African unions of NED and more particularly in institutions in the WAUM.

By the end of the sixties, there were fewer than a thousand students in the division's primary schools outside Africa, just 3 per cent of the more than 32,000 primary-school students, 84 per cent of whom were in WAUM schools. In the Ethiopian Union there were

---

3   *YB 1935*, pp. 156 249; *YB 1937*, pp. 150, 169, 230, 240; *YB 1938*, pp. 153–54, 171, 248. While Advent-Missionsseminar is both listed as a Baltic Union institution and appears in the lists of NED institutions in the 1938 *YB*, it no longer has its own entry in the 'Institutions: Educational' section, which names board and staff members. This suggests ownership of the property but suspension of teaching, which would reconcile the reports in *SDAE*, I, 514 (closure of the Latvian school in 1937) and Kleimanis, 'Latvia', p. 144 (training continuing into the 1940s, though this may merely reflect a faulty oral tradition).

4   G. A. Lindsay, 'The Light of the Advent Shines in Northern Europe', *ARH*, 125.32 (5 Aug. 1948), 9, 19.

5   R. Unntersten, 'When Figures Are Not Dry' and table 'Report of the Educational Institutions for the Year 1965', *Northern Light*, 16.6, Statistical Supplement (1966), unpaginated [pp. 2, 6].

31 Adventist primary schools; in the West African Union, 153; whereas in the six unions of Europe and the Iceland Conference there were 22 (with none in two unions, the PUC and SUC). In contrast, those homelands had seven of seventeen secondary schools (with at least one in each union), educating slightly more than 40 per cent of secondary students in the NED. Still, overall, only 5 per cent of all students in Adventist schools in the NED were in what would soon become the Northern Europe section. At tertiary level, too, there was an imbalance thanks to the Adventist Seminary of West Africa (ASWA) and to teachers' and nurses' training colleges (Illustrations 10.3 and 10.4), the home of exactly three-quarters of the students at the NED's higher education institutions; Newbold and the 'junior colleges' or seminaries elsewhere in the division had 22 per cent of its tertiary student body.[6]

This major imbalance partly reflected the fact that there was free, high-quality public education throughout the division's core countries, whereas in Africa the church was one of the major providers of schools; church leadership put a great emphasis on providing schools. The imbalance between institutions and enrolments in Africa and Europe is important, historically, firstly as an indicator of the lack of priority given to Adventist education across most of Northern Europe by the sixties, in sharp contrast to the situation in most of the Adventist world, or indeed to the situation in the NED in the twenties and thirties. It is still the case today that church schools are not prioritised in the TED. The availability of good public education in Europe is cited as though this negated a need for Adventist schools. State schools educate only the mind, whereas Adventist education is wholistic – and it is also a major contributing factor to retention, as revealed by recent studies of former and current church members.

The imbalance that developed between Adventist education in the NED's homelands and its mission fields is historically important,

---

6   *ASR*, 107 (1969), 24.

secondly, because of its problematic nature. It was difficult to find sufficient staff for Adventist schools and colleges in the African mission fields. There was an increasing pool of local graduates from the church's colleges (especially primary school teachers), but the number of schools kept increasing, and consequently a large number of teaching positions (particularly in colleges and secondary schools) in NEWAD's West Africa Section continued to be filled by missionary appointees from its Northern Europe Section right through the sixties and seventies.[7] Yet Adventist education was reducing its footprint in Europe, and so struggled to support its mission-field sister institutions. The lack of big-picture thinking about education across the division as a whole, of a real division-wide educational strategy, was a problem in the past, and arguably in the present.

There has been an ongoing challenge: to keep educational institutions on track. This was true in three ways: intellectually or academically, financially, and theologically or spiritually. The last could not be taken for granted. Many Protestant denominations and missionary societies, finding it difficult to make conversions, concentrated on schools and clinics. For most missionaries, at least when starting in a country or region, education and health were intended to be instrumental, a means to effect the goal of conversion. Instead, in many cases, in many countries, the provision of education, or health care, became ends, rather than means.

The danger of mission drift was not restricted to Adventists, of course. Missionaries of other denominations were aware of the trajectory that mission schools often followed. In 1937 for example, an Anglican missionary in Uganda, working not far from Upper Nile Union Training School in Mubende, and across the lake (Victoria

---

7   See D. O. Babalola, 'The Seventh-day Adventist Church in Yorubaland, Nigeria (1914–1984)' (PhD thesis, University of Ibadan, 1988), pp. 142–43; Abiodun Ayodeji Adesegun, 'Christian Education in the Seventh-day Adventist Church in Remo, Ogun State, Nigeria, 1959–2004' (PhD thesis, University of Ibadan, 2009), pp. 52, 54; Phillips, 'British Adventists Overseas', p. 23; and Chapter 7.

Nyanza) from Kamagambo Training School in Kisumu and Kendu Hospital in Gendia, wrote of twin hazards, that the local 'people [would] regard the schools as a semi-secular side line; and that, on the other [hand], some of our extremely fine Christian schools [...] eclipse the pastorate'.[8] The tendency for schools and universities to become havens for divergent and heterodox thinking is one that Adventists faced. On the whole, under NED and NEWAD, the church's African institutions not only thrived in terms of student numbers, finances, and physical plant, they also remained distinctly Adventist and contributed powerfully to mission in Africa. This should be regarded as one of the success stories in the TED's history. In institutions in Europe, the compass needle has swung between the poles of emulating state education, and following the Adventist 'blueprint'. Examples of success in the latter endeavour, in the face of financial difficulties and, sometimes, the scepticism of church members, include Ekbyholm in Sweden in the eighties and Stanborough Park in Britain in the nineties.[9] Newbold's orthodoxy was not in doubt and, for the TED's first sixty years, its leaders showed their faith in the college by sending family members to study there. American missionary Ernest Dick, secretary of the NED from 1932 to 1936, sent his son to Newbold, as did Jan Paulsen in the early 1990s, while president of the TED.[10]

In terms of academic or intellectual rigour, African church schools were regarded as being examples of best practice; colleges, too, had little difficulty recruiting because of a lack of higher-education alternatives. In Europe, Newbold and the other, smaller, colleges and seminaries have had to struggle with the perception, widespread among Adventist church leaders, that research is a luxury, or indeed likely to lead to heterodox opinions. However, on the whole there has been support for high standards from the TED officers. Walter Read was

---

8   H. D. Hooper, circular letter, 11 Oct. 1937, DUL, MS SAD 29/7/118.
9   Bertil Wiklander, 'Ekbyholmsskolan and Work/Study in the 1980s', in *HRSDAE*, pp. 226–28.
10   Dick to M. E. Kern, 8 Apr. 1936, in appointee file 'Dick, E. D.', GC Ar., RG 21, box no. 947, file no. 45602; author's personal knowledge.

a scholar by vocation and, eventually, by profession. Erwin Roenfelt was a man of keen if largely undeveloped intellect, who (unlike some church leaders then and since) was not suspicious of educators with higher degrees.[11] Three division presidents – Scragg, Paulsen, and Wiklander – had doctoral degrees, as did three secretaries: Seton, Beach, and Bruinsma.

Accreditation in Europe has proved more of a challenge; so, too, have financial factors (considered in the next section). As a result, leadership of Adventist academic institutions has historically been very difficult; Newbold, for forty years the only division institution in this division, has persistently presented a challenge to administration (both of the TED and of the college itself).[12] In the nineties, Newbold attained national accreditation in Britain after almost a century of solely denominational accreditation. Newbold had previously obtained validation agreements with American Adventist colleges, despite the significant differences between the European and American approaches to higher education.[13] The shift to British accreditation was a blessing in many ways and facilitated the offering of extension programmes elsewhere in the TED. This included the Baltic republics, which had not been able to resurrect their own colleges per se, but provided locations at which Newbold staff conducted theological and ministerial training.

Church administrators have been supportive of the theological, spiritual, intellectual, and academic aspects of church education, but by their nature, these are realms in which church leaders tend not to be directly involved. But the financial and logistical side of affairs

---

11 Marshall, 'Read', p. 14; Roenfelt to E. S. Cubley, 20 Sept. 1950, GC Ar., RG 21, Secretariat Correspondence, box no. 3449, fld. 'Middle East Union Officers, 1950'.
12 See Derek C. Beardsell, 'A Study of Selected Administrative Issues in the History and Development of Newbold College' (PhD dissertation, Andrews University, 1983).
13 Derek Beardsell, 'The Beginnings of Newbold College', in *HRSDAE*, pp. 44–45.

is rather different. Here, leaders of the church's organisational units and, above all, of the division, have been heavily involved. It is to the financial support of institutions, and not only of educational institutions, that we now turn.

Newbold and Skodsborg

Newbold

Even though Newbold, for roughly the first fifty years after its founding in 1901, was a British Union institution, from the very beginning of the NED the division was closely involved in managing 'the British college'.[14] Gradually the division's considerable financial involvement led to the adoption of Newbold as a division college.

Minutes of union and division executive committees and property-holding corporation boards all testify to the sums, often substantial, disbursed to improve, maintain, and sometimes expand schools and colleges. Early in the division's history, when institutions were small and had limited financial resources, almost any building project necessitated a request for funds to the parent union or to the division. In February 1938, the Newbold College board formally requested, and was granted by the British Union, £77 13s. 4d. towards the cost of 'a new chimney for the steam boiler'. The college was obliged to establish a special 'Boiler Chimney Repair Fund', which speaks eloquently of how even relatively minor construction or repairs could be too much for internal financial resources, but was so specific it did not help the following year when Newbold needed a new oven (including chimney); fortunately, £280 was granted from NED funds towards the expense.[15]

---

14 E.g., NED Winter Council, 4 Nov. 1929, NEDCOM-WCM 1929, p. 21.
15 BAM Board Meetings, 17 Feb. 1938, 26 Sept. 1938, and 1 July 1939, RGL, BMB 1938–47, fols. 11ʳ, 22ʳ, 27ʳ.

Soon after the outbreak of World War II, the gymnasium at Newbold College was taken over by the armed forces, for use in training recruits. The rest of the Newbold Revel property in Warwickshire, the site of the college campus, remained in church hands, though not unscarred: in 1940 it was surrounded by barbed wire entanglements, probably against the danger of a landing by German paratroopers. In January 1942, the whole property, except for the farm, was appropriated by the Royal Air Force. The staff and students were obliged at little notice to leave and, 'under most difficult conditions', move through thick snow twenty-five miles to a former boys' school, Packwood Haugh, which the church had been able to secure and hastily put 'in order for the use of the school'. Some education continued but Packwood was inadequate. The college property was surrounded by barbed wire until late in 1943, by which time it had become clear that the United Kingdom would not be invaded.[16] It was also looking increasingly likely, however, that Newbold Revel would not be restored.

In the summer of 1945, church leaders learned that, despite of the end of hostilities in Europe, the British government indeed intended to retain Newbold Revel. As leaders noted, 'our inability to secure the return of Newbold from the Air Ministry' was a blow, 'inasmuch as Packwood was entirely unsatisfactory for our scholastic work'. Accordingly, it was decided to sell the Newbold estate (which included farm land not being used by the air force training institute) to the UK government and use the proceeds of the sale to 'establish the College at the new place'.[17] By the autumn of 1945, the decision had been taken to buy Moor Close, a country house and associated estate in Binfield, in the southern county of Berkshire – and by the

---

16 BUC Committee meeting, 10 Feb. 1942, mins. in GC Ar., RG NE 1, fld. 'British Union Conference Minutes 1942', pp. 8–9; BAM Board Meeting, Nov. 17, 1943, RGL, BMB 1938–1947, fol. 171^r; cf. Porter, 'Church in the Age of Dictators', p. 18.

17 BAM Board Meeting, 3 and 9 July 1945, RGL, BMB 1938–1947, fols. 192^r–95^r.

winter, the sale of Newbold Revel for £50,000 and purchase of the Binfield property for some £25,000 had proceeded. Thus, Newbold College, having left the property that was its namesake, found its long-term and current home (Illustration 10.5).[18]

The move to Binfield in January 1946 was a huge challenge: the new property had to be tailored to educational needs, books and equipment had to be transferred, student accommodation set up, the majority of its staff had to be moved and rehoused, and in consequence, a major building programme was essential, while further purchases of ancillary property around Binfield were deemed necessary. For all this to take place required the expenditure of very considerable sums, the creation of a complex set of new church policies, the obtaining of planning approval from the local government authority in Berkshire, and the whole process spun out rather longer than British church leaders originally expected.[19] There was need for considerable and sustained investment. From where was it to come?

It was natural to look to the church in America for help and the union leaders had kept GC administration in the loop since the summer of 1946. As it became clearer that the British Union was likely to be attached directly to the GC, the union leadership turned to the world church. Having almost certainly received informal encouragement from Ernest Dick, the GC (and former NED) secretary, when he visited Britain in the winter of 1946, after the BUC's direct relationship to the GC was accepted at the 1946 Session, the BUC requested a special appropriation of £25,000 'for College rehabilitation' – this was a huge sum (equivalent to at least £1 million in

---

18 BAM Board Meetings, 6 Nov. and 4 Dec. 1945, RGL, BMB 1938–1947, fols. 205ʳ–7ʳ; M. L. Anthony, 'Decades of Change', in *Seventh-day Adventists in the British Isles*, ed. by Marshall, p. 26.

19 Anthony, ibid.; BAM Board Meetings, 2 Jan., 26 Feb. and 4 Mar. 1946, RGL, BMB 1938–1947, fols. 209ʳ–12ʳ, [214]ʳ, 221ʳ; BUC Committee meetings, 26 Feb., 11 July, 1, 11, 16 and 25 Aug., and 9 Sept. 1946, GC Ar., RG NE 1, fld. 'British Union Conference Minutes 1946', pp. 23–24, 59, 61, 79, 82–83, 91, 99.

2018) and 55 per cent of the annual BUC budget as proposed to the GC. The world church eventually helped – and kept on helping for several years.[20]

In the aftermath of World War II, however, the GC was bombarded with requests for funding from around the world. One concomitant of world-church support was that Newbold had to have a larger role. In 1949, while the British church was still independent of the NED, the GC affirmed a BUC request to 'raise the status of Newbold Missionary College to that of a senior college', but wanted it to serve as 'a training school [...] not alone for Great Britain, but [...] Northern Europe and West Africa'; and the GC officers told the BUC president, E. B. Rudge, that the college's status would 'depend on what should be decided re the Union organisation in relation to the Northern European Division'.[21] By the time, a committee had investigated further and reported, the BUC was back in the NED; and so Newbold indeed became the senior training school for Northern Europe as well as the British Isles.

Once Newbold became a division institution, emergency needs were channelled directly to the division, but there was some continuity in necessities. Boilers, pipes, and chimneys had been expensive items in the thirties; in the early seventies the college needed extra funds for 'renewal of [a] sewage pipe', an internal fire escape, and to replace boilers. The Northern Europe-West Africa Division granted £1675 – and requested the South England Conference to add an extra £200, since Newbold Primary School would benefit from the new sewage line. It helped, no doubt, that the Newbold board and

20 See minutes of GCC meeting, 12 July 1945, GCC Proc., xvi, vii, 1966; BAM Board Meeting, 26 Feb. 1946, RGL, BMB 1938–1947, fol. 214ʳ; BUC Committee meetings, 26 Feb. and 16 Aug. 1946, GC Ar., RG NE 1, fld. 'British Union Conference Minutes 1946', pp. 23-24, 83; GC Officers' Meeting, 18 Apr. 1949, GCOM, p. 49-100. Dick attended the 26 Feb. meetings of the BAM Board and BUC Committee. For conversions into 2018 values, see <www.measuringworth.com>.

21 GC Officers' Meetings, 3 and 18 Apr. 1949, GCOM, pp. 49-80, 49-100; GCC meeting, 25 April 1949, GCC Proc., xvii, vi, 1966.

267

NEWAD Executive Committee membership were almost identical and, on this occasion, the executive committee actually adjourned and met briefly as the Newbold board, before adjourning that in turn and reconvening as the division executive committee, which unsurprisingly voted to approve the requests that the same men had just approved while meeting as the college board.[22] By the end of the 1970s, Newbold needed much more substantial sums to construct married student housing and £202,655 in funding was approved.[23]

By the early 2000s, as well as money for capital projects, Newbold increasingly turned to the TED for appropriations to strengthen working capital and liquidity, and to cover shortfalls in operating budgets and losses in some academic years. Special appropriations ranged from £65,000 to £750,000 and even £1,000,000; they could not be sustained indefinitely and were one reason for the repeated rounds of cost-cutting, staff redundancies, and administrative and curricular rationalisation, from 2005 until 2014.[24]

Skodsborg under NED and NEWAD

It was a health care institution, Skodsborg Badesanatorium in Denmark, which rivalled Newbold for division investment. Although never formally a division institution, at times the relationship was so close that formal distinctions were blurred. And in the case of

---

22 NEWAEC meeting, 8 Sept. 1971, NWDMC-ECM 1971, pp. 132–33.
23 NNESC meeting, 13 June 1979, NWDM-ESC 1979, §§ 21–22, p. 14. The expenses of similar projects forty years earlier were rather more moderate: BAM Board Meeting, 27 Jan. 1938, RGL, BMB 1938–47, fol. 7ʳ.
24 E.g., TEDEC Spring Meeting, 16 May 2005, Treasurer's Report and special appropriation, TEDMC-EC 2005, §§ 15, 19, pp. 26–27; TEDEC Winter Meeting 2007, 20 Nov. 2007, Treasurer's Report, and 22 Nov., special appropriation, TEDMC-EC 2007, §§ 50, 186, pp. 26, 129–30; TED ADCOM, 16 Jan. 2008, TEDMC-AC 2008, §§ 14–15, pp. 7–8; TEDEC Annual Council, 20 Nov. 2013, TEDMC-EC 2013, § 91, p. 33; Financial Statement, 31 Dec. 2014, and 'Online Framework Proposal', p. 1, both presented at TEDEC Spring Meeting, 18 May 2015, appended to TEDMC-EC Minutes.

Skodsborg, it generated income for the division, as well as requiring funds from it.

The sanitarium had been founded in 1898, in a former Danish royal palace not far from Copenhagen, by a charismatic and capable medical entrepreneur, Dr Carl Ottosen, who had studied at Battle Creek College and Sanitarium under John Harvey Kellogg. For ninety years the institution and other institutions and enterprises that clustered around it were at the heart of Danish Adventism and, for much of the period, were central to Northern European Adventism.[25]

Skodsborg appears regularly in the minutes of the NED, NEWAD, and TED Executive Committee which regularly met at the sanitarium, often voted appropriations to it, and sometimes received funds from it. Where Newbold's needs were basic – for pipes and boilers – Skodsborg's needs reflected both its palatial accommodations and exclusive clientele. In 1937, for example, the NED voted an appropriation of DKr 1000 for improvements to the dining room.[26] There is little doubt that such investments paid off in a sense, since Skodsborg attracted clients from the highest class of society in Sweden and elsewhere in Scandinavia, as well as in Denmark.[27] But Skodsborg was more than the sanitarium alone; that was just the core, income from which sustained a whole range of programmes, including health food manufacturing, health education, a physiotherapy school, initiatives to feed and clothe the poor, and evangelistic projects. Unfortunately, the expenses for these continued to come in, even when income from the Badesanatorium patients declined; and the Skodsborg complex was not always as well managed as it could have been.

As a result, the sanitarium, the Danish Conference, and the West Nordic Union had recourse to the NED and GC. The drain

---

25 Hans-Jorgen Schantz, 'Denmark', in *HRSDAE*, pp. 73–74.
26 NED Home Committee, 2 Mar. 1936, in NEDCOM Mins., 1935–1936, p. 28.
27 See Medical Secretary's Report, NED Winter Council, 20 Dec. 1936, NEDCOM-WCM 1936, p. 36.

on division and world-church resources supporting 'Skodsborg Sanitarium and its allied philanthropies' prompted a degree of cynicism from GC leaders, evident in the unusually candid observation in the minutes of an officers' meeting in the spring of 1939: 'The board members of that institution seem now really to want good management and an improved plan of operation.'[28] However, the war quickly hit Skodsborg hard. Barely three months into the conflict (and while Denmark was still neutral), it had suffered such a collapse in patronage by patients that management had perforce 'reduced the number of workers in every department of the institution', in all 'reducing the number of workers by over one hundred', while also cutting the remaining 'workers' wages […] in spite of the fact that the costs of living have risen in the country'. The NED president, W. E. Read, requested help from the General Conference.[29]

Skodsborg's management, overseen by the WNUC leadership, eventually navigated the financial shoals of the thirties and first half of the forties, steering the institution into calmer waters during the prosperity of the fifties and sixties, when it flourished. In 1948, it had total income equivalent to SKr 1,954,210 (the NED's official currency at the time). By the end of 1950, the Sanitarium had 'become free of debt and […] been able to repay' a loan of DKr 150,000 to the WNUC.[30] It had meanwhile become the centre for the extraordinary aid and relief operation mounted by the Seventh-day Adventist Church in post-War Europe, which is described in Chapter 11. While its role in the late forties was unsurpassed, it was just the beginning. For the next forty years, Skodsborg really did support a range of 'allied philanthropies'. Some of the substantial and steady revenue stream from the sanitarium was diverted to other quarters and other

---

28 Meeting 16 Mar. 1939, GC Ar., GCOM, ii, 3238.
29 See summary of letter from Skodsborg Superintendent 'Dr. A. Andersen', read at General Conference Officers' Meeting, 26 Nov. 1939, GC Ar., RG 2, GCOM, ii, 3655.
30 See Medical Department Report, NEDCOM meeting, 2 Jan. 1950, in NEDCOM mins., 1947–1950, p. 332; Letter from Skodsborg management, printed in *Northern Light*, 1.1 (March 1951), 5.

needs. Its impact was profound: 'Thousands of people [were] helped and many [were] won for the SDA Church.'[31] Much of the history is specific to the Danish Conference and the West Nordic Union, but the NED as well as the WNUC used Skodsborg as a resource. In 1958, for example, two missionaries were called to Greenland: 'Miss Anna Hogganvik of the West Nordic Union [... and] Miss Ella Praestin' were both nurses and the NED acted partly because it was 'understood that the Skodsborg Sanitarium management' would, 'for the first year' meet a large part of their salaries and expenses.[32] The Badesanatorium itself provided a wonderful facility that was regularly a venue for NED Winter Councils and other meetings, and frequently used by the division for seminars and training courses of various kinds.[33]

To maintain such a major institution, located in an historic building, at the lavish level expected by the clients whose patronage helped drive Skodsborg's profitability was inevitably very costly. Skodsborg benefited from the generous social welfare and health care policies of the Danish government in the heyday of Scandinavian social democracy, but private clients were an important source of revenue. In 1971, the NEWAD Executive Committee received a proposal from 'Skodsborg Badesanatorium which has served the denomination for three quarters of a century', but which was 'urgently in need of modernisation [in order] to continue to operate successfully'. The proposal was for major building works, the cost of which totalled an extraordinary DKr 9,700,000 (almost US$1.3 million, or £540,000). Some funds were contributed by the GC, and a large portion by NEWAD, but considerable sums were also borrowed.[34] Reading the

---

31 Schantz, 'Denmark', p. 74.
32 NEDCOM meeting at Skodsborg, 9 Nov. 1958, NEDCOM mins., 1958, p. 76.
33 E.g., NEDCOM Winter Meeting, 1 Dec. 1964, NEDCOM mins., 1964, p. 171; TEDEC meeting, 11 Mar. 1992, TEDMC-EC 1992, § 46, p. 32.
34 NEDCOM meeting, 8 Sept. 1971, NEDCOM mins., 1971, pp. 133–35 (p. 135).

minutes, one sees a foreshadowing of future trauma, but at the time it was not foreseen and, for the moment, all seemed well.

Union Institutions

It was not only Newbold and Skodsborg that frequently came cap in hand for extra funds to the division. When their income, or union reserves, did not suffice for their needs, the unions passed on the needs of their institutions to the NED, NEWAD, and TED.

In 1938, for example, the British health food company, Granose, like Newbold around the same time, had to construct a new oven chimney; it, too, like Newbold had to request (and was granted) funds, in this case £76 10s.[35] Forty years later, Nutana, the chief Scandinavian health-food company, with subsidiaries in both Denmark and Norway, undertook rapid expansion. It was a WNUC institution and distinct from Finn-Nutana, the Finland Union's health-food company; Nutana's Danish factory 'was the largest of its kind in Denmark'. But the expansion of the late seventies was perhaps too rapid. Nutana was obliged to borrow DKr 2 million 'from retirement funds' on 'the understanding that this will be repaid within 3 years' – a major and risky course of action that required (and received) division approval (but was not without consequence, as we will see later in this chapter).[36] In the 1970s, the Adventist Seminary of West Africa was verging on being a second division institution, at least informally, though not officially, for it served the entire West Africa Section of the division, rather than one or other of the two unions. This meant ASWA, too, came to the division for funds, though at times, as in 1976, it was NEWAD administration which raised the issue of 'the depleted state of the operating capital and liquid assets at ASWA' – and provided the funds that were needed.[37]

---

35 BAM Board Meeting, 26 May 1938, RGL, BMB 1938–1947, fol. 21ʳ.
36 Schantz, 'Denmark', p. 75; NED meeting, 10 June 1981, NEDCOM mins., 1981, § 293, p. 73.
37 NWASC meeting, 8 Jan. 1976, NWDM-WSC 1976, § 9, p. 4.

Secondary and further education institutions in the unions often play a vitally important part in the local Adventist culture, so that strong emotions can be aroused when church leaders or local church members discuss their futures. These institutions included the Polish Union seminary (which after the end of the Cold War evolved into a successful College of Theology and Humanities), Stanborough School in the UK, the four Nordic 'junior colleges' (an American term), and the old Yugoslav Union junior college at Maruševec in Croatia (Illustration 10.6), currently grandly titled 'Adriatic Union College', all of which essentially are, or have on their campuses, secondary schools, but which also offer (or at points in their history offered) post-secondary training (especially for pastors). All of these still exist at the time of writing. The Netherlands Union school and seminary, and the Iceland secondary school, were founded soon after World War II (Illustrations 10.7, 10,8), but closed in the mid-nineties.[38] At various points all of these educational institutions had their own line items in division annual appropriation budgets.[39] In addition, over the years, the division made large appropriations for special purposes, or actually bailed out, Toivonlinna Junior College in Finland, Vejlefjord in Denmark, Ekbyholm in Sweden, Tyrifjord in Norway, and Maruševec in Croatia (Illustrations 10.9–10.13).[40]

In Africa, mission clinics, dispensaries, and hospitals were on the front line of mission. In the 1930s, Dr G. A. S. Madgwick oversaw the development of Kendu Hospital on the shores of Victoria Nyanza, an EAUM institution. In 1940, George Madgwick was called to Nigeria where he established Ile-Ife Hospital, a WAUM

---

38 See Hugh Dunton, 'Iceland', *HRSDAE*, pp. 131–32; Bruinsma, 'The Netherlands', p.159; cf. *YB 1994*, p. 330; *YB 1995*, pp. 327, 334; *YB 1996*, p. 413. The NUC seminary closed in 1994, the Iceland school in 1995.

39 E.g., NNESC Appropriations Budget for 1978, NEWAD Winter Meetings, NNESC, 25 Nov. 1977, NWDM-ESC, p. 38, action no. 84, budget on pp. 39–45 (pp. 40–41).

40 NNESC meeting, 2 Feb. 1977, NWDM-ESC, p. 1, action no. 3; NEWAEC meeting, 17 Mar. 1977, NWDM-ECM, p. 22, action no. 76.

institution (Illustration 10.14). Jengre Hospital, in the largely Islamic far north of Nigeria, was founded as a dispensary in 1931 by John J. and Louisa Hyde; it was one of the first mission stations intended to reach the Fulani people, who had been ignored while the work concentrated on the Ibo and Yoruba (see Chapter 12). Later, their son, Dr John A. Hyde, oversaw the development of Jengre into a hospital (Illustrations 10.15 and 10.16). Although founded by British missionaries, by the NEWAD years Jengre was largely staffed by doctors from the Nordic nations, though nurses also came from the USA and the UK, including one of the first British missionaries of Caribbean ethnicity, Yvonne Eurick, who also served at Ile Ife, and at Kwahu Hospital in Ghana, which had been founded by J. A. Hyde in 1955 (Illustration 10.17). These institutions and others like them were strongholds of Adventist mission in what were, initially, hostile surrounds.[41] Although union institutions, they still required support from NEWAD in managing matters such as accreditation by nursing and medical councils.[42]

In Europe, the ScUC and then the ENUC (later the SUC and Finland Union) and WNUC all operated sanitariums. As early as the mid-thirties, church leaders recognised that the presence of these 'large medical institutions' meant a heavy responsibility on the shoulders of the respective union treasurers as well as of the institutional treasurers, though this had the virtue of being good preparation for higher responsibilities (and it is notable that there have been more

---

41 See Phillips, 'British Adventists Overseas', pp. 23–24; *sub* 'Ile-Ife', 'Jengre Seventh-day Adventist Hospital', 'Kendu Adventist Hospital', 'Madgwick, George Alex Sheridan', and 'Seventh-day Adventist Hospital Ile-Ife', *SDAE*, I, 829, 856, II, 5–6, 589–90; Dick, 'Visiting Our Missions in West Africa', pp. 2–3, 5; files for 'Hyde, John J.', 'Hyde, John Ashford', and, e.g., 'Johnson, Larry', GC Ar., RG 21, Secretariat Appointee Files, nos. 46085, 46086, and 15514; David Marshall, 'Winds of Change', in *Messenger*, Souvenir Special, *100 Years of Mission 1906–2006* (2006), pp. 17–18 (p. 18); Anita and David Marshall, 'Yvonne Eurick: A Vision of Africa', ibid., p. 19.
42 See e.g., Edward Moon (Ile-Ife Director of Nursing) to Deputy Registrar, General Nursing Council, 9 July 1972, NAUK, DT 18/392.

Scandinavian division treasurers than secretaries or presidents).[43] In Scandinavia, sanitariums accorded with a wider cultural emphasis on preventive medicine, physiotherapy, and water cures. After World War II, moreover, the Nordic social democracies funded lavish rehabilitation for those recovering from surgeries. Several Adventist sanitariums were retitled as health centres and/or rehabilitation centres. In the 1940s there were nine; in the sixties, eight, rising to nine again in the 1970s: one in Denmark, two in Finland, two in Sweden, and three (rising to four) in Norway. Many were located in beautiful settings consistent with the ideals of Ellen White. They had caring and capable staff, in many cases products of the physiotherapy school located at Skodsborg (Skodsborg Fysioterapiskole), which over the years trained more than 2000 physiotherapists.[44]

Health care expenses, however, became more and burdensome – for rehabilitation centres, not just for acute-care hospitals. The unions turned to the division for help. In 1977, for example, NEWAD approved 'building and financial plans' presented by the SUC 'for a new building at Hultafors Sanitarium'. Historically, Hultafors had been the most profitable sanitarium after Skodsborg (Illustration 10.18). The total cost amounted to SKr 3.3 million, or $741,573.03; the division voted to 'pass [the plans] on to the General Conference', so it evidently hoped the GC would contribute towards the SKr 600,000 to be invested by the church, which left more than four-fifths of the funds to be raised through loans.[45] The willingness to take on a significant burden of debt was to prove unfortunate in the

---

43 See, e.g., L. H. Christian, 'Change in the Division Treasury', *Advent Survey*, 7.6 (June 1935), 8.
44 Medical Department report for 1948, NEDCOM mins., 1947–1950, pp. 332–33; *YB 1970*, pp. 204–05; *YB 1977*, pp. 244–45; *YB 1986*, p. 348; Schantz, 'Denmark', pp. 74–75. In 1985, the author visited Skodsborg, Hultafors Hälsocenter in Sweden, and Jeloy Sanitarium (Jeloy Kurbad-Fysikalsk-Medisinsk Rehabilitering) in Moss, Norway.
45 NNESC meeting, 28 Feb. 1979, NWDMC, §2, p. 2. Cf. e.g., NEDCOM meeting, 2 Jan. 1950, Medical Department Report, NEDCOM mins., 1947–1950, p. 332.

end for Nordic Adventist health care institutions. As a result of rising costs, even the Nordic countries in the nineties cut back generous social and health care programmes. Reduced income combined with debts were a bad mix.

Added to this was the intertwining of the financial affairs of various West Nordic Union institutions, which were propped up, in effect, by Skodsborg – strictly speaking by the Nordisk Filantropisk Selskab (Nordic Philanthropic Society), which 'comprised the three legal entities, Skodsborg Badesanatorium, Skodsborg Fysioterapiskole and Nutana'. Nutana was thus a subsidiary of Skodsborg. Poor management of the company, an inability 'to respond positively to the rigors of [...] market forces', and profligate borrowing, resulted in very heavy 'operational losses' for both Nutana-Denmark and Nutana-Norway, which in three years and nine months (1988–1991) respectively totalled DKr 29.8 million and 22.4 million Norwegian *kroner*. This resulted in blow-back for the Nordic Philanthropic Society, the sanitarium, and the West Nordic Union. Poor financial management was not limited to Nutana. The level of oversight by the WNUC, in particular, or indeed by the TED, was not what it ought to have been; the Badesanatorium took on a level of debt that it could probably have survived, all other things being equal, but not when part of a wider cluster of debts and 'excessive losses'. So great were the liabilities, added to which were similar factors affecting Nutana-Norway and one of the Norwegian sanitariums, that the WNUC was 'stretched beyond its own financial resources'. Other WNUC sanitariums took on debts in an attempt to sustain Skodsborg. Yet in the end, Nutana-Denmark, Nutana-Norway, and then Skodsborg Sanitarium itself, were all sold.[46]

The TED was obliged to loan DKr 4 million to the West Norwegian Union to help it meet its obligations. This was intended to be a

---

46 'Report of Financial Survey Commission – West Nordic Union Conference', 20–22 Jan. 1992, received by TEDEC, 27 Jan. 1992, TEDMC-EC 1992, § 18, pp. 11–16 (pp. 11–12); TEDEC meeting, 11 Mar. 1992,

bridging loan until the WNUC's finances were put back in order, and it was supposed to be repaid relatively quickly – only for the TED to have to repeatedly postpone the repayment. The division administration was sufficiently exasperated that, on the third occasion, the Executive Committee stipulated 'that the Division will not be financially involved in assisting the West Nordic Union Conference to make full and final settlement of the outstanding debt', while the wording of its voted action was to 'reluctantly extend the repayment period'! Such evidence of impatience in the normally staid pages of committee minutes is revealing. Later the division had to partly bail out the union's retirement fund. The financial crisis led to the merging of conferences in Denmark as a cost-saving measure and, by helping to foster mistrust between Danish and Norwegian Adventists, was a factor in the eventual establishment of separate Norwegian and Danish unions.[47]

The immediate results had been disastrous. Yet that was not an end to it. Adventist health care in Northern Europe was weakened by knock-on effects of the attempts to save Skodsborg for the church. There was, moreover, not always the most effective or business-minded approach by union and institutional leaders at a time when the health care sector was becoming increasingly specialised and expensive. Adventist institutions met industry standards in care, but not always in marketing or management. The combination of these factors was doubly unfortunate, because in the late eighties and early nineties, economic trends and market forces contributed to a new approach to government social and health care in the Nordic social democracies. Under the pressure of challenges from outside and weaknesses within,

---

TEDMC-EC 1992, § 47, p. 34; Torkelson, 'Norway', pp. 165–66; Schantz, 'Denmark', pp. 74–75.
47 TEDEC meetings, 15 and 27 Jan., 15 Apr., and 18 Sept. 1992, TEDMC-EC 1992, §§ 3, 19, 76–77, 223, pp. 2, 16, 48, 123–24 (quotation § 76, p. 48); 'Report of Financial Survey Commission', ibid., pp. 15–16. See Chapter 9, above.

the Adventist health care sector declined. By 1995, only five of the sanitariums survived; today just one, in Norway, still operates.[48]

Managing Properties and Employees

Although its name is little known among church members at large, World Wide Advent Missions Ltd (WWAM) has been important in the TED's history, thanks partly to the decision to locate the headquarters in Britain. In English law, the division had no separate legal existence; it needed a corporate existence in order to hold properties and conduct financial business. World Wide Advent Missions is the division's legal, corporate identity.

Doubtless because of the complications with setting up the new headquarters in the spring of 1929, WWAM was not incorporated until later in the summer, even though the need to do so had been identified late in 1928 and steps had certainly begun by the spring of 1929.[49] The title helped associate it with the 'Mission Board of Seventh-day Adventists', which was the legal entity through which the GC operated its missions, especially in imperial territories where colonial officials were accustomed to dealing with Mission Boards. By the start of World War II, if not earlier, C. H. Anscombe, the GC transportation agent in London, was also the secretary of the Seventh-day Adventist Mission Board in Britain (and for the NED), and treasurer of WWAM.[50]

---

48 *YB 1995*, pp. 323–25, 328, 333: still two in Sweden, but only one in Finland, two in Norway, and none in Denmark. *YB 2017*, p. 476: Skogli Health and Rehabilitation Center (Helse-og Rehabiliteringssenter).

49 NED Minority Committee, 8 Dec. 1928, 18 Mar. 1929, NEDCOM mins., 1928, p.17, 1929, p. 16; WWAM Certificate of Incorporation, no. 241146, 18 July 1929, Companies House, London, digital copy available at <https://beta.companieshouse.gov.uk/company/00241146>.

50 This is not set out clearly in NEDCOM mins., but see Anscombe to Secretary of State for India, 14 June 1939, British Library, IOR/L/PJ, file 2915/39; and above, Chapter 4. On the continuation of the Mission Board 'for necessary legal business', see D. J. B. Trim, 'General Conference Secretariat and Foreign Missionaries', ASTR Research Papers (2017), p. 6.

Meanwhile, at its Winter Council in 1929, the NED executive committee had formally 'accept[ed] the association bearing the name of "The World Wide Advent Missions Limited" as our legal society in the Division' and established the principal that its officers should be 'the officers of the Northern European Division'. It also established the principle, which still applies, that all properties, including those in the mission field, would be purchased and held by WWAM, rather than by the General Conference Association.[51] This was an important innovation in terms of contemporary practice by world divisions, and a departure from then-standard practice. It enabled the division to take action without waiting on the GC, a valuable option that has sometimes been exercised. In practice, it took time for some mission-field properties to be transferred to WWAM. In 1938, according to board minutes of British Advent Missions Ltd, the legal corporation by which the BUC did business, 'the government of Tanganyika territory looks to this Company as being responsible for Seventh-day Adventist properties in Tanganyika'. By the mid-forties, however, most if not all properties in British colonies seem to have been transferred to WWAM ownership.[52]

In practice, the line between WWAM and the division was blurred. The NED Executive Committee was the constituency for WWAM, the WWAM board was often simply the division officers (as is the case currently), and in practice, decisions that might have been taken by a separately constituted board devolved onto the full Division Committee, or the Minority Committee. The exception was during the interlude in which the church in Britain was removed from the NED, when, after hesitation and joint study by the GC and BUC officers, WWAM was placed under the BUC Executive

---

51 NED Winter Council, 4 Nov. 1929, NEDCOM-WCM, 1929, pp. 21–22. The GC Association was the predecessor of today's General Conference Corporation.
52 BAM Board Meeting, Feb. 15, 1938, RGL, BMB 1938–47, fol. 10ʳ. See WWAM report to BUC Committee, 11 July 1946, GC Ar., RG NE 1, fld. 'British Union Conference Minutes 1946', pp. 55–59.

Committee.⁵³ Thereafter, it was the division Executive Committee that engaged with WWAM matters for the next forty years, until, in 1991, a TED ADCOM was introduced. In its absence, just managing the division office, the homes associated with it, and other properties vested in WWAM, all took up time and money. The time taken up was that of the Division Committee, to which decisions came, as well as to the WWAM board.

Some of the matters were routine, but still had to be processed. The properties owned by the division were an ongoing issue that took up the time of in-house division committees and, often, of the Executive Committee. Up to 1965, repairs of, rental payments for, local government negotiations concerning and, in some cases, sales of, NED-owned homes in Hazel Gardens, and in Riverdene and Windsor Avenue (both streets less than half a mile from the division office), all came before NEDCOM: whether to authorise action by WWAM, or, at times, to meet considerable operating deficits that arose from operating the 'staff houses in Edgware' as a service rather than a profit-making venture.⁵⁴

After the move to St Albans, there was for many years a NEWAD/TED 'House Committee', the function of which was to deal with the headquarters building and the houses around it, though it also at times dealt with expenses relating to the staff who worked in the

---

53 GC Officers' Meeting, 18 Apr. 1949, GCOM, p. 49–101; GCC meeting of 19 Apr. 1949, GCC Proc., xvii, v, 1464. This formal decision was taken only a little more than a year before the BUC was reassigned to the NED, but in practice WWAM had started treating the BUC as its constituency as soon as the union was attached directly to the GC by the 1946 Session: e.g., WWAM report to BUC Committee, cited in fn. 52.

54 Operating deficit: NEDCOM meeting, 21 Oct. 1958, NEDCOM Mins., 1958, p. 71. On the NED's return to Edgware, 'rental charges […] to workers occupying Division owned homes in Edgware' had been set at 10 per cent of salary: NEDCOM meeting, 14 Jan. 1951, NEDCOM mins., 1951, p. 8. Homes in Riverdene and Windsor Ave.: e.g., NEDCOM meetings, 17 Dec. 1951 and 15 Sept. 1955, NEDCOM mins., 1951, p. 143, 1955, pp. 106–7 (setting an amount for rentals rather than a percentage of salary – this required negotiations with the local authority rent tribunal).

division office. It was not only Newbold College that had pipes and boilers in need of repairs or replacement: in January 1982 (perhaps motivated by expenses resulting from wintry cold weather), the NED spent £1682.35 on converting the boiler in the division office from oil to gas. But office expenses were not only for hardware or engineering; the same month, expenditure of £500 was authorised 'for the redecorating of the two offices of the Communication Department and the two offices of the Health Department'.[55] The staff who filled clerical and more minor administrative positions needed to be taken care of; in 1979, the division committee saw fit to organise 'an Office Secretaries' Seminar [...] for secretaries serving in Northern Europe'.[56]

Accommodations for staff also continued to require the investment of time and money. In June 1979, for instance, NEWAD was obliged to spend no less than £5000 on an underground water tank and associated new pump for the 'staff flats' near the division office.[57] Among other business processed by the House Committee was authorising 'the purchase of a postage scale at a cost of £256'; the expenditure of £150 to put up fencing at one of its houses in St Albans; and approving a loan of £2500 to one employee to enable him to buy a car. In 1981, the issue of purchasing the division office's first computer went to the NED Executive Committee, which eventually authorised a Rank Xerox Word Processor Model 850 that cost £3605.25 (equivalent to £13,570 in 2018 values). With such mundane matters was the time of the division executive officers and even

---

55 NED House Committee, 13 Jan. 1982, TEDArc., House Committee Minutes binder, 1982 §§ 1–2, p. 1.
56 NNESC meeting, 25 Apr. 1979, NWDM-ESC 1979 § 9, p. 6.
57 NED House Committee, 13 June 1979, TEDArc., House Committee Minutes binder, 1979, § 45, p. 11. Although this was a sizeable sum, it was not subsequently taken to NEWAEC; thus, the House Committee had considerable financial authority delegated to it.

its executive committee occupied, before, as we saw in Chapter 9, the Administrative Committee was introduced in 1991.[58]

There were, however, thorny legal and practical issues that to be worked through because of the Adventist tendency for properties owned by the corporate body of one ecclesiastical organisational unit to be utilised by another. Although the houses in Edgware had been bought for division office personnel, in practice they were made available to BUC employees by the 1940s (if not earlier). By the 1970s, the shoe was on the other foot: NEWAD had taken over management of properties built and owned by the BUC, with the division renting them to NEWAD employees and missionaries on furlough. All this muddied the waters at various points through the twentieth century.[59] As late as the twenty-first century, a major property in London, being used by the South England Conference, was actually owned by WWAM and the need to resolve its status legally eventually had to be taken to the TED Executive Committee.[60]

None of these matters was mission critical, yet all had to be dealt with. The history of the TED – indeed of any division – is always about more than ambitious programs, strategic visions, bold initiatives, nurture of church members, enterprising evangelism, and sustaining institutions as they engage in the teaching and healing ministry of Christ. The history of a division is also about preparation

---

58   NEWAD House Committee, 10 Jan. and 13 June 1979, TEDArc., House Committee Minutes binder, 1979, §§ 1, 46–47, pp. 1, 11: the meeting of 13 June was chaired by NEWAD President Scragg with Secretary Beach present at the meeting; Beach (Illustration 10.19) chaired the 10 Jan. meeting. NEDCOM meeting, 28 July 1981, in NWDC-EC 1981, § 352, p. 88 (£3135 before VAT, which was 15 per cent). For conversion of sterling values see <www.measuringworth.com/calculators/ukcompare/relativevalue.php>. Not coincidentally, the last House Committee was appointed in 1990: TEDEC meeting, 31 Oct. 1990, TEDMC-EC, 1990, § 252, p. 125.
59   See, e.g., BUC Committee meeting, 9 Sept. 1946, minutes in GC Ar., RG NE 1, fld. 'British Union Conference Minutes 1946', p. 99; NEWAD House Committee, 10 Jan. 1979, TEDArc., House Committee Minutes binder, 1979, § 2, p. 1.
60   Treasurer's report, TEDEC Spring Meeting, 20 May 2019.

of agendas for and minutes of winter councils, regular executive committee meetings, and various boards. It is about property management and financial investment, about processing the transmission of funds from unions to the division and thence to the GC, about transferring world-church funds to the division and its appropriations to the unions and to institutions. A division history is about paying, housing, and caring for office staff. If these mundane matters are not taken care of, then the division headquarters will not function, the relationships between different parts of the church will break down, and eventually mission will suffer, if not cease. Taking care of routine business is one of the foundations of success in more exciting areas of the work of the church.

Chapter 11
Engaging with Society

One of the major developments in the TED during the late twentieth century and early twenty-first century has been the prominence of the Adventist Development and Relief Agency: ADRA. This has been a story, not of rise and fall, but rather of ADRA's rise and rise. In the words of one historian of Adventist missions in Africa: 'In recent years the tide of missionaries flowing from Europe to the developing world has slowed to a trickle'; young women and men of the Seventh-day Adventist Church in the TED, members of what is 'now very much a multicultural organisation' in many countries, 'are volunteering their unpaid part-time help or making career choices full-time for the ADRA phenomenon all over the world.'[1]

The church's aid, development, and relief work began to gain an increased profile in Europe in the 1970s, before the title ADRA had been adopted for the church's agency responsible for those lines of work. But, in the 1990s and early 2000s, ADRA achieved a kind of ascendancy; it sometimes seemed as if, for many Adventists, ADRA *was* the church. It drew numerous European Adventist recruits, especially (though not only) Newbold graduates, who once would have volunteered to be missionaries.

Why was this so? Humanitarianism and relief were socio-culturally acceptable terms and concepts in Europe, whereas, in the Western world at large but perhaps especially in Europe, 'missionary' was now a bad word (as discussed in Chapter 1). To many Gen X and Millennial Adventists, ADRA was mission service for the post-imperial age. The type of work it does is consistent with longstanding Adventist approaches to mission, not least wholistic thinking about health, and is consistent, too, with the church's conscious effort to

---

1   Jack Mahon, 'A Century of British Seventh-day Adventist Missions' in *A Century of Adventism*, ed. by Marshall, p. 19.

reflect the healing and the teaching ministries of Jesus Christ. As understood and practiced by Adventist missionaries, 'medical missionary work' had long incorporated aspects that today would be addressed by relief and development agencies, because the Adventist approach to 'the ministry of healing' was both preventive and ameliorative.[2] The traditional Adventist understanding that education should be practical meant there was always an emphasis on training, including in agricultural techniques and light industrial skills, and thus inherent in the work of Adventist missionaries in 'mission fields' were some kinds of development. Adventist mission, in short, although always explicitly conversionary and other-worldly as far as ultimate goals went, was never divorced from this-worldly concerns.

All this meant that there were aspects of Adventist ministry – ones valued by church members across the theological spectrum – which lent themselves to moving towards a strongly humanitarian focus in church work. As a result, ADRA was the perfect *via media* for Adventists in the TED. For those postmodern church members who were instinctively leaning towards a doctrine-lite version of their faith and increasingly doubting the legitimacy of 'conversion', while still appreciating and valuing the Adventist message of wholeness and hope in Christ, ADRA was the perfect way to square the circle: whether supporting ADRA with prayer and donations; having ADRA as the aspect of the church they would talk about, without embarrassment, to friends of other churches and faiths, or none; or working for ADRA (as opposed to 'the Church', as though the two were somehow distinct). As one ADRA veteran told the European Mission Conference in 1997, ADRA provided 'opportunities for church members to engage in society and feel comfortable about doing so'.[3]

---

2   Ellen G. White, *The Ministry of Healing* (Mountain View, Calif.: Pacific Press, 1942 [1909]), esp. the third chapter: 'Medical Missionaries and Their Work'; for a good summary of how this worked in practice, see Charles Teel, 'Revolutionary Missionaries in Peru: Fernando and Ana Stahl', *Spectrum*, 18.3 (Feb. 1988), 50.

3   David Syme, 'ADRA and Mission', in *Re-visioning Adventist Mission in Europe*, ed. by Baumgartner, pp. 163–66 (p. 165).

For those more traditional church members who had no doubt about the beauty of the Fundamental Beliefs, ADRA was a way of delivering historic Adventist priorities, even while still proclaiming the prophetic truths of the angels of Revelation 14; and for them, too, it could be an entering conversational wedge with unchurched or otherchurched friends and colleagues (to whom they might otherwise have had nothing of mutual interest to say).

In sum, then, one Adventist reaction to the rise of secularist and postmodernist values in the territory of the TED was a concomitant rise in the importance of humanitarian relief and development. ADRA was embraced, including by people who assumed that supporting it meant supporting the conversionary mission of the church, when in fact that was not always the case, certainly not directly.

* * *

The prominence of ADRA probably seems unprecedented to many Adventists in the TED. Yet it is not. The greatest impact this division has had in relieving mass suffering came in the 1940s when the leaders of the NED, supported by its unions, conferences, and institutions, took a leading role in the relief of Europe in the aftermath of World War II.

The Post-War Crisis and the Church's Response

In the early twentieth century, many local church organisations and individual missionaries engaged in what would now be called humanitarian assistance and development in what today is often known as the Global South, which includes the TED's historic mission fields in Africa. But humanitarian relief was done largely on an individual, localised basis. The first major, coordinated, sustained international relief effort by the Seventh-day Adventist Church was undertaken in the aftermath of World War II. Many parts of the world church contributed to feeding, aiding, and rebuilding Europe, but the part played by the church in the TED was unequalled. The unions and institutions in the division, church members in the Scandinavian countries, the NED headquarters: all were actively involved, some in providing resources, others in managing how they were utilised, but both sides were necessary.

The unparalleled scale and extent of destruction and of human suffering caused by the Second World War necessitated a similarly unprecedented response; a systematic and international approach to relief was needed. Such an approach was indeed adopted by the United Nations Relief and Rehabilitation Administration (UNRRA), created in 1943 (before the current United Nations was formally organised) in order to deal with the humanitarian disaster that the American, British, and Canadian governments knew would face them after they defeated the Axis powers. The UNRRA is an appropriate point of comparison for the Adventist Church, for UNRRA was international, drawing staff, funds, and other resources from multiple countries; it began its preparations in 1943, well before the war was over, and it continued major operations after the war's end, into 1947.[4] These points are also true of the Seventh-day Adventist Church; the nature of the human catastrophe likewise evoked a systematic, international, effort by the worldwide Adventist Church, which started gathering clothing and food, and raising money, in 1944. While official church engagement in post-war Europe did not start until 1946, which was slow compared to other churches and non-denominational religious organisations, the church's role, through the NED, continued to be very active until well into 1949.[5]

4　Susan E. Armstrong-Reid and David Murray, *Armies of Peace: Canada and the UNRRA Years* (Toronto & London: University of Toronto Press, 2008); *Relief in the Aftermath of War*, ed. by Jessica Reinisch, special issue of *Journal of Contemporary History*, 43. 3 (July 2008).

5　For other religious groups, see e.g., Paul Weindling, '"For the Love of Christ": Strategies of International Catholic Relief and the Allied Occupation of Germany, 1945–1948', in *Relief in the Aftermath of War*,

Initially, materials and money were collected in America and sent directly to the former war zones; later it was mainly money that was sent to Europe, with North America remaining the largest (though not unique) source for funds. But how would funds be used to best effect? How would food and other needed items purchased with the funds get where they were needed? A structure was necessary; the NED headquarters and the Adventist Church in Denmark and Sweden supplied one that worked superbly well.

The history of Adventist relief work in post-war Europe has largely been ignored by scholars.[6] It provides a counterpoint to recent work by historians of the role of American Protestantism in post-war Europe, which emphasises American, and minimises European, agency in the delivery of aid.[7] This chapter only scratches the surface, to give some indication of a crucial chapter in the TED's history. It draws partly on the archive of the NED 'Relief Committee', preserved for many years at the Swedish Union headquarters and now in the TED archives.[8] It is to be hoped that these and other sources will be exploited and an exhaustive history of this extraordinary episode written.

Rebuilding and Resettling

The church involved itself in aid and relief in several ways. The most important was in the area of provision of food and clothing,

ed. by Reinisch, 477–92; Johannes-Dieter Steinert, 'British Humanitarian Assistance: Wartime Planning and Postwar Realities', ibid., 421–35 (pp. 423–24, 426–28, 432).

6 It is briefly considered by Audrey Andersson, 'The Scandinavian Influence on the Trans-European Division', in *Faith in Search of Depth and Relevancy: Festschrift in Honour of Dr Bertil Wiklander*, ed. by Reinder Bruinsma ([St Albans]: Trans-European Division of Seventh-day Adventists, 2014), pp. 393–94; there is only a short paragraph in the *SDAE* article on 'Adventist Development and Relief Agency', *SDAE*, I, 12–14 (p. 13).

7 Hans Krabbendam, 'Opening a Market for Missions: American Evangelicals and the Re-Christianization of Europe, 1945–1985', *Amerikastudien / American Studies*, 59 (2014), 154.

8 References in this chapter that cite TEDArc. are all of this collection of papers.

289

which was also the most sustained form of aid and the form that most involved the church in the NED, and will be explored later in this chapter. Other kinds of assistance were also rendered however, which provide the context.

Firstly, showing considerable foresight, the 1942 Autumn Council established the Rehabilitation Fund to cover the cost of replacing or repairing physical infrastructure, from local churches to institutional buildings. In each of the next three years, the GC Executive Committee set aside extra funds; a Rehabilitation Offering, taken on 3 February 1945 (though in the Western Hemisphere and South Africa only), brought in $1,035,000; funds raised by unions, institutions, conferences, and local churches in North America added more than another million dollars. As a result, by 1 January 1946, the Rehabilitation Fund totalled the extraordinary sum of $4,847,856.04 – but fundraising continued and, among the Rehabilitation Offerings taken all around the world, £1500 was raised from churches in the British Union.[9] The fund was accessed widely as Adventists tried, in the most literal sense, to rebuild in the years following the war; it provided money for reconstruction in the TED's territory, including Britain, Ethiopia, Finland, Netherlands, Norway, and Poland.

Secondly, the church made an effort to help resettle Displaced Persons and to find new families for war orphans. To lead this work, the GC chose Walther Ising, a German Adventist who had served as CED secretary and president in the 1920s–30s and been moved to the world headquarters in 1938, partly to save him from arrest by the Nazis. As the war ended, Ising was of retirement age, but he was

---

9 W. E. Nelson, 'The Treasurer's Report', Forty-Fifth GC Session, second meeting, 6 June 1946, *ARH*, 123.34, General Conference Report, no. 2 (7 June 1946), 24, 29–30 (p. 29); A. V. Olson, 'Rehabilitation Offering', *Canadian Union Messenger*, 15.4 (21 Aug. 1946), 3–4; BUC Committee meeting, 26 Feb. 1946 GC Ar., RG NE 1, fld. 'British Union Conference Minutes 1946', p. 23. The Jan. 1946 value is worth at least $67.6 million in 2018: <https://www.measuringworth.com/calculators/uscompare/relativevalue.php>.

kept on salary and for four years the church paid (or reimbursed) his expenses as he shuttled back and forth between North America and Europe, and across Europe. His knowledge of the languages and cultural contexts was invaluable. He found homes and jobs in the United States and US visas for 'about 250 displaced persons' (including some from the TED's territories); he also made arrangements for care of orphans, some of them in Adventist homes in Switzerland, others in America.[10]

This pales into insignificance in contrast with Roman Catholic resettlement of DPs in North America and it is probable that the Seventh-day Adventist Church could have done more to assist refugees of various kinds and from diverse countries. That said, however, the Adventist effort was not negligible, given the disparity between both the institutional infrastructure of the two churches, and their influence with American military and immigration officials. Further, Adventists (like Catholics) concentrated on helping to resettle their own co-religionists, who were rather fewer in number than Catholics.[11] Ising certainly gave it his all. Exhausted by his efforts, he died in 1950 at the age of 69.

Giving Generously

In the United States and Canada, individual Seventh-day Adventists, local Adventist churches and Dorcas societies, and organisational units, all played a role in assembling and sending to Europe large quantities of clothing and food. This, too, was initiated before the end of the war and the actual despatch of items of food and clothing

---

10 Obit., *ARH*, 127.51 (26 Oct. 1950), 20; GC Treasurer W. E. Nelson's statement to GCC Spring Meeting, 18 Apr. 1947, GCC Proc., XVII, ii, 472. Ising's diary for 1946 is in GC Ar., Personal Collections, no. 93. Instance of his expenses being reimbursed: GC Famine Relief Committee meeting, 6 June 1948, mins. in GC Ar., RG 25, box MIN 80 (unpaginated).

11 See Todd Scribner, '"Pilgrims of the Night": The American Catholic Church Responds to the Post-World War II Displaced Persons Crisis', *American Catholic Studies*, 124.3 (Fall 2013), 1–20.

from the United States seems to have largely ceased by the end of 1946. Thereafter, there was an emphasis on donating money that could be sent to Europe and used there, giving greater flexibility and the ability to respond directly to identified needs.

Planning began soon after the Allied invasion of Normandy, an event which indicated that the end of the war, while not imminent, would not be far off. The treasurer of the General Conference, W. E. Nelson, steered the initial planning (Illustration 11.1).[12] He also chaired the GC Famine Relief Committee (discussed more below). Nelson reported to the 1946 GC Session that Adventist relief efforts had begun in August 1944 and consisted of gathering clothing. By the time of the session, nearly two years later, the church had already shipped '118 tons of clothing and food' overseas, mostly to Europe. Church leaders knew that given the 'very severe famine' conditions in much of Europe, more clothing and food would be needed in 1947.[13] Thereafter, however, it was mostly money, rather than actual foodstuffs, articles of clothing, or household items, that was given by church members. One reason was that by the end of 1946 there was already a system in place in Scandinavia to identify needs, purchase the necessary items, transport them where they were needed, and distribute them to those who had most need of them. This was the NED Relief Committee.

While its operations were vital and will be briefly examined later in this chapter, it could not have worked as successfully as it did without a steady stream of funds. This came both from within and

---

[12] The 'Special Committee – Post War Relief', chaired by Nelson, met for the first time on 28 June 1944: mins. in GC Ar., RG 25, box MIN 314, fld. 'W Misc'.

[13] See W. E. Nelson, 'Report of Relief Work Carried on by the General Conference During and Since the End of the War', *ARH*, 123.24, General Conference Report no. 2 (7 June 1946), 34–35 (quotations p. 34); Henry F. Brown, 'A Call for Continued Clothing Drive', *Canadian Union Messenger*, 15.4 (21 Aug. 1946), 1; and 'Thanks for Relief', voted action, NED Winter Council, 14 Feb. 1947, NEDCOM mins., 1947–1950, p. 31.

from without Europe. By the end of 1946, a total of $1,266,768.04 (or more than $16 million in 2018 dollars) had been given by Canadian and American churches and church members.[14] But the GC officers realised, even before year's end, that even more would be needed. James Cummins, the secretary of the Famine Relief Committee, was 'advised by the headquarters [of] the UNRRA' that it was 'largely discontinuing its activities abroad', leaving 'a much heavier responsibility on the volunteer agencies who have been doing this work'.[15] Nelson travelled to Europe in the autumn following the GC Session, accompanied by Vice-President Lewis Christian. Amongst other cities, they visited Berlin, and Berne in Switzerland, making the first visit to the SED headquarters by officers of the GC since before the war. From the consultations there and from the horrifying scenes they witnessed, Nelson urged on colleagues that 'the famine situation' in Europe was worse than they had thought and that the church needed to 'do more than last year', as otherwise 'thousands of our members will succumb this winter and spring'. By the end of the year, North American leaders renewed appeals to Adventist church members in North America to donate more money, clothing, and non-perishable food.[16]

As we will see, the emergency situation was addressed in 1947, but that was not an end to world-church financial support for the relief effort in Europe. For the rest of the forties, the GC and divisions set aside a Sabbath annually for a special offering for the Famine Relief Fund. North American Adventists thus continued to be generous for the needs of their brethren and sisters in Europe. While the sums given decreased as the decade wore on (and the need became less

---

14 Statement of GC Treasurer Nelson, GCC Spring Meeting, 18 Apr. 1947, GCC Proc., XVII, ii, 471; conversion of 1946 to 2018 dollars: <www.measuringworth.com>.
15 James F. Cummins, 'Reduction in Price on Relief Packages to Europe', *Northern Union Outlook*, 8 Oct. 1946, p. 2.
16 Nelson to J. F. Cummins, telegram 1 Dec. 1946, text printed on the front pages of *Columbia Union Visitor*, 19 Dec. 1946 and *Central Union Reaper*, 17 Dec. 1946.

urgent), in the first nine months of 1947, $624,966.43 was donated in the North American Division, while some relief projects additionally received funds from the separate Missions Extension offering and from Ingathering.[17]

They were not, however, alone; church members in Northern Europe also gave and collected for European relief. Swedish Seventh-day Adventists gave generously, a manifestation of a wider trend in their country, which, in the words of Gustav Lindsay, ENUC president in the forties, 'was one of the few countries in Europe that escaped the horrors of war devastation or occupation'. Aware both of their good fortune and of the fate of their neighbours, 'all classes of people [...] all parties and creeds [were] ready and eager to play the part of the good Samaritan.' One result was that, as Lindsay told the 1946 GC Session, 'our people responded with liberal offerings for relief work', initially to help refugees who arrived in Sweden 'poor and destitute'; then, once the war was over, to help the rest of Europe.[18]

As we will see, this general Swedish charitableness towards war-torn Europe was a resource the NED would draw on and work synergistically with.[19] As for church members in the NED, the 1947 relief offering, given in Danish and Norwegian *kroner* and in Swedish *kronor* (including a small contribution from Finland but none from the Netherlands or Poland) came to the equivalent of $20,231.96.

17   Untitled financial summary (n.d., but for 1 Jan. –30 Sept. 1947), with Famine Relief Committee mins., 1947, GC Ar., RG 25, box MIN 80.
18   Forty-Fifth Session, third meeting, 6 June 1946, *ARH*, 123.24, General Conference Report, no. 2 (7 June 1946), 36, and text of report: G. A. Lindsay, 'The East Nordic Union Conference', ibid., 39–40 (p. 39). Lindsay's view of Swedish attitudes is borne out by an informed secular observer: E. J. L. 'Some Trends in Post-War Sweden', *The World Today*, 2.7 (1946), 313–30 (pp. 324–25).
19   By the autumn of 1945, the Swedish Red Cross and other Swedish organisations were already involved in distributing aid in the Netherlands and Germany, and a coordinating committee of 34 Swedish aid organisations was founded: see 'Some Trends in Post-War Sweden', *art. cit.*, p. 326; Banning, 'Food Shortage and Public Health', p. 110; Steinert, 'British Humanitarian Assistance', pp. 431–32. The NED's Relief Committee actively collaborated with these bodies: see below.

The relief offering in 1948 raised sums in all the NED's unions, including the PUC and NUC, equivalent to $15,610, nearly double the $8750 'goal set by the General Conference' for the NED. When miscellaneous donations are included, church members in Northern Europe had given the equivalent of $37,515 since the war's end.[20] This was 3 per cent of the donations given in North America to the end of 1946 alone, while the NED membership in 1946 was equal to 8.5 per cent of the NAD membership, but these offerings were from territories fought over and occupied.[21]

Oversight and Leadership

Leaders of the world church recognised that it was not enough to throw money at a problem. Part of the story of post-war relief is the people who managed it.

It is an Adventist Church nostrum that the denomination has a committee system not a presidential system of governance. As we have seen, in Chapters 5 and 7, that does not mean that presidents, especially of the General Conference or of divisions, do not have a great deal of influence and authority; and yet at its heart it is true, and a strength of the Seventh-day Adventist Church. Thus, important steps towards aiding war-torn Europe were the establishment of two committees. But committees were not enough; the church also sent workers to direct and undertake the necessary relief work.

There had been ad hoc committees in the GC headquarters, chaired by Treasurer Nelson and Assistant Treasurer Cummins, that had been working since the summer of 1944.[22] But in April 1946, President McElhany, by virtue of a GC Executive Committee action,

---

20 NED, 1947/48 and 1949 Winter Councils and 1948 Spring Council, 1–2 Jan. 1948, 22 Apr. 1948, and 30 Dec. 1949, NEDCOM mins., 1947–1950, pp. 89, 100, 135–36, 316. There is no report in NEDCOM mins. on the 1949 offering.
21 *ASR*, 84 (1946), 2.
22 'Special Committee – Post War Relief', and 'War Relief Committee', mins. in GC AR., RG 25, box MIN 314, fld. 'W Misc'.

appointed the Famine Relief Committee, which Nelson chaired. A committee with wide-ranging terms of reference was needed to process the various requests that came in from church leaders and committees at the basic levels of structure; identify and prioritise needs and formulate a strategy for meeting them; agree action plans and have them endorsed by appropriate executive committees; and then have the plans implemented. The same action that served as warrant for the Famine Relief Committee also provided that J. J. Strahle should 'go to Europe as director of our relief work, and that [Viggo] Thomsen and [Möller] Christensen of Denmark be associated with him as a committee'. This as yet unnamed small committee was, after the 1946 GC Session and rebirth of the Northern European Division, enlarged and became the NED Relief Committee.[23] A powerful local committee was probably indispensable to facilitate cooperation between the different levels of church structure in the many countries and several divisions in Europe; indeed it would have been difficult to coordinate the considerable enthusiasm for relief work that existed among church workers and institutions in Sweden and Denmark, because they were in two different unions (ENUC and WNUC).

The man the GC officers had chosen as director of European relief (and only asked two days before it was ratified by the executive committee) was John-Jacob Strahle (Illustration 11.2).[24] Although he had been born and bred in Nebraska, his family roots were in Germany, he spoke German, and he had extensive experience of Europe, including as an NED departmental secretary in the thirties.[25] The Famine Relief Committee recognised that, were the church to buy stocks of food in

---

23 GCC meeting, 2 Apr. 1946, GCC Proc., xvii, i, 2357; meeting of GC Officers with Famine Relief Committee, 4 Apr. 1946, GCOM, second series, p. 6385; report from NED committee, Jan. 1947, in GC Famine Relief Committee mins., GC Ar., RG 57, box MIN 80, fld. 'Famine Relief 1947'.
24 GC Officers' Meeting, 31 Mar. 1946, GCOM, second series, p. 6383.
25 Obit., under 'In Remembrance', *ARH*, 137.47 (24 Nov. 1960), 27. Strahle had been elected NED Publishing secretary at the 1930 GC Session and served until the 1936 Session, when he was called to the world

North America and have them 'processed and packaged and shipped to Europe, it would require many weeks and possibly months', and so Strahle was directed 'to purchase large quantities of food in Denmark and Sweden', two of the least war-torn parts of the continent of Europe, in order to expedite matters.[26] Adventists in Denmark and Sweden were well organised and active; thanks to the decisions of the 1946 Session in Takoma Park, a new headquarters for the whole region was about to be based in Stockholm for the rest of the forties; Skodsborg, as we will see later, provided a strong institutional base. From Copenhagen, Strahle directed the whole relief operation, a huge task! Another American missionary, J. J. Aitken, was sent to Switzerland, to represent Strahle in Central Europe, while a Danish Adventist, Rye Andersen, who had served as a missionary in Uganda from 1929 to the mid-1930s, was assigned to work directly under Strahle; later D. G. Rose, a German-American pastoral worker, was sent to assist Aitken.[27]

Strahle was only in Europe for two months, then returned to North America to report on initial progress to the officers' councils prior to the GC Session. The new General Conference Committee reappointed him, 'for such time as may be necessary', and he went back to Scandinavia.[28] He remained in Europe for several months, but was back in the US in December, where he 'visited a number of our large churches' in the Lake Union, which had a very large proportion of members of Scandinavian ethnicity. He 'told them how thousands of lives had been saved through the welfare work', urging them to give

headquarters as associate secretary of the Publishing department. Examples of correspondence in German include Lars Ivarsson to Strahle, 1 Oct. 1946, and Otto Brozio to same, 21 Oct. 1946, TEDArc.
26 Nelson, 'Report of Relief Work', p. 34.
27 See J. J. Strahle, 'Distributing Food in Europe', *ARH*, 123.35 (11 July 1946), 16; GC Officers' Meeting, 11 Aug. 1946, GCOM, second series, p. 6494; Nelson, 'Report of Relief Work', p. 34; 'Some Statistics and Information Concerning Our Missions in Africa', appended to end of NEDCOM-WCM, 1929.
28 GCC meeting, 16 June 1946, GCC Proc., XVII, ii, 3; and see GC Officers' Meeting, 26 June 1946, GCOM, second series, p. 6459.

more for 'the needs of our starving people in Europe'. He returned there again in mid-January 1947, attended the first winter council of the 'newly re-organized Northern European Division' in Stockholm in February, then stayed in Sweden and Denmark until the end of March before reverting to the United States. This concluded his work in Europe.[29] Strahle retained the title 'Director of European Relief', exercised loose oversight from the world headquarters in Washington, DC, and liaised between the Relief Committee and committees at the GC.[30]

As this summary indicates, Strahle's time in Europe was quite limited; the success that followed owed less to him than to a group of gifted Scandinavian church workers who took on the task of relieving the hungry and the (almost) naked. Strahle's achievement lay in recognising their talent and energy, and giving them their head. In addition to the two original (Danish) committee members, Christensen, a treasury official in the West Denmark Conference, and Thomsen, the treasurer of Skodsborg Sanitarium, church officials in Sweden soon became involved; they included David Carlsson and Alf Karlman, respectively president of the North Swedish Conference and secretary-treasurer of the ENUC, which shared the same headquarters.[31] Karlman was only 42 when he began to work with Strahle, and energetic, but had ten years' experience as secretary-treasurer. He rapidly took the lead 'in buying and shipping food'. Viggo Thomsen's role quickly went beyond committee membership to a more active role, at first buying food for Strahle, then traveling in Germany to assess

---

29 Strahle to Karlman, 20 Dec. 1946, TEDArc.; GCC meeting, 30 Dec. 1946, GCC Proc., XVII, ii, 348; Strahle report to NEDCOM Winter Council, 11 Feb. 1947, NEDCOM mins., 1947–1950, p. 2. 'European Relief', schedule 1, 'J. J. Strahle Expenses 1947, paid by Skodsborg Sanitarium', n.d., TEDArc.
30 E.g., Strahle to Alf Karlman, 13 Apr. 1947, and reply, 21 Apr. 1947, TEDArc.
31 *YB 1946*, pp. 139–40, 283; *YB 1947*, p. 139; Jacqueline Dusing to Carlsson, 28 Apr. 1946, TEDArc.

where church members were, their wants, and how best to supply them.[32]

As a result, despite the GC's active role in 1945 and early 1946, and North America's ongoing importance as a source of funds, from the middle of 1946 it was the NED, both administratively, through the Relief Committee, and more generally, in terms of individuals and institutions in the division, that became responsible for providing food and clothing throughout Europe.

The European Relief Committee

Each year, for the first five years after the end of World War II, several hundred thousand dollars' worth of foodstuffs were purchased in Denmark and Sweden, or imported from around the world, and then distributed in Austria, Czechoslovakia, Hungary, Poland, Romania, and all four occupied zones of Germany. A large part of the necessary funding came from the world church, but Adventists in Northern Europe raised funds as well, the region's Adventist health institutions took responsibility for expenses, and the European Relief Committee, based in the NED, guided and administered the whole process. As the relief effort matured, moreover, assistance began to be provided to all those needing it, rather than only to church members.

Aiding Adventists

The first priority was to distribute food to 'our starving brethren' in Northern Europe. This is how W. E. Nelson, treasurer of the General Conference and first chairman of the Famine Relief Committee, reported to the 1946 Session. But it is also evident in instructions

---

32 'In Remembrance', 'Karlman, Alf M.', *ARH*, 142.26 (1 July 1965), 24; Strahle, 'Distributing Food', p. 16; D. G. Rose telegram, quoted in W. E. Nelson, 'What Will You Do for Famine Relief?', *Atlantic Union Gleaner*, 9 Sept. 1947, p. 1.

from the GC officers and the Famine Relief Committee to Strahle.³³ Further, those responsible for relief in Europe did, in practice, prioritise 'bringing relief to our people' during 1945–1947; the beneficiaries were tens of thousands of 'needy Seventh-day Adventists'.³⁴

Over the winter of 1945/46, the GC purchased some 4000 packages of food in New York, which were shipped to 'Finland, Poland, and Holland'.³⁵ The decision to prioritise the church members of these three countries was pragmatic and compassionate. Denmark was largely untouched, and Norway had suffered oppression and privation, but not much damage to infrastructure. In contrast, parts of both Finland and the Netherlands had been the scenes of heavy fighting, and then both countries suffered severe food shortages, while Poland, as noted in Chapter 4, had experienced almost total devastation, perhaps the worst of any European country. The Netherlands, with its large Atlantic ports, received sufficient supplies of food and clothing (and medicines), relatively quickly. Finland and Poland were harder to reach, due in part simply to distance and shattered infrastructure, but also in part to obstruction of UNRRA by Soviet soldiers and officials. It was thanks to the relief effort steered from Stockholm and Skodsborg that Finnish and Polish church members received clothing and food in 1946 and 1947.

Finland was still under severe rationing in the summer of '47 – at a large gathering of Finnish Adventists, Francis Nichol, the visiting editor of the *Review & Herald*, was told that all the 800 church

---

33 Nelson, 'Report of Relief Work', p. 34. See mins. of GC Officers' Meeting, 30 June 1946, GCOM, second series, p. 6642.

34 Treasurer Nelson's statement, and report of J. J. Strahle, to GCC Spring Meeting, 18 Apr. 1947, GCC Proc., XVII, ii, 471–72. See anon., 'In Appreciation', *Canadian Union Messenger*, 15.4 (21 Aug. 1946), 1–2; W. E. Nelson, 'Famine Relief', ibid., pp. 2–3. In addition, the minutes of the GC Famine Relief Committee for 1947 show that it authorised expenditure on many items *specifically* for Seventh-day Adventists (e.g., suits for workers, Sabbath dresses for ladies): GC AR., RG 25, box MIN 80.

35 Home and Foreign Officers' Meeting, 26 May 1946, GCOM, second series, p. 6428; Nelson, 'Report of Relief Work', p. 34; Strahle, 'Distributing Food', p. 16.

members attending – men, women, and children – were wearing clothes sent from America and had survived on American food aid the previous winter.[36] Church members in Poland particularly benefited from the largesse of the church in North America. By the autumn of 1947, 'the help which has been received' by 'Polish Adventists [from] the General Conference and [...] Division' already totalled, according to the PUC president, 69,757 kilogrammes of relief clothing 'and many tons of food'.[37] It was Danes and Swedes, however, who were instrumental in distributing aid and deploying funds from America; they were sending food and domestic items across Europe; and increasingly the aid reaching Finnish and Polish Adventists had its origins in the Northern European, not the North American, Division. The PUC Executive Committee recognised this in 1948, voting to 'express their very warm and heartfelt thanks' to the Northern European Division, 'for all the relief supplies sent to them' in the preceding year. The NED Relief Committee was still sending boxes of clothing from Sweden to Finland in 1949.[38]

Meanwhile, however, by the late summer of 1946, food had started to 'be delivered in large quantities' to 'our believers', in Austria, Czechoslovakia, and the French and American occupation zones in Germany, as well as Finland and Poland (Illustration 11.3). Much of it was being distributed by James Aitken and a team operating from Berne.[39] But Switzerland could not supply the volumes of food

---

36 F. D. Nichol, 'Adventist Activities in the North Lands', *ARH*, 124.30 (24 July 1947), 3–4.
37 In his report to the 1947/48 NED Winter Council, 1 Jan. 1948, NEDCOM mins., 1947–1950, p. 83.
38 NED Winter Council, 1 Dec. 1948, NEDCOM mins., 1947–1950, p. 165; T. Heinonen (secretary-treasurer of the East Finland Conference) to A. Karlman, 21st of [month illegible], 1949, TEDArc.
39 See, e.g., W. E. Nelson, 'Results in Food and Clothing Relief', *Lake Union Herald*, 3 Sept. 1946, pp. 1–2; idem, 'Serious Plight of European Believers', *Columbia Union Visitor*, 5 Sept. 1946, p. 1–3 (p. 3); idem, 'German Believers Receive Supplies', *North Pacific Union Gleaner*, 10 Sept. 1946, pp. 1–2; cf. Strahle, 'Distributing Food', p. 16.

in question; much of what was being distributed was coming from Scandinavia.⁴⁰

Making It Happen

In the winter of 1947, the Executive Committee of the provisional NED noted 'that our churches in the countries where there is plenty are doing a great work [...] sending many tons of food and clothing to Germany, Austria and Hungary beside what we send to Poland and Finland' (i.e., NED Adventists were helping not only countries in the same division but also those in other divisions).⁴¹ These tons were largely sent from Denmark and Sweden and went to several other countries as well as those named. Adventist relief work in Central and East-Central Europe represented the realisation of plans made in Northern Europe.

There are several hundred pages of documents relating to the work of the Relief Committee in the TED archives. There are other documents in the GC Archives and references in the NED Minutes. All I have been able to do here is to sketch out the broad outlines and to give a few examples which are indicative or interesting.

In the autumn of 1947, Alf Karlman became NED secretary-treasurer. He became the administrative mainstay of the Relief Committee and, with Strahle in America, was in effect the real director of European relief. Viggo Thomsen and Rye Andersen were the committee's chief agents in the field, gathering information about needs, letting Aitken and Rose in Berne know what supplies and/or money they would receive for their part of the distribution, and themselves overseeing some distribution of goods and foodstuffs. Thomsen travelled widely; just in the month of October 1947, for example, he visited Prague, Vienna, and Warsaw, before returning to Skodsborg, traveling

---

40   Nelson's report to the Home and Foreign Officers' Meeting, 26 May 1946, GCOM, second series, p. 6428.
41   NED Winter Council, 14 Feb. 1947, NEDCOM mins., 1947–1950, p. 31.

by both plane and train.[42] Thomsen also had a management role, however, chairing a subcommittee based at Skodsborg, which played a crucial role.

In Denmark and Sweden, large volumes of foodstuffs, particularly non-perishables, were assembled locally or imported from parts of the world less hard hit by conflict. They were then exported (or re-exported) to Central and Eastern Europe, either shipped into German or Polish ports, or transported by road, sometimes in semi-trailers with signage that ostentatiously proclaimed their Danish origin [see Illustration 11.4].

The main Relief Committee in Stockholm administered the money – the transfer of funds and charges back and forth between the NED, GC, SED and partner institutions – and managed the purchase of food, shoes, clothing, and household items in Sweden. Thomsen's subcommittee at Skodsborg Badesanatorium managed most of the import of food from outside Europe, and exports into Europe south of the Baltic. The reasons may have been partly to do with different regulatory frameworks for Danish and Swedish commerce; but they probably also reflected the strong institutional finances, which meant Skodsborg could pay large sums up front. 'In 1943 the Germans took two thirds of the sanitarium', yet Skodsborg continued to receive and treat patients, suffered limited infrastructural damage, and emerged from the war in reasonable physical and financial condition; its finances soon were thriving as it took in more and more patients.[43]

Skodsborg was not the only institution involved. Hultafors Sanatorium in Sweden contributed to the relief work as well. In the winter of 1946/47, it sent a large stock of medications to Germany:

42 D. G. Rose to A. Karlman, 22 Apr. 1948; 'European Relief', schedule 5, 'V. Thomsen travellexpenses [sic] 1947'; both in TEDArc.
43 See WNUC report, Forty-Fifth GC Session, third meeting, 6 June (p.m.) 1946, *ARH*, 123.24, General Conference Report, no. 2 (7 June 1946), 36, and text of report: P. G. Nelson, 'The West Nordic Union', ibid., 43–44 (p. 43); Medical Department Report, NEDCOM meeting, 2 Jan. 1950, in NEDCOM mins., 1947–1950, p. 332.

analgesics, cold remedies, sleeping tablets, and homeopathic anxiety remedies – all applicable to the health situation in post-war Germany. Hultafors took this on because the 'scarcity of medicine' in Denmark meant drugs could not be exported from there, and Hultafors bore the initial cost (which may not have been reimbursed).[44]

It was Skodsborg, however, that took on the biggest share of the burden. In 1947 there were thirty-four shipments from Denmark, comprising 30,868 parcels, which had cost almost DKr 650,000; total shipping expense came to another DKr 84,000. One in three parcels was sent to the British Occupation Zone in western Germany, with smaller proportions sent to the American-French Zone in the south, the Soviet zone in the east, to Austria, Hungary, and Poland; more than 12,800 parcels, 40 per cent, went to the eastern side of the Iron Curtain.[45] The total expense incurred in those thirty-four shipments was DKr 732,439; all of these sums were disbursed by Skodsborg Sanitarium. At the 1947 exchange rate of DKr 4.79 to the dollar, this amounted to $152,910 – a prodigious sum for the 1940s.[46]

Clothing was distributed, much of it sent from North America. In the four-year period, 1945–1948, a total of 1,668,265 lbs of clothing were sent from the GC's New York warehouse to Europe. Germany was by far the largest single beneficiary, receiving 858,783 lbs of clothing.[47] When it came to food, there was naturally a preference for non-perishables. The NED (which probably meant the Relief Committee) was a regular purchaser of powdered milk in Sweden. In the

---

44 Dr A. Andersen (Skodsborg) to Dr Isaac Unhäll and Afl. Karlmann [sic], 16 Dec. 1946, and Karlman to Strahle, 2 Jan. 1947, TEDArc.
45 'European Relief 1947', schedule 6, 'Cost of Shipments from Denmark', n.d., TEDArc. Winston Churchill had already used the term 'Iron Curtain' for the East-West divide in Europe in a famous speech in Fulton, Missouri, on 5 March 1946: Reynolds, *In Command of History*, pp. 43–44.
46 'European Relief: Summary of expenses: paid by Skodsborg Sanitarium 1947', and schedule 6, TEDArc.
47 'Summary of Clothing Shipments Overseas for Relief', Jan. 1, 1945–Dec. 31, 1948, with GC Relief Committee mins., GC Ar., RG 25, box MIN 80.

autumn of 1948, the subcommittee in Skodsborg arranged to import walnuts, pistachios, sesame seeds, dried white beans, dried apricots, raisins, and dates, from Iran for delivery in January and thus presumably for distribution in February and March, when food stocks would be lowest.[48] The provisions shipped from Skodsborg in 1947 included small amounts of honey and chocolate; the largest quantities were of sugar, rolled oats, margarine and vegetable fats. Interestingly, however, small quantities of animal fat, sardines and dried fish, and even veal, were among the items the Adventist Church supplied![49]

Other items that Skodsborg paid out for give insights into what was involved in the nuts and bolts of famine and disaster relief. In 1947, the sanitarium paid, *inter alia*, to translate letters from Hungarian, to buy butter and eggs to recompense drivers (payment in kind), to purchase and develop photographic film and to ship movie film to the USA (all for PR purposes). It spent DKr 17.44 on storing 'marmelade' [jam], 202.33 on storing 'soybean milk', and 7.38 on '[e]xpenses for powd[ered] milk'. It reimbursed the NED more than DKr 600 (the largest single item) for exchange rate losses in converting $22,571; and it bore the NED's costs in cabling back and forth across the Atlantic.[50] In 1947, it also covered DKr 1222.27 of Viggo Thomsen's travel expenses (to Austria, Czechoslovakia, Germany, Hungary, Poland, Romania, and Sweden) and his international telephone calls and telegrams; and DKr 2149 in travel expenses and telephone bills

---

48   See letter of 10 Oct. and multiple quotes, 20 Oct. 1948, from Samuel Akmal Trading Co., Tehran. In October the GC Relief Committee authorised the purchase of 'thirty tons of raisins' (10 Oct. 1948, GC Ar., RG 25, box MIN 80), but not for other items for which the European Relief Committee had contracted, which presumably means the cost was borne by NED or Skodsborg.

49   See 'Report on Relief Work', 'Shipments of food from Denmark November 47–March 1948' and 'Shipments of food from Denmark Jan–Dec. 1947'; and document, no title, listing shipments into Germany, n.d.; all TEDArc.

50   'European Relief', schedule 4, 'Sundry Expenses 1947 paid by Skodsborg Sanitarium' (totalling DKr 2745.07), n.d., TEDArc.

for Rye Andersen (which were not the total of his travel expenses as some were paid directly by the NED).[51]

In 1949, Denmark became a founding member of NATO, which limited what could be done from Skodsborg, since Communist governments in Eastern Europe became suspicious of Western aid efforts. Swedish neutrality meant, though, that it was still possible to send relief 'shipments from Sweden to eastern Germany and to Czechoslovakia'. As late as 1950, the GC Famine Relief Committee directly subsidised food parcels for Polish church members. Thereafter, the Iron Curtain proved largely impermeable to Western relief efforts.[52]

Helping Everyone

A large proportion of all these provisions would have been consumed by people who were not Adventists. Relief inevitably went beyond the ranks of church members, though initially to a limited degree. At first, food began to be distributed *through* church members rather than only *to* members.[53] Then, increasingly, as the needs of church members were being met, Adventists started to feed and clothe the needy of any denomination, or none.

In the spring of 1948, for example, Rye Andersen worked with city officials in Cracow, Poland, to identify nearly 400 widows and orphans of concentration camp victims, who were furnished with food, clothes, and shoes. But this was not new, for 'city officials spoke very highly of the relief work that the Adventist Church in America and Scandinavia had done in Poland during the last two years'.[54]

---

51 'European Relief', schedule 2, 'B. Rye Andersen expenses, paid by Skodsborg Sanitarium 1947', and schedule 3, 'V. Thomsens [sic] Expenses 1947 paid by Skodsborg Sanitarium', TEDArc. GC Famine Relief Committee meeting, 2 June 1947, mins. in GC Ar., RG 25, box MIN 80, p. 119.
52 GC Famine Relief Committee meeting, 28 Mar. 1949, mins. in GC Ar., RG 25, box MIN 80; NEDCOM meeting, 30 Jan. 1950, NEDCOM mins., 1947–1950, p. 352.
53 Nelson, 'Famine Relief', p. 3.
54 G. A. Lindsay, 'Relief Work in Poland', *ARH*, 125.24 (10 Jun 1948), 15.

This aid was particularly disinterested given that Poles were 'overwhelmingly Catholic' and that the great bulk of aid from America was donated by Polish Americans (who were not a significant group among American Adventists, in contrast to Scandinavians and Germans) and channelled through Catholic fraternal organisations.[55] This was humanitarian in its purest sense – or perhaps we might instead call it Christ-like.

Furthermore, the Relief Committee actively worked with other humanitarian and charitable organisations, which would not have had any sectarian restrictions on those whom they would aid. In particular, the NED Relief Committee worked in Germany with the *Hilfswerk der Evangelischer Kirchen in Deutschland* ('Relief Organisation of the Protestant Churches in Germany'), which assisted in shipping and delivery of items (including, for example, medications sent from Hultafors Sanitarium to Krankenhaus Waldfriede, the Adventist hospital in Berlin). In Sweden the church cooperated closely with the Swedish Red Cross,[56] and with two charities: the *Hjälpkommittén for Tysklands Barn* ('Aid Committee for German Children') and the *Hjälp Krigets Offer* ('Help War Victims!') organisation. In the first half of 1947, the *Hjälpkommittén for Tysklands Barn* sent 128.81 kilos of clothes, 32.85 kilos of shoes, 716.75 kilos of food, and 26 kilos of medicines and household utensils to Germany from Stockholm, plus a further 117 kilos of unspecified goods from Gothenburg. The total was valued at SKr 8,145,298, with the committee acting as a coordinating body to bring together funding, food, and items, from other charities – including the Seventh-day Adventist Church.[57] Later that year, the NED made a cash donation to the *Hjälpkommittén*, while in the following spring, the NED Executive Committee voted a small appropriation of SKr 500 to *Hjälp Krigets Offer* 'for a contribution

---

55 Bradley E. Fels, '"Whatever Your Heart Dictates and Your Pocket Permits": Polish-American Aid to Polish Refugees during World War II', *Journal of American Ethnic History*, 22.2 (Winter 2003), 3–30 (p. 5).
56 W. R. Soderberg to Gertrud Pedersen, 23 Dec. 1948, TEDArc.
57 'Export översikt', 15 July 1947, TEDArc.

for the sending of seed to the British Zone in Germany'.[58] In January 1948, *Hjälp Krigets Offer* acted as shipping agent for the ENUC for a cargo shipped from New York to Helsinki – presumably to save money either on shipping or on customs duties.[59]

Expenses and Funding

By the end of May 1947, the GC had remitted a total of $635,606.64 to Strahle, Rose, the NED, and the SED, and a further $10,623.23 directly to Skodsborg.[60] But funding also came from within Northern Europe and not just from the Relief Offering. As will have already become apparent, Skodsborg in particular made a major contribution.

The total expenses incurred by Skodsborg in 1947 totalled in excess of DKr 900,000. It received a grant of $100,000 from the GC, while the GC reimbursed an extra DKr 53,398 (or $11,147) through the WNUC; the NED reimbursed it DKr 146,518 ($30,388.39). The sanitarium itself contributed DKr 200,000 of its own funds in 1947 alone.[61] This was no small sum, since the following year Skodsborg's total charitable donations came to DKr 125,312, though its profit on nearly DKr 2 million of income was doubtless also deployed towards the cost of European relief.[62] In the first quarter of 1948, the Skodsborg subcommittee had incurred expenses equivalent to almost $60,000 but had received $50,000 from the GC, transferred to the

---

58 *Hjälpkommittén* receipt, 12 Aug. 1947, TEDArc.; NEDCOM meeting, 23 Apr. 1948, NEDCOM mins., 1947–1950, p. 139.
59 Invoice from *Hjälp Krigets Offer* to East Nordic Union Conference, 30 January 1948, TEDArc.
60 Report to GC Famine Relief committee, 18 June 1947, mins. in GC Ar., RG 25, box MIN 80, p. 122.
61 'European Relief: Summary of expenses', 1947, TEDArc.
62 From the Medical Department Report for 1948, given at NEDCOM meeting, 2 Jan. 1950, which reported income in Swedish *kronor*, the division currency at the time, which I have converted to Danish using the exchange rates used by the NED in 1948 (and 1949): see NEDCOM mins, 1947–1950, pp. 106, 226, 332.

NED.[63] The NED also incurred expenses directly, some of which were reimbursed by the GC or taken from funds transferred by the GC for relief.[64]

By 1948, operations were beginning to wind down in much of Central Europe, but in Poland conditions were such that the NED Committee agreed 'to retain Brother Rye Andersen as Relief Secretary in Poland after April 1' and until the end of the quadrennium, his salary to be paid not by the PUC but by the division.[65] There was an extra cost to this relief work, beyond the financial one. Both Andersen and his wife were killed in a car crash in Poland on 18 February 1949, leaving two parentless children.[66]

The European Relief, Overview

This chapter in European Adventist history is significant for several reasons. First, the scope of the aid delivered was extraordinary – and not only in the extraordinary sums of money and immense amounts of material aid delivered, but also in transcending the developing 'Iron Curtain' to include parts of Eastern Europe. In this regard, it was surely crucial that much of the relief was directed not from the United States, but from the NED headquarters in Stockholm, so that relief was associated more with neutral Sweden and less with the Western powers.

Second is the huge sums of money raised by American Adventists for relief, most of which was used to materially help suffering European church members. This generosity has largely been forgotten on both sides of the Atlantic, yet deserves to be remembered, not

---

63 'Financial statement for quarter ending March 31, 1948', TEDArc.
64 E.g., GC Famine Relief Committee meeting, 2 June 1947, mins. in GC Ar., RG 25, box MIN 80, p. 119.
65 NEDCOM Spring Council, 22 Apr. 1948, and meeting, 1 June 1948, NEDCOM mins., 1947–1950, pp. 135, 145.
66 *YB 1950*, p. 486; NEDCOM meeting, 12 April 1949, and President's Report, NED Winter Council, 28 Dec. 1949, NEDCOM mins., 1947–1950, pp. 245, 292.

least during the periodic episodes of cultural and theological tension between the church on different sides of the Atlantic. Third is the nature of the church's relief effort: systematic, and organisational, rather than ad hoc, local, or individual. This set a precedent for subsequent developments in Adventist engagement with disaster relief, development of infrastructure, and food security. Indeed, it is no exaggeration to say that the modern Adventist engagement with aid, disaster relief, and sustainable development, which culminates with ADRA, began in Europe in the late forties.

A final factor of significance is that no question was raised about the theological propriety of this massive involvement in helping suffering humanity. No one doubted that it was right to expend a huge amount of effort and funds – much of it, admittedly, to help fellow believers, but not all. Further, stopping human suffering and needless death was seen as a positive good, in and of itself. There was complete moral, ethical, and theological clarity, unmuddied by some traditional Adventist concerns about involvement in easing wider social ills.

Neither apocalypticism nor Adventist a-politicism created obstacles; in the latter case probably because it was *people* who were directly aided, not governments; in the former case because no theological tension was perceived – indeed just the opposite. General Conference general vice-president, L. H. Christian, a veteran of Europe and of the NED, saw in Berlin in the autumn of 1946, not a contradiction, but a connection, between the Adventist apocalyptic message of eschatological urgency, and meeting needs here and now 'in the lands of suffering and want'. Lewis Christian did have an instrumental view of relief and reconstruction, as ways to win as many as possible before the imminent *eschaton*, but he had no doubt it was right to stop human suffering. In any case, other church leaders did not see merely means to an end. GC treasurer, W. E. Nelson, told the 1946 Session, in his report on relief efforts: 'We believe that many lives will be saved as the result of our famine relief program in Europe'. He advanced no other rationale; this was sufficient justification, an apt objective for the church, in its own right. This spirit actuated all that the GC and NED did. The editor of the church's flagship journal, the *Review*, summarised the standard view of church leaders in an article reporting on the Relief Committee's work: 'It is wonderful that we could send to needy people the bread of life to save their souls. It is equally a part of good religion that we should send them bread for empty stomachs and clothes for naked bodies.'[67]

In many ways, then, this massive relief effort, maintained over five years, and drawing on church resources from around the world, was important for the precedents it set as well as for what it achieved (remarkable as that was). The idea that the church should be involved in humanitarian relief simply as an expression of Christian love, rather than as an aid to conversionary strategies, laid the groundwork for the subsequent creation of SAWS (Seventh-day Adventist World Service). In 1949 and 1950, the General Conference officers decided to make the Famine Relief Committee permanent, though under the title 'Disaster Relief Committee', and it deployed funds to help refugees affected by new wars, far from Europe, and the victims of natural disasters.[68]

But it also laid the foundations for the importance of ADRA to the church in the NED – and, indeed, for ADRA's work in the NED's territories. Although most church members are not aware of it, the roots for the extraordinary relief, courageously provided, in Bosnia in the first half of the nineties and in Kosovo at the end of the decade, and of the development work undertaken in Albania throughout the decade, lay in Central and Eastern Europe in the late forties. Identities

---

67 L. H. Christian, 'Rebuilding God's Work in a Shattered Land', *ARH*, 124.30 (24 July 1947), 1, 17–18 (p. 1); Nelson, 'Report of Relief Work', p. 34; Nichol, 'Adventist Activities in the North Lands', p. 4.
68 GC Officers' Meetings, 16 Feb. and 27 Feb. 1949, 8 Mar. and 12 Apr. 1950, GCOM, pp. 49-28, 49-41, 50-57, 50-98.

have shifted: from Relief Committee, to SAWS, to ADRA.[69] Organisational structures have changed. Yet the concern for helping people, as Christ helped them, is the same.

ADRA

Recently, ADRA has had an unusual impact in the TED, partly because of its structure and partly because of the nature of European society. ADRA is a network, with autonomous national offices, and draws much of its funding from Western governments. European governments are among the most generous with funding for foreign aid. The Adventist Church in a country that funds development generously has scope for action that is unrelated to the size of its membership or tithe receipts. Three of the outstanding examples worldwide of national ADRA offices achieving a major impact with a small footprint in the home country are ADRA-Denmark, ADRA-Sweden, and ADRA-UK. Each has an extraordinary record of identifying needs and then obtaining national and European Union funding for projects. Delivering projects is done by local workforces, which is one reason why these two national offices, with relatively small memberships and budgets from the respective unions, have been able to punch above their weight. That they have done so is also in part because, in the last two-to-three decades, there have been ADRA leaders in the BUC, Denmark, Sweden, and at the TED headquarters, possessed both of a high degree of professionalism and of impressive vision.

The work of ADRA is largely overseas and out of sight, unlike Adventist Community Services, which had a high profile and a positive impact in several countries of the TED in the last thirty years. There are those in European Adventism who are sceptical about the missional value of ADRA, as opposed to Community Services. However, as well as manifesting Christ's love to suffering people, the

---

69 *Sub* 'Adventist Development and Relief Agency International', *SDAE*, 1, 13.

successes of national ADRA offices gives the British, Danish, and Swedish churches a profile in their homelands that is disproportionate to their size. The work of ADRA gives the Adventist Church a chance it probably would not otherwise have had, to leverage favourable publicity from projects abroad to promote mission in the homeland. How to make the most of this opportunity is a challenge that faces media and communications specialists at the unions and at the TED.

In the 2010s, there has been a backlash, in the media and academe, against aid and development NGOs (non-governmental organisations). Maybe an 'ADRA moment' has been and gone, without it being recognised – though perhaps it will continue from strength to strength. But perhaps, too, there is more scope for ADRA to act within in its homelands and to be more directly missional. In the South Pacific and South America, ADRA has cooperated closely with local conferences and local congregations in community projects, an approach now fostered by ADRA International. It also now encourages, where possible, that initiatives be openly associated with the Adventist Church, as well as the Adventist Development and Relief Agency.[70] Involvement in church projects in the TED's core territories, particularly its big cities, might enable ADRA to make a more direct impact inside the TED. It would also represent something of a return to the past, when the Northern European Church took a lead in feeding, sheltering, clothing, and caring for millions of survivors of the most destructive war in history.

---

70   Cf. Kimi Roux-James, 'ADRA's 2019 Annual Council Gears Toward Growth, Embraces New Purpose', *ARH*, 196.5 (May 2019), 9–10.

Chapter 12
Adaptation and Innovation

I have become all things to all men, that I might by all means save some. – 1 Cor. 9:22 (RSV)

A noble purpose inspires sacrifice and stimulates innovation. – Gary Hamel, 2013 Annual Council[1]

In a division of the TED's historic size and complexity, dealing with diversity has always been a crucial issue. The sheer number of 'nations, tribes, tongues and peoples' could have been bewildering and daunting. But leaders at all levels have historically been willing to embrace diversity and engage with its practical implications for the work of the church. In the historic mission fields, this included what missiologists now call contextualisation, but it has been true more widely. There has been an openness to hearing and learning from a wide variety of perspectives. International and widely spread as the TED has been, it has been characterised by a great willingness to look even farther afield, to utilise experienced and expert church leaders from outside the division, and to learn from them – even as the best of them also learned from their time in the Trans-European Division. Advised, encouraged, and often funded by leaders at the TED headquarters, the division as a whole has actively sought to encompass people of all ethnicities, languages, nationalities, ages, and both genders, in the ministry and mission of the Seventh-day Adventist Church.

---

1   Gary Hamel, 'Thriving in the Midst of Turbulence', address to the 2013 Leadership Education and Development Conference, GC Executive Committee Annual Council, 10 Oct. 2013. A different (and longer) version is better known, being quoted in Richard L. Daft, *The Leadership Experience*, 6th edn (Stamford, CT: Cengage Learning), p. 409, citing Gary Hamel, 'Hole in the Soul: Leaders Either Cause It or Fix It', *Leadership Excellence*, Oct. 2011, p. 3.

Intercultural Interactions

Is it possible to speak of a 'Trans-European approach' to cross-cultural mission? I suggest that it is: that in spite of inevitable diversity in praxis given the different times and places where people have served, and the different places from whence they came, there are sufficient commonalities and continuities that we can speak of a common NED/TED approach to mission, embracing the practice of many individual missionaries and the views of division leaders.

This approach was characterised by considerable willingness to adapt the Adventist message to local contexts, communicating the three angels' messages in local languages both literally and figuratively, both verbally and conceptually. This was true of individual missionaries on the ground, in mission stations on the leading edge of Adventist expansion in Africa, such as Aba and Awtun, Agona and Koforidua, Kireka and Kakoro, Wollo and Wollega.[2] But it was also true, to a degree some might think remarkable, of the division leaders in London, St Albans, and Stockholm; they acknowledged almost as early as mission leaders in Ibadan, Nairobi, and Addis Ababa that the institutional church, as well as individual missionaries, had to adapt to different cultures, and that it had to provide support to enable contextualisation at the basic level. The first division administration recognised, and in the next half century successive administrations sustained the awareness, that more than Western methods or missionaries were necessary in order to fulfil the commitment made as the NED came into existence; if the division's Adventists were, indeed, 'to carry the Advent Message to the many millions' in the NED, especially 'its large mission fields', then it was essential to adapt to local contexts. Doing so was part of 'making every effort' to reach 'the unwarned millions'.

---

2   Mission stations of the mid-to-late 1930s: Aba = south-eastern Nigeria; Awtun = western Nigeria; Agona and Koforidua = Gold Coast (Ghana); Kireka and Kakoro = Uganda; Wollo and Wollega = western Ethiopia.

Did missionaries from the TED and church leaders in the TED always get things right? No; but they tried very hard, and often with considerable success.

Developing an Indigenous Workforce

From the beginning, the division leadership wanted to develop African pastors and workers. In this era, Adventists unapologetically referred to them as 'natives'. By the 1960s they had adapted their language and spoke instead of 'national' workers. Whatever the terminology, the division leadership's goal was achieved; there is no doubt that by fostering a strong indigenous workforce they laid the foundations for later growth and for the present strength of the church in countries like Ghana, Kenya, Nigeria, and Uganda.

In Chapter 4, we saw the emphasis put by the division on making use of talented locals in Tanganyika and Uganda. This was part of a wider trend to give far greater emphasis to the development of local workers than the old European Division had done. As the NED came into existence there were fifty-two workers in all its African mission fields, East and West, both missionaries and 'natives'.[3] By the end of 1933, Ernest Dick, secretary of the NED (and a missionary to South Africa before coming to Europe) was able, with some satisfaction, to inform the NED Winter Council:

> *We now have 55 missionaries in the field and under appointment. Our force of African workers includes 11 ordained ministers, 22 licentiated* [sic] *ministers, 75 licentiated missionaries, 230 African teachers, and a large number of colporteurs.*[4]

---

3   *ASR*, 66 (1928), 8.
4   Secretary's Report to NED Winter Council, 22 Nov. 1933, NED-COM-WCM, p. 2.

In other words, in four years the work force had increased sevenfold and while there were now more missionaries than there had been total workers in 1928, the largest increase must, clearly, have been in the 'force of African workers'.

Aware of the value of example and cultural affinity, British mission leaders in the forties began to call African-American missionaries ('workers from our colored constituency in the States') to the WAUM. They were employed without the racially inspired distinctions that pertained in North America for they were called 'on the same basis as European workers are called to the mission field in both wages and allowances [and] in all respects'. They were praised by W. E. Read for 'their devotion and […] their plans for progressive work'. As we saw in Chapter 7, one such black missionary of the sixties, C. Dunbar Henri, was an articulate and early advocate of greater Africanisation.[5] Henri was a missionary to West Africa for nineteen years (1945–1964) and in 1973 was elected a general vice-president of the General Conference (Illustration 12.1). In all there were at least sixty-seven black American missionaries who answered calls from NED/NEWAD to its territories in Africa, from 1945 up to the points when first the Ethiopian Union and then the two unions in West Africa went their respective ways.[6]

The British and Scandinavian missionary leaders and administrators at the division did not seek to impose a glass ceiling on indigenous African talent and did not merely desire African pastors and literature evangelists to serve as the foot soldiers of mission. Veteran missionaries noted with delight the spread of 'training schools

---

5 J. I. Robison to J. J. Hyde, 18 Aug. 1946, in GC Ar., RG 21, Secretariat Appointee Files, no. 46086; W. E. Read, 'Dawn of a New Day in Liberia', *ARH*, 124.30 (24 July 1947), 17.

6 Obit. from *ARH* is reproduced at <www.blacksdahistory.org/c--dunbar-henri.html>. DeWitt S. Williams, *Precious Memories of Missionaries of Color*, vol. 2 (N.p.: TEACH Services, 2015): of these 67, only five (7.5 per cent) served in Ethiopia, the rest in West African countries. These figures do not include a large number who served as missionaries only in the African territories of other divisions.

and colleges where full theological training is given' and the fact that they were preparing men not only for 'the ordained ministry and administrative positions'.[7] There was recognition, though, that advanced training would be needed, which would need to be in the United States. Already by the early 1950s, the WAUM and NED were investing financially in talented Africans 'to proceed to America [...] to meet [their] educational needs [... and] the needs of the West African field'. It was not only talented theologians or potential administrative leaders whose study in the United States was partly or wholly funded, but also capable educators, indicative of awareness that investing in this sphere would enable production of home-grown talent later, though at this point it was masters' degrees that were being funded.[8] When the Seventh-day Adventist Theological Seminary (by now under the leadership of W. G. C. Murdoch) conducted its first extension school at Newbold in 1964, the NED paid for C. B. Mensah, president of the Ghana Mission to attend.[9]

It was clear, though, that more was needed. In the mid- to late sixties, the NED and WAUM took the first steps to make advanced training available to a wider group of pastors; continuing theological and missiological education was provided to previously qualified pastors via field schools held in Ghana, Liberia, Nigeria, and Sierra Leone. A Norwegian missionary serving at ASWA, Jan Paulsen (later division secretary and president, and GC president), played a key part in establishing this programme that enabled professional development of African ministers.[10] In the 1970s, the division made provision for funding 'Doctoral or Advanced Degrees' though this was usually still in the United States.[11] By this time, even though few Afri-

---

7 Vine, 'Opportunity Knocks Again', p. 1.
8 NEDCOM meeting, 26 July 1951, NEDCOM mins., 1951, p. 82. E.g., I. K. Ansong: see Chapter 7, fn. 37.
9 NEDCOM meeting, 22 Jan. 1964, NEDCOM mins., 1964, p. 15.
10 Jan Paulsen, 'Field Schools in West Africa', *Northern Light*, 16.12 (Dec. 1966), 8.
11 GCC meeting, 27 July 1972, GCC Proc., xxiii, iv, 72-1035; NWASC meeting, 26 Apr. 1979, NWDM-WSC 1979, § 31, pp. 8–9.

cans were serving on NEWAD's West African Section Committee, talented indigenous Adventists were already beginning to take over leadership positions in Africa itself. This trend, which accelerated in the eighties, was thanks to the forward-thinking policies adopted by the NED in the fifties and sixties, and fostered further by NEWAD in the seventies.

Today the challenge may be to develop a stronger indigenous church work force in Europe. Already in some countries of the TED, in both its south-eastern and north-western sections, a substantial proportion of pastors are from different countries – even different continents – and/or are from ethnic groups that are a minority of the wider population. Just as special measures were taken in the past to develop and promote African pastors and leaders, which resulted in greater church growth in the mission fields of sub-Saharan Africa, so church leaders today might do well to introduce special measures to foster national leadership in several countries in Europe.

Translating the Third Angel's Message

Church leaders in Northern Europe invested time and money in providing excellent, idiomatic translations of church materials, in as many languages as possible. This was far from straightforward, requiring subtlety and cultural insight as well as linguistic skill. What is the best equivalent of God the Father, for example, to some Nigerian peoples for whom the senior male relative is the father's older brother rather than the actual father?[12] What does the Lord's Prayer metaphor of 'forgive us our debts' mean to people to people living in simple societies with very basic, non-monetary, economies?[13] Interpretation is the better term, rather than translation, for what is required to convey the underlying thoughts, not merely the actual

---

12 I owe this insight to Leonard Clemonds, a missionary in Nigeria for many years.
13 Cf. Gottfried Oosterwal, *The Lord's Prayer Through Primitive Eyes* (Nampa, ID: Pacific Press, 2009).

words. This kind of work required thought, sensitivity, experience in the field, and mental flexibility.

Making the Bible available in local languages was of course fundamental. Gilbert Lewis, who the NED called to Kenya in 1929, then served on a mission station for fourteen years, became expert in the local vernacular, and achieved the first translation of the New Testament into Kisii. Other missionaries to Kenya, including Grace Clark, were enlisted by the British and Foreign Bible Society for its translation of the Bible into Luo. There was need for translations in Europe as well as Africa. The NED formally approached the Society and asked it to translate the Bible into Lithuanian.[14] In 1932, the NED, not the Baltic Union, recognised that mission in Latgale, the eastern region of Latvia, which Adventists had only entered in 1924 (thirty years after evangelistic work in Riga began), would benefit if the Bible were available in Latgalian, the regional language. Printing in Latgalian had been banned from 1865–1904; the language was dismissed as a dialect by the elite in Riga; and by the early 1930s Latvian was officially favoured. All this lessened the likelihood of local translation and publication. The NED undertook to 'negotiate with the British and Foreign Bible Society in London to have the Bible printed in the Latgalian language' – this necessarily involved a financial commitment, one that would have been beyond the Baltic Union's means.[15]

Other examples could be given of the urge to make the Word available in words everyone could understand. But there was a wider and deeper desire, which went beyond biblical translation, to articulate

---

14 C. T. J. Hyde, 'East African Publishing House', *British Advent Messenger*, 27 Mar. 1964, p. 5; Phillips, 'British Adventists Overseas', p. 23; Mahon, 'A Century of British Adventist Missions', p. 17; idem, 'What Happened in 1906?', pp. 8–9; NED Winter Council, 4 Nov. 1929, NED-COM-WCM 1929, p. 24.

15 NED Winter Council, 17 Nov. 1932, NEDCOM-WCM 1932, p. 24; *sub* 'Latvia', *SDAE*, 1, 906; Metuzāle-Kangere and Ozolins, 'The Language Situation in Latvia', pp. 317, 321–23.

the Adventist message in terms that everyone could understand and that would contribute to the spiritual life of ordinary people in different places. That desire was often achieved imperfectly, or not at all, and took different forms in different places and at different times, but it was shared by church leaders in most of the division for most of its history. It was part of their passion for mission and has been a driving force, despite its diverse forms, over the ninety years. The division provided funds, for example, to translate the writings of Ellen G. White not only into the major languages of its territory, but also, at various times, into 'Lapp' (probably Northern Sami) and Greenlandic. The NED encouraged unions (and periodically provided subsidies) to make other materials, too, available in local languages, including 'Lappish [sic], Greenlandic, Faroese, Welsh and Gaelic'.[16] Yet these are not the only ways in which the desire to communicate the Adventist message, and do so in ways that anybody would comprehend and find appealing, has been put into practice in the Trans-European Division.

Contextualisation Through Song

Having argued that the impulse to contextualise was fundamental in the TED's history, it could be exemplified in a number of ways. One lens through which it can be seen at work, over many years and in very dissimilar locations and contexts, is that of music. Preparing hymnals and songbooks in local languages was an effort the division consistently supported, partly perhaps because there was an understanding that singing hymns together has a rare power to promote spirituality and to foster community. The examples that follow are not comprehensive but illustrative – they say something about Adventist love of music and the history of Adventist hymnody, but they do rather more. They speak to the willingness of church leaders in the

---

16 NEWAD Spring Meeting, 10 May 1973, NWDM-ECM 1973, § 170, p. 56; NEDCOM meeting, 15 Apr. 1981, and NED Winter Meeting, 23 Nov. 1982, NEDCOM mins., 1981, § 157, p. 35 and 1982, § 471, p. 156.

TED to emulate the Apostle Paul. In this division, Adventists have been ready to 'become all things to all men and women that [they] might by all means save some' (1 Cor. 9:22).

Shortly after the NED was established, it arranged for the publication of a songbook in Yoruba, the language of a major ethnic group spanning southwestern Nigeria and what today are Benin and Togo. In 1929, however, there were only 582 Seventh-day Adventists in Nigeria and none in French Togo and Dahomey, as they were then called (both then part of the NED), so this initiative demonstrates forward thinking. The British Adventist missionaries who led the Nigeria Mission were keenly aware that other Protestant missionary societies were well established in contrast: 'We have only a very meagre beginning', they recorded in 1929, 'and other societies take advantage of this to prejudice people against us.' As they were also well aware, British Protestant missionaries had been publishing hymnals, prayerbooks, and psalters (including musical settings) since the 1850s, with revised editions appearing as recently as 1916. One of their needs was met with the publication, with the backing of the NED Publishing department, of *Iwe orin ti awon ijo S.D.A.* It was only forty-eight pages long, mostly songs from a Church Missionary Society Yoruba hymnal, and printed in Britain by the press that had published in Yoruba in the past; yet, while not as distinctively Adventist as it might have been, it demonstrates a desire to adapt to the local context.[17]

Ten years later, a more substantive step towards indigenising Adventism was taken by the recently founded Nigerian Union Mission (as it had become), when it issued a much longer hymnbook

---

17 *ASR*, 67 (1929), 14; Nigerian Mission Committee, 'Memorial', n.d., reviewed by NEDCOM, 2 Apr. 1929, copy in NEDCOM mins., 1929, p. 6; NED Winter Council, 4 Nov. 1929, NEDCOM-WCM, 1929, pp. 38–39. *Iwe orin ti awon ijo S.D.A.* (Exeter & London: James Townsend & Sons, n.d [1929]); the only copy on WorldCat is James White Library, Andrews University, BV510.Y6 I9. Searching on WorldCat reveals six psalters, songbooks, and prayerbooks published in Yoruba by British missionary societies, starting in 1854 (<www.worldcat.org/

in Yoruba.[18] By this time, Adventist schools in southwest Nigeria had started teaching in Yoruba, while the union had also established its own publishing house, Advent Press, in Ibadan.[19] There were now 3000 members in the union, three-quarters of whom were in the Southeast Nigerian Mission, where the majority language would have been Ibo (a language in which Adventist pamphlets were being published), so the decision to issue a book in Yoruba surely signifies a determination to do better at reaching this other major ethnic group.[20] The new hymnal, *Iwe orin ti awon ijo onireti-bibo Jesu (Seventh-day Adventist)*, was 214 pages long, it comprised 260 hymns, and though all were translations, not new compositions in Yoruba, it was printed in Nigeria by Advent Press.

The new hymnbook speaks to the nature of the West African Adventist Church at this time. The great majority of hymns were from the *Advent Hymnal*, a product of the British Adventist Church (with most from the revised 1928 edition, but some from the 1915 edition); other sources were three American Adventist hymnals, *Christ in Song*, *Gospel in Song*, and *Hymns and Tunes*, though some came from different editions of the Sankey-Moody hymnbook,

---

oclc/85076081>), with the latest in 1916 (<www.worldcat.org/oclc/649946480>). James Townsend & Son had printed a 1907 book in Yoruba: <www.worldcat.org/oclc/1079830153>.

18 *Iwe orin ti awon ijo onireti-bibo Jesu (Seventh-day Adventist)* (Ibadan: Nigeria Union Mission of Seventh-day Adventists, n.d. [1940?]); the only copy on WorldCat, which I examined, is DUL, Pratt Green Collection, 783.9F4 IWE.

19 See William Hyde to W. L. Pascoe, 5 Mar. 1965, GC Ar., RG 21, box 9864, fld. 'Hyde, W. T. B.'; Adesegun, 'Christian Education', p. 51.

20 Membership numbers and distribution are in *ASR*, 77 (1939), 12; see E. D. Dick's recollection in 1946 that 'in 1935 […] in the Yoruba country, in western Nigeria, the people were indifferent': Dick, 'African West Coast Union Mission', p. 16. For a short overview of the printing of Adventist literature in Yoruba, see Babalola, 'Seventh-day Adventist Church in Yorubaland', pp. 168–73; and, on publications in Igbo and success reaching Igbo people, see A. S. Maxwell, 'British Publishing House', *Advent Survey*, 2.5 (May 1930), 2–3 (p. 2) and J. Clifford, 'Camp-Meetings in Southern Nigeria', ibid., 3; E. D. Dick, 'In the Ibo Country', *Advent Survey*, 5.7 (July 1933), 2–4 (p. 3).

which was prodigiously popular among Protestants in Britain and America.[21] Adventism in Nigeria was thus not, in any simple sense, culturally American; although David Babcock, the first missionary to the country, was an American, subsequently Nigerian Adventism was shaped by its relationships to the BUC and NED. This connection helps to explain the lively and generally warm memories in West Africa of the historical connection with the TED (see Chapter 7). In considering cultural questions, however, what is clear is that British and Northern European leaders in Europe and Africa were feeling their way, from an early stage, towards what missiologists now call 'critical contextualisation' or 'faithful contextualisation'.[22]

Further evidence of the interest in contextualisation through song includes the translation, by missionaries in Liberia, of Adventist songs into Kpelle, one of the local languages, and the initiative by church leaders in the Gold Coast Union Mission to translate and publish their own 'new hymnal' – aided by an appropriation for the purpose from the NED.[23] As the unions in Africa matured it is probable that further translation and contextualisation of hymnals and songbooks was done locally. In 1972, however, the division provided a special appropriation to the West African Union Mission for production of an Ibo hymnal.[24]

In Europe, too, there was a recognition of the role music could play in mission and of the concomitant need to have hymns that

---

21 *Iwe orin ti awon ijo onireti-bibo*, passim; on Sankey-Moody see, e.g., Mary G. de Jong, '"I Want to Be like Jesus": The Self-Defining Power of Evangelical Hymnody', *Journal of the American Academy of Religion*, 54 (Autumn, 1986), 461.
22 The bibliography of works on contextualisation is vast; a good starting point is Gorden A. Doss, *Introduction to Adventist Mission* (Berrien Springs, MI/Silver Spring, MD: Department of World Mission, Seventh-day Adventist Theological Seminary/Institute of World Mission, General Conference of Seventh-day Adventists, 2018), pp. 211–21.
23 Wogu, 'Forgotten Trailblazers', p. 20; NEDCOM meeting, 29 Mar. 1938, NEDCOM mins., 1938, p. 2.
24 NEWAD 1972 budget, NEWAEC Winter Council, 13 Nov. 1971, NWDM-ECM 1971, p. 210.

spoke to the local context – which in Britain could include hymns and 'gospel songs' that were familiar to Britons (a persistent issue since American Adventist hymnals often used hymns known in Britain but with different tunes). In 1940 the BUC, prompted by the 'need for a small hymn book for use by our Evangelists in their campaigns', put considerable resources into 'the production of such [a] hymn book', consisting of 150 songs of which one-third were to be 'new Gospel songs [and] Choruses' familiar to British audiences. The NED secretary, James Robison, and the Sabbath School and YPMV leader, William Bartlett, were present and voting when the BUC took this action, so it had the division's support.[25]

In 1983, the NED provided a special appropriation for the Iceland Conference to translate the *Church Hymnal*.[26] In addition, from the mid-seventies onwards, the division (whether in NEWAD, NED, or TED guise) supported the translation and publication of two Polish hymnbooks;[27] new editions of the Dutch hymnal,[28] and Swedish hymnal;[29] and a brand new Polish hymnal.[30] There is a long history of the translation of Adventist texts and documents into Northern European languages, pre-dating missions to Africa, and the creation of the NED or indeed of the European Division. What is striking in these cases is that division approval was required for initiatives taken by unions, in each case in a language that could only benefit that particular union – and in each case approval was given. The involvement of NEWAD in what might be seen as the internal affairs of a union reflected the desire of division leaders, articulated in an action

---

25 BUC council, 31 Jan. 1940, GC Ar., RG NE BR 1, fld. 'British Union Conference Minutes 1940', pp. 15–16.
26 NEDCOM meeting, 17 May 1983, NEDCOM mins., 1983, § 226, p. 58.
27 NEWAD Winter Meeting, 25 Nov. 1976, NWDC-ECM 1976, p. 241; NEWAEC meeting, 25 July 1979, NWDC–ECM 1979, p. 75.
28 NEDCOM meeting, 21 July 1982, NEDCOM mins., 1982, § 336, p. 107.
29 TEDEC meeting, 25 Nov. 1986, TEDMC-EC 1986, § 828, p. 358.
30 TEDEC meeting, 7 Jan. 1987, TEDMC-EC 1987, § 14, p. 4.

voted in 1977, that 'the hymnals and song books produced and used in the Division' needed 'refinement and updating and *indigenisation*'. This action was taken, moreover, as part of the creation of an 'overall strategy to use music as a positive [...] influence in the life of the church and community'.[31] Even before this strategy was created, part of the division's wider strategy for mission was the indigenisation of one of the core acts of worship, one of the most emotive parts of spiritual life, and one with a power to unite people: praising God together.[32]

Intellectual and International Interchange

In Chapter 6 we considered the important extent of the interchanges between the NED, especially Britain, and the wider world church during the 1950s–'60s. In those decades, perhaps as never since, administrators, educators, and thought leaders from the NED influenced the development of Adventist theology considerably, and also shaped world-church administration. Yet, the difference between those decades and others in the division's history was of degree and not of kind. For most of the TED's ninety years it has sponsored the injection of fresh blood, and with it fresh thinking, into the division with largely positive impacts on Adventist thought and practice in the TED. Yet this has also been a history of give and take: leaders developed in the TED have gone on to share good ideas and good praxis, and to practice good leadership, outside the division.

The interchange of ideas, and introduction of different approaches, has had a powerful and positive impact, though it diminished in the twenty-first century. The TED may, to some extent, have become

---

31 NEWAD Winter Meeting, 23 Nov. 1977, NDWC-ECM 1977, pp. 163–64 (p. 164, italics supplied). Eventually *Working Policy* was amended to make 'publication of church hymnals and major songbooks for general use in the churches [...] controlled by the Division': TEDEC Spring Meeting, 6 May 1996, TEDMC-ECM 1996, p. 37.
32 See Coralie, 'Understanding Adventist Worship'.

instinctively sceptical of ideas if they came from outside. Yet this is a relatively recent departure. The NED was intentional about interchange literally from its conception. In 1928, the NED-Committee-in-waiting voted that the officers should consult with the Australasian Division, 'concerning the transfer of labourers in the hope that an arrangement can be made whereby these two Divisions can co-operate in transferring labourers as between their fields.' This was endorsed by the GC Executive Committee and was quoted the following year, when NEDCOM voted 'to renew our request to the General Conference that an exchange of workers be effected from time to time between the British Isles and English-speaking countries'.[33] In 1937, the division executive committee endorsed a resolution from the previous year's GC Session, adopting it but adding to the language:

> *Experience of many years has proven that unity of the Advent Movement is best preserved when there is an interchange of workers of different Countries. [...] in the manning of our own Division an excellent example of this has been given by employing a large number of workers from different countries with their varied gifts.*[34]

This concept was taken seriously by church leaders throughout the TED's history.

External Influences

The early external influences at the highest level were American. Missionaries from the United States had of course been crucial in the early years, right across Northern Europe, but their numbers decreased in the 1920s.

Still, American influence remained strong in the division. To be sure, L. H. Christian was not only the first division president but also

---

33 NEDCOM meeting, 10 Sept. 1929, NEDCOM mins., 1929, p. 50; Annual Council, 3 Oct. 1928, GCC Proc., xiii, ii, 720.
34 NED Winter Council, 17 Dec. 1936, NEDCOM-WCM, p. 16.

the last born in America.³⁵ Yet when Walter Read resigned as division secretary in 1932 after being elected president of the BUC, it was an American missionary-educator serving in the Southern Africa Division, E. D. Dick, who was called as Read's replacement and served for six years. In 1935, Ellis Colson became the NED treasurer; he was from a Swedish-speaking family and had served as a missionary in Sweden, but he was American born and bred. Meanwhile, on Dick's election to the GC secretaryship at the 1936 GC Session, he was succeeded as secretary by James Robison, another American educator serving Africa (in this case Rhodesia, following previous service in South Africa). Both Colson and Robison served until the 1941 GC Session when they were called to positions in North America.³⁶

Meanwhile, in early 1933, Henry L. Rudy, an American missionary, had been elected president of the Baltic Union Conference, at the young age of 31. Rudy been born in Schöndorf, an ethnically German community in western Russia (near the border with Ukraine) but had emigrated to the United States when he was six years old. Rudy went to Eastern Europe as a missionary in 1925. He served as president of the Polish seminary and a PUC conference president, nearly two years as a departmental secretary at the NED headquarters (1931-1932) during which time he also served as acting division secretary, bridging the gap between Read's departure and Dick's arrival. Rudy was then president of the Baltic Union for nearly three years, until the end of 1935. His service in Poland and the Baltic states speaks to the significance of German-speaking Adventists in those countries. Rudy later served as president of the Central European

---

35 As noted in Chapter 5, Gustav Lindsay, NED president 1946–1950, though Swedish born, was a US citizen, having emigrated at age 17.
36 'Dick, E. D.', GC Ar., RG 21, Secretariat Appointee Files, no. 45602, box 9842; NED Minority Committee, meeting of 2 Mar. 1932, NEDCOM mins., 1932, p. 15; Colson obit., 'In Remembrance', *ARH*, 139.4 (25 Jan. 1962), 22.

Division (1938–1940) and as a GC general vice-president from 1950 to 1958 (Illustration 12.2).[37]

All of these Americans in senior positions in the NED served up to World War II. There was thereafter a steep decline in the number of Americans serving in the European homelands of the NED. This may seem a natural trend, yet notably it is in contrast to the pattern of other evangelical Protestant denominations based in America (and the Jehovah's Witnesses and Mormons), all of which witnessed a marked post-war increase in numbers of American missionaries to Europe. This reflected the dawning realisation that Europe was no longer Christendom, but instead was, as one Baptist missionary wrote, 'over-civilized, pagan, and de-Christianized'.[38] The Adventist trajectory was thus unusual in some respects.

What it was not, however, was a trend towards purely local leadership. Even though fewer Americans served in the TED, church leaders from English-speaking regions other than North America were called to leadership positions. In roughly the middle third of its organisational existence, the TED had a series of church leaders from the Southern Hemisphere, a point we touched on in Chapter 6, since it was especially notable in the five quadrennia from 1950–1970; but it continued through almost to the end of the NED nomenclature. In the thirty-three years from the re-founding of the NED in 1950 to the election of Jan Paulsen as TED president in 1983, there seemed to be an unspoken rule that the Trans-European Division should have either a South African or an Australian as its president. The only

---

37 See 'Former V.P. Dies in Oregon', *ARH*, 159.12 (25 Mar. 198), 24; obit., *ARH*, 159.15 (15 Apr. 1982), 21; Naturalisation Records of the U.S. District Court for the Eastern District of Washington, 1890–1972, Ancestry.com, *U.S., Naturalization Records, 1840–1957* [database on-line] (Provo, UT: Ancestry.com Operations, 2010); Staats Archiv Bremen, *Bremen Passenger Lists*, archive ID nr., AIII15-03.01.1936_N, *Bremen Passenger Lists* <http://212.227.236.244/passagierlisten/index.php?lang=en>; and annual editions *YB, 1929–1940*.

38 Krabbendam, 'Opening a Market for Missions', pp. 154–5, 162–66 (quotation at p. 164).

exception was Alf Lohne in the mid-seventies. The South Africans, Tarr and Eva, served nineteen years in total; each was succeeded by Australians, Roenfelt and Scragg (twelve years together). If Tarr's election by the 1950 GC Session was the result of circumstance (see Chapter 6), he was so successful that thereafter the leaders of the British and Nordic unions that were the powerhouses of the NED were open to a division president brought in from outside, though apparently with a definite preference for experienced administrators who were English-speakers but not Americans.

Floyd Tarr has been discussed earlier. Duncan Eva became president in 1966, succeeding Erwin Roenfelt. Eva had worked in his native South Africa, Rhodesia, and Kenya (as president of the EAUM). For eleven years (1954–1965), he was secretary of the Trans-Africa Division, working alongside Robert Pierson, before going to the GC as associate secretary; after just one year he was elected to the NED presidency. W. D. Eva was president of NED and NEWAD for seven years. He returned to the GC in 1973 as a general vice-president, serving in that capacity for seven years, first under his old boss, Pierson, and later, Neal C. Wilson. Both drew on his immense experience to chair crucial committees: for example, Eva oversaw the drafting and approval of the Church's Statement of Fundamental Beliefs; GC presidents kept using him into the early nineties as a troubleshooter for sensitive issues around the world. Duncan Eva was attentive to detail, intelligent, perceptive, and personally warm, able to inspire affection even in those who disagreed with him.[39]

Eva was succeeded mid-session by the division secretary, Alf Lohne, a Norwegian (Illustration 12.3). When the 1975 GC Session in Vienna elected Lohne to follow Eva to Washington, DC, as

---

39 See 'Former GC Vice-President Dies', *ARH*, 174.32 (Aug. 1997), 21; fld. 'Eva, William Duncan', GC Ar., RG 21, Secretariat Appointee/IDE Files, no. 12483; *Fundamental Belief 6: Creation*, ed. by D. J. B. Trim and Benjamin J. Baker, General Conference Archives Finding Aids, 1 (Silver Spring, Md.: General Conference of Seventh-day Adventists, Office of Archives, Statistics, and Research, 2014).

a general vice-president, it also elected Walter Scragg as president of NEWAD. After pastoral work and radio evangelism in New Zealand, where he was born, and Australia, of which he was a citizen, he was called to the GC in 1966, aged just 40, as associate departmental secretary for Radio and Television. The 1970 Session elected him to lead the department and, under Pierson's reformist presidency, Scragg was responsible for the major departmental reorganisation that merged Radio and Television with the Public Relations department, at every level of the church; he then became the first department secretary of the newly created Communication department. Meanwhile, in 1971, he played a key role in the creation of Adventist World Radio. After his election in Vienna, Scragg served eight years as division president, overseeing the separation from Africa and reversion to being the NED; he then returned to Australia as president of the South Pacific Division. After initially retiring, he was called back to the GC to serve as president of Adventist World Radio.[40] Scragg, too, was a capable leader (Illustration 12.4).

In 1983, Paulsen's election broke the pattern and for the next thirty-one years the TED had Scandinavian-born presidents – Paulsen the second Norwegian and Bertil Wiklander the first Swede, but just the third and fourth division nationals to serve as its first officer (Illustrations 12.5–12.6). In electing Raafat Kamal in 2014, some might have thought custom was being breached, but instead, an older tradition was being restored. The TED has had presidents who were citizens of one of the countries in its territory for less than half of its history.

In particular, there has been a longstanding Australian connection. Literally from the TED's earliest days, it has called successful evangelists from Australia, initially for service in the British Union. Until recently, most Australians were of British stock, while many

---

40 See fld. 'Scragg, W. R. L.', GC Ar., RG 21, GC Secretariat Appointee/IDE Files, no. 3313; David Gibbons, 'Walter R. L. Scragg, 84 Division President and Church Leader, Dies', *ARH*, 187 (21 Oct. 2010), 10; obit., *Record*, 20 Nov. 2010, p. 23; and see above, Chapter 8.

Antipodean Adventists had close relations in, and sentimental attachment to, the 'old country', as it was widely called in Australia and New Zealand up to the 1960s. Later, Australians served as evangelists and church planters more widely across the TED. The first call for Australian evangelists to serve in the BUC was approved by the Division Committee at its fifth meeting, only two weeks after the NED formally came into being.[41] One of the first two was Roy Anderson, who served in the BUC from 1930 to 1936, where he had a considerable impact as an evangelist, both in his results, and in his approach and style. As we saw in Chapter 6, while GC Ministerial Association secretary, he was instrumental, along with Read and Froom, in the evangelical dialogues of the mid-fifties. Anderson already had a deep interest in British history before he arrived in the UK and retained an affinity for England, where he remained a popular speaker, until the end of his life.[42]

The profound Australian influence in the TED has included two division presidents, Roenfelt and Scragg, while E. B. Rudge was secretary, having previously been BUC president. There was an especially strong tradition of Australians serving as evangelists and Ministerial Association secretaries, a custom that continued until recently. After Anderson, T. J. (Tom) Bradley and E. L. (Len) Minchin served for eight years apiece, each man spending four years in the BUC and four at the NED (1946–54). J. F. (John) Coltheart worked at NED/NEWAD for nine years (1965–1974) until his sadly premature death, aged not yet 50 (Illustration 12.7). Russell Kranz served in the BUC for ten years (1968–1978), C. R. (Ray) Stanley in the Finland Union, WNUC, and BUC for five years (1978–1981, 1985–1987), A. D. C. (David) Currie in the BUC and at the TED for ten years

---

41   NEDCOM, 15 Jan. 1929, NEDCOM mins., 1929, p. 7.
42   See fld. 'Anderson, Roy A.', GC Ar., RG 21, Secretariat Appointee Files, no. 5248; Anderson's personal files on 'British Israelites', late 1920s, and 'New Gallery (London)', CAR, Roy Allan Anderson Papers, box 31, fld. 1 and box 44, fld. 3; J. R. Spangler, 'Tribute to a Great Australian', *South Pacific Record*, 8 Mar. 1986, p. 13; short obit., 'Deaths', *ARH*, 163.12 (20 Mar. 1986), 21.

(1975–1979, 1990–1995), and Peter Roennfeldt, his successor at the division, for almost another ten years (1996–2005). Additionally, in the twenty-first century, R. J. (Roy) Richardson was ADRA director for four and a half years (2001–05). At the division's institution, Newbold, Kevin Howse (1982–1989) and Stephen Currow (2002–2011) were inspirational teachers of religion and mission.[43]

If there was a particularly strong Antipodean connection, the TED also continued to draw periodically on church leaders from America. Bert B. Beach was division secretary from 1973–1980; of the fourteen division secretaries, his is the fourth-longest tenure of the office (Illustration 12.8). Beach was an American, but Swiss-born, fluent in French, with a PhD from the Sorbonne; he had been Education and Sabbath School departmental secretary at the NED from 1960–1973. He went to the GC in 1980, becoming a hugely respected director of the Public Affairs and Religious Liberty department until nominally retiring in 1995. Given that Beach had twenty years at the TED headquarters versus fifteen at the GC, he could be regarded as an example both of external influence on the TED and of its role in the wider church. Harold L. Calkins was elected BUC president in 1981, having previously served solely in the United States (primarily in California); his one five-year term was the last American presidency of one of the TED's 'homeland' unions.[44] Meanwhile, in 1985, Mark A. Finley became TED Ministerial Association secretary. He

---

43 See sources cited in Chapter 6, above; the respective appointee/IDE files, GC Ar., RG 21, Secretariat: Bradley, no. 45296; Coltheart, no. 13153; Currie, no. 18564; Currow, no. 92743; Kranz, no. 10719; Richardson, no. 38499; Roennfeldt, no. 40775; Stanley, no. 31511 (also AVS file no. 115858: Stanley returned to conduct an evangelistic campaign in Norway in his 89th year); Ormond K. Anderson, 'Life Sketch of Pastor John Coltheart', *Australasian Record*, 23 Dec. 1974, pp. 13–14; fld. 'Richardson, Roy J.' and fld. 'Roenfelt [sic] Peter and Judith Ann', GC Ar., RG 32, Transportation & International Personnel Service files, nos. 119417, 119419. Howse's time at Newbold was cut short by brain cancer and he died aged 42: see brief obit., 'Deaths', *ARH*, 168.1 (3 Jan. 1991), 29.

44 Obit., *Redlands Daily Facts*, 21 Jan. 2008: <https://www.redlandsdailyfacts.com/2008/01/21/harold-calkins-87/>; Arthur, 'Profile of the Church 1981–1992', pp. 35, 37.

served one five-year term, before going on to a distinguished career that eventually included service as a GC general vice-president and special assistant to the GC president (Illustration 12.9).[45]

This list is not definitive; there have undoubtedly been others who spent time working in parts of the TED and/or its headquarters. We might add Raafat Kamal, division president since 2014, born in what is now the Middle East North Africa Union (Illustration 12.10). However, since he was educated at Newbold, married a Norwegian, and gained most of his experience in church work in the TED, there is a case for considering him a local. He undoubtedly brought a somewhat different perspective to leadership, however, and in that sense fits with the pattern we have explored, of the TED benefiting from leaders who could look at challenges and opportunities in a different way.

TED in the Wider Adventist World

The TED has also been well represented at high levels outside the division. This is partly a side-effect of relatively large numbers of British, Danish, Dutch, Finnish, Norwegian, and Swedish missionaries serving around the world. Well into the 1960s, missionaries were disproportionately likely to be tapped to fill leadership positions, whether in the mission or union office, or one of the institutions that were founded as Adventist mission spread. This created a large pool of talented men (and they *were* mostly men in this period) who had leadership experience. As the numbers of missionaries from the TED declines, it may well be that the incidence of TED-born world-church leaders will diminish. It is also the case, however, that historically the TED has simply produced numbers of high-calibre leaders who were called to work at the GC, its institutions, or at other divisions.

---

45   See fld. 'Beach, Bert' and fld. 'Finley, Mark Alan', GC Ar., RG 21, Secretariat Appointee/IDE Files, nos. 3386, 12766.

The first were George Keough and Walter Read, but they were far from the last. Many gave distinguished service; those whose wider influence was exercised up to the 1960s have been discussed already (Chapter 6). What follows will give some sense of the ways in which the TED has influenced the Adventist church worldwide during the last fifty years.

At the 1966 GC Session, Bernard Seton, then serving in departmental administration at the SED, was elected the secretary of the NED; he served only a year before accepting election as president of the BUC (following in both positions, and in the sequence, in the footsteps of his mentor, W. E. Read). At the 1970 GC Session, Seton was elected associate secretary of the GC and served in that capacity for eight years; he was highly influential in the drafting of the church's statement of Fundamental Beliefs, from 1976–1979.[46] In 1973, Victor Cooper accepted a call to the GC as associate in the recently created Communication department; he must have been chosen by Walter Scragg. Cooper served fifteen years as associate director of the GC Communication department, retiring in the spring of 1989.[47] Seton and Cooper are both remembered at the GC as remaining quintessentially English (Illustrations 12.11–12.12).

Overlapping with Cooper and Sparrow was Alf Lohne. A Norwegian, his service was entirely in Scandinavia until chosen as Seton's successor in 1967. Lohne was NED/NEWAD secretary for six years: 1967–73. Even though his only experience of Africa came from short visits during that time, he was elected to succeed Eva as NEWAD president in 1973. He must have been a powerful personality, for at

---

46 David Marshall, '"A Warm-Hearted Intellectual": An Appreciation of the Life of Dr Bernard Seton', *Messenger*, 4 June 2004, pp. 6–7; fld. 'Seton, Bernard E.', GC Ar., RG 21, Secretariat Appointee/IDE Files, no. 17091; Read to Dederen, 16 Aug. 1972, GC Ar., Personal Collection 25, Box 10826, fld. 'Dederen Mrs Louise'; Trim and Baker, *Fundamental Belief 6*, pp. 1–2, 7, 20–22, 25, 35–37.

47 See fld. 'Cooper, Victor Herbert' and fld. 'Cooper, Victor H.', GC Ar., RG 21, Secretariat Appointee/IDE files, no. 14469, RG 32, Transportation & International Personnel Service files, no. 19655.

the 1975 GC Session, after just two years as division president, he was elected a general vice-president for the GC. Lohne served two terms (1975–1985) before retiring.[48] He was the third TED-born president but the first citizen of a country on the mainland of Europe to serve as first officer of the division.[49]

Following in this group's footsteps was C. D. Watson. As noted in Chapter 7, Watson was president of the Afro-Mideast Division for one term but, at the 1980 GC Session in Dallas, he was elected an associate secretary of the General Conference. An Englishman, Charles Watson had previously served seven years (1968–1975) in the GC Temperance department. He served in GC Secretariat for twelve years before retiring in 1992, making nineteen years in a senior position at the world headquarters.[50]

Two years after Watson retired, Ray Dabrowski, a Pole who was then serving as Communication director for the TED was called to the GC. During his sixteen years as director of the Communication department (1994–2010), the world headquarters embraced the internet and the world church successfully finessed the crisis occasioned by the questionable conduct of Robert Folkenberg, Sr, as GC president. Subsequently, the creation of the Adventist News Network was also overseen by Dabrowski (Illustration 12.13).

Folkenberg's successor was Jan Paulsen. He had been TED president for twelve years before, in 1995, following in Lohne's footsteps to become the second TED-born general vice-president of the GC. In 1999, after Folkenberg's resignation, Paulsen became the sixteenth president of the General Conference of Seventh-day Adventists, filling

---

48 There is a very short obit. notice, 'Two Former GC Vice-Presidents Die', *ARH*, 170.50 (16 Dec. 1993), 7. See fld. 'Lohne, Alf', GC Ar., RG 21, GC Secretariat Appointee/IDE files, no. 44344.
49 After the Briton, Walter Read, and the Swedish-born US citizen, Gustav Lindsay.
50 Obit., *Messenger*, 7 Aug. 2009, p. 15; obit., *ARH*, 9 June 2009; fld. 'Watson, Charles Douglas', GC Ar., RG 21, Secretariat Appointee/ IDE files, no. 39764.

that office until 2010. He was only the second president who was a foreign national.⁵¹ A former missionary to West Africa, principal of Newbold, secretary and president of the TED, and GC general vice-president and president, Jan Paulsen has surely had the greatest influence on the world church of any leader to come out of the TED.

As Paulsen left office at the GC, the third Norwegian national to serve as a GC officer was elected as the third TED-born associate secretary of the General Conference. Elected by the 2010 Session, Harald Wollan was truly a son of the old NED; born in Eritrea to parents serving as missionaries in the Ethiopian Union, he worked in the WNUC and WAUM, before going as union president to Bangladesh. In 2001, he was elected secretary of the TED, holding that office for nine years before serving at the GC for a five-year term, and then retiring (Illustration 12.14).

Meanwhile, in 1984, Bryan W. Ball had been called from Newbold to become president of Avondale College. This led to his election at the 1990 GC Session as president of the South Pacific Division. He served for seven years until retiring in 1997, having overseen considerable institutional development (Illustration 12.15). Ball had followed in the footsteps of another TED missionary to Australia, Jan Knopper of the Netherlands. After service in the Congo and Tanzania as well as the NUC, the 1975 GC Session elected him Publishing director for the Australasian Division. A champion of literature evangelism, he served in this capacity until he retired in 1990 (Illustration 12.16). In 1993, however, Knopper went to the new Euro-Asia Division as publishing director; he also served as special assistant to the division president for a year, helping to actually establish the division and its headquarters.⁵²

---

51 Although the third born outside America and second born in Norway: Ole A. Olsen, the fifth president, was Norwegian born, but emigrated to the United States with his family as a small child.

52 D. J. B. Trim, "B. W. Ball: Evangelist, Administrator, Scholar', in *A Century of Adventism*, ed. by Marshall, p. 31; J. T. Knopper, 'A Challenge', *Australasian Record*, 9 Feb. 1976, p. 1; fld. 'Knopper, Jan Theunis', GC Ar.,

Natives of the Trans-European Division have also played a role in Adventist education, especially theology, disproportionate to the number of members in the TED's territory. In Chapter 6 we briefly explored the influential careers of Read, Lowe, Keough, Murdoch, and Heppenstall, who were all British. Since 1970, Danish and Dutch theologians had the greater influence, before, more recently, Britons have again played a part. These educators and theologians included V. Norskov Olsen, the first Danish (or indeed Scandinavian) principal of Newbold (1960–1966). A church historian, he was one of the rare Adventist scholars to win critical praise for his scholarship outside Adventist circles.[53] In 1974, V. N. Olsen was appointed president of Loma Linda University, a position he held for ten years, preserving what was described as 'a rich, resonant Danish brogue' (Illustration 12.17).[54]

In 1966, as Olsen went to the United States, so too did Hans K. LaRondelle. A native of the Netherlands, where he served as a pastor and evangelist, he was mentored by William Murdoch, on whose advice he began postgraduate studies in theology at the Free University of Amsterdam. His move to North America was to study at the Seventh-day Adventist Theological Seminary; there he came under the influence of Edward Heppenstall, but LaRondelle's brilliance meant he was soon appointed to the faculty himself. Apart from a brief return to his homeland to complete his doctoral studies in Amsterdam, LaRondelle served on the Seminary faculty for twenty-four years, before becoming Professor Emeritus. His teaching and published scholarship made him the most influential Adventist theologian for the post-war (Baby Boomer) generation of American Adventist teachers of theology and religion, as Heppenstall had been

RG 21, Secretariat Appointee/ IDE files, no. 27816.
53 V. Norskov Olsen, *John Foxe and the Elizabethan Church* (Berkeley, Los Angeles & London: University of California Press, 1973).
54 LoVae Pray, 'Olsen Inaugurated as LLU President', *San Bernardino County Sun*, 5 Dec. 1974; obit., *Pacific Union Recorder*, May 2000, p. 43; fld. 'Olsen, V. N.', GC Ar., RG 21, Secretariat Appointee/IDE/AVS files, no. 30263.

for the previous generation. LaRondelle's work on soteriology has proved particularly influential.[55]

Not long after LaRondelle moved to the Seminary, he was joined by Gottfried Oosterwal. Another native of the Netherlands, and also with a PhD from a Dutch university (the University of Utrecht), he and his wife Emilie had spent seven years as missionaries in the Far East Division. From 1968, he taught in the Department of World Mission at the Seminary and, as a colleague later put it, 'grew and developed the Institute of World Mission', which offers the Seventh-day Adventist Church's official training programme for missionaries. He also provided consultancy and advice on mission strategy and missionary recruiting for the GC Secretariat (Illustration 12.18).[56]

Norskov Olsen had been the first native of the TED to lead a GC institution, but he was not the last. Niels-Erik Andreasen, a Dane like Olsen, became president of Andrews University in 1994, though unlike Olsen, who had served in the TED, Andreasen never did; after graduating from Newbold College with a BA in 1963, his entire career was in the United States.[57] After a record twenty-two years as president of Andrews, Andreasen's successor in 2016 was Andrea Luxton, a former head teacher of Stanborough School, Education director for the BUC, and Newbold principal (1997–2001). Luxton had later served as an associate director of the Education department

---

55 Hans K. LaRondelle, *Perfection and Perfectionism: A Dogmatic-Ethical Study of Biblical Perfection and Phenomenal Perfectionism* (Berrien Springs, Mich.: Andrews University Press, 1971). See Laurence A. Gilmore, 'The Gentle Theologian', *Australasian Record*, 21 May 1973, p. 5; Malcolm Bull and Keith Lockhart, 'The Intellectual World of Adventist Theologians', *Spectrum*, 18.1 (Oct. 1987), 32–37 (pp. 34–35); Michele Jacobsen, 'Andrews University Board Reelects President', *ARH*, 168.14 (4 April 1991), 21.
56 'In Memoriam: Gottfried Oosterwal' and Russell Staples, 'Gottfried Oosterwal – Inspirational Missiologist', both in *Journal of Adventist Mission Studies*, 11.2 (2015), v–xi.
57 This can be documented partly through his GC Secretariat Appointee file, which exists thanks to interest in missionary appointments, none of which he accepted: GC Ar., RG 21, file no. 2981.

at the General Conference, in which capacity she was followed in 2006 by Lisa Beardsley-Hardy, born in England and an alumna of Newbold. Beardsley-Hardy was later elected director of the GC Education department by the 2010 GC Session, a post she has filled since.

Also in 2010, Derek Morris was appointed editor of Ministry magazine, becoming an associate secretary of the Ministerial Association at the GC. Morris is a native of Britain and a graduate of Newbold, though most of his career in ministry was in the United States. He was appointed president of the Hope Channel in 2016 – the same year that Jeff Brown, who had worked in pastoral ministry in Britain and taught at Newbold College, was called to the GC as associate editor of Ministry and Ministerial Association associate secretary.

As well as church administrators, there was also A. S. ('Uncle Arthur') Maxwell, whom we already encountered in Chapters 3 and 4 when he was editor of the British Adventist publishing house. In 1936, he accepted a call to the United States and never returned to the territory of the TED except to visit. Maxwell never had the profound intellectual, theological, or administrative influence of some others (two of his sons arguably among them), but thanks to the astonishing success of his books (which sold millions of copies), he was, up to his death in 1960 (and probably for many years after), to virtually all Seventh-day Adventists worldwide, probably the best-known native son of the NED.[58]

To adopt a popular saying, what happens in the TED didn't stay in the TED – and that was generally a positive thing for the Seventh-day Adventist Church worldwide. The TED's sons and daughters, when they went out into the world, took a unique perspective with them. It was partly innate, the fruit of the cultures in which they were raised. In most cases it also reflected their experience in a division that, truly, is unlike any other.

---

58 David Marshall, 'Arthur S. Maxwell: The Great Communicator', in *A Century of Adventism*, ed. idem, p. 15; *sub* 'Maxwell, Arthur Stanley', *SDAE*, II, 44–45.

International and Intellectual Influence and Interchange: Conclusions

By intentionally bringing international influences to bear, the division achieved two things.

First, it helped within the division. Leaders came with different experience and different perspectives. Leaders from the Southern Hemisphere brought more of a willingness to take risks and try innovations. A sense of this can be gained from looking at the ninety-year trend in growth rates, illustrated in Figure 13, in which the annual percentage growth rate is calculated by comparing the territory of any given year with the equivalent territory in the previous year (ignoring changes in alignment between one year and the next); growth rates have then been calculated as five-year moving averages in order to smooth out the volatility that inevitably occurs in rates from year to year. All this means that less account is taken of the deductions of whole unions in 1970, 1980, and 2011, and addition of new unions in 1985, 1993, and 1995, though because of the moving averages they have an impact (as do the audits in the late nineties). The thirty-three years when the division was led by South Africans and

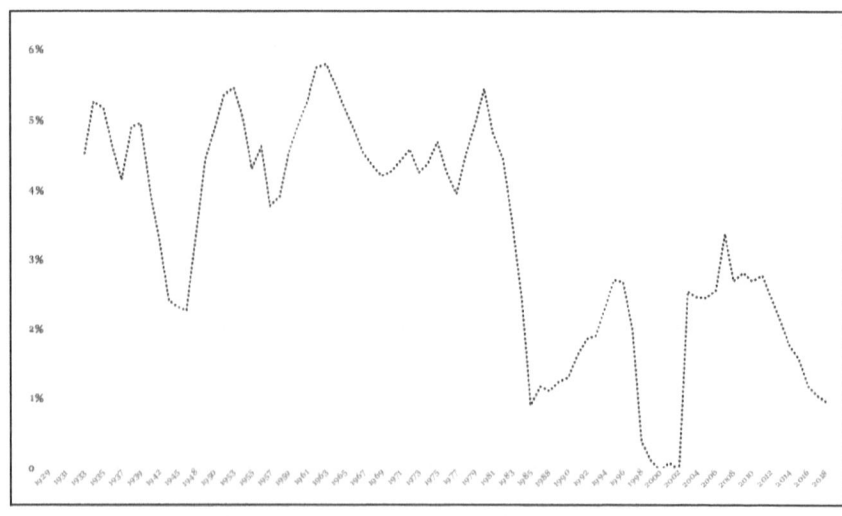

Figure 13: Growth-Rate Trend in the TED, 1929–2018

Australians were years of growth in sub-Saharan Africa and an era when evangelism was somewhat easier in Europe, so a simple comparison with the thirty-five years that followed cannot meaningfully be made. Nevertheless, the data do suggest that the TED's leaders do not necessarily have to be from its territory for the division to experience growth. Perhaps they also suggest that substantial experience in pastoring (as was the case up to 1983), as opposed to academic and church administration (the case since 1983), is a valuable asset for presidents of the division.

Second, by supporting the interchange of ideas and personnel, the TED increased its own influence in the world church. Those leaders who had been brought in from outside the division often later moved onto positions in other divisions or at the General Conference. They took with them fond memories of their time in the TED; who can doubt that in several cases their own approach to church business and wider attitudes was also adapted as a result of experiencing the distinctive Northern European way of doing things. They could also be a voice speaking on the TED's behalf: not necessarily out of bias but because they understood, from first-hand experience, what working in its territories was like, what the needs were, and what the impact of proposed policies would be. This last comment is also true, of course, of the many leaders from the TED who went on to influential careers in the world church, both in other divisions and at the world headquarters.

In sum, the internationalisation we have described – very much a two-way street – has been an important aspect of the history of the Trans-European Division, not least as it relates to the wider Seventh-day Adventist Church.

Gender

As we have seen, a consistent characteristic of Adventism in the TED's European territory has been a strong desire to take the gospel 'into all the world'. One result of the passion for mission has historically been, especially in Scandinavia, the Baltic, and Britain, openness to innovation. This has existed in tension with the natural Adventist tendency to conservatism and a propensity, at certain points in the division's history, to move slowly in order to ensure consensus. But at times there has been boldness, a readiness to try new methods, and above all a desire to mobilise all available talent, given the small number of Adventists in the TED's territory. One manifestation of this has been a willingness to use women in leadership roles that has been present from the beginning of the church in what became the Trans-European Division.

Women in Leadership up to the 1950s

In 1898, when the British Conference was established, a woman, Edith Adams, was elected secretary-treasurer; nine years later, when the Russian Union Conference was organised in Riga, two women were elected as both secretary and treasurer: the latter was an American missionary, but the secretary, Sophie Bojanus, may have been a German-Latvian.[59] In the Seventh-day Adventist Church in the late nineteenth and early twentieth centuries, it was by no means unheard of for women to be elected as officers of organisational units, though always as secretary, treasurer, or secretary-treasurer; none was ever elected a conference or union president. Every year for fifteen years, 1897 to 1911, the percentage of conference, mission, or union officers, worldwide, who were women was in double digits, with more than 11 per cent in 1910 and 1911, while the latter year, with forty-nine female officers, was the peak year in absolute numbers (and probably remained so until quite recently). In the 1910s, however,

---

59 Nigel Barham, 'British Isles', in *HRSDAE*, p. 32. Guy Dail; 'Another European Conference', *ARH*, 85.5 (30 Jan. 1908), 16.

the percentage began to drop and in the 1920s the downward trend accelerated.[60]

It is striking, then, that when one of the TED's unions (and a constituent union of the NED), the Baltic Union Conference, was organised in 1923, the first treasurer elected was a woman, Martha Raba. She later served as Estonian Conference treasurer (Illustration 12.19).[61] In 1929 or 1930, the Estonian Conference elected another woman treasurer, Amanda Sohvie Nuka (and that was not the end of her career, as we will see).[62] In 1929, too, the Polish Union Conference elected a woman treasurer, Miss M. Babinska, who had previously been treasurer of two PUC conferences.[63] These two decisions demonstrate not just an historic inclination of the church in the new NED's territory, but a willingness at the NED itself to use women in leadership. It is made crystal clear by the election in 1928, by the newly formally established Northern European Division Committee, of one of the faculty members at Stanborough College, Miss Mary Wharrie, as treasurer of the East African Union Mission (Illustration 12.20). She subsequently crossed to the other side of Africa, serving as secretary-treasurer of the Nigerian Union Mission, before she met an 'untimely death'.[64]

Given the statistics of women in leadership noted above, the election of these women was not wholly exceptional, yet it was highly

---

60 See Kit Watts's groundbreaking article, 'The Rise and Fall of Adventist Women in Leadership', *Ministry,* 68.4 (Apr. 1995), 6–10; more data are in D. J. B. Trim, 'The Ordination of Women in Seventh-day Adventist Policy and Practice, up to 1972', paper read at the Theology of Ordination Study Committee meeting, 21–23 July 2013, table on p. 24; available to download at: <https://www.adventistarchives.org/the-ordination-of-women-in-Seventh-day-adventist-policy-and-practice.pdf>.
61 *YB 1924,* p. 83; *YB 1925,* p. 92; *YB 1926,* p. 95.
62 *YB 1930,* p. 207. Nuka is not in *YB 1929* but may have been elected after the cut-off point for reporting.
63 *YB 1924,* p. 102; *YB 1925,* p. 107; *YB 1926,* p. 116; *YB 1927,* pp. 125–26; *YB 1928,* p. 131; *YB 1929,* pp. 134–35, 137.
64 NED Minority Committee meeting, 23 Dec. 1928, NEDCOM meetings, 6 and 10 Jan. 1929, and NED Home Committee meeting, 23 Nov. 1935, NEDCOM mins.: 1928, p. 19, 1929, p. 1, 1935–1936, p. 61.

unconventional, especially because the wider trend in the church during the twenties was away from utilising women in officer positions of church organisational units. The NED's willingness to use talented women, especially in what might be regarded as mission fields, continued. For example, M. Babinskaya continued as PUC treasurer through 1937; this included re-election at the 1936 Polish Union Session when a GC field secretary, F. C. Gilbert, was present, so that her election was clearly within the bounds of what was seen as acceptable. The change in 1938, moreover, was that she became PUC secretary-treasurer and subsequently joined the board of the Polish seminary. Sister Babinskaya, whose first name we do not know, disappears from church records in 1940 and may have been a casualty of the war.[65]

In 1931, Amanda Nuka (Illustration 12.21) was called from the Estonian Conference to serve as treasurer of the Nigerian Union Mission. For reasons that remain unclear, in the end the division executive committee appointed her treasurer of the Sierra Leone Mission (though the fact that she took a course in tropical medicine is a reminder of how pioneering missionaries had to be all-rounders). When she went to Sierra Leone, however, it did not mean a woman did not go to the Nigerian Union headquarters. Instead, the NED Committee appointed a British woman, Miss (Ruth) Jessie Bowles, as secretary-treasurer of the Nigerian Union Mission. Both Bowles and Nuka were just 27 years old when they were entrusted with their respective responsibilities.

Jesse Bowles served eighteen months as union treasurer, then, in 1933, married Charles Bartlett, a British-American missionary. For the next six years, as she later noted in one of the forms the church had missionaries complete, she was a 'Missionary's wife assisting in

---

65 *YB 1931*, pp. 223–24; *YB 1932*, pp. 200–01; *YB 1933*, p. 154; *YB 1934*, p. 155; *YB 1935*, p. 157; *YB 1936*, pp. 169–70; Wm. Czembor, 'The Polish Union Session', *Advent Survey*, 8.11 (Nov. 1936), 3; *YB 1937*, pp. 162–63; *YB 1938*, pp. 164–65; *YB 1939*, p. 169; *YB 1940*, pp. 170–71, 281.

office, educational, medical and evangelistic work in various [mission] stations [in] Nigeria'. But, starting in 1939, she served as treasurer of the short-lived Gold Coast Union Mission, continuing as treasurer of the Gold Coast Mission until 1946. While on furlough she was replaced and then Charles was called to Sierra Leone and Jessie did not serve in a senior administrative position again. In 1949, Jessie's successor as treasurer of the Gold Coast Mission was himself replaced as treasurer – by none other than Amanda Nuka! In 1936, she had returned to Europe, to serve as secretary-treasurer of the Baltic Union after the crisis caused by government repression in Latvia – the fact that it was the NED which moved her back to the Baltic to help handle a crisis situation speaks eloquently about how they regarded her talents. She later returned to Africa and spent several years in teaching, but eventually returned to Treasury work. The following year, after a furlough, she went back to the Sierra Leone Mission as secretary-treasurer. There she was active not only in administrative duties but also in training pastors and teachers. This led in due course to a faculty appointment at the Nigerian Training College (one of the predecessor institutions of Babcock University). Jessie Bartlett's missionary appointment ended only in 1953, Amanda Nuka's not until 1959.[66] They gave their lives to the church's mission in the NED.

Although the 1950s are usually regarded as an era of conservatism in the church, Nordic Adventists continued to elect women to serve as officers. In the mid-fifties, for example, both conferences in

---

66 Sources for this and the preceding paragraph: NED Minority Committee meetings, 27 Apr., 2 and 20 July, and 16 Aug., 1931, NEDCOM mins., 1931, pp. 20, 36, 43, 51–52; joint meeting, NED Home Committee and Baltic Union Committee, 21 Jan. 1936, in NEDCOM mins., 1935–1936, p.10; fld. 'Bartlett, Charles A.' and fld. 'Nukka [sic], Miss A.', GC Ar., RG 21, Secretariat Appointee Files, nos. 45194, 48848; J. R. Bartlett, completed 'Biographical Information Blank', 22 Sept. 1947, GC Ar., RG 21, 'Personal Information Forms and Biographical material', box no. 7298, fld. 'B to Bea'; *YB 1937*, p. 149; *YB 1946*, p. 219; *YB 1949*, p. 234; *YB 1950*, p. 239; *YB 1951*, p. 162; *YB 1952*, p. 256; A. F. Tarr, 'Itinerating in West Africa', *Northern Light*, 1.1 (March 1951), 10.

Sweden had women as secretary-treasurer: Lisa Soderberg and Anna Sundqvist.[67]

Women in Ministry

The women in leadership should not be seen as aberrations even though their numbers were very much a minority of leaders in the NED. Women also were involved in outreach. In the inter-war Baltic Union, for example, women were leaders in the publishing work. Publishing had been important in the Baltic states since the church's beginnings. The Estonian Conference, for example, perhaps uniquely in the world church, classified the 'Book and Bible House' as a department and the conference also had its own small publishing house, which printed only in Estonian, in addition to the Baltic Union publishing house in Riga, which printed predominantly in Latvian. Pastors essentially were figureheads in the publishing work; it was laypeople who were the driving force and thus the women were able to take leadership roles.

In Finland, right from the start, women had 'an active role in evangelism and in other areas of Church work'.[68] In World War II, however, they became very prominent. The ENUC president, Gustav Lindsay reported to the 1946 GC Session:

> *When but two ministers were left free to engage in public work, our good sisters in the Bible work came to fill the gaps in the ranks of the evangelists. They were sent out two by two to work as the brethren had done, holding series of evangelistic meetings and preaching [...] with force and enthusiasm.*

He highlighted the case of 'two young sisters', who 'were successful in bringing 100 souls to the truth in five years in a district

---

67 E.g., *YB 1955*, p. 125; *YB 1956*, p. 133.
68 Esa Rouhe, 'Elsa Luukkanen and the Role of Adventist Women in Finland', in *HRSDAE*, pp. 95–97 (p. 96).

where there was no Adventist church before'.[69] While Lindsay left these two unnamed, it is likely that one was Elsa Luukkanen. She became famous for her evangelistic campaigns across Finland, in which 'hundreds of people were converted, and a number of churches established'.[70]

Luukkanen was only in her twenties when the war began, so the Finnish church had turned to youth, as well as to women. One of the division's Australian departmental leaders wrote in 1951, with a degree of surprise:

> *Finland is the only country in the world that I know of where we have lady evangelists. We have several in this land. One in particular is a young woman who has done a remarkable work and for a number of years has been bringing into the truth from fifty to eighty souls from each mission she holds. She has had, we believe, a real experience with the Holy Spirit and her gifts have been sanctified and enlarged. The spirit of revival is found in many of our churches in Finland. Large crowds of people are coming out to hear our evangelists who are few in number, but who are proclaiming the truth with power.*[71]

Again, the unnamed woman is probably Luukkanen, but other women also played a role in soul winning, conducting Bible studies with those swayed by the evangelistic preaching of Luukkanen or others. One admiring journalist wrote:

Denominational periodicals of the fifties pay tribute to the work done by Finnish women. Their reputation even extended to the

69   G. A. Lindsay, 'The East Nordic Union Conference', report to 1946 GC Session, *ARH*, 123.24, General Conference Report, no. 2 (7 June 1946), 39.
70   Rouhe, 'Elsa Luukkanen and Adventist Women in Finland', p. 96. There is a short autobiography, 'as told to' E. Olavi Rouhe, *Elsa, Sweet Singer of Finland* (Mountain View, Calif.: Pacific Press, 1980), which is inspiring but of limited value as an historical source.
71   E. L. Minchin, 'Itinerating in Sweden and Finland', *Northern Light*, 1.1 (March 1951), 10–11.

United States of America, thanks to a trip Luukkanen and a colleague made to the 1958 General Conference Session in Cleveland, Ohio, at which they were introduced to the delegates during the NED report (illustration 12.22). This provided an opportunity to tour Canada and the northern Midwest, known for its Finnish émigré communities.

> Miss Elsa Luukkanen and Miss Aino Lehtoluoto [...] have, by the blessings of God, won more than 500 people to this truth in the last 16 years in their home country. The speaker of the team is Elsa Luukkanen and she has a powerful voice and deep personal experience in the things of God and wonderful evangelistic appeal in her preaching. Aino Lehtoluoto has served as Bible teacher and co-laborer during this entire period. [...] During the war [...] all of our ministers were called into military service and no workers were available to answer evangelistic appeals. Miss Luukkanen was pressed into service on what was thought to be a temporary basis but after the conference leaders returned to their duties they insisted that these two ladies continue their work. In Helsinki three meetings were held every Sunday for a number of weeks to accommodate the crowd. In other places the Finnish team remained long enough in locations where no Adventist church existed to see that the people were baptized and a church building provided before moving on to the next field of labor.[72]

Luukkanen and Aino Lehtoluoto later toured Canada again in 1964 and Florida in 1965, receiving much attention from American church members (Illustration 12.22).

It is worth noting that, at this juncture, there were at least twenty-two female Bible Instructors in the Finland Union, as opposed to

---

[72] R. M. Whitsett, 'Finnish Evangelists Visit Minnesota', *Northern Union Outlook*, 17 June 1958, pp. 6–7; see also Louise C. Klenser, 'Bible Instructors at Cleveland', *Ministry*, 31.10 (Oct. 1958), 30–31 (p. 30).

eighteen ordained and licensed pastors (and another six Bible Instructors whose gender is not clear from their names).[73] So it is plain that a large part of the heavy lifting of evangelism was being done by the women. In 1968 (a year whose significance is noted below), there were still eighteen active women Bible Instructors (plus three who held honorary credentials, meaning they were retired), and twenty-eight licentiates and ordained ministers. The Swedish Union in 1968, in contrast, had six female Bible Instructors; the West Nordic Union four, the Netherlands and Polish Unions, none.[74]

The Role of Women and the TED in Historical Context

In this history, I do not go into the controversial subject of women's ordination, on which there is no consensus among church leaders and church members in the TED, much less the world church.
It is important to note, however, from an historical perspective, firstly, that the election and appointment of women as conference and union officers was done without refence to ordination. There is no evidence that any of the women discussed so far sought to be ordained to gospel ministry. But to focus on this certainly significant point would be to miss another, equally significant: lack of ordination did not stop women from the countries around the Baltic and from Britain being used in leadership. They were used and their regular re-elections show they were effective in the Secretariat and Treasury. Secondly, it must also be noted that this is the historical context of the 1968 action by the Finland Union Conference Executive Committee 'to inquire of the General Conference through the Division, whether the sisters who are working in preaching ministry could be ordained as ministers'. The NED requested 'counsel regarding ordination of women', since 'the question has arisen in Finland'.[75] In light of the qualita-

---

73 *YB 1958*, pp. 135–36.
74 *YB 1968*, pp. 182–85, 189–91.
75 Meeting, Finland Union Committee, 20 Feb. 1968, Minutes §§ 19–20, quoted in Rouhe, 'Luukkanen and Adventist Women', pp. 96–97; GC Officers' meeting, 8 Apr. 1968, GCOM, p. 68-183.

tive and quantitative evidence briefly reviewed above, the interest of Finnish church leaders in ordaining women is understandable, whatever view one takes of it theologically.

The fact that the inquiry about ordination did not receive an affirmative response did not matter to women in Finland and in Sweden. In 1969, Luukkanen introduced Adventist Community Services to Finland and had a tremendous impact; she also kept up evangelistic preaching into the 1980s.[76] In 1983, Anna-Liisa Helevaara, a Finnish literature evangelist, was praised by the General Conference Executive Committee as the 'world champion literature evangelist', after selling $285,000 worth of books in 1982.[77] The 1990 GC Session elected Anna-Liisa Halonen, who had been serving as general manager of the Finland Publishing House, as TED treasurer.[78] This was almost unprecedented. In the 1870s–'80s, women had served as GC treasurers; as we have seen, in the fifty years thereafter, there had been female union treasurers. All these examples were well in the past. Halonen was the first female *division* treasurer and the first woman to serve as an executive officer of any division in the Seventh-day Adventist Church.[79] In September 2003, the Swedish Union Executive Committee elected Audrey Andersson as its executive secretary; she was then re-elected by the Union Session in June 2005.[80] In 2010, the GC Session elected her the secretary of the TED. This was almost unparalleled. Although Halonen provided the precedent of a female executive officer, Andersson is the first woman to serve as a

---

76 Short obit., 'At Rest', *ARH*, 174.21 (22 May 1997), 29; Rouhe, 'Luukkanen and Adventist Women', p. 96.
77 GCC meeting, 6 Jan. 1983, GCC mins., p. 83-6.
78 Fifty-Fifth Session, twelfth meeting, 12 July 1990, *ARH*, 163.34 (17 July 1990), 19; cf. *YB 1990*, p. 525.
79 Family circumstances meant she only served two years before accepting a call back to the Finland Union Conference as treasurer: TEDEC meeting, 27 Mar. 1992, TEDMC-EC 1992, § 53, p. 36.
80 SUC Executive Committee meeting, 10 Sept. 2003, Executive Committee mins., 2003: § 179; SUC Union Session, 14 June 2005, Session mins. 2005: § 56 (I am indebted to Rainer Refsbäck for these references).

division secretary – the second officer of a division – anywhere in the world church (Illustrations 12.24–25).

Events do not occur and ideas do not arise in a vacuum. There are some Adventists who believe that the sole context for the push to ordain women in the TED is increasing secularisation in the Nordic countries, the Netherlands, and the United Kingdom. But this betrays lack of awareness of the TED's history. An equally significant context is the time-honoured readiness of Seventh-day Adventists in those countries – and, too, in the Baltic and Polish Unions – to make use of women in leadership positions and in literature and public evangelism. Given the small memberships, historically, throughout the TED, if only men, or only ordained ministers, were used in these roles, then Adventists would *not* have been able to follow through on the founding premise of the division: to 'carry the Advent Message to the [...] unwarned millions'.

* * *

A significant part of the history of the Trans-European Division has been how it has dealt with diversity. Multiplicity made for complexity and, potentially, for perplexity. As we saw earlier (Chapters 6, 8, and 9), there have been times and places in which ethnicity posed challenges to church members and leaders alike; with hindsight, it is plain that the response of church leaders was not always wise, humane, or Christlike. If one takes the division as a whole, however, and over the whole ninety years, what stands out is the willingness of leaders at all levels to embrace diversity (though youth are rather embraced less in the TED's organisational structures at present than they have been at some points in the past).

The issue of diversity will continue to be one with which the Seventh-day Adventist Church in the territory of the TED will have to successfully engage. That is dictated by broader forces: the movement of peoples across the world and within Europe, and the shifting nature of what is increasingly a global culture but continues to have distinctive national, regional, and local manifestations. History suggests that success will not come easily, but it also shows that the TED has succeeded in this area before – and that should give confidence for the future.

Chapter 13
Conclusion

This has been, truly, a story of struggles, defeats and victories.[1] It began in the heyday of the age of empires, an era of authoritarian nationalism and communism; it continued through the Great Depression, genocide, World War, and Cold War, into the era of the War on Terror, climate change, and resurgent nationalism. Today, the TED seeks to reach the southeast and northwest of a Europe that is post-colonial, post-communist, post-Christian. Much has changed. There have been successes along the way, and setbacks, but the constant has been struggle. Yet through it all, tens of thousands of people have been brought to know Jesus Christ as their Lord, Saviour, High Priest, Great Physician, and soon-coming King.

Having examined separate periods and themes of the division's history, then, what can we say about ninety years of the Trans-European Division? Viewing the period as a whole, what trends can be identified and what conclusions drawn?

Complexity

First, the history of the Seventh-day Adventist Church in the Trans-European Division territory is complex, more so than that of any other division – not least because this division has probably experienced more, and more sweeping, changes of territory than any other division. Put simply, despite the use of 'Northern Europe' in the division's title for its first fifty-five years, it has always included territories outside the north and northwest of Europe. Nevertheless, as suggested in Chapter 1, for the whole of its history, the heartland of this division has been the church in Britain, Denmark, Finland, Norway, and Sweden, joined since 1951 by the Netherlands; from

---

1 Cf. White, *Patriarchs and Prophets*, p. 596; see above, Chapter 1.

these six countries the bulk of tithes and offerings, and foreign missionaries, has come. The European base has often been a blessing, because Western Europe in the last century has generally enjoyed liberal political and religious freedoms, but there has also been much prejudice against what has been perceived as an American implant, and Adventists have persistently faced a range of powerful pressures: persecution and parochialism in the early days, and still today in parts of Eastern Europe; pluralism and postmodernism today in the British Isles, the Netherlands, and the Nordic and Baltic countries. The two World Wars were incredibly destructive to society in general, and disruptive of the denomination's mission, in particular. The Seventh-day Adventist Church has also, however, suffered internal strains, including theological controversies and ethnic tensions (with the latter sometimes exacerbating the former). Ethnic tensions were felt both between the core European territories and the mission fields, and within the European heartland.

As noted in Chapter 3, there are indications that national pride was a factor in relations between the church in the Nordic countries, which may explain the separation of the Scandinavian Union into the ENUC and WNUC in 1931. Cultural and linguistic differences were factors in the dissolution of the ENUC in the sixties, after Swedes and Finns parted company (Chapter 6); cultural tensions played a part in the dissolution of the WNUC into Danish and Norwegian Unions in the early nineties (Chapters 9, 10); and at the same time, the knock-on effects of resurgent Nationalist politics broke asunder the Yugoslavian Union Conference (Chapter 9). Population movements have, however, caused a larger strain than longstanding national differences within Northern Europe. In the late twentieth century, most countries in the TED were affected by migration. Homogeneous societies became diverse and the same dynamic was at work in the church. Many Adventist immigrants into Europe came from Africa and the Caribbean, where the Adventist Church is strong, and they brought a sense of vigour and purpose that had started to dwindle in the TED's core territories. Meanwhile, church membership in Hungary and the Balkans was diminished by migration within Europe, though church members from south-eastern Europe, along with the rather larger numbers of Adventist immigrants from outside Europe, increased church membership in north-western Europe. Yet tensions sometimes ensued, not least in Great Britain and the Netherlands. Issues such as national identity, race relations, and membership (or not) of the European Union, will continue to make for considerable complexity.

In addition, at times denominational organisational structures have created their own difficulties. The perceived need to attach mission fields to European countries made sense in the age of empires, when having a headquarters in the capital of an empire had many advantages for obtaining visas, travel permits, operating authority in colonies, even interceding with higher authorities for contracts and planning permission. Shipping lines usually linked imperial metropoles with their far-flung colonies. But having African mission territories part of supposedly 'European' divisions was utterly out of step with the 'wind of change'-era in Africa that began in the late 1950s, gathered pace in the sixties, and resulted in independence for one-time colonies across the African continent. In addition to political embarrassment, however, there was also potential for incoherence: administratively, culturally, and missiologically.

In the case of the NED and then TED, the fact that it included the United Kingdom had unforeseen consequences. Britain's empire was so large that, when the assignment of mission-field territories was based on imperial connections, it meant that much of Africa and Asia could, on the face of it, be reasonably assigned to the British Union Conference and its parent division. Even after decolonisation, the presence of the English language in certain territories made a connection with the TED more logical than with the Southern European or Euro-Africa Divisions. The anglophone connection and commercial and cultural affinities help to explain the attachment of the Middle East and Pakistan to the TED well after the sun had set on the British Empire.

All this, though, meant in turn that the NED and then TED became the historic foster parent for orphaned fields which, for whatever reasons, did not neatly fit into other divisions: Liberia in 1932, Pakistan in 1985, and the Middle East in 1995 are the obvious examples, though one could add French Equatorial Africa all the way back in 1929, and make a case for the Netherlands in 1946, though that turned out to be adoption rather than fostering. Providing a temporary home for unwanted unions and fields was a service the division historically provided to the world church, though it is probably an under-appreciated one. The TED's territory has historically spanned from the icy climes of the Arctic Circle to the tropics, reaching from Greenland in the west to Pakistan in the east; from North Cape in Norway, to south of the Equator in what is now Tanzania. In encompassing Zanzibar and Svalbard, Lake Tanganyika and Lake Ladoga, the sheer geographical extent and cultural variety of territories assigned to British and Scandinavian leaders has been unmatched anywhere else in the world church. To provide leadership to territories characterised by so great geographic, linguistic, and ethnic differences is inevitably demanding; it creates its own challenges, beyond those that emerge from social or ecclesiastical contexts.

The TED has often been disjointed, in not just geographic, but also missional terms: was its chief work to convert Lutherans in the Scandinavian countries? Catholics in Poland, Croatia, and Hungary? Members of the Orthodox Churches in Greece, Montenegro, and Serbia? Adherents of other ancient Christian traditions in Egypt, Lebanon, and, up to 1970, Ethiopia? Or, right up to 1980, followers of African traditional religions in West or East Africa? Or Muslims in Africa and then, after 1985, in Pakistan and across the Middle East? Or, latterly, postmodern neo-pagans or secular humanists across

Europe? The outreach methodology that would serve well for any one of these would be detrimental if used for almost any of the others. And, unlike any of the three American divisions or the Southern Asia Division, for example, there has been limited long-term stability in the populations the division organisation has served and endeavoured to evangelise, since the territory has been regularly reconfigured: in 1970, 1980, 1985, 1994, 1995, 2011 – six times in less than a half century. In attempting to create resources and strategies, then, division leaders have for many years face a moving target, as well as one that is so broad that it is difficult to focus efforts.

Mission Success

In spite of prejudice, war, secularism, indifference, financial difficulties, theological controversies, and other challenges, the Third Angel's Message has taken root in European soil. In 1901, when the Scandinavian Union Conference was organised, there were just over four thousand Seventh-day Adventists in Europe: around one for every 62,600 Europeans. When the European Division was split into four, the ratio had improved to 4750 to 1, but if one looks at the figures for 1929 in the TED's current territory (rather than the NED's as it was in 1929), so as to have a proper comparison with today, there were 22,400 church members and a general population of 165 million: the ratio was 7365 to 1 – worse than in Europe as a whole but, for the this division, immensely improved on 1901. Today's 88,100 church members in the TED are a fraction of the total population, estimated by demographers at some 206 million. Yet that means the ratio today is 2340 people for every church member. Put another way, there are now 42.7 Seventh-day Adventists per 100,000 people in the TED in contrast to 13.5 Adventists per 100,000 in 1929 (and 1.6 per 100,000 in 1901!). The share is 300 per cent of what it was ninety years ago when the division began. This means that the church not only has grown, it has also grown faster than the population at large.

There is no doubt, though, that where the division historically grew fastest was sub-Saharan Africa. In 1929, 13.2 per cent of the NED's 24,228 members were in the division's mission fields in Africa. By 1980, when the West African territories of NEWAD were detached and the division re-renamed NED, 67.9 per cent of its 87,389 members were in the two West African unions, each of which had more members than the division's six European unions put together.[2] In one sense, this was to be regretted, because it reflects the relative decline of Christianity in Europe – a phenomenon that is not unique to the Seventh-day Adventist denomination. However, even though one wishes that Europeans were much more receptive to the Third Angel's Message, the transformation in the Adventist Church in Africa was wonderful. It was a matter of the growth of the church, in terms of members, but also its growth in the sense of a maturing process. Once, African countries needed foreign missionaries to act as ministers and administrators – now, missionaries typically are used in medical and technical positions. The numerical growth and the self-sufficiency are alike outcomes undoubtedly desired by early missionaries to Africa, men and women such as William Bartlett, Ruben and Hanna Bergström, Charles and Jessie Bartlett, Jesse and Catherine Clifford, Gunnar and Marit Gudmundsen, Per Lindegren, William McClements, George Madgwick, Amanda Nuka, Valdemar and Minnie Toppenberg, and others; were they still alive, they would undoubtedly praise God for this ultimate conclusion to their life work.

How was it achieved? It was because church leaders followed through on their pledge of 1928, quoted in Chapter 2: 'to make every effort to carry the Advent Message to the many millions in the countries of the Northern European Division, including its large mission

---

2   *ASR*, 118 (1980),16.

fields.' It was a huge and hugely bold undertaking for church leaders from the countries fringing the Baltic, on the Scandinavian Peninsula, and in the British Isles, in which lived just over 24,200 Seventh-day Adventists, to commit themselves to taking the Third Angel's Message to an area that, as Walter Read told the first division Winter Council, covered 'fully 5000 miles from east to west and 2000 miles from north to south', and was inhabited by 165 million people. It could easily have just been words. But here is the remarkable thing: they did it. They did make every effort. And the efforts of the hundreds of missionaries from the TED's mission homelands had a powerful effect.

In celebrating expansion and progress across Africa, it is vital not to forget how much is owed to those missionaries. The most rapid church growth came after local believers took responsibility for 'carrying the Adventist message' to their own compatriots. Yet they built on foundations laid, quite literally, with toil, tears, and sweat. Individual missionaries from NED/NEWAD offered their lives as living sacrifices, as the apostle Paul urged believers; not only in their own division, either, for numbers of church members went as missionaries to other divisions' territories. Their personal commitment was matched by, indeed was part of, a corporate commitment – by the church *qua* church – to the mission fields assigned to it: an ongoing and considerable commitment of funds and personnel. In many cases, too, the people the division sent were the church's best and brightest. Their willingness to 'go into all the world', to endure privation and isolation, and to face the prospect of disease and death – this was heroic and laid the foundations of today's flourishing Adventist presence in Ghana and much of Nigeria, in Ethiopia and Uganda, Kenya and Tanzania. Without their commitment, without the years and decades of service missionaries gave, even the toeholds the church has in Pakistan and the Middle East might not exist.

Their sacrifices are, sadly, largely forgotten across the division's historic homelands. Despite the TED's longstanding and substantial investment in the Ellen G. White Research Centre at Newbold, which is dedicated to wider Adventist history in Europe as well as the Spirit of Prophecy, and in spite, too, of the efforts of enthusiasts and amateur archivists in Scandinavia,[3] there is little doubt that, as discussed in Chapter 7, the history of the TED's NED/NEWAD years is better remembered in West Africa than Northern Europe, at least at the administrative level.

But here is a troubling thought: the extraordinary flourishing of the church in Ethiopia, Kenya, Uganda, South Sudan, Sierra Leone, Ghana, Nigeria, and Cameroon, all of which initially were, and in some cases for several decades remained, under the TED, was due in large part to a massive injection of people and money from Northern Europe. Was the outflow of resources to Africa too much for the good of the church back in the core countries of the TED? Did the prominence given to converting 'the heathen' mean that insufficient emphasis was given to evangelising Europeans? Did church growth in the African mission fields come at the expense of church growth in the mission homelands? It would be difficult if not impossible to reach a definite conclusion; one would have to take into account positive influences on the church in the homelands, as well as evidence that is often indeterminate; but this disquieting question at least has to be considered.

Here is another question: was as much time, effort and money put into 'translating' Adventism into the cultural idiom of Northern Europe as it was into contextualising in Nigeria or Somalia, in Uganda or Ghana? The idea that Adventism needed to 'learn to speak the language of Europe' (see Chapter 9) did not refer merely to mastering actual dialects. It means cultural adaptation not only linguistic translation. Both were done with great success in West Africa. Contextualisation was also attempted, though less successfully, in the

---

3   E.g., Historisk Arkiv för Sjundedags Adventistsamfundet: see <https://www.adventist.se/historiskt-arkiv/747/1>; Stichting Historisch Archief Nederlandse Adventkerk: see <http://shana.adventist.nl/>.

Middle East and Pakistan. Is it possible that as Europe grew less and less Christian, so that American ideas and methodologies became less likely to work here, the institutional church did not engage as much as it might have – as much as it ought to have – in its homelands, in the kinds of exercise it engaged in, with distinction, in the mission fields?

Challenges

It is to Europe, to the core countries of the TED, and to its mission homelands that we now turn, as we draw to a conclusion. Table 13.1 shows both the total membership and the equivalent proportion of division membership for the eleven countries that at the beginning were, and currently are, part of the division: four were in the ScUC historically, and have evolved via the ENUC and WNUC, eventually, into four unions; three were and are in the Baltic Union Conference; two were and are in the BUC; with Iceland and Poland the others.[4]

These statistics could be understood in various ways, and a positive or negative spin put on them, but their presentation here is not intended as a basis for apportioning praise or blame. Given the upheavals those ninety years have witnessed, along with the fact that the TED includes some of the most secular countries and cultures in the world, that there has been growth at all is a matter for profound gratitude. In considering, however, as we have, the history of what was long called the 'Northern European Division', it is striking that the northernmost parts of the division are becoming proportionately ever less significant.

---

4   Iceland was in a personal union with the Danish crown up to 1944; it never formed part of the state of Denmark.

Table 13.1: Ninety-Year Trend: January 1929 to 1 January 2019

Original Organisation	Membership			Current Organisation	Divisional Share	
	1929	2019	Growth		1929	2019
Denmark Conference	2,665	2,445	-8.25%	Union of Churches	10.92%	2.77%
Finland Conference	1,490	4,657	+212.55%	Union of Churches	6.65%	5.3%
Norway Conference	2,367	4,536	+91.64%	Union Conference	10.6%	5.15%
Sweden Conference	1,883	2,928	+55.50%	Union of Churches	8.4%	3.33%
Scandinavian Union Conference	8,405	14,566	+73.30%	Four unions	37.52%	16.53%
Baltic Union Conference	3,768	5,950	+57.91%	Union Conference	16.82%	6.75%
British Union Conference	4,473	38,594	+762.82%	Union Conference	19.97%	43.80%
Polish Union Conference	2,260	5,836	+158.23%	Union Conference	10.09%	6.62%
– Iceland Mission	307	465	+51.47%	Conference	1.37%	0.53%
(Northern European Division	22,402	88,099		Trans-European Division)		

Sources: *ASR*, 66 (1928), 8; *YB 1929*, pp.137–41; *ASR*, Advance Release of Membership Statistics by Division for 2018 (2019), pp. 16–17.

Note: The European Division's year-end statistical report for 1928 does not include conference breakdowns, only total union figures. The conference figures are taken from the 1929 *YB*, which gives a slightly larger total for the Scandinavian Union than the ASR figure, reflecting that the two publications had different cut-off points. As the total is only 25 more than the ASR union membership, I have used the *YB* figures.

The balance of membership between the different unions and countries, with their different cultures, can affect how the division does business, who becomes its leaders, their modus operandi in dealing with the component unions, how they relate to the General

Conference, and the role that leaders from across the division play in world-church decision-making processes.[5] The statistics, then, disclose a development of historic significance, while the trajectories they reveal (also shown in Figure 14) are likely to shape the division's future.[6]

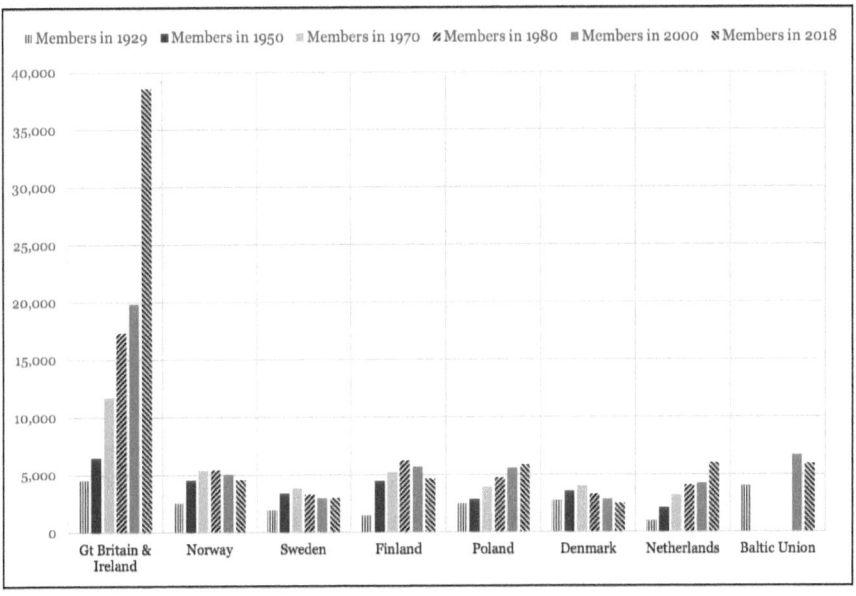

Figure 14: Membership Trajectories in the TED's Core Countries since 1929

The change in the relative importance of the Nordic countries is partly the result of the reassignment of the Netherlands to the NED at the end of World War II and the addition to the TED in the mid-eighties of two (now three) unions and two attached fields in Eastern Europe. When the NED was constituted, Africa supplied about 15

---

5 Andersson, 'Scandinavian Influence on the Trans-European Division', is suggestive in this regard.
6 The next five paragraphs are drawn from *ASR*, 66 (1928), 8; *ASR*, 67 (1929), 12–15; *YB 1929*, pp. 131–34, 137–41; *ASR*, 117 (1979), 16; *ASR*, 127 (1989), 22; *ASR*, 154 (2018 for 2016–2017), 31–49; *ASR Advance Release 2018* (2019), pp. 6–7 *et passim*; TED, 'Treasurer's Statistical Report – Annual – 2018', 9 Jan. 2019, GC Ar., RG 29.

per cent of total membership, whereas at present 25 per cent – one in four church members – are from Holland, Hungary, or the Balkans. The balance is 10 percentage points lower than ninety years ago. The overall Scandinavian share is bound to be less. A graphic sense of the shifting demographic balance within the TED is provided by Figure 14, which shows the membership in the historic, core countries of the division at certain pivotal moments in its history: at the beginning; twenty years later, in 1950, when the NED was re-founded; another two decades on, in 1970, as East Africa was detached; in 1980, as West Africa was separated; a further twenty years on, at the turn of the millennium; and nearly twenty years later again, as the TED marked its ninetieth anniversary.

The Netherlands Union proved a valuable addition to the TED. It was the third-largest union in terms both of membership and of tithe contributions in 2018 (though the Dutch totals were 6.8 per cent and 7.5 percent, respectively, of the TED totals). It also punches above its weight for the world church: as well as Dutch missionaries (though their numbers have dwindled in the last three decades), there is also the financial contribution. While international comparisons are difficult because all tithes and offerings are converted into US dollars, so that union contributions are subject to the vagaries of currency conversion, it is nevertheless striking that, out of 137 unions worldwide, the Netherlands Union of Churches currently has the 122nd-largest membership, yet is the 85th-largest contributor of tithes and offerings. The addition of the Balkans in 1985 also played a part in altering the relative importance of Scandinavia in the TED; the South-East European Union Conference was the division's second-largest union in terms of membership as of 1 January 2019.

The major development, though, has undoubtedly been the growth in both absolute and relative terms of the British church: from not quite 4500 members when the NED started, to a fraction under 14,000 at its golden jubilee in 1979, and now, forty years later, approaching 40,000 (see Figure 14). In the first half century, British membership increased 300 per cent, but this was from a low base; the 120 per cent growth in the last four decades in some ways is more impressive, representing 525 additional members per year, as opposed to 260 per year in the preceding five decades. Equally significant is the BUC's share of division membership: it was 20 per cent in 1929; it had declined to 11 per cent fifty years later, but this was distorted by the dramatic and disproportionate growth in the West African mission fields, home to two-thirds of NEWAD's membership; ten years later, in 1989, the BUC had 26 per cent of TED's members, slightly higher than in 1929. Yet it is now 44 per cent – more than doubling its share of division membership since the NED was founded, a dramatic demographic-geographical shift. The BUC's share of tithe rose from 36.3 per cent in 1929 to 48.4 per cent in 2018. British members gave one-third of the division's first mission offering; by 2018 their contribution had risen to 46.6 per cent. In all, 48.1 per cent of the TED's total tithes and offerings in 2018 were returned or given in the British Union.

This shift in the division's centre of gravity is striking. Of its original six unions, the ScUC was not just the largest: it had more members than the second and third largest, the British and Baltic Union Conferences, combined. In 1929, the Scandinavian Union's share of NED tithe was 44.33 per cent and of mission offerings, 40 per cent; in 2018, the combined share of the four unions that had been conferences of the ScUC was 24.6 per cent of tithes and 17 per cent of mission offerings. The shift has been away not only from Scandinavia in general, but from Denmark in particular. Denmark was where Adventist history in the TED began. More, it was the historic hub, first of the ScUC and then of the NED. This was partly due to the role of Skodsborg (analysed in Chapters 10 and 11). Denmark's pivotal role in what was the foundation of the division is evident especially in statistics. Today, of the four countries that constituted the old ScUC, Finland has the largest membership, Norway the second largest (and it is the biggest financial contributor of the four); combined they amount to 10 per cent of the total TED membership. In contrast, in January 1929 the Denmark Conference had 11 per cent of NED membership. It had a larger membership than the East African, Ethiopian, or Polish Unions (or the combined West African missions). Denmark's share of the division's total tithe was 16.6 per cent; Danes gave 14.26 per cent of the NED's mission offering. Just this one conference was the source of 12 per cent of all tithes and offerings in the division. In 2019, as Table 13.1 shows, not quite one in thirty-three members in the TED were in the Danish Union of Churches, which in the last quarter-century of its life has had only two years of positive growth, declining from 2922 members in 1997 to the 2445 of 1 January 2019, considerably less than the membership on the same day ninety years before.

In sum, whereas the Scandinavian Union, initially, and then for decades the East and West Nordic Unions, were the engine driving the NED and then TED, those days are in the past. Yet paradoxically, their influence has been preserved in the division's ecclesiastical polity, because the four countries, each a conference in 1929, eventually became four unions. Among the issues that future TED leaders will need to resolve are the weight that ought to be given to denominational membership and resources as opposed to missional need. Which should be more important in church structure: the population of church members to be served, or the wider population to be reached? Whatever one's perspective, the trajectory in the TED is away from its historical heartland in Scandinavia, which heightens the need for the issues to be studied, discussed, and addressed.

At the same time, the trajectory of the TED as a whole is back to the homelands. The organisational and conceptual model that indelibly moulded the division was of a homeland responsible for distant mission fields. This model took structural shape, yet it also took mental and cultural forms, transcending a mere template and approaching an archetype. Its influence was especially evident in administration, finances, governance, and representation: the external trappings of an ecclesiastical organisation. But it was also internalised, shaping the imagination of generations of Adventists dispersed widely across Europe, but sharing a passion for mission. The pattern endured for half a century and overall has characterised seventy-seven of the TED's ninety years, restored in revised form after the brief five-year interval of 1981–1985, after which the location of the mission fields changed, but not the essential nature of the dynamic. In 2011, though, the mould was broken. It is unlikely ever to be recast.

To a great extent, the division's *raison d'être* was to mobilise the time, talents, and money of Adventists in its northern homelands and deploy them to its African appendages. That is not how it would ever have been stated; in principle, financial and personnel assets were also to be applied to evangelising the regions that supplied most of the resources. There was, though, a prevailing assumption that Europe was already Christian, already evangelised; the urgent necessity seemed to be to reach the 'nations, tribes, and peoples', who had never heard the gospel, much less the distinctive Adventist understanding of the prophetic message of the angels of Revelation 14. The romance of the mission field, the pathos of 'the unwarned millions', and perhaps the fact that, ultimately, mission was rather more successful in what was supposedly the 'dark continent' than in what had once been Christendom, all helped to make unclear what was central and what peripheral in what is now the Trans-European Division.

When the energies and assets of the homelands (a concept discussed in Chapter 1), were being largely applied to the apparently marginal mission fields, which region really took precedence? If power lay principally in Britain and Scandinavia, the needs of Africa set the agenda. At first, that meant the need for European leaders in Africa; gradually, national leadership took over but continued to request and receive missionaries and money. The upshot was an effect that turned the mental world of European Adventists upside down. The church grew rapidly in the pagan periphery, while it plateaued in the homeland. Indeed, the mental world of European Adventists was turned upside down. Today, large parts of the African territories that came under the NED are more Christian than post-Christian Europe. Instead of mission being something done from or by Europe to Africa, the Caribbean, and Asia, since the 1980s, East and West Africans and West Indians have made significant contributions to the church in the Netherlands and the United Kingdom, and played their part, too, in Denmark, Norway, and Sweden.

I suggest that, in some ways, the attitudes and thinking of the days when the division was known as NED, NEWAD, and NED again, linger in the TED still today, even as, sadly, the youngest members in the TED have little or no idea of the heritage of missional involvement in Africa, and beyond. It is these which have to be overcome if the Trans-European Division is to be a truly European division.

In 1937 a Danish author, Karen Blixen, published *Out of Africa*, her memoir of seventeen years living in Kenya (then the colony of British East Africa). Blixen believed she had settled there permanently, but in the end returned to her homeland. The book was a best-seller and made into an Academy Award-winning movie. In some ways, it could stand for the history of the NED and TED. The gradual trajectory has been out of Africa; while the division was, of course, always European in one sense, its energies and resources were constantly being directed to Africa. It seemed that the Danes – and the Britons, Norwegians, Swedes and others – were in Africa to stay, but in the end, the control of the African Adventist church by paternalistic authorities 8000 miles (12,800 kilometres) away proved to be fleeting, like the British and French occupation of African lands. There was an imperial Adventist moment. But it passed.

Today, Europe's Adventists have to adjust mentally to the fact that they are out of Africa, even as many African church members are literally going out of Africa, emigrating to Europe. It is not easy, however, to shake off seventy-seven years of history. Perhaps there is still a sense, among some of the older generation, that deference is due to the old homelands, even to the old heartlands. Church members are on the move into Europe and the TED, indeed as they are moving *within* Europe, between the TED's far-flung territories, which extend from Karelia and Cyprus to Ireland and Iceland, from Lake Balaton to the Lake District. As they move, these Adventist immigrants may to be more sensitive to the cultural context of their new homes. If they are serious about winning majority populations, they will need to adjust, making a conscious effort in the way that missionaries from Northern Europe made a studied effort to adjust to the cultural setting of the one-time mission fields.

There is a need to get past nostalgia, for it will be of limited value in evangelising the people groups that presently are the TED's principal missional target. Neither native Europeans nostalgic for the old days when they controlled the church on other continents, nor émigrés nostalgic for the way people in their homeland 'did church' before they departed (and ignoring the changes that have taken place there since they left) will be well placed to bring together people of very diverse, sometimes radically different, ethnicities, cultures, ages, life experiences, and theological perspectives to work together. Wistfulness for the past needs to be left behind. Church members need to work unitedly and effectively if they are to saturate Europe's southeast and far north and the several North Atlantic archipelagos with the distinctive Adventist message of wholeness and hope in Christ and His soon return.

In concluding this section on challenges, here are two more disquieting questions, I fear even provocative ones, but I think they need to be asked. First, are European Adventists in the early twenty-first century able to adjust to these historic shifts? Second, will those same Adventists, themselves in many cases postmodern to a great degree, drawn from a range of different ethnicities and cultures (including many members of African descent), and drawn, too, from geographically, culturally, and linguistically diverse territories, be able to work together effectively, to evangelise Europe as their forefathers and foremothers once did tropical Africa. At its crux, the challenge is whether the Trans-European Division can now simply be European.

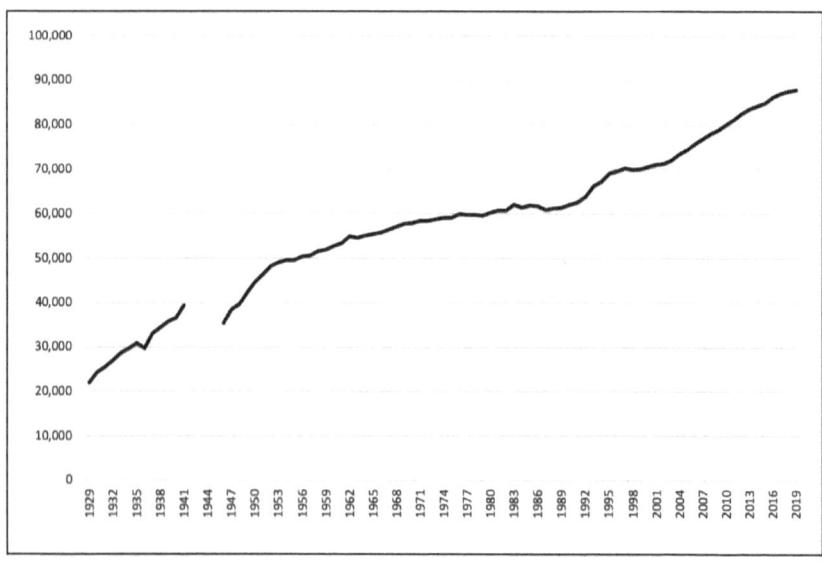

Figure 15. TED, Current Territory, Membership on New Year's Day, 1929–2019

Concluding Thoughts

Having highlighted challenges, I want to stress a very simple point, about success. In the face of widespread absolute indifference to religion – which may well be more difficult to overcome than outright hostility – the Seventh-day Adventist Church survives, and in some places is starting to find ways to thrive, in the northwest and southeast of Europe. There is a church presence in the countries of the Trans-European Division today because of the fidelity and fortitude of generations of faithful Adventists, who, in the face of the vicissitudes of depression and recession, world war and cold war, theological controversies, persecution, pluralism, parochialism, and postmodernism, kept the flame alive in Europe and took it to much of Africa.

This book has contained many statistics and many graphs. Here is a last one (Figure 15). It shows the TED's membership on New Year's Day of each year, starting with 1929 and continuing through 2019, but with the membership based on its current territorial configuration. As noted in Chapter 12, simply plotting on a graph the membership reported by the division starting in 1929 is utterly unmeaningful, because of the frequent changes in its territory. The statistics graphed in Figure 14 are for all ninety years, for the 29 nations and autonomous regions that make up the present-day TED, regardless of their divisional affiliation in the past. This shows the real growth of the Seventh-day Adventist Church in the Trans-European Division. Colleagues in some parts of the world might look at this and be unimpressed; but then, they *are* in other parts of the world; they do not live and work in Europe. Growth has been slow at times, but it has been steady. If there is no room for complacency, certainly, there is room for some satisfaction. The Third Angel's Message has taken root in European soil.

If we take all the statistics we have reviewed, they are troubling in many ways, yet they reveal that the Seventh-day Adventist Church in Europe has staying power. Much of the credit goes, as it must, to church members, to pastors and elders. But some of the credit, perhaps a great deal of it, is due to the leadership that provided direction from London and St Albans for ninety years.

Still, it would be self-deceptive to end on too triumphalist a note. Not only is the missional challenge to the church in Europe formidable, but in addition, even though this history reveals that passion for mission is embedded deep in European Adventist DNA, there is no room for complacency. It cannot be assumed that Seventh-day Adventists born in the Trans-European Division in the twenty-first century will inevitably share the passion their predecessors had for outreach.

There is evidence that the post-Christian condition of Europe is having an effect on the church. There are Seventh-day Adventists in the TED who seem to doubt some distinctive Adventist doctrines, or at any rate to question whether their neighbours really need to hear them. Reacting against this, other Adventists fail to distinguish between ecclesiological minutiae and the 'weightier matters of the law'; they anathematise fellow believers regardless of whether diversity is in areas of substance or style. This makes life difficult for other Adventists again, who *are* trying to communicate in the present-day European idiom. They are endeavouring, in the jargon of missiologists, to 'contextualise critically': that is, to uphold and promote Adventist doctrinal fundamentals, but to express them in ways that, while new or unfamiliar to other Adventists, could help draw into the community of believers those who currently outside it. At times it seems that church members at both ends of the Adventist theological spectrum have turned inwards, becoming so invested in debating each other, that they have little time for reaching out beyond the community of believers.

It can be the great difficulties – the struggles and defeats – that prompt some European Adventists to introspection, or to despondency; the victories seem long ago and our best days behind us. But perhaps future historians, instead of concluding that this division's best days were decades ago, will find them in days that still lie ahead of us. The following suggest themselves from the TED's ninety-year history, as lessons that could be drawn on in working towards a bright future.

- If Seventh-day Adventists in this division concentrate on their connection with Christ.
- If they take pride in their extraordinary record of missionary service in Africa and Asia, and are inspired by it, without letting it define them.
- If they focus their energies on becoming as fluent in the cultural idioms of Europe as in its linguistic tongues and dialects.
- If they can recognise and accept the shifts that have taken place both in the world church and within the division, and will work with the church as it now.
- If they are willing to move on from the power structures, mental topographies, and evangelistic methodologies of a past century.
- If they remember and reignite their traditional passion for mission.
- If church organisation and structure are geared so that mission is prioritised over management and expansion over conservation.
- If the division officers, church officers, and church members in the Trans-European Division now truly focus their energies on being European.

Christ's ultimate commission to His followers ('Go', in order to 'make disciples of all nations' and 'preach the gospel to all creation', Matt. 28:19, Mark 16:15) is what impelled this church's founders 150 years ago and the division's originators ninety years ago. Nothing must stand in the way of witnessing to the risen Christ and calling people to become His disciples. It is why the church exists; why the Seventh-day Adventist Church exists; and it is and always has been why the Trans-European Division exists. In acknowledging and acting on this principle, Adventists from Lake Peipus to Loch Ness, from Nicosia to Narvik, will be impelled by our Lord and Saviour's last command to His disciples; but they can also be inspired by the example of those who have gone before.

Photographs

Photo 1.1: General Conference President W. A. Spicer wearing a pith helmet at Malamulo Mission Station in British Central Africa [Malawi], May 1924.

Photo 1.2: Baptism in Lake Victoria [Victoria Nyanza], 1930s: the boats and men with spears are positioned to prevent crocodile attacks.

Photo 2.1: Delegates to the European Division Council, Darmstadt, 1928.

Photo 2.2: Oliver Montgomery, GC general vice-president, photographed c.1928: Montgomery was an expert in church organisation.

Photo 2.3: Lewis H. Christian, first NED president (1929–1936), photographed in 1925. He later served as a general vice-president of the GC (1936–1946).

Photo 2.4: William A. Spicer, GC secretary (1903–1922), then president (1922–1930), from a photograph taken while serving as world-church president. Spicer played a key role in the negotiations in 1928 that resulted in the creation of the NED.

Photo 2.5: Christian Pedersen, first NED treasurer, (having previously served as European Division treasurer), from a photograph taken in 1922.

Photo 2.6: Walter E. Read, first NED secretary (and later first TED national to serve as division president, 1936–1942), from a photograph taken soon after his election as NED president.

Photo 4.1: Ernest D. Dick, NED secretary (1932–1936), GC secretary (1936–1950), from a photograph taken towards the end of his term as NED secretary.

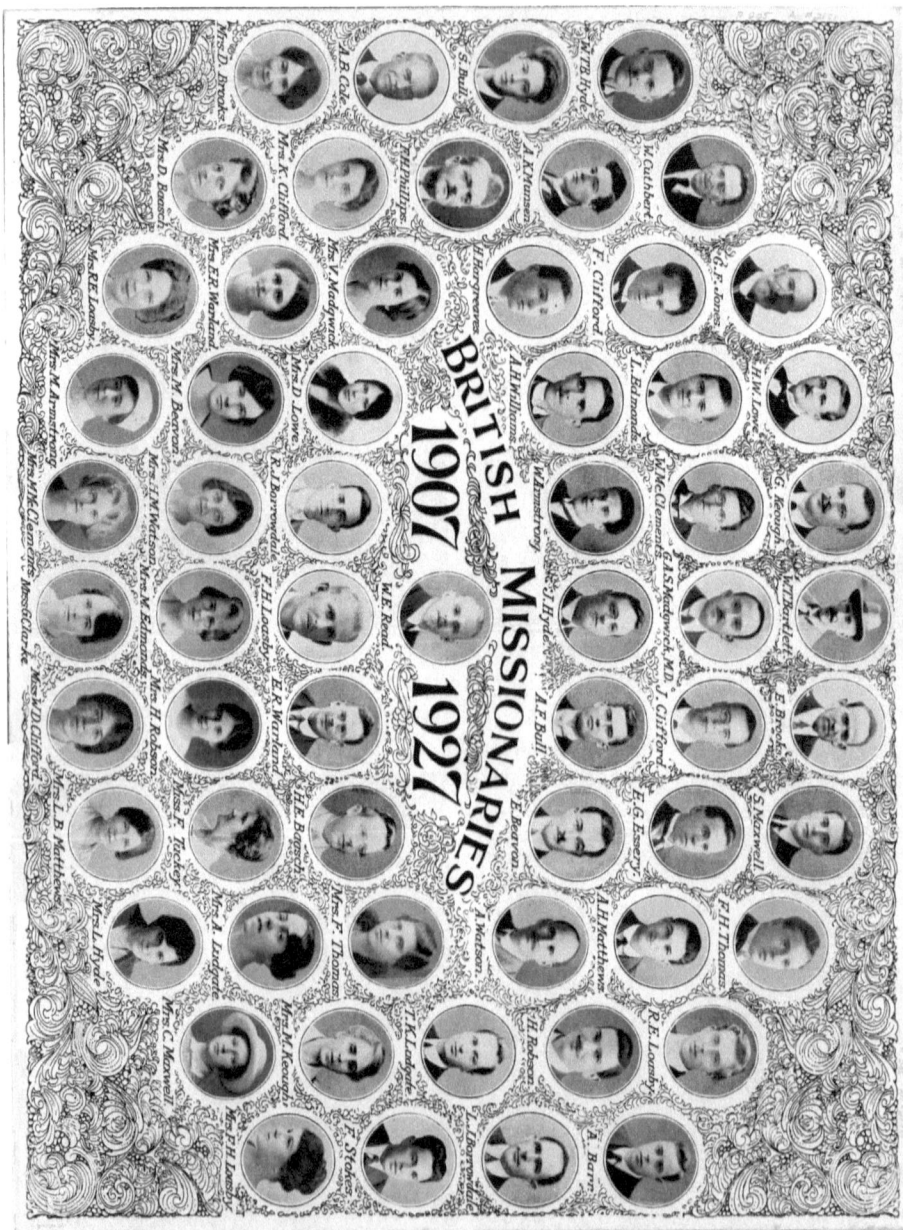

Photo 2.7: 'British Missionaries 1907–1927' — an image created by the British Union and used to promote missionary recruiting.

Photo 3.1: This photograph of the new Northern European Division office in Edgware, taken in 1929, shows clearly its origins as a converted home.

Photo 3.2: This is the photograph of the division headquarters building (taken 1930) that the division used most frequently in public relations.

Photo 3.3: NED President Christian and Secretary Read, with A. Carey, BUC secretary-treasurer, A. S. Maxwell, Stanborough Press manager, and R. A. Anderson, South England Conference evangelist, delivering a petition against Sunday laws to Number 10 Downing Street (official residence of the British Prime Minister).

Photo 4.2: James I. Robison, NED secretary (1936–1941) and later GC associate secretary (1946–1958), photographed in 1953.

Photo 4.3: Ellis R. Colson, NED treasurer (1935–1941).

Photo 4.4: Arthur S. Maxwell, editor of Present Truth (1920–1936) and manager of Stanborough Press (1925–1932) (later better known as 'Uncle Arthur'), photographed in 1932, before moving to the USA.

Photo 4.5: Paul M. Knudsen: after seven years as NED assistant treasurer (1934–1941) he was briefly NED secretary-treasurer (1941).

Photo 4.6 William T. Bartlett, pioneer missionary to East Africa (1920–1930), NED field secretary (1932–1943). Bartlett represented the GC and NED in Britain after the NED was placed in suspended animation during World War II.

Photo 4.7: William H. Branson, president of the African Division (1920–1930), GC general vice-president (1930–1938 and 1940–1946), China Division president (1938–1940 and 1946–1949), GC president (1950–1954). As vice-president, Branson chaired the Provisional Division Committee for Detached Missions (1944–1946), which oversaw the Ethiopian Union and West African Union when the NED was in suspended animation; as GC president he was instrumental in the reunification of the NED in 1950.

Photo 4.8: William and Mary Anne McClements, pioneer missionaries to Nigeria (1920–1943), photographed at the 1946 GC Session, three years into William's period as WAUM president (1943–1951).

Photos 4.9 and 4.10: Ruben and Hanna Bergstrom, who were pioneer missionaries to northern Cameroon, from photographs taken in 1931 at their mission station in Cameroon (*Advent Survey*, January 1931).

Photo 5.1: Gustav A. Lindsay, NED president (1946–1950) and treasurer (1950–1958).

Photo 5.2: Alf M. Karlman, NED treasurer (1946) and secretary-treasurer (1947–1950).

Photo 5.3: Edwin B. Rudge, Australasian Division president (1944–1946), BUC president (1946–1950), NED secretary (1950–1958).

Photo 5.4: A. Floyd Tarr, Southern Asia Division secretary (1941–1950), NED president (1950–1962), and GC associate secretary (1962–1966), from a photograph taken at the end of his presidency.

Photo 6.1: George D. King, NED secretary (1956–1962).

Photo 6.2: Floyd Tarr, photographed on an itinerary in Africa, 1946.

Photo 6.3: Tarr as NED president in the late 1950s.

Photo 6.4: Tarr (with ostrich eggs) in Ethiopia, 1961.

Photo 6.5: Erwin E. Roenfelt as a young man in Australia, where he later became president of the Australasian Union Conference, before he was called to the GC.

Photo 6.6: E. E. Roenfelt, GC associate secretary (1946–1962) and NED president (1962–1966), photographed during his presidency.

Photo 6.7: Walter E. Read, shown in later life, while serving as GC field secretary.

Photo 6.8: Roy A. Anderson, Australian who served as an evangelist in the BUC (1930–1936) and was GC Ministerial Association associate secretary (1946–1950) and secretary (1950–1966), from a photograph taken in 1947.

Photo 6.9: Harry W. Lowe, BUC president (1936–1946), GC field secretary (1962–1966), photographed at the 1946 GC Session where he was elected GC Sabbath School associate departmental secretary.

Photo 6.10: William G. C. Murdoch. For fifty years from 1927, Murdoch had a remarkable and influential career as an educational administrator and theologian, including as principal of Newbold Missionary College, president of Australasian Missionary College, and Dean of the Seventh-day Adventist Theological Seminary.

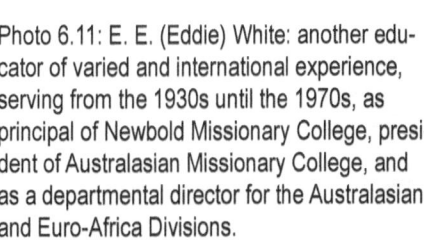

Photo 6.11: E. E. (Eddie) White: another educator of varied and international experience, serving from the 1930s until the 1970s, as principal of Newbold Missionary College, president of Australasian Missionary College, and as a departmental director for the Australasian and Euro-Africa Divisions.

Photo 6.12: Edward Heppenstall, perhaps the most influential Adventist theologian of the post-war era.

Photo 6.13: George D. Keough, pioneer missionary to the Middle East, theologian, and missiologist: this photograph was taken in Lebanon in the 1950s, when he was in his early seventies.

Photo 6.14: Keough is pictured here with Newbold students, in a photograph taken around 1960.

Photo 6.15: Emanuel W. Pedersen, NED secretary (1962–1966), GC field secretary (1966–1973), photographed while division secretary.

Photo 6.16: Stanisław Dabrowski, charismatic and capable president of the Polish Union Conference in the 1960s.

Photo 6.17: W. Duncan Eva, Trans-Africa Division secretary (1954–1965), GC associate secretary (1965–1966), NED president (1966–1973). GC general vice-president (1973–1980), pictured just after his election to the NED presidency.

Photo 7.1: Robert H. Pierson, Southern Asia Division president (1950–1954), Southern Africa Division president (1958–1966), GC president (1966–1978), shown in a photograph taken early in his presidency. Pierson greatly influenced the history of the TED, driving the reshaping of the NED into NEWAD, initiating the review that led to the shrinking of NEWAD back to NED, and in beginning the integration of the church in the British Isles.

Photo 7.2: Walter R. Beach, Southern European Division secretary (1936–1946), and president (1946–1954), GC secretary (1954–1970). W. R. Beach was influential in the reorganisation discussions during 1966–1970; his son, B. B. Beach, was serving at the NED in that period (see Photo 7.7).

Photo 7.3: Magdalon E. Lind, NED Sabbath School and YPMV departmental secretary (1954–1965), Trans-Africa Division secretary (1965–1970), Afro-Mideast Division president (1970–1975).

Photo 7.4: Charles D. Watson, Afro-Mideast Division president (1975–1980), GC associate secretary (1980–1992), photographed in 1975.

Photo 7.5: John Muderspach, missionary to West Africa (1956–1969), NED/TED treasurer (1980–1990).

Photo 7.6: Reinder Bruinsma, missionary to West Africa (1985–1991), TED Secretary (1995–2001), missiologist and theologian.

Photo 7.7: Bert B. Beach, NEWAD secretary (1973–1980), with a map showing the the educational institutions in each of the unions in Europe

Photo 8.1: Jan Paulsen, NED secretary (1980–1983), NED/TED president (1983–1995) (and later GC vice-president and president), photographed at the time of the 1985 GC Session.

Photo 8.2: GC President Pierson photographed in 1977, around the time of his decisive intervention in British church affairs.

Photo 8.3: Orville Woolford, director TED Education Department (1985–2005) (and other departmental responsibilities in this timeframe) and field secretary (2002–2005): first black departmental director or officer at the TED.

Photo 8.4: Cecil R. Perry, path-breaking and bridge-building church leader in Britain for more than a quarter of a century, and first black president of a union in the TED.

Photo 10.1: Newbold College of Higher Education (pictured in winter 2003–2004): Newbold is the only division institution in the TED.

Photo 10.2: Skodsborg Badesanatorium, in its mid-century heyday, from a contemporary postcard: Skodsborg was an institution of considerable significance in the history of the Seventh-day Adventist Church in Northern Europe and beyond.

Photo 10.3: Student-teachers at Nigerian Training College study a map of Africa, 1954.

Photo 10.4: Students and teacher at Kwahu Hospital School of Nursing and Midwifery, sometime in the 1960s.

Photo 10.5: Newbold Missionary College, soon after moving to Binfield in 1946.

Photo 10.6: Adventistički Seminar Dvorac Maruševec/Yugoslavian Adventist Seminary, c.1986: Photo published originally in the *Journal of Adventist Education* and titled 'The Theology School Among the Trees'.

Photo 10.7: Netherlands Missionary School, 1950. Students make their way to the school building at Huize Zandbergen.

Photo 10.8: Students in Bible class at Hlíðardalsskóli/Iceland Mission School, 1962.

Photo 10.9: Toivonlinnan Kristillinen Opisto/Toivonlinnan Christian Institute/Finland Mission School, 1960. Young men transport wood by sleigh towards the school.

Photo 10.10: Students in a natural history class at Vejlefjord Højskole/Danish Mission School (later Danish Junior College), 1954.

Photo 10.11: Ekbyholmsskolan/Swedish Junior College and Seminary, 1962. Students make their way to class and worship through the snow.

Photo 10.12: Tyrifjord Høyere Skole/Norwegian Junior College, 1962. Students at Tyrifjord skate with the school in the background.

Photo 10.13: Adventistički Teološki Fakultet [Adventist Theology Faculty]/Adriatic Union College, Maruševec, 2018.

Photo 10.14: Ile-Ife Mission Hospital, c.1960s.

Photo 10.15: John Jacob and Louisa Hyde with their son, John Ashford, photographed at Jengre Mission Station in 1933 (*Advent Survey*, June 1933).

Photo 10.16: Jengre Seventh-day Adventist Hospital with patients, 1960s.

Photo 10.17: Nursing staff at Kwahu Hospital, c.1970.

Photo 10.18: Hultafors Sanitarium, 1946 (photograph from Vänersborgs Museum).

Photo 10.19: Bert B. Beach, NED secretary (1973–1980), speaking to a gathering of church leaders in 1979.

Photo 10.20: Beach pictured in 1970, when NED Education and Sabbath School departmental secretary.

Photo 10.21: Group photo from Northern European Division Teachers Convention, Tyrifjord, July 1965.

Photo 11.1: William E. Nelson, GC treasurer (1936–1950), and chair of the GC Famine Relief Committee (1945–1950).

Photo 11.2: John-Jacob Strahle, NED Publishing department secretary (1930–1936), director of European Relief (1946–1950).

Photo 11.3: 'Food Depot in Vienna, 1946' (*ARH*, 7 July 1946).

Photo 11.4: 'Big Motor Trucks Used for Carrying Food Parcels From Copenhagen to Vienna, June, 1946. These Trucks Brought the First Relief to Our Churches at Vienna' (*ARH*, 7 July 1946).

Photo 12.1: C. Dunbar Henri in 1981, shortly after retiring. He and his wife Lorraine were missionaries in the WAUM (1945–1964) and in the EAUM (1970–1973); he then served as general vice-president of the GC (1973–1980).

Photo 12.2: Henry L. Rudy in 1939. An American of German-Russian ethnicity, Rudy was a missionary to Eastern Europe, church leader at various levels in the NED (1929–1935), president of the Central European Division (1938–1940), and GC general vice-president (1950–1958).

Photo 12.3: Alf Lohne, NED secretary (1967–1973), and president (1973–1975), GC general vice-president (1975–1985).

Photo 12.4: Walter R. L. Scragg, NEWAD/NED president (1975–1983), South Pacific Division president, 1983–1990.

Photo 12.5: Jan Paulsen in 1991 when TED president: he later served as GC general vice-president (1995–1999) and president (1999–2010).

Photo 12.6: Bertil Wiklander, who succeeded Paulsen as TED president in 1995 and served until 2014.

Photo 12.7: John F. Coltheart, Australian who served as evangelist in the BUC (1965–1967), and as division evangelist and Ministerial Association secretary for the NED/NEWAD from 1965 until he died in 1974; from a photograph taken not long before his death.

Photo 12.8: Bert Beach pictured in 1999, when GC director of Inter-Church Relations.

Photo 12.9: Mark A. Finley, TED Ministerial Association secretary (1985–1990), GC general vice-president (2005–2010).

Photo 12.10: Raafat Kamal, TED president since 2014.

Photo 12.11: Bernard Seton, NED secretary (1966–67), GC associate secretary (1970–1978).

Photo 12.12: Victor Cooper, GC Communication associate director (1973–1988), pictured in 1982.

Photo 12.13: Ray Dabrowski, GC Communication department director (1994–2010), pictured in 2005.

Photo 12.14: Harald Wollan, TED secretary (2001–2010), GC associate secretary (2010–2015).

Photo 12.15: Bryan W. Ball, church historian and theologian, South Pacific Division president (1990–1997).

Photo 12.16: Jan T. Knopper in 1976: missionary to East Africa in the 1960s, Publishing secretary/director, Australasian/South Pacific Division (1975–1990), special assistant to the president, Euro-Asia Division (1993).

Photo 12.17: V. Norskov Olsen, church historian and administrator, in 1982, when president of Loma Linda University, a post he held from 1974 to 1984, having previously served as principal of Newbold College from 1960 to 1966.

Photo 12.18: Hans K. LaRondelle, Dutch theologian and educator, photographed when a visiting professor at Avondale College in Australia, in 1973.

Photo 12.20: Margaret Wharrie: a missionary administrator in Africa, she served as EAUM treasurer (1929–1933) and then as Nigerian Union Mission secretary-treasurer until her death there in 1935.

Photo 12.19: Estonian Conference officials and laypeople, c.1926: Martha Raba (left), Estonian Conference treasurer and later secretary-treasurer of the Estonian Tract Society; with Pastor M. Bärengrub (centre), secretary, later editor of the Estonian Publishing House and departmental secretary for 'Book and Bible House' (which, unusually, was a department in the Estonian Conference); and E. Lillioja (right), Field Mission department secretary for the conference and later worker at the Estonian Publishing House. Raba and Lillioja were both laypeople and undertook translations into Estonian.

Photo 12.21: Amanda Nuka: a pioneering female church administrator and educator, she served in many capacities from 1929 until 1959, including as Estonian Conference treasurer, Sierra Leone Mission treasurer and secretary-treasurer, Baltic Union Conference secretary-treasurer, and Gold Coast Mission treasurer.

Photos 12.22–23: Else Luukkanen and Aino Lehtoluoto, remarkably successful Finnish evangelistic workers.

Photo 12.22 (left) photographed while being introduced at the 1958 GC Session.

Photo 12.23 (below) pictured in Finnish national costume during a tour of the United States in 1959.

Photo12.24: Anna-Liisa Halonen, TED treasurer (1990–1992) (and first female treasurer of any division).

Photo 12.25: Audrey Andersson, TED secretary since 2010 (and first female secretary of any division).

Appendices

APPENDIX I:
Countries and Ecclesiastical Organisational Units

Table A.1 Nations, Dependencies, and Autonomous Polities in the Northern European Division, 1929

Abyssinia [Ethiopia]*	Kenya
Åland Islands	Latvia
Dahomey [Benin]	Lithuania
Denmark	Niger
Eritrea	Nigeria
Estonia	Norway
Faroe Islands†	Poland
Ethiopia	St. Thomas and Group [São Tomé & Príncipe]
Fernando Pó; Elobey, Annobón and Corisco**	Sierra Leone
French Equatorial Africa, northern [Chad]††	Somaliland, British [Somaliland]
Finland	Somaliland, French [Djibouti]
Gambia	Somaliland, Italian [Somalia]
Gold Coast [Ghana]	Sudan, Anglo-Egyptian
Greenland	Sudan, French [Mali]
Guernsey	Sweden
Guinea, French [Guinea]	Tanganyika [Tanzania]
Iceland	Togo
Irish Free State	Uganda
Isle of Man	United Kingdom of Great Britain & Northern Ireland
Ivory Coast [Côte d'Ivoire]	Upper Volta [Burkina Faso]
Jersey	Zanzibar [Tanzania]

* 'Abyssinia' was the title used in official church documents in 1929.
** Insular territories of Spanish Guinea [Equatorial Guinea].
† 'Faroe' Islands was the church's official spelling in 1929.
†† French Equatorial Africa to the north of 10º North, this is roughly equivalent to Chad.

Table A.2: Unions and Polities in Northern European Division, 1933

Baltic Union Conference
Estonia, Latvia, Lithuania

British Union Conference
Irish Free State, United Kingdom of Great Britain and Northern Ireland and its dependencies (Channel Islands, Isle of Man)

East African Union Mission
Kenya Colony and Somaliland (Italian)

East Nordic Union Conference
Finland, Sweden

Ethiopian Union Mission
Eritrea, Ethiopia, Somaliland (British and French), Sudan (parts not in Uganda Union)

Gold Coast Union Mission
Dahomey, Gold Coast, Ivory Coast, Upper Volta

Nigeria Union Mission
British Cameroon, Niger, Nigeria

Polish Union Conference
Poland

Sierra Leone Union Mission
French Guinea, French Sudan, Gambia

Uganda (later Upper Nile) Union Mission
Uganda, plus most of the southern provinces of Sudan

West Nordic Union Conference
Denmark and its dependencies (Faroes, Greenland, Iceland), Norway

French Equatorial Mission (attached to NED)
French Cameroon and French Equatorial Africa, north of the 10th Parallel

Table A.3: Major Ecclesiastical Organisational Units in the Reorganised Northern European Division, 1951

British Union Conference	Polish Union Conference
East Nordic Union Conference	West African Union Mission
Ethiopian Union Mission	West Nordic Union Conference
Netherlands Union Conference	Iceland Mission (Attached)

Table A.4: Nations, Dependencies, and Autonomous Polities in the Northern Europe-West Africa Division, 1971–1980 (Contemporary Church Nomenclature)

Dahomey	Liberia
Denmark	Netherlands
Eire [Republic of Ireland]	Nigeria
Faroe Islands	Norway
Finland	Poland
Gambia	Sierra Leone
Ghana	Sweden
Greenland	Togoland
Iceland	United Kingdom of Gt Britain & N. Ireland
Ivory Coast	Upper Volta

Table A.5: Major Ecclesiastical Organisational Units in the Northern Europe-West Africa Division, 1971–1980

British Union Conference	Polish Union Conference
Finland Union Conference	Swedish Union Conference
Netherlands Union Conference	West African Union Mission
Nigerian Union Mission	West Nordic Union Conference
	Iceland Conference

Table A.6: Major Ecclesiastical Organisational Units in the Northern European Division, 1981

British Union Conference	Polish Union Conference
Finland Union Conference	Swedish Union Conference
Netherlands Union Conference	West Nordic Union Conference
Iceland Conference	

Table A.7: Ecclesiastical Organizational Units in the Northern European Division, 1991

British Union Conference North British Conference, South England Conference, Irish Mission, Scottish Mission, Welsh Mission	*Swedish Union Conference** *West Nordic Union Conference* East Denmark Conference, East Norway Conference, North Norway Conference, West Denmark Conference, West Norway Conference, Greenland Mission
Finland Union Conference Finland Finnish Conference, Finland Swedish Conference, Lapland Mission	
Hungarian Union Conference Duna Conference, Tisza Conference	*Yugoslavian Union Conference* North Yugoslavian Conference, South Yugoslavian Conference, Southwest Yugoslavian Conference, West Yugoslavian Conference
*Netherlands Union Conference**	
Pakistan Union Section North Section, South Section	*Attached to TED* Greek Mission, Iceland Conference, Israel Field*
Polish Union Conference East Polish Conference, South Polish Conference, West Polish Conference	* There were no longer any conferences in either the Netherlands or Swedish unions

Table A.8: Major Ecclesiastical Organisational Units in the Northern European Division, Early 1995

Baltic Union Conference	South-East European Union Conference
British Union Conference	Swedish Union Conference
Danish Union of Churches	*Attached*
Finland Union Conference	Albanian Mission
Hungarian Union Conference	Croatian-Slovenian Conference
Netherlands Union Conference	Greek Mission
Norwegian Union Conference	Iceland Conference
Pakistan Union Section	Israel Field
Polish Union Conference	Macedonian Mission

Table A.9: Major Ecclesiastical Organisational Units in the Northern European Division, 1999

Adriatic Union Conference	Norwegian Union Conference
Baltic Union Conference	Pakistan Union Section
British Union Conference	Polish Union Conference
Danish Union of Churches	South-East European Union Conference
Finland Union Conference	Swedish Union Conference
Hungarian Union Conference	Greek Mission (attached)
Middle East Union Mission	Iceland Conference (attached)
Netherlands Union Conference	Israel Field (attached)

Table A.10: Nations, Dependencies, and Autonomous Polities in the Trans-European Division, 2019

Åland Islands	Isle of Man
Albania	Jersey
Bosnia and Herzegovina	Kosovo
Croatia	Latvia
Cyprus	Lithuania
Denmark	Montenegro
Estonia	Netherlands
Faeroe Islands*	North Macedonia
Finland	Norway
Greece	Poland
Greenland	Serbia
Guernsey	Slovenia
Hungary	Sweden
Iceland	United Kingdom of Great Britain and Northern Ireland
Ireland, Republic of	

* 'Faeroe' Islands is the official spelling in 2019

Table A.11: Major Ecclesiastical Organisational Units in the Trans-European Division, 2019

Union Conferences	Unions of Churches
Adriatic	Danish
Baltic	Finland
British	Netherlands
Hungarian	Swedish
Norwegian	*Attached*
Polish	Cyprus Section
South-East European	Greek Mission
	Iceland Conference

APPENDIX II:
Division Administration 1929 – 2019

Northern European Division:	Jan. 1929 – July 1950
North Atlantic Division:	July 1950 – Oct. 1950
Northern European Division:	Oct. 1950 – May 1971
Northern Europe-West Africa Division:	May 1971 – Oct. 1980
Northern European Division:	Oct. 1980 – Dec. 1985
Trans-European Division:	Jan. 1986 – present

Presidents

1929 – 1936	Lewis H. Christian
1936 – 1942	Walter E. Read
1942 – 1946	--
1946 – 1950	Gustav A. Lindsay
1950 – 1962	(Albert) Floyd Tarr
1962 – 1966	Erwin E. Roenfelt
1966 – 1973	(William) Duncan Eva
1973 – 1975	Alf Lohne
1975 – 1983	Walter R. L. Scragg
1983 – 1995	Jan Paulsen
1995 – 2014	Bertil Wiklander
2014 – present	Raafat Kamal

Secretaries

1929 – 1932	Walter E. Read
1932 – 1936	Ernest D. Dick
1936 – 1941	James I. Robison
1941	Paul M. Knudsen (as secretary-treasurer)
1942 – 1946	--
1947 – 1950	Alf M. Karlman (as secretary-treasurer)
1950 – 1956	Edwin B. Rudge
1956 – 1962	George D. King
1962 – 1966	Emanuel W. Pedersen
1966 – 1967	Bernard E. Seton
1967 – 1973	Alf Lohne
1973 – 1980	Bert B. Beach
1980 – 1983	Jan Paulsen
1983 – 1987	Pekka Pohjola
1987 – 1995	Karel C. van Oossanen
1995 – 2001	Reinder Bruinsma
2001 – 2010	Harald Wollan
2010 – present	Audrey Andersson

Treasurers

1929 – 1935	Christian Pedersen
1935 – 1941	Ellis R. Colson
1941	Paul M. Knudsen (as secretary-treasurer)
1942 – 1946	--
1946 – 1950	Alf M. Karlman (as secretary-treasurer from 1947)
1950 – 1958	Gustav A. Lindsay
1958 – 1964	Alf M. Karlman
1964 – 1980	Roland Unnersten
1980 – 1990	John Muderspach
1990 – 1992	Anna-Liisa Halonen
1992 – 2000	Graham M. Barham
2000 – 2003	William M. Olson
2003 – 2013	Jóhann E. Jóhannsson
2013 – present	Nenad Jepuranović

APPENDIX III:
Division Headquarters Locations

1928 – 31 March 1929

Box 60, Berne 16
Switzerland
(temporary)

1 April 1929 – 1941

41 Manor Gardens (later Hazel Gardens)
Edgware, Middlesex
England

1941 – 1946

Temporarily administered from the GC headquarters in Washington, D.C.; Edgware office retained with minimal presence

1946 – 1947

Tunnelgatan 25
Stockholm, Sweden
(temporary)

1947 – 1950

Bergstigen 25
Stocksund, Stockholm
Sweden

1951 – 30 April 1965

41 Hazel Gardens
Edgware, Middlesex
England

1 May 1965 – Present

119 St. Peters Street
St. Albans, Hertfordshire
Great Britain

Notes

1. The address is given as 41 Manor Gardens in the *Yearbooks* of 1929–1931; it was regularly published in issues of *Advent Survey* for its first two years, 1929–1930. In the 1932 edition of the *Yearbook*, however, the address is given as 41 Hazel Gardens; but to complicate matters, 41 Manor Gardens continued to be given as the address for the NED's legal association, 'World Wide Advent Missions', until 1935; in 1936, the registered address of WWAM was also given as 41 Hazel Gardens. Today, Google Maps shows no Manor Gardens in Edgware, though there is a Manor Park Gardens; however, photographs of 41 Hazel Gardens are an exact match for photos from 1929 and 1930 of the division office said to be at 41 Manor Gardens. Thus, it seems clear that, though no official church records mention it, the street was renamed Hazel Gardens. It is likely that neither the NED nor GC secretariats noticed the inconsistent address for World Wide Advent Missions, which occurs in a separate part of the *Yearbook*, and, absent any correction, was therefore continued (as is practice with the *Yearbook*) until eventually noted and corrected in the 1936 *Yearbook*.

2. The 1947 edition of the *Yearbook* gives the NED office address as: '(Temporarily) Tunnelgatan 25, Stockholm Sweden', which is also the address given for the ENUC union office. At some date by the late spring of 1947 the division office had moved to Bergstigen 25 in Stocksund, which a visiting GC dignitary described as a suburb of Stockholm.[1]

3. The exact date of the return to Edware is uncertain, but it had taken place before NEDCOM met at 41 Hazel Gardens on 14 January 1951 and voted actions, *inter alia* about 'Division-owned homes in Edgware'.[2]

---

1 *YB 1947*, p. 133; F. D. Nichol, 'Adventist Activities in the North Lands', *ARH*, 124.30 (24 July 1947), 4.
2 NEDCOM mins., 1951, pp. 7–8.

Bibliography Part I

Select Bibliography of Secondary Sources on Seventh-day Adventist History in the Present-Day Territory of the Trans-European Division

Andersson, Audrey, 'The Scandinavian Influence on the Trans-European Division', in *Faith in Search of Depth and Relevancy: Festschrift in Honour of Dr Bertil Wiklander*, ed. by Reinder Bruinsma ([St Albans]: Trans-European Division of Seventh-day Adventists, 2014), pp. 381–95

Anthony, Martin L., 'Decades of Change', in *The Story of Seventh-day Adventists in the British Isles 1902–1992*, ed. by D. N. Marshall (Grantham, UK: Stanborough Press, 1992), pp. 26–31

—— 'A century of evangelism', in *A Century of Adventism in the British Isles,* ed. by David Marshall (Grantham, UK: Stanborough Press, 2000), pp. 10–14

Arasola, Kai, 'Finland', in *Heirs of the Reformation: The Story of Seventh-day Adventists in Europe*, ed. Hugh Dunton, Daniel Heinz, Dennis Porter, and Ronald Strasdowsky (Grantham, UK: Stanborough Press, 1997), pp. 89–94

Arthur, W. J., 'Profile of the Present-Day Church: 1981–1992', in *The Story of Seventh-day Adventists in the British Isles 1902–1992*, ed. by D. N. Marshall (Grantham, UK: Stanborough Press, 1992), pp. 35–40

Barham, Nigel G., 'The Progress of the Seventh-day Adventist Church in Great Britain 1878–1974', (PhD dissertation, University of Michigan, 1976)

—— 'Walter E. Read and the British Union Conference', *Adventist Heritage*, 5.1 (Summer 1978), 16–24

—— 'Opening the British Mission', *Adventist Heritage*, 9.2 (Fall 1984), 12–18

Barham, Nigel, 'British Isles', in *Heirs of the Reformation: The Story of Seventh-day Adventists in Europe*, ed. by Hugh Dunton, Daniel Heinz, Dennis Porter, and Ronald Strasdowsky (Grantham, UK: Stanborough Press, 1997), pp. 30–40

Baumgartner, Erich W., ed., *Re-visioning Adventist Mission in Europe* (Berrien Springs: Andrews University Press, 1998)

Beardsell, Derek C., 'A Study of Selected Administrative Issues in The History and Development of Newbold College' (PhD dissertation, Andrews University, 1983)

—— 'The Beginnings of Newbold College', in *Heirs of the Reformation: The Story of Seventh-day Adventists in Europe*, ed. by Hugh Dunton, Daniel Heinz, Dennis Porter, and Ronald Strasdowsky (Grantham, UK: Stanborough Press, 1997), pp. 44–45

Billington, Louis, 'The Millerite Adventists in Great Britain, 1840–1850,' *Journal of American Studies*, 1 (1967), 191–212

Bruinsma, Reinder, *Ontstaan en Groei van de Adventbeweging* ['Origin and Growth of the Advent Movement'] (Den Haag: Boekhuis 'Veritas', n.d.)

—— 'The Netherlands', in *Heirs of the Reformation: The Story of Seventh-day Adventists in Europe*, ed. by Hugh Dunton, Daniel Heinz, Dennis Porter, and Ronald Strasdowsky (Grantham, UK: Stanborough Press, 1997), pp. 156–60

—— 'Past Patterns of European Mission Involvement', in *Re-visioning Adventist Mission in Europe*, ed. by Erich W. Baumgartner (Berrien Springs: Andrews University Press, 1998), pp. 32–37

Christian, L. H., *Pioneers and Builders of the Advent Cause in Europe* (Mountain View, Calif.: Pacific Press, 1937)

Dabrowski, Ray, 'Albania', in *Heirs of the Reformation: The Story of Seventh-day Adventists in Europe*, ed. by Hugh Dunton, Daniel Heinz, Dennis Porter, and Ronald Strasdowsky

(Grantham, UK: Stanborough Press, 1997), p. 17

Dabrowski, R. L. and B. B. Beach, eds, *Michael Belina Czechowski, 1818–1876* (Warsaw: Znaki Czasu, 1979)

Davidson, Keith, 'The British Experience in Britain: *Windrush 2000*', in *A Century of Adventism in the British Isles*, ed. by David Marshall (Grantham, England: Stanborough Press, 2000), pp. 22–24

Davis, Anthea N., 'West Indian Immigrants and Administrative Politics in the Seventh-day Adventist Church in Britain c.1950–1980' (MA dissertation, University of London, 2003)

Delafield, D. A., *Ellen G. White in Europe* (Washington DC: RHPA, 1975)

Dunton, H. I., 'The Millerite Adventists and Other Millenarian Groups in Great Britain 1830–1860' (PhD thesis, University of London, 1984)

—— 'Iceland', *Heirs of the Reformation: The Story of Seventh-day Adventists in Europe*, ed. by Hugh Dunton, Daniel Heinz, Dennis Porter, and Ronald Strasdowsky (Grantham, UK: Stanborough Press, 1997), pp. 131–33

—— 'Millennial Hopes and Fears: Great Britain 1780–1960', *Andrews University Seminary Studies*, 37 (Autumn 1999), 181–210

Dunton, Hugh, Daniel Heinz, Dennis Porter, and Ronald Strasdowsky, eds, *Heirs of the Reformation: The Story of Seventh-day Adventists in Europe* (Grantham, UK: Stanborough Press, 1997)

Griffiths, Herbert, 'The Impact of African Caribbean Settlers on the Seventh-day Adventist Church in Britain 1952–2001' (PhD thesis, University of Leeds, 2003)

—— 'The Implication of Mission from a Black Seventh-Day Adventist Perspective, with Reference to Britain, the Caribbean, and Africa', in *Christianity in Africa and the African Diaspora: The Appropriation of a Scattered Heritage*, ed.

by Afe Adogame, Roswith Gerloff, and Klaus Hock (London: Continuum, 2008), pp. 293–303

Hagstotz, Gideon David, *The Seventh-day Adventists in the British Isles, 1878–1933* (Lincoln, NE: Union College Press, 1936)

Kleimanis, Isaak, 'Latvia', in *Heirs of the Reformation: The Story of Seventh-day Adventists in Europe*, ed. by Hugh Dunton, Daniel Heinz, Dennis Porter, and Ronald Strasdowsky (Grantham, UK: Stanborough Press, 1997), p. 143–46

Koning, Danielle, 'Place, Space, and Authority: The Mission and Reversed Mission of the Ghanaian Seventh-day Church in Amsterdam', *African Diaspora* 2 (2009), 203–26

Koning, G. Henk, *Enige markante gebeurtenissen uit de geschiedenis van het Kerkgenootschap der Zevende-dags Adventisten in Groningen* ['Some striking events from the history of the Seventh-day Adventist Church in Groningen'] (Groningen: Kerkgenootschap der Zevende-dags Adventisten, 1983)

—— 'It Has Been Done', in *Re-visioning Adventist Mission in Europe*, ed. by Erich W. Baumgartner (Berrien Springs, Mich.: Andrews University Press, 1998), pp. 208–12

Leonard, Harry H., 'John N. Andrews and England's Seventh Day Baptists: "We are Brethren"', *Adventist Heritage*, 9.1 (Spring 1984), 50–56

—— 'Andrews and the Mission to Britain', in *J. N. Andrews: The Man and the Mission*, ed. idem (Berrien Springs, Mich.: Andrews University Press, 1985), pp. 225–60

—— 'Evangelizing in Tough Territory', in *The Story of Seventh-day Adventists in the British Isles 1902–1992*, ed. by D. N. Marshall (Grantham, UK: Stanborough Press, 1992), pp. 2–6

—— 'The Foundations of Adventism in the British Isles', in *A Century of Adventism in the British Isles*, ed. by David

Marshall (Grantham, UK: Stanborough Press, 2000), pp. 5–7

—— 'The Adventist Rubicon: John N. Andrews and the Mission to Europe', in *Pluralism, Parochialism and Contextualization: Challenges to Adventist Mission in Europe (19th–21st Centuries)*, ed. by D. J. B. Trim and Daniel Heinz Adventistica: Forschungen zur Geschichte und Theologie der Siebenten-Tags-Adventisten, 9 (Oxford, Bern, Berlin, Brussels, Frankfurt am Main, New York & Vienna: Peter Lang, 2010), pp. 31–50

Lindén, Ingemar, 'Sweden', in *Heirs of the Reformation: The Story of Seventh-day Adventists in Europe*, ed. by Hugh Dunton, Daniel Heinz, Dennis Porter, and Ronald Strasdowsky (Grantham, UK: Stanborough Press, 1997), pp. 216–25

Luukkanen, Elsa, and E. Olavi Rouhe, *Elsa, Sweet Singer of Finland* (Mountain View, Calif.: Pacific Press, 1980)

Lyko, Zachariasz and Hugh Dunton, 'Poland', in *Heirs of the Reformation: The Story of Seventh-day Adventists in Europe*, ed. by Hugh Dunton, Daniel Heinz, Dennis Porter, and Ronald Strasdowsky (Grantham, UK: Stanborough Press, 1997), pp. 170–79

McFarlane, D. W., 'The Past and the Future', in *The Story of Seventh-day Adventists in the British Isles 1902–1992*, ed. by D. N. Marshall (Grantham, UK: Stanborough Press, 1992), pp. 43–46

—— 'Some Challenges Facing the British Church in the Twenty-First Century', in *A Century of Adventism in the British Isles*, ed. by David Marshall (Grantham, UK: Stanborough Press, 2000), pp. 26–28

—— 'Evangelism in the British Union During the Last 25 Years', *Messenger*, Souvenir Special, *100 Years of Mission 1906–2006*, ed. by D. N. Marshall (2006), pp. 22–25

Mahon, Jack, 'A Century of British Seventh-day Adventist Missions' in *A Century of Adventism in the British Isles*, ed. by

David Marshall (Grantham, UK: Stanborough Press, 2000), pp. 15–21

—— 'What Happened in 1906?', in *Messenger*, Souvenir Special, *100 Years of Mission 1906–2006*, ed. by D. N. Marshall (2006), pp. 3–11

Marshall, Anita and David, 'Yvonne Eurick: A Vision of Africa', in *Messenger*, Souvenir Special, *100 Years of Mission 1906–2006* (2006), p. 19

Marshall, David, 'Arthur S. Maxwell: The Great Communicator', in *A Century of Adventism in the British Isles*, ed. idem (Grantham, UK: Stanborough Park, 2000), 15

—— 'Dr Edward Heppenstall (1901–1994): Theologian and Thought Leader', in *A Century of Adventism in the British Isles*, ed. idem (Grantham, UK: Stanborough Press, 2000), p. 20

—— 'Orville Woolford: Headmaster, Motivator, Church Leader', in *A Century of Adventism in the British Isles*, ed. idem (Grantham, UK: Stanborough Press, 2000), p. 31

—— 'Top Stories of the Century', in *A Century of Adventism in the British Isles*, ed. idem (Grantham, UK: Stanborough Press, 2000), p. 2

—— 'W. E. Read (1883–1976): Administrator and Scholar' in *A Century of Adventism in the British Isles*, ed. idem (Grantham, UK: Stanborough Press, 2000), p. 14

—— '"A Warm-Hearted Intellectual": An Appreciation of the Life of Dr Bernard Seton', *Messenger*, 4 June 2004, pp. 6–7

—— 'Winds of Change', in *Messenger*, Souvenir Special, *100 Years of Mission 1906–2006* (2006), pp. 17–18

Marshall, D. N., ed., *The Story of Seventh-day Adventists in the British Isles 1902–1992* (Grantham, UK: Stanborough Press, 1992)

—— ed., *A Century of Adventism in the British Isles* (Grantham, UK: Stanborough Press, 2000)

—— ed., *Messenger*, Souvenir Special, *100 Years of Mission*

1906–2006 (2006)

Mirilov, Branislav. 'Croatia, Bosnia, Serbia and Other Former Yugoslavian Regions', in *Heirs of the Reformation: The Story of Seventh-day Adventists in Europe*, ed. by Hugh Dunton, Daniel Heinz, Dennis Porter, and Ronald Strasdowsky (Grantham, UK: Stanborough Press, 1997), pp. 55–62

Oster, Yvonne, *Till jordens yttersta gräns: Svenska adventistmissionärers liv och verksamhet* ['To the uttermost ends of the earth: The life and activities of Swedish Adventist missionaries'], Historisk Arkiv för Sjundedags Adventistsamfundet serien, 5 (Stockholm: Skandinaviska Bokförlaget, 2018)

Page, Kevin and Ronald Strasdowsky, 'Lithuania', in *Heirs of the Reformation: The Story of Seventh-day Adventists in Europe*, ed. by Hugh Dunton, Daniel Heinz, Dennis Porter, and Ronald Strasdowsky (Grantham, UK: Stanborough Press, 1997), pp. 147–52

Papaioannou, Kim, 'Greece', in *Heirs of the Reformation: The Story of Seventh-day Adventists in Europe*, ed. by Hugh Dunton, Daniel Heinz, Dennis Porter, and Ronald Strasdowsky (Grantham, UK: Stanborough Press, 1997), pp. 116–24

Peake, Christopher, 'Seventh-day Adventists in Britain in Relation to their Host Community in the Early 20th Century', in *Pluralism, Parochialism and Contextualization: Challenges to Adventist Mission in Europe (19th–21st Centuries)*, ed. by D. J. B. Trim and Daniel Heinz Adventistica: Forschungen zur Geschichte und Theologie der Siebenten–Tags–Adventisten, 9 (Oxford, Bern, Berlin, Brussels, Frankfurt am Main, New York & Vienna: Peter Lang, 2010), pp. 93–115

Phillips, Brian Pugh, 'A Century of Adventism in Wales 1885–1985: A History of Seventh-day Adventism in Wales and the

Border Counties' (PhD thesis, University of Glamorgan, 1992)

—— 'British Adventists Overseas' in *The Story of Seventh-day Adventists in the British Isles 1902–1992*, ed. by D. N. Marshall (Grantham, UK: Stanborough Press, 1992), pp. 22–24

Porter, D. S., *A Century of Adventism in the British Isles: A Brief History of the British Union Conference of Seventh-day Adventists*, *Messenger*, Centennial Historical Special (Grantham, UK: Stanborough Press, 1974)

—— 'The Church in the Age of Dictators', in *The Story of Seventh-day Adventists in the British Isles 1902–1992*, ed. by D. N. Marshall (Grantham, UK: Stanborough Press, 1992), pp. 14–18

Rajki, Zoltán and Jenő Szigeti, *Szabadegyházak története Magyarországon 1989-ig* ['History of Free Churches in Hungary until 1989'] (Budapest: Gondolat, 2012)

Riches, Rex, *Establishing the British Mission of the Seventh-day Adventist Church 1863–1887* (Greensboro, NC: for the author, 1997)

Rijn, H. G. van, *Advent Exposé. 100 Jaar Adventkerk in Nederland* ['Advent Exposé. 100 Years of the Adventist Church in the Netherlands'] (Bosch en Duin: Uitgeverij 'Veritas', 1987)

Roennfeldt, Peter, 'Can Adventism Learn the Language of Europe?', in *Pluralism, Parochialism and Contextualization: Challenges to Adventist Mission in Europe (19th–21st Centuries)*, ed. by D. J. B. Trim and Daniel Heinz Adventistica: Forschungen zur Geschichte und Theologie der Siebenten–Tags–Adventisten, 9 (Oxford, Bern, Berlin, Brussels, Frankfurt am Main, New York & Vienna: Peter Lang, 2010), pp. 199–205

Rouhe, Esa, 'Elsa Luukkanen and the Role of Adventist Women

in Finland', in *Heirs of the Reformation: The Story of Seventh-day Adventists in Europe*, ed. by Hugh Dunton, Daniel Heinz, Dennis Porter, and Ronald Strasdowsky (Grantham, UK: Stanborough Press, 1997), pp. 95–97

Schantz, Hans Jorgen, 'Denmark', in *Heirs of the Reformation: The Story of Seventh-day Adventists in Europe*, ed. by Hugh Dunton, Daniel Heinz, Dennis Porter, and Ronald Strasdowsky (Grantham, UK: Stanborough Press, 1997), pp. 70–77

Snorrason, Bjorgvin Martin Hjelvik, 'The Origins, Development, and History of the Norwegian Seventh-day Adventist Church from the 1840s to 1889' (PhD dissertation, Andrews University, 2010)

Spalding, Arthur Whitefield, *Captains of the Host* (Washington, DC: RHPA, 1949)

────── *Christ's Last Legion* (Washington, DC: RHPA, 1949)

Strayer, Brian E. *J. N. Loughborough: The Last of the Pioneers* (Hagerstown, MD: RHPA, 2013), chaps. 11–12

Šušljić, Milan, *Bićete mi svedoci: prilozi za istoriju Hrišćanske adventističke crkve na području Jugoistočne Evrope* ['You will be Witnesses to Me: Contributions to the History of the Christian Adventist Church in South-Eastern Europe'] (Beograd: Preporod, 2004)

Szigeti, Jeno, '*Steps to Christ* Has Interesting History in Hungary', *Adventist Review*, 160.5 (3 Feb. 1983), 19

──────. 'Hungary', in *Heirs of the Reformation: The Story of Seventh-day Adventists in Europe*, ed. by Hugh Dunton, Daniel Heinz, Dennis Porter, and Ronald Strasdowsky (Grantham, UK: Stanborough Press, 1997), pp. 125–28

Szilvási, József and Tibor Tonhaizer, *Az Adventmozgalom története* ['The History of the Advent Movement'] (Pécel: Katica Könyv Műhely, 2017)

Theobald, Robin, 'The Politicisation of a Religious Movement:

British Adventism under the Impact of West Indian Migration', *British Journal of Sociology*, 32 (1981), 202–223

Torkelson, Edwin, 'Norway', in *Heirs of the Reformation: The Story of Seventh-day Adventists in Europe*, ed. by Hugh Dunton, Daniel Heinz, Dennis Porter, and Ronald Strasdowsky (Grantham, UK: Stanborough Press, 1997), pp. 161–68

Trim, D. J. B., 'Adventist Mission in Europe in Historical Perspective', in *Parochialism, Pluralism, and Contextualization: Challenges to Adventist Mission in Europe (19th–21st Centuries)*, ed. by Trim and Daniel Heinz, Adventistica: Forschungen zur Geschichte und Theologie der Siebenten–Tags–Adventisten, 9 (Oxford, Bern, Berlin, Brussels, Frankfurt am Main, New York & Vienna: Peter Lang, 2010), pp. 9–29

—— '"Plans for a Larger Work": Adventism in the Trans-European Division', *Adventist World*, 9.7 (July 2013), 20–21

Trim, D. J. B., and Daniel Heinz, eds, *Pluralism, Parochialism and Contextualization: Challenges to Adventist Mission in Europe (19th–21st Centuries)*, Adventistica: Forschungen zur Geschichte und Theologie der Siebenten-Tags-Adventisten, 9 (Oxford, Bern, Berlin, Brussels, Frankfurt am Main, New York & Vienna: Peter Lang, 2010)

Viirsalu, Voldemar, 'Estonia', in *Heirs of the Reformation: The Story of Seventh-day Adventists in Europe*, ed. by Hugh Dunton, Daniel Heinz, Dennis Porter, and Ronald Strasdowsky (Grantham, UK: Stanborough Press, 1997), pp. 78–84

Wiklander, Bertil, 'Ekbyholmsskolan and Work/Study in the 1980s', in *Heirs of the Reformation: The Story of Seventh-day Adventists in Europe*, ed. by Hugh Dunton, Daniel Heinz, Dennis Porter, and Ronald Strasdowsky (Grantham, UK: Stanborough Press, 1997), pp. 226–28

Winandy, Pierre, et al., *Centennial Symposium: Ellen G. White and Europe, 1885/1887–1987* (Bracknell, UK: Ellen G. White Research Centre, Europe, 1987)

Woolford, Orville, 'The 70s Struggle: A Black Perspective', in *The Story of Seventh-day Adventists in the British Isles 1902–1992*, ed. by D. N. Marshall (Grantham, UK: Stanborough Press, 1992), pp. 34–35

Bibliography, Part II
Additional Primary and Secondary Sources Cited

Adesegun, Abiodun Ayodeji, 'Christian Education in the Seventh-day Adventist Church in Remo, Ogun State, Nigeria, 1959–2004' (PhD thesis, University of Ibadan, 2009)

'Adventist Theologian Heppenstall Dies', *ARH*, 171.36 (8 Sept. 1994), 6–7

Altink, Wim and Rudolf H. Dingjan, 'Understanding the Dutch Society', in *Re-visioning Adventist Mission in Europe*, ed. by Erich W. Baumgartner (Berrien Springs: Andrews University Press, 1998), pp. 221–28

'An Afternoon with the Provisional Division', *ARH*, 123.29, General Conference Report, no. 7 (13 June 1946), 147–48.

Anderson, Clarence V., 'Meetings in the Baltic Union', *Advent Survey*, 4.8 (Aug. 1932), 7

Anderson, Godfrey, *Spicer: Leader with the Common Touch* (Washington, DC: RHPA, 1983)

Anderson, Ormond K., 'Life Sketch of Pastor John Coltheart', *Australasian Record*, 23 (Dec. 1974), 13–14

Armstrong-Reid, Susan E. and David Murray, *Armies of Peace:*

Canada and the UNRRA Years (Toronto & London: University of Toronto Press, 2008)

Atkin, John, *The Foreign Exchange Market of London: Development Since 1900* (New York: Routledge, 2005)

Babalola, D. O., 'The Seventh-day Adventist Church in Yorubaland, Nigeria (1914–1984)' (PhD thesis, University of Ibadan, 1988), pp. 142–43

Bang-Andersen, Arne, Basil Greenhill, and Egil Harald Grude, eds., *The North Sea. A Highway of Economic and Cultural Exchange: Character – History* (Stavanger: Norwegian University Press and Oxford: Oxford University Press, 1985)

Banning, C., 'Food Shortage and Public Health, First Half of 1945', *Annals of the American Academy of Political and Social Science*, 245, *The Netherlands during German Occupation* (May 1946), 93–110

Bartlett, W. T., 'East Africa Union Mission', *Quarterly Review of the European Division of the General Conference of Seventh-Day Adventists*, 12.1 (1926), 5

—— 'The Winter Council', *Advent Survey*, 8.2 (Feb. 1936), 2

Beach, B. B., 'An Open Bible in Thousand-Year-Old Poland', *Northern Light*, 16.12 (Dec. 1966), 5

Beevor, Anthony, *The Battle of Arnhem* (New York: Viking, 2018), pp. 372–79

Blaich, Roland, 'Religion under National Socialism: The Case of the German Adventist Church', *Central European History*, 26 (1993), 255–80

Bodley, John H., 'A Transformative Movement among the Campa of Eastern Peru', *Anthropos*, 67 (1972), 220–28

Branson, W. H., 'The Provisional Division', *ARH*, 123.27, General Conference Report, no. 5 (11 June 1946), 123–24

'The British Union and the North Atlantic Division', *British Advent Messenger* (Union Session Bulletin no. 5), 13 Oct. 1950, pp. 13–14

Brown, Clifford, 'Twentieth-Century Adventure', *The Youth's Instructor*, 94.17 (23 Apr. 1946), 1, 17–18

Brown, Henry F., 'A Call for Continued Clothing Drive', *Canadian Union Messenger*, 15.4 (21 Aug. 1946), 1

Bruce, Steve and David Voas, 'Do Social Crises Cause Religious Revivals? What British Church Adherence Rates Show', *Journal of Religion in Europe*, 9 (2016), 26–43

Bull, Malcolm and Keith Lockhart, 'The Intellectual World of Adventist Theologians', *Spectrum*, 18.1 (Oct. 1987), 32–37

Casteel, James E., 'The Russian Germans in the Interwar German National Imaginary', *Central European History*, 40 (2007), 429–66

Christian, L. H., 'Change in the Division Treasury', *Advent Survey*, 7.6 (June 1935), 8

—— 'Rebuilding God's Work in a Shattered Land', *ARH*, 124.30 (24 July 1947), 1, 17–18

'Church Mourns Loss of Theologian', *Record*, 17 Sept. 1994, p. 5

Clifford, J., 'Camp-Meetings in Southern Nigeria', *Advent Survey* 2.5 (May 1930), 3

'Closing Report of the Mission Schools', *Advent Survey*, 1.3 (Sept. 1929), 11

Conway, Martin, 'The Rise and Fall of Western Europe's Democratic Age, 1945–1973', *Contemporary European History*, 13 (2004), 67–88

Coralie, Alain, 'Understanding Adventist Worship: A Liturgical Theology' (PhD thesis, Trinity College/University of Bristol, 2018)

Cottrell, Raymond F., 'The Bible Research Fellowship: A Pioneering Seventh-day Adventist Organisation in Retrspect', *Adventist Heritage*, 5.1 (Summer 1978), 39–52

Cummins, James F., 'Reduction in Price on Relief Packages to Europe', *Northern Union Outlook*, 8 Oct. 1946, p. 2

Czembor, Wm., 'The Polish Union Session', *Advent Survey*, 8.11 (Nov. 1936), 3

Daft, Richard L., *The Leadership Experience*, 6th edn (Stamford, CT: Cengage Learning 2015)

Dail, Guy, 'Another European Conference', *ARH*, 85.5 (30 Jan. 1908), 16

—— 'At the Baltic Union School', *ARH*, 102.52 (24 Dec. 1925), 20

de Jong, Mary G., '"I Want to Be like Jesus": The Self-Defining Power of Evangelical Hymnody', *Journal of the American Academy of Religion*, 54 (Autumn, 1986), 461–93

Dick, E. D., 'African West Coast Union Mission', *ARH*, 123.3 (17 Jan. 1946), 16–17

—— 'In the Ibo Country', *Advent Survey*, 5.7 (July 1933), 2–4

—— 'Our Losses in Ethiopia', *Advent Survey*, 8.2 (Feb. 1936), 1–2

—— 'Visiting Our Missions in West Africa', *Advent Survey*, 5.6 (June 1933), 1–5

Doss, Gorden A., *Introduction to Adventist Mission* (Berrien Springs, MI/Silver Spring, MD: Department of World Mission, Seventh-day Adventist Theological Seminary / Institute of World Mission, General Conference of Seventh-day Adventists, 2018)

Douglass, Herbert Edgar, *A Fork in the Road. 'Questions on Doctrine': The Historic Adventist Divide of 1957* (Coldwater, Mich.: Remnant Publications, 2008)

Down, Goldie, 'Adventist Youth', in *Seventh-day Adventists in the South Pacific 1885–1985*, ed. by Noel Clapham (Warburton, Vic.: Signs Publishing, 1985), pp. 126–43

Drake, H. A., *Constantine and the Bishops* (Baltimore, MD: Johns Hopkins University Press, 2000)

Eastcott, Ella M., 'North Cameroons Mission', *Advent Survey*, 3.1 (Jan. 1931), 5–6

Ellis, John, *The World War II Databook* (London: BCA, 1993)

Emmerson, W. L., 'The Tide of Time', *Present Truth*, 10 Mar. 1938, pp. 2–3

Eva, W. Duncan, 'Progress in Poland', *Northern Light*, 16.12 (Dec. 1966), 1–2

—— 'Report of the Northern European Division', Fifty-first GC Session, *ARH*, 147.27, suppt., *GC Session Bulletin* (16 June 1970), 94–96

'Fall Council Election', *ARH*, 123.52 (7 Nov. 1946), 23

Fels, Bradley E., '"Whatever Your Heart Dictates and Your Pocket Permits": Polish-American Aid to Polish Refugees during World War II', *Journal of American Ethnic History*, 22.2 (Winter 2003), 3–30

Figuhr, R. R., 'A Report from Africa', *ARH*, 138.2 (12 Jan. 1961), 1

Finlan, Alastair, *The Collapse of Yugoslavia 1991–1999* (Oxford: Osprey, 2004)

'Former GC Vice-President Dies', *ARH*, 174.32 (Aug. 1997), 21

'Former V.P. Dies in Oregon', *ARH*, 159.12 (25 Mar. 1982), 24

'From Home Base to Front Line', *ARH*, 137.26 (30 June 1960), 22

Gammon, K., '"For Such a Time as This": Great Conference Youth Rally', *British Advent Messenger* (Union Session Bulletin no. 5), 13 Oct. 1950, pp. 9–10

Gibbons, David, 'Walter R. L. Scragg, 84 Division President and Church Leader, Dies', *ARH*, 187 (21 Oct. 2010), 10

Gilmore, Laurence A., 'The Gentle Theologian', *Australasian Record*, 21 May 1973, p. 5

'Gleanings from the Winter Council held in Warsaw', *Advent Survey*, 2.1 (Jan. 1930), 8

Greenleaf, Floyd, *A Land of Hope: The Growth of the Seventh-day Adventist Church in South America* (Tatuí, Brazil: Casa Publicadora Brasileira, 2011)

—— *The Seventh-day Adventist Church in Latin America and the Caribbean*, 2 vols (Berrien Springs, Mich.: Andrews University Press, 1992)

Gribben, Crawford, *Evangelical Millennialism in the Trans-Atlantic World, 1500–2000* (Basingstoke: Palgrave Macmillan, 2011)

Hamel, Gary, 'Hole in the Soul: Leaders Either Cause It or Fix It', *Leadership Excellence*, Oct. 2011, p. 3

Hart, Nicky, 'Famine, Maternal Nutrition and Infant Mortality: A Re-examination of the Dutch Hunger Winter', *Population Studies*, 47 (1993), 27–46

Henri, C. D., Editorial, *West African Advent Messenger*, 8.5 (May 1960), 8

'He Served the World Church', *Southern Asia Tidings*, 1 Oct. 1980, 17

Hitchcock, William I., *The Bitter Road to Freedom: A New History of the Liberation of Europe* (New York: Free Press, 2008)

Hobsbawm, Eric, *The Age of Revolution 1789–1848* (orig. edn, 1962; New York: Vintage Books, 1996)

Höschele, Stefan, *Christian Remnant – African Folk Church: Seventh-day Adventism in Tanzania, 1903–1980*, Studies in Christian Mission, 34 (Leiden: Brill, 2007)

Hyde, C. T. J., 'East African Publishing House', *British Advent Messenger*, 27 Mar. 1964, pp. 4–6

Iacob, Norel, 'World Church Welcomes Back Hungarian Splinter Group', *ARH* Online, 2 July 2015

'In Appreciation', *Canadian Union Messenger*, 15.4 (21 Aug. 1946), 1–2

'In Memoriam: Gottfried Oosterwal', *Journal of Adventist Mission Studies*, 11.2 (2015), v–ix

Isaac, J., 'Success in Spite of Difficulties', *Advent Survey*, 2.3 (Sept. 1930), 4, 8–9

Iwe orin ti awon ijo onireti-bibo Jesu (Seventh-day Adventist) (Ibadan: Nigeria Union Mission of Seventh-day Adventists, n.d. [1940?])

Iwe orin ti awon ijo S.D.A. (Exeter & London: James Townsend & Sons, n.d [1929])

Jacobsen, Michele, 'Andrews University Board Reelects President', *ARH*, 168.14 (4 April 1991), 21.

James, S., 'A Tribute to Pastor Albert Floyd Tarr', *Southern Asia Tidings*, 1 Oct. 1980, p. 12

Johnsson, William G., 'Britain — the Church Changes', *ARH* (13 July 1989), 13–15

—— 'Changing Times in Great Britain', *Adventist Review*, 178.6 (8 Feb. 2001), 8–13

Jordal, Odd, 'Glimpses from the Netherlands', *Northern Light*, 10.12 (Dec. 1960), 5–6

Joyce, S. G., 'Ireland: Great Britain's Neediest Mission Field', *Missionary Worker*, 6 Feb. 1931, pp. 1–2

Karstrom, Henning. 'God's Precious Gift', *Northern Light*, 16.6 (June 1966), 1–3, 7

Kaufmann, Eric, Anne Goujon, and Vegard Skirbekk, 'The End of Secularization in Europe? A Socio-Demographic Perspective', *Sociology of Religion*, 73 (2012), 69–91

Kinzer, Stephen, 'For Dutch, It's O.K. to Despise Germans', *New York Times*, 8 Feb. 1995, national edition, p. A0013

Klemann, Hein A. M., 'The "Tommies" or the "Jerries": Dutch Trade Problems in the Inter-War Period', in *Unspoken Allies: Anglo-Dutch Relations Since 1780*, ed. by Nigel John Ashton and Duco Hellema (Amsterdam University Press, 2001), pp. 101–20

Klenser, Louise C., 'Bible Instructors at Cleveland', *Ministry*, 31.10 (Oct. 1958), 30–31

Klinge, Matti, 'Aspects of the Nordic Self', *Daedalus*, 113.2 (1984), 257–77

Knight, George, ed., *Questions on Doctrine* (Berrien Springs, MI: Andrews University Press, 2003)

Knopper, J. T., 'A Challenge', *Australasian Record*, 9 Feb. 1976, p. 1

Knott, William M., 'Foot Soldier of the Empire: Hannah More and the Politics of Service' (PhD dissertation, George Washington University, 2006)

Krabbendam, Hans, 'Opening a Market for Missions: American Evangelicals and the Re-Christianization of Europe, 1945–1985', *Amerikastudien /American Studies*, 59 (2014), 153–75

L., E. J., 'Some Trends in Post-War Sweden', *The World Today*, 2.7 (1946), 313–30

Land, Gary, 'Coping with Change, 1961–1980', in *Adventism in America*, ed. idem, (Grand Rapids, Mich.: Wm. B. Eerdmans, 1986), pp. 208–30

LaRondelle, Hans K., *Perfection and Perfectionism: A Dogmatic-Ethical Study of Biblical Perfection and Phenomenal Perfectionism*, Andrews University Monographs, 3 (Berrien Springs, Mich.: Andrews University Press, 1971)

Larsen, Timothy, *Christabel Pankhurst: Fundamentalism and Feminism in Coalition* (Woodbridge, Suffolk: Boydell Press, 2002)

Lee, Michel Sunhae, 'Contesting the Sabbath: A History of Sacred Times in America, 1848–1920' (PhD dissertation, University of Texas, Austin, forthcoming)

'Life-Sketch of Edwin Lennard Minchin', *South Pacific Record*, 30 May 1987, p. 12

Lindén, Ingemar, *The Last Trump: An Historico-Genetical Study of Some Important Chapters in the Making and Development of the Seventh-day Adventist Church*, Studien zur interkulturellen Geschichte des Christentums / Studies in the Intercultural History of Christianity, 17 (Frankfurt am Main, Bern & Las Vegas, NV: Peter Lang, 1978)

Lindsay, G. A., 'The Advent Message in Uganda', *Advent Survey* 3.8 (August 1931), 6–7

—— 'The East Nordic Union Conference', report to 1946 GC Session, *ARH*, 123.24, General Conference Report, no. 2 (7 June 1946), 39–40

—— 'The Light of the Advent Shines in Northern Europe', *ARH*, 125.32 (5 Aug. 1948), 8–9, 19

—— 'Relief Work in Poland', *ARH*, 125.24 (10 Jun 1948), 15

Lohne, Alf, 'Big Scale Evangelism in Continental Europe', *Northern Light*, 18.4 (April 1968), 1–2

—— 'Phenomenal Booksales in Norway', *Northern Light*, 10.3 (March 1960), 6

—— 'West Nordic Union', *Northern Light*, 11.1 (Jan. 1961), 8

Lowe, H. W., 'The British Union Conference', report to 1946 GC Session, *ARH*, 123.24, General Conference Report, no. 2 (7 June 1946), 41–42

Maangi, Eric Nyankanga, 'The Contribution and Influence of the Seventh-day Adventist Church in the Development of Post-Secondary Education in South Nyanza, 1971–2000' (EdD dissertation, University of South Africa, 2014)

Maberly, Nalissa, 'Former Avondale College Principal Dies', *Record*, 5 Apr. 2003, p. 5

McChesney, Andrew, 'Adventist Church in Hungary Reconciles with Breakaway Group After 40 Years', *ARH* online, 1 May 2015

McGraw, Paul, 'Born in Zion?: The Margins of Fundamentalism and the Definition of Seventh-day Adventism' (PhD dissertation, The George Washington University, 2004)

Manners, Bruce, 'Evangelism and Health Pioneer Dies', *Record*, 16 Aug. 2003, p. 7

Maxwell, A. S., 'British Publishing House', *Advent Survey* 2.5 (May 1930), 2–3

—— 'European Council', *ARH*, 100.36 (Sept. 6, 1923), 8–9

—— 'Is Britain going Fascist?', *Present Truth*, 5 July 1934, pp. 6–7

—— 'The March of Events', *Present Truth*, 10 Sept. 1936, p. 2

Mazower, Mark, *The Balkans: A Short History* (New York: Modern Library, pb edn, 2002)

Mbwana, Geoffrey, 'Like a Mustard Seed: Adventism in the East-Central Africa Division', *Adventist World—NAD*, 10.4 (April 2014), 40–41

Metuzāle-Kangere, Baiba and Uldis Ozolins, 'The Language Situation in Latvia 1850–2004', *Journal of Baltic Studies*, 36 (2005), 317–44

Mihas, Elena, *Upper Perené Arawak Narratives of History, Landscape, and Ritual* (Lincoln: University of Nebraska Press, 2014)

Minchin, E. L., 'Itinerating in Sweden and Finland', *Northern Light*, 1.1 (March 1951), 10–11

Mirilov, Branislav, 'An Examination of the Response of the Seventh-day Adventist Church to some Contemporary Socio-Political Issues in the Light of Two Distinctive Adventist Doctrines: A Comparison of North America and Former Yugoslavia' (PhD thesis, University of Birmingham, 1994)

Montgomery, Oliver, *Principles of Church Organization and Administration* (Washington, DC: RHPA, 1942)

Morris, Kevin, 'Fascism and British Catholic Writers 1924— 1939: Part 2', *New Blackfriars*, 80 (1999), 82–95

Murdoch, W. G. C., 'News from Stanborough College', *Missionary Worker*, 9 Jan. 1931, p. 6

Nam, Juhyeok Julius, 'Reactions to the Seventh-day Adventist evangelical conferences and *Questions on Doctrine*, 1955– 1971' (PhD dissertation, Andrews University, 2005)

—— '*Questions on Doctrine* and M. L. Andreasen: The Behind-the Scenes Interactions', *Andrews University Seminary*

Studies, 46 (2008), 229–44

Nelson, P. G., 'The West Nordic Union', report to 1946 GC Session, *ARH*, 123.24, General Conference Report, no. 2 (7 June 1946), 43–44

Nelson, W. E., 'German Believers Receive Supplies', *North Pacific Union Gleaner*, 10 (Sept. 1946), 1–2

—— 'Report of Relief Work Carried on by the General Conference During and Since the End of the War', *ARH*, 123.24, General Conference Report no. 2 (7 June 1946), 34–35

—— 'Results in Food and Clothing Relief', *Lake Union Herald*, 3 Sept. 1946, pp. 1–2

—— 'Serious Plight of European Believers', *Columbia Union Visitor*, 5 Sept. 1946, pp. 1–3

—— 'What Will You Do for Famine Relief?', *Atlantic Union Gleaner*, 9 Sept. 1947, p. 1

Nichol, F. D., 'Adventist Activities in the North Lands', *ARH*, 124.30 (24 July 1947), 3–4

Nix, James R., *Memorable Dates from our Adventist Past* (Silver Spring, Md.: North American Division Office of Education, 1989)

Nixon, J. W., 'The Publishing Department', *Northern Light*, 11.1 (Jan. 1961), 5

Numbers, Ronald L., *Prophetess of Health: A Study of Ellen G. White and the Origins of Seventh-day Adventist Health Reform*, rev. 2nd edn. (Knoxville: University of Tennessee Press, 1991 [1976])

Olsen, V. Norskov, *John Foxe and the Elizabethan Church* (Berkeley, Los Angeles & London: University of California Press, 1973)

—— 'The Lord's Day in the Second Century', *ARH*, 139.4 (25 Jan. 1962), 1, 4–5

Olson, A. V., 'First Detailed Postwar Report from Southern

Europe', *ARH*, 123.3 (17 Jan. 1946), 1, 17–18

—— 'Rehabilitation Offering', *Canadian Union Messenger*, 15.4 (21 Aug. 1946), 3–4

Oosterwal, Gottfried, *The Lord's Prayer Through Primitive Eyes* (Nampa, ID: Pacific Press, 2009)

Oswald, L. F., 'Our God is Able', *Advent Survey*, 2.3 (Sept. 1930), 1

Parsons, Neil, *King Khama and the Great White Queen: Victorian Britain through African Eyes* (Chicago & London: University of Chicago Press, 1998)

'Pastor E. B. Rudge', *Northern Light*, 10.12 (Dec. 1960), 8

Paulsen, Jan, 'Field Schools in West Africa', *Northern Light*, 16.12 (Dec. 1966), 8

Pfeiffer, Baldur Ed., 'The Coming of the Mission to East Africa', in *Seventh-day Adventist Contributions to East Africa, 1903–1983*, ed. idem (Frankfurt am Main, Bern and New York: Peter Lang, 1985), pp. 27–32

Pierson, Robert H., 'Heart to Heart', *Southern African Division Outlook*, 59.8 (Aug. 1961), 2

—— 'New division formed during Autumn Council', *ARH*, 148.44 (4 Nov. 1971), 46

Plaat, Jaanus, 'Religious Change in Estonia and the Baltic States during the Soviet Period in Comparative Perspective', *Journal of Baltic Studies* 34.1 (2003): 52–73

Porter, Dennis S., 'Crisis in the British Union', *Spectrum*, 11.4 (1981), 2–12

Pound, Reginald and A. J. A. Morris, 'Gibbs, Sir Philip Armand Hamilton (1877–1962), Writer and Journalist', *Oxford Dictionary of National Biography* (Oxford: Oxford University Press, 2004)

Pray, LoVae, 'Olsen Inaugurated as LLU President', *San Bernardino County Sun*, 5 Dec. 1974

Price, Bruce, 'Life-Sketch of Pastor Erwin E. Roenfelt', *Record*, 7

Nov. 1987, p. 13

Rea, Walter L., *The White Lie* (Turlock, Calif.: M & R Publications, 1982)

Read, W. E., 'Another New Year', *Advent Survey* 10.1 (Jan. 1938), 1–2

—— 'Dawn of a New Day in Liberia', *ARH*, 124.30 (24 July 1947), 17

—— 'Missionary Sailings', *Advent Survey*, 1.3 (Sept. 1929), 3–4

—— 'Off to the Far-Away Fields', *Quarterly Review of the European Division of the General Conference of Seventh-Day Adventists*, 12.3 (1926), 4

—— 'Some Changes at the General Conference', *Advent Survey*, 12.3 (Oct. 1941), 3

Reinisch, Jessica, ed., *Relief in the Aftermath of War*, special issue of *Journal of Contemporary History*, 43.3 (July 2008)

Reynolds, David, *In Command of History: Churchill Fighting and Writing the Second World War* (New York: Basic Books, 2007 [2005])

Reynolds, Keld J., 'The Church Under Stress, 1931–1960', in *Adventism in America*, ed. by Gary Land (Grand Rapids, Mich.: Wm. B. Eerdmans, 1986), pp. 182–94

Robison, J. I., 'Items from the Secretary's Report at the Winter Council', *Advent Survey*, 10. 1 (Jan. 1938), 4–5

Roennfeldt, Peter, 'The Secular Person as a Target for Mission', in *Re-visioning Adventist Mission in Europe*, ed. by Erich W. Baumgartner (Berrien Springs: Andrews University Press, 1998), pp. 59–69

Roux-James, Kimi, 'ADRA's 2019 Annual Council Gears Toward Growth, Embraces New Purpose', *ARH*, 196.5 (May 2019), 9–10

Rudy, H. L., 'Our Foreign Missions Campaigns in 1931', *Advent Survey*, 4.2 (Feb. 1932), 2–3

Salazar, Ph.-J. and Brett Syndercombe, 'Harold Macmillan,

"The Wind of Change"', *African Yearbook of Rhetoric*, 2.3 (2011), 27–39

Salvador, Eyezo'o, 'Un paramètre de l'histoire du Cameroun: La Mission Adventiste (1926–1949)', (MA thesis, University of Yaoundé, 1985)

Santos-Granero, Fernando, 'The Enemy Within: Child Sorcery, Revolution, and the Evils of Modernization in Eastern Peru', in *Darkness and Secrecy: Witchcraft and Sorcery in Native South America*, ed. by Neil L. Whitehead and Robin M. Wright (Durham, NC: Duke University Press, 2004), pp. 272–305

Schantz, Børge, 'Adventism in a New Eastern Europe', in *Adventist Mission in the 21st Century*, ed. by Jon L. Dybdahl (Hagerstown, Md.: RHPA, 1999), pp. 298–306

Scragg, Walter R. L., 'Consultative Group in Britain Opts for Integration', *Northern Light*, 28.5 (May 1978), 7

Scribner, Todd, '"Pilgrims of the Night": The American Catholic Church Responds to the Post-World War II Displaced Persons Crisis', *American Catholic Studies*, 124.3 (Fall 2013), 1–20

Serraillier, Ian, *The Silver Sword* (London: Jonathan Cape, 1956)

Seton, B. E., 'By the Editor', *Northern Light*, 16.12 (Dec. 1966), 2

Seventh-Day Adventists Answer Questions on Doctrine (Washington, DC: RHPA, 1957)

Sicking, Louis, *et al.*, *Dutch Light in the 'Norwegian Night': Maritime Relations and Migration across the North Sea* (Hilversum: Verloren, 2004)

Spangler, J. R., 'Tribute to a Great Australian', *South Pacific Record*, 8 Mar. 1986, p. 13

Spicer, William, *Our Story of Missions for Colleges and Academies* (Mountain View, Calif.: Pacific Press, 1921)

—— *Miracles of Modern Missions: Gathered out of Mission Records* (Washington, DC: RHPA, 1926)

Standish, Russell R. and Colin D. Standish, *Adventism Challenged*, 2 vols. (Rapidan, VA: Hartland Institute, n.d. [*c.*1985])

—— *Deceptions of the New Theology* (N.p.: Hartland Publications, 1989)

Staples, Russell, 'Gottfried Oosterwal — Inspirational Missiologist', *Journal of Adventist Mission Studies*, 11.2 (2015), ix–xii

Steinert, Johannes-Dieter, 'British Humanitarian Assistance: Wartime Planning and Postwar Realities', in *Relief in the Aftermath of War*, ed. by Jessica Reinisch, special issue of *Journal of Contemporary History*, 43.3 (July 2008), 421–35

Strahle, J. J., 'Distributing Food in Europe', *ARH*, 123.35 (11 July 1946), 16

Syme, David, 'ADRA and Mission', in *Re-visioning Adventist Mission in Europe*, ed. by Erich W. Baumgartner (Berrien Springs: Andrews University Press, 1998), pp. 163–66

Szilvási, József, 'Church Policy in East-Central Europe after the Collapse of Communist Regimes', paper presented at the conference 'Memory, History and Reconciliation in the Light of the Papal Declaration on "Memory and Reconciliation"', Newbold College, 20 Oct. 2000

Tarr, A. F., 'Greetings from the President', *Northern Light*, 1.1 (March 1951), 1

—— 'Itinerating in West Africa', *Northern Light*, 1.1 (March 1950), 10.

—— 'Winds of Change Over Africa', *Northern Light*, 10.4 (April 1960), 4–5

Teel, Charles, 'Fernando and Ana Stahl — Mediators of Personal and Social Transformation', in *Adventist Mission in the 21st Century*, ed. by Jon L. Dybdahl (Hagerstown, MD: RHPA, 1999), pp. 278–85

—— 'Revolutionary Missionaries in Peru: Fernando and Ana

Stahl', *Spectrum*, 18.3 (Feb. 1988), 50–52

Thaden, Edward C., 'Finland and the Baltic Provinces: Elite Roles and Social and Economic Conditions and Structures', *Journal of Baltic Studies*, 15 (1984), 216–27

Thomsen, Viggo, 'Denmark', *Northern Light*, 7.11 (Nov. 1957), 5–6, 13

Timm, Alberto R. and James R. Nix, eds., *Lessons from Battle Creek: Reflections after 150 Years of Church Organization* (Silver Spring, MD: Review & Herald, 2018)

Trim, D. J. B., *Adventist Mission in the Middle East: A History* (Silver Spring, MD: General Conference Archives Monographs, forthcoming)

—— 'B. W. Ball: Evangelist, Administrator, Scholar', in *A Century of Adventism in the British Isles*, ed. by David Marshall (Grantham, England: Stanborough Press, 2000), 31

—— 'Church Member Survey 2017–18: Trans-European Division in the Context of the World Church', presentation at the Trans-European Division Executive Committee Midyear Meeting, 21 May 2019: <https://www.adventistresearch.org/sites/default/files/CompressedGCMS%202017-18%20TED%20in%20Context%20edited-compressed.pdf>

—— 'General Conference Secretariat and Foreign Missionaries', ASTR Research Papers (2017)

—— *A Living Sacrifice: Unsung Heroes of Adventist Mission* (Nampa, ID: Pacific Press, 2019)

—— 'Modernism and Post-Modernism in Western Thought and Culture: From "Buttoned-Up Tight" to "ad hoc Tattooed"', in *Journeys to Wisdom: Festschrift in Honour of Michael Pearson*, ed. by Andreas Bochmann, Manuela Casti Yeagley, and Jean-Claude Verrecchia (Bracknell: Newbold Academic Press, 2015), pp. 45–72

—— '"Nothing to fear … except": Understanding the past and

applying it to the future', *College and University Dialogue*, 30.2 (2018), 21–23

—— 'Officers' Meetings: History and Character', ASTR Research Report (March 2019)

—— 'The Ordination of Women in Seventh-day Adventist Policy and Practice, up to 1972', paper presented at the Theology of Ordination Study Committee meeting, 21–23 July 2013, table on p. 24; available to download at: <https://www.adventistarchives.org/the-ordination-of-women-in-Seventh-day-adventist-policy-and-practice.pdf>

—— 'Stones of Meaning', part 1, 'Why History Matters: Sacred History', part 2, 'Why *Our* History Matters: Seventh-day Adventists and History', *ARH*, 188 (9 and 16 June 2011), 500–02, 529–29

Trim, D. J. B. and Benjamin J. Baker, eds, *Fundamental Belief 6: Creation*, General Conference Archives Finding Aids, 1 (Silver Spring, Md.: General Conference of Seventh-day Adventists, Office of Archives, Statistics, and Research, 2014)

Trim, John B., 'Pillars of the Faith Strengthened', *Australasian Record*, 3 Mar. 1958, pp. 1–2

Trim, Marye and D. J. B. Trim, 'Revival and the Holy Spirit: The 1939 Australasian Revival', *Ministry*, 89.2 (Feb. 2017), 16–18

'Two Former GC Vice-Presidents Die', *ARH*, 170.50 (16 Dec. 1993), 7

Unntersten, R., 'When Figures Are Not Dry', *Northern Light*, 16.6, Statistical Supplement (1966), unpaginated

Vine, A. C., 'Opportunity Knocks Again', *British Advent Messenger*, 27 Mar. 1964, pp. 1–2

Vine, R. D., 'The British Union', *Northern Light*, 11.1 (Jan. 1961), 8

—— 'Disarming Prejudice', *Northern Light*, 10.3 (March 1960), 4–5

Warren, Edgar A., 'More Wheelchairs', *West African Adventist Messenger*, 25.1 (Jan. 1971), 5

Watts, Kit, 'The Rise and Fall of Adventist Women in Leadership', *Ministry* 68.4 (Apr. 1995): 6–10

Weigley, Russell F., *The American Way of War: A History of United States Military Strategy and Policy* (Bloomington: Indiana University Press, 1977)

Weindling, Paul, '"For the Love of Christ": Strategies of International Catholic Relief and the Allied Occupation of Germany, 1945–1948', in *Relief in the Aftermath of War*, ed. by Jessica Reinisch, special issue of *Journal of Contemporary History*, 43.3 (July 2008), 477–92

White, Arthur L., 'Further General Conference Actions on Race Relations', *ARH*, 143.16 (21 Apr. 1966), 6–8

White, E. E., 'In Memoriam: William G. C. Murdoch', *Messenger*, 20 Apr. 1984, pp. 13, 16

White, Ellen G., *Life Sketches* (Mountain View, Calif.: Pacific Press, 1943)

—— *The Ministry of Healing* (Mountain View, Calif.: Pacific Press, 1942 [1909])

—— 'Our Missions in Europe', *ARH*, 64 (6 Dec. 1887), 753

—— *Patriarchs and Prophets* (Mountain View, Calif: Pacific Press, 1913)

—— *Testimonies for the Church*, 9 vols. (Mountain View, Calif.: Pacific Press, 1948)

Whitsett, R. M., 'Finnish Evangelists Visit Minnesota', *Northern Union Outlook*, 17 June 1958, pp. 6–7

Williams, David A., 'Worship Music as Theology: An Examination of Music in the Liturgy of Black and White Adventists in the United States from 1894 to 1944' (PhD dissertation, Seventh-day Adventist Theological Seminary, 2018)

Williams, DeWitt S., *Precious Memories of Missionaries of Color*, vol. II (N.p.: TEACH Services, 2015)

Winandy, Pierre, 'After 100 Years, Europe Still Finds Ellen White Relevant', *ARH*, 165.12 (24 Mar. 1988), 17–18

'Winter Council of the Northern European Division', *Northern Light*, 1.1 (March 1951), 5

Wogu, Chigemezi Nnadozie, 'Forgotten Trailblazers: Unearthing Stories of Our Mission Pioneers', *Mission 360º*, 7.2 (2019), 20–21

Woodberry, Robert D., 'The Missionary Roots of Liberal Democracy', *American Political Science Review*, 106 (2012), 244–74

www.ingramcontent.com/pod-product-compliance
Lightning Source LLC
Chambersburg PA
CBHW031053080526
44587CB00011B/665